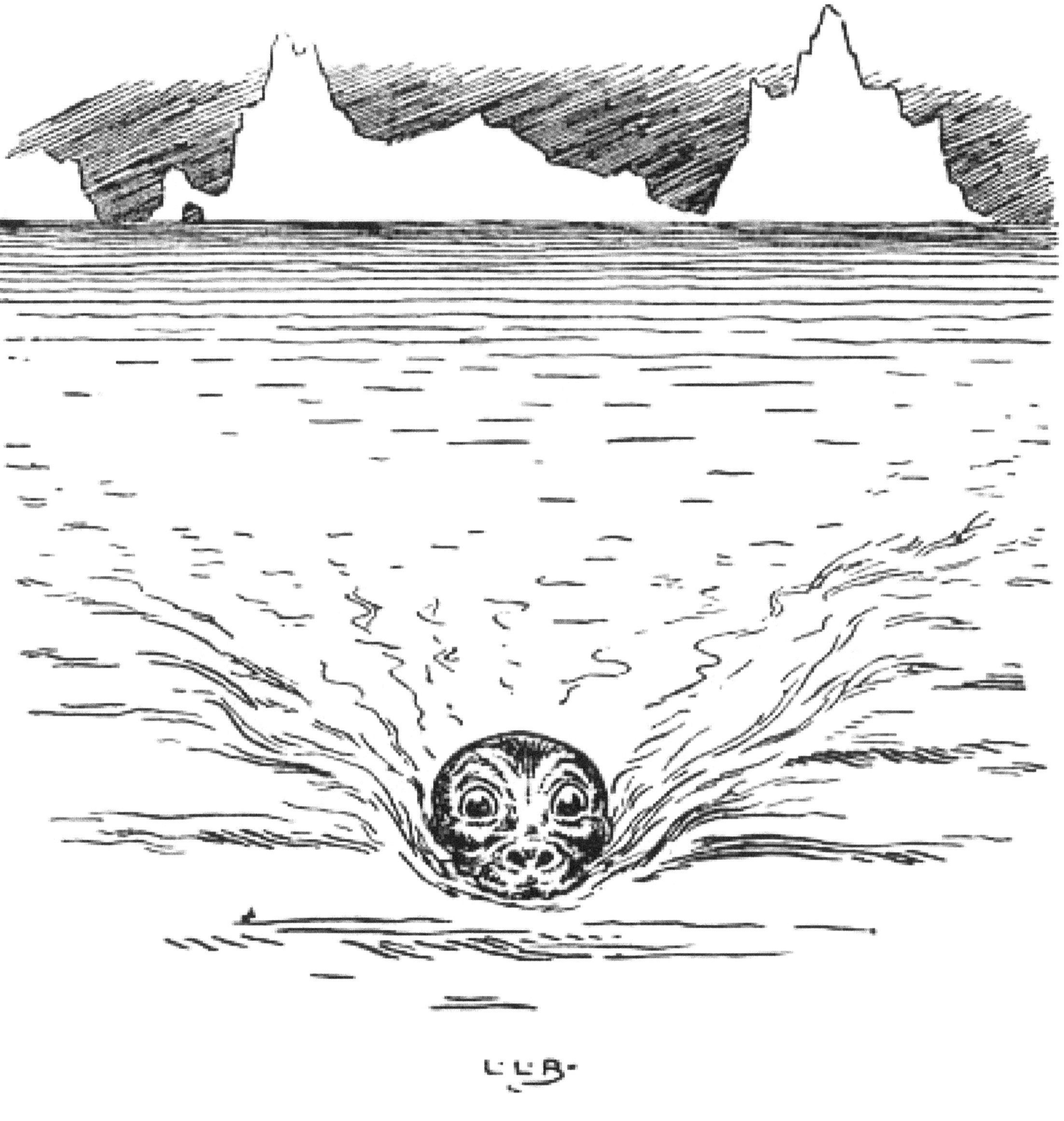

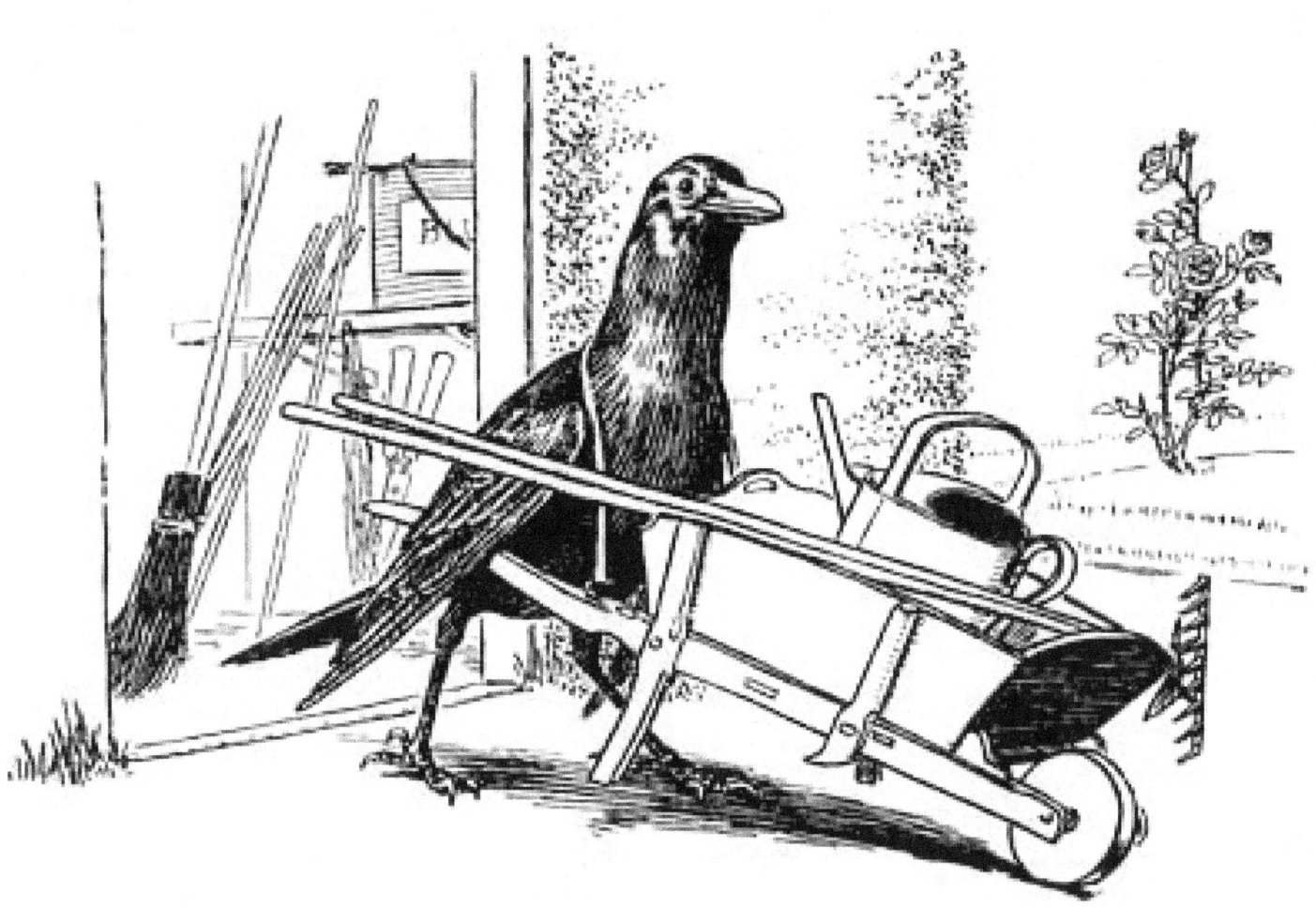

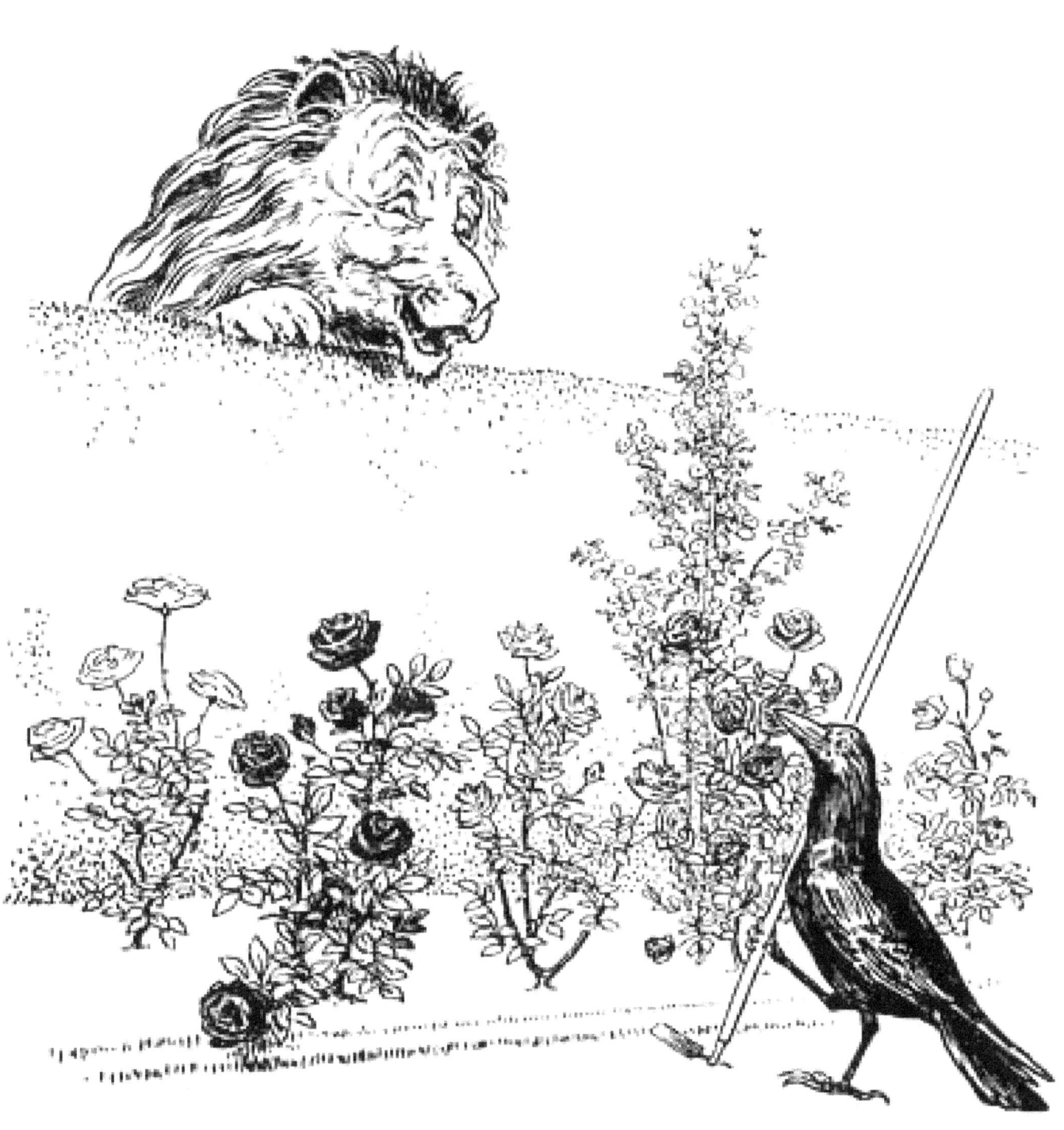

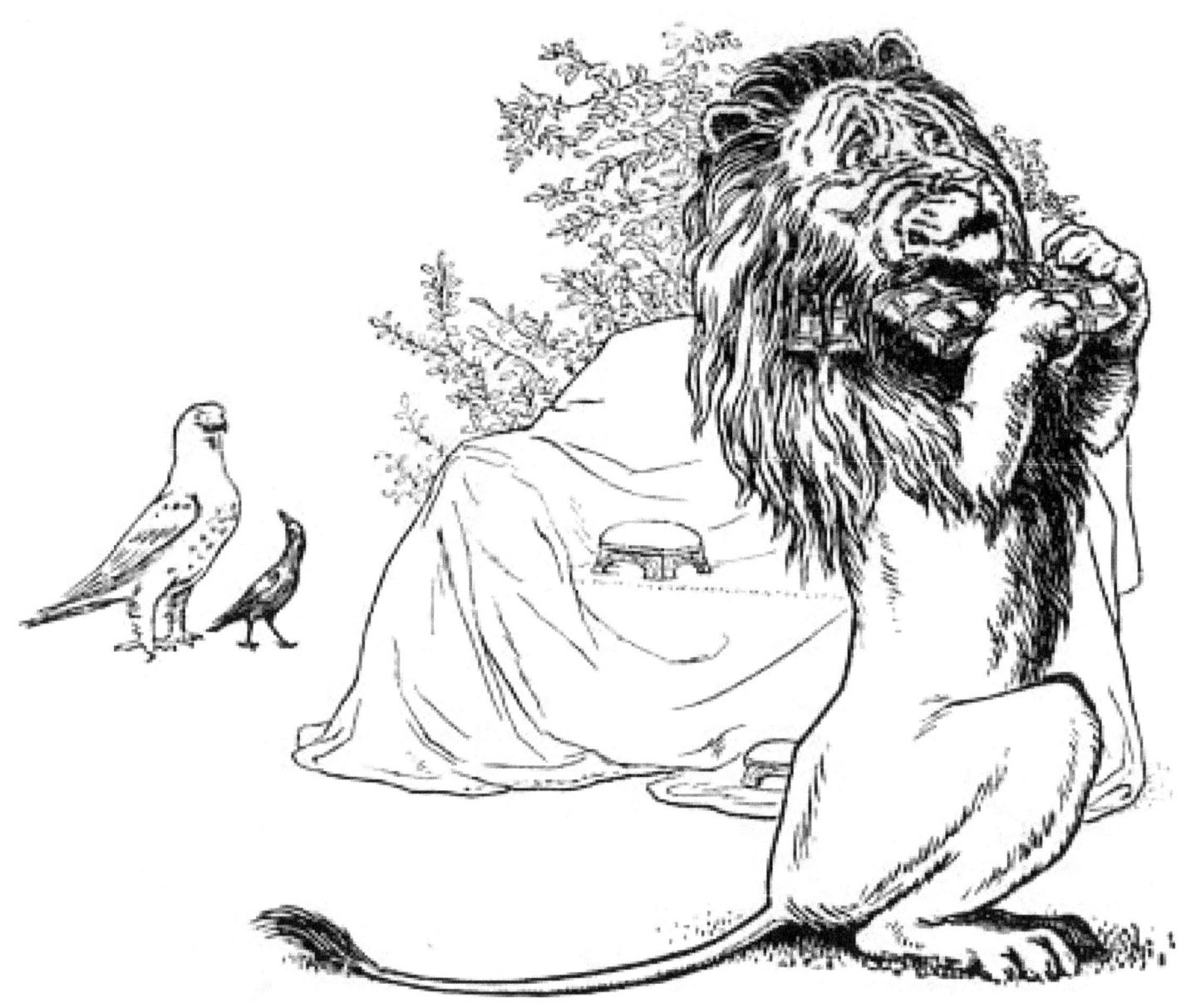

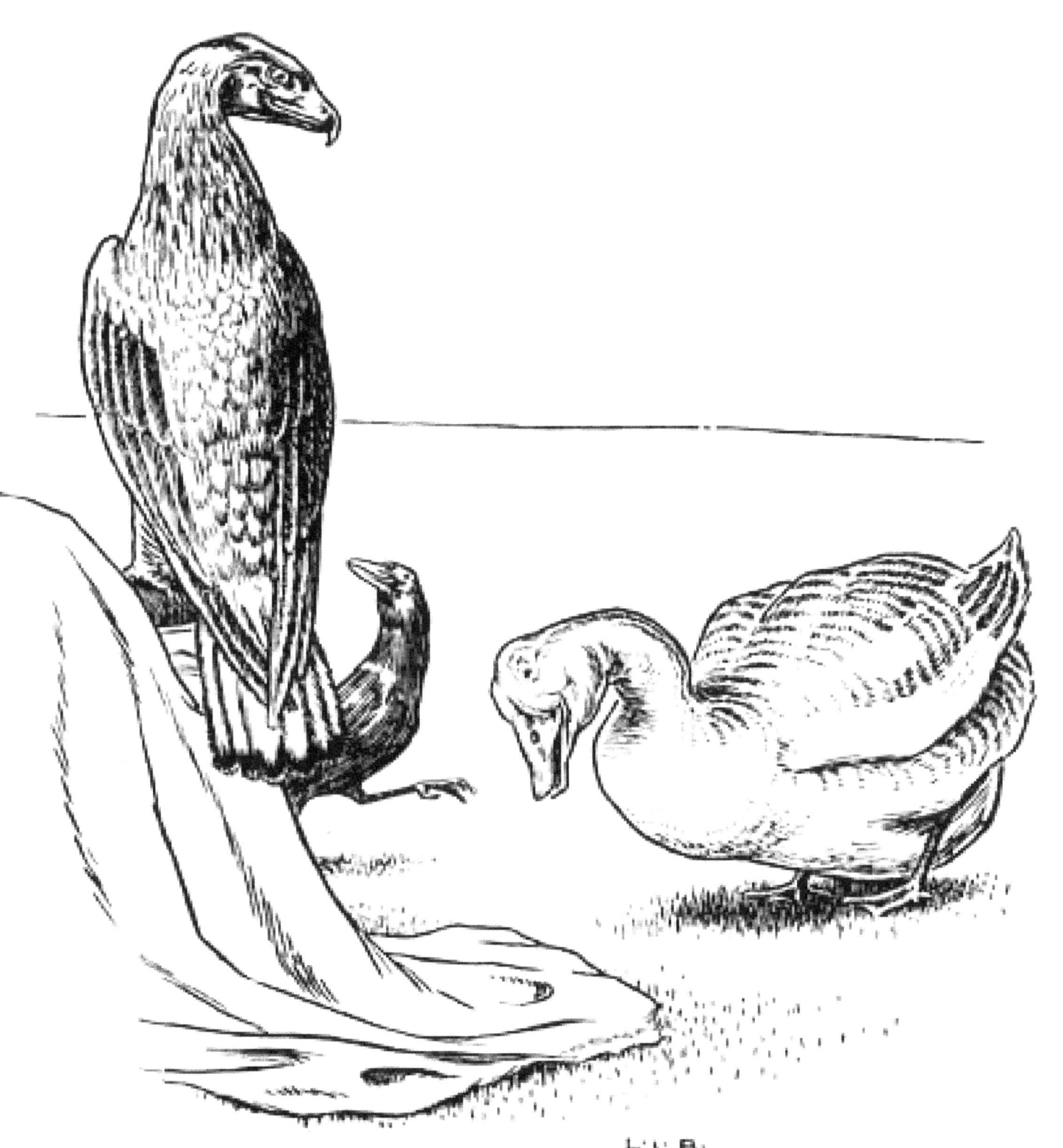

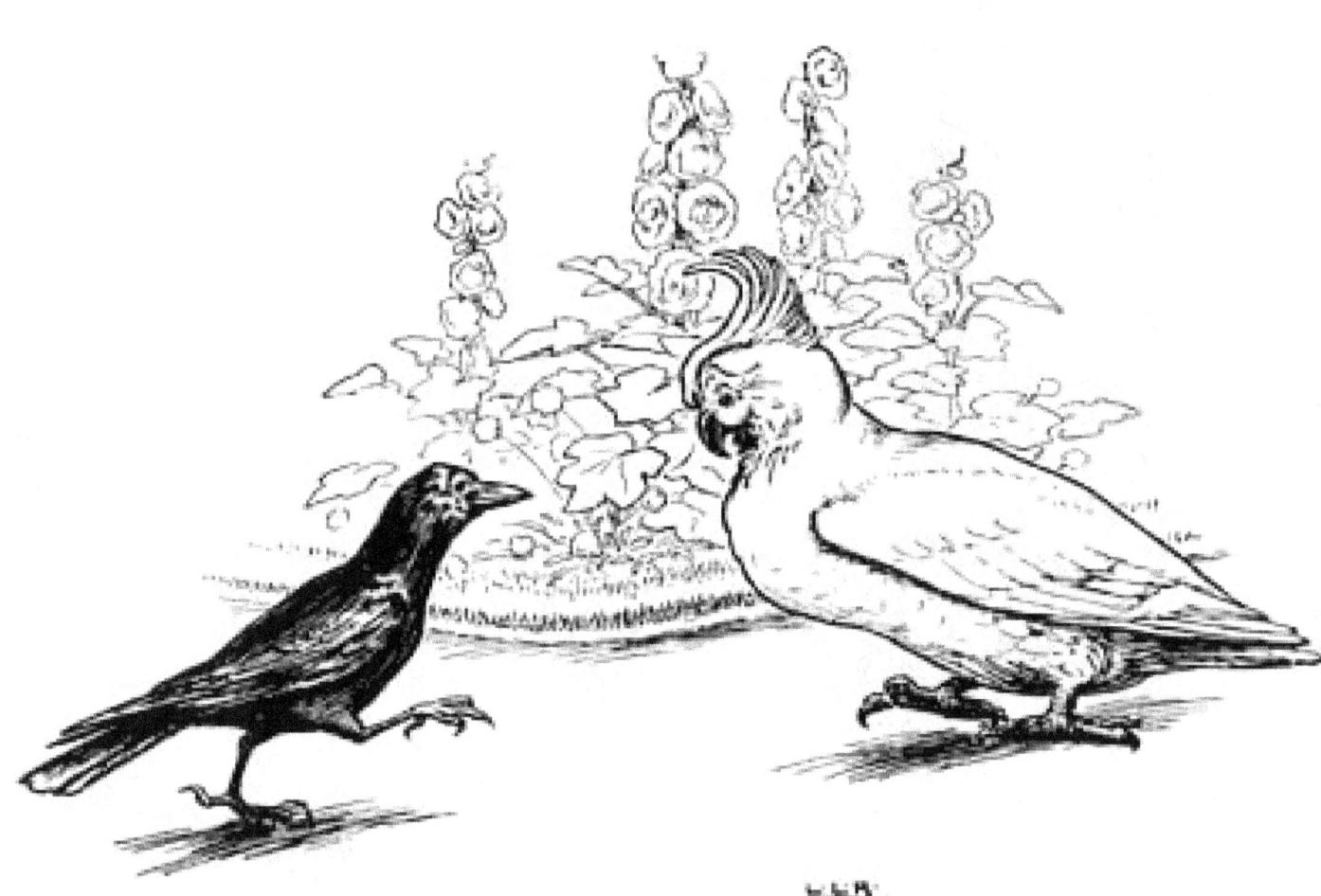

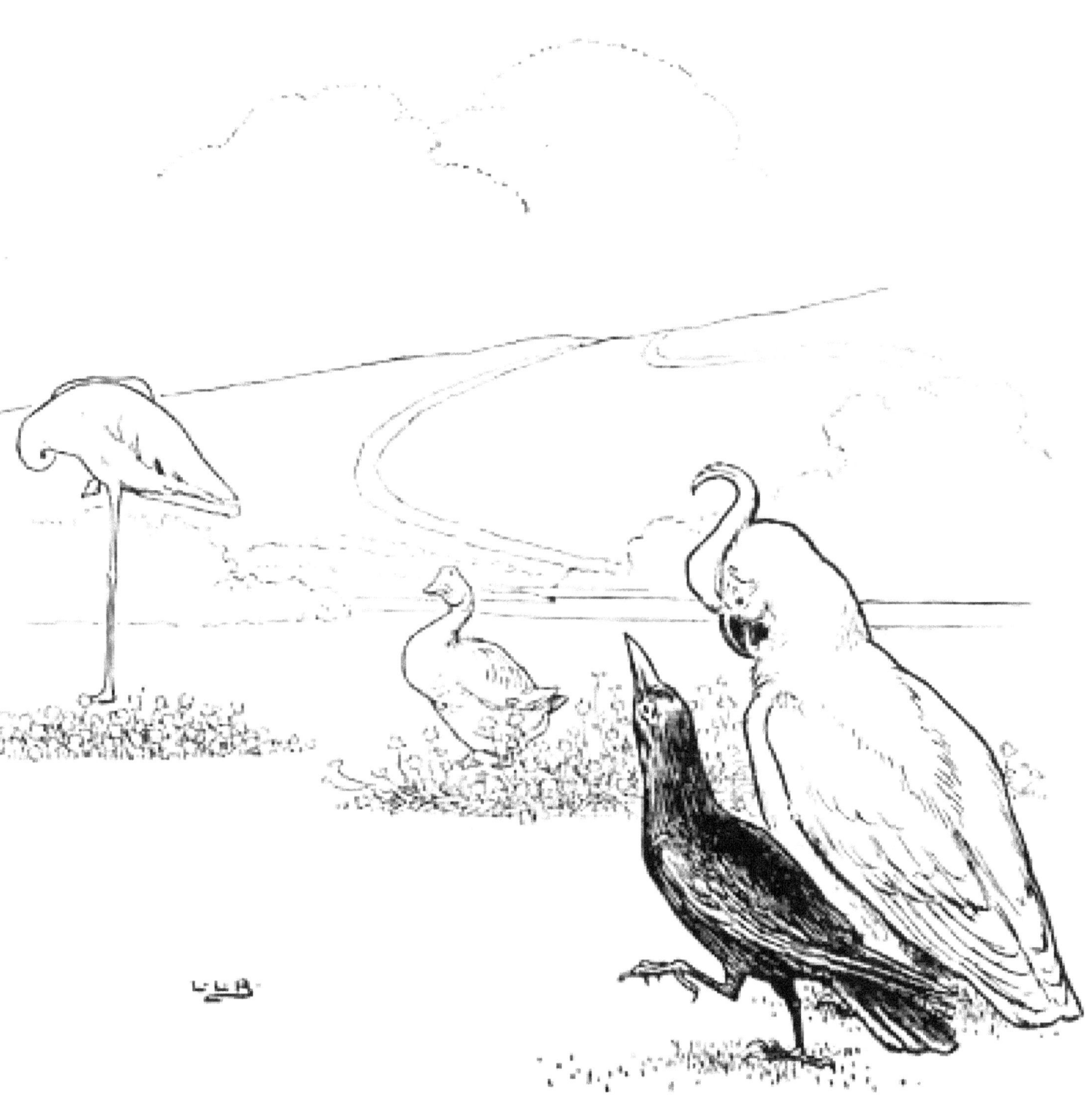

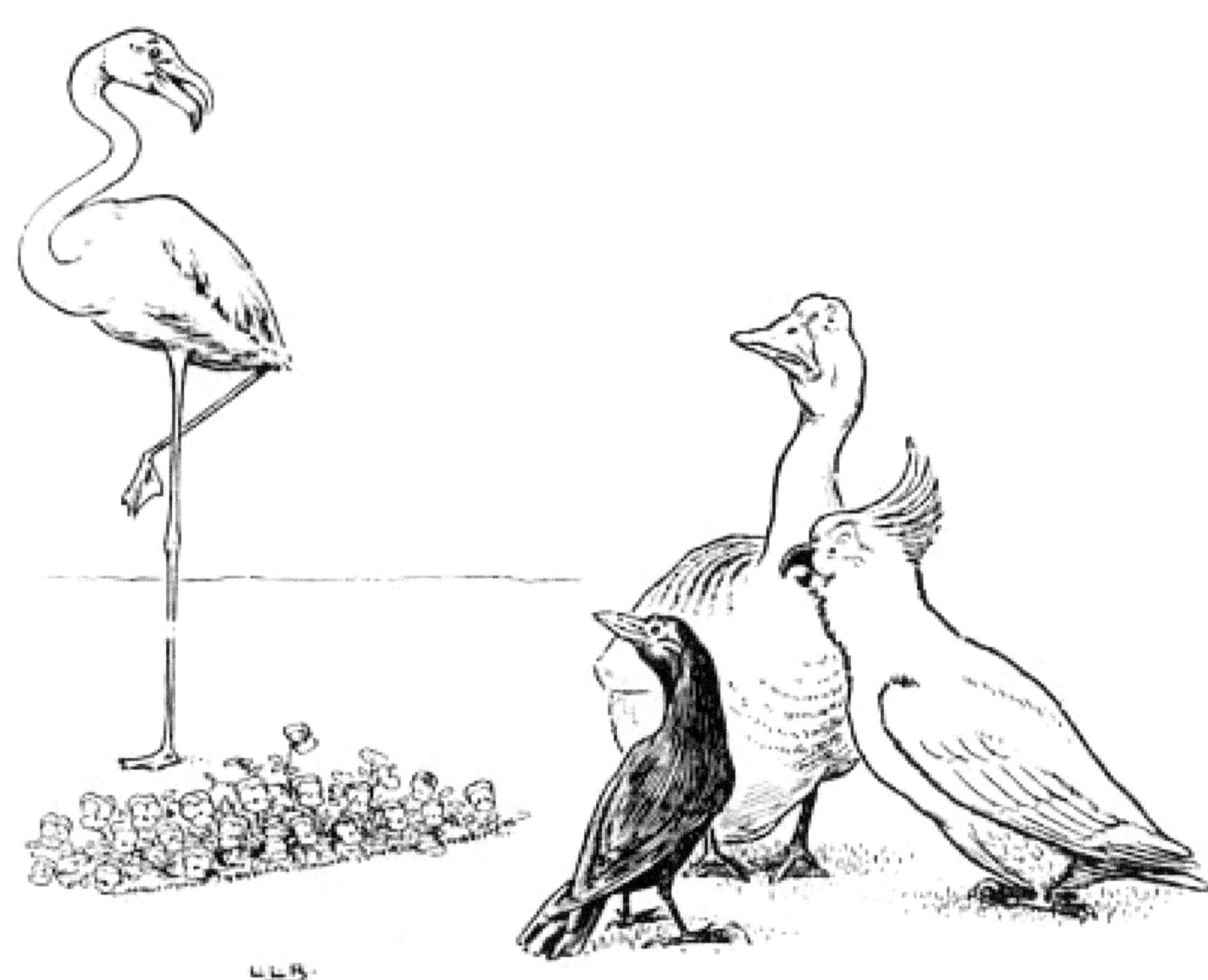

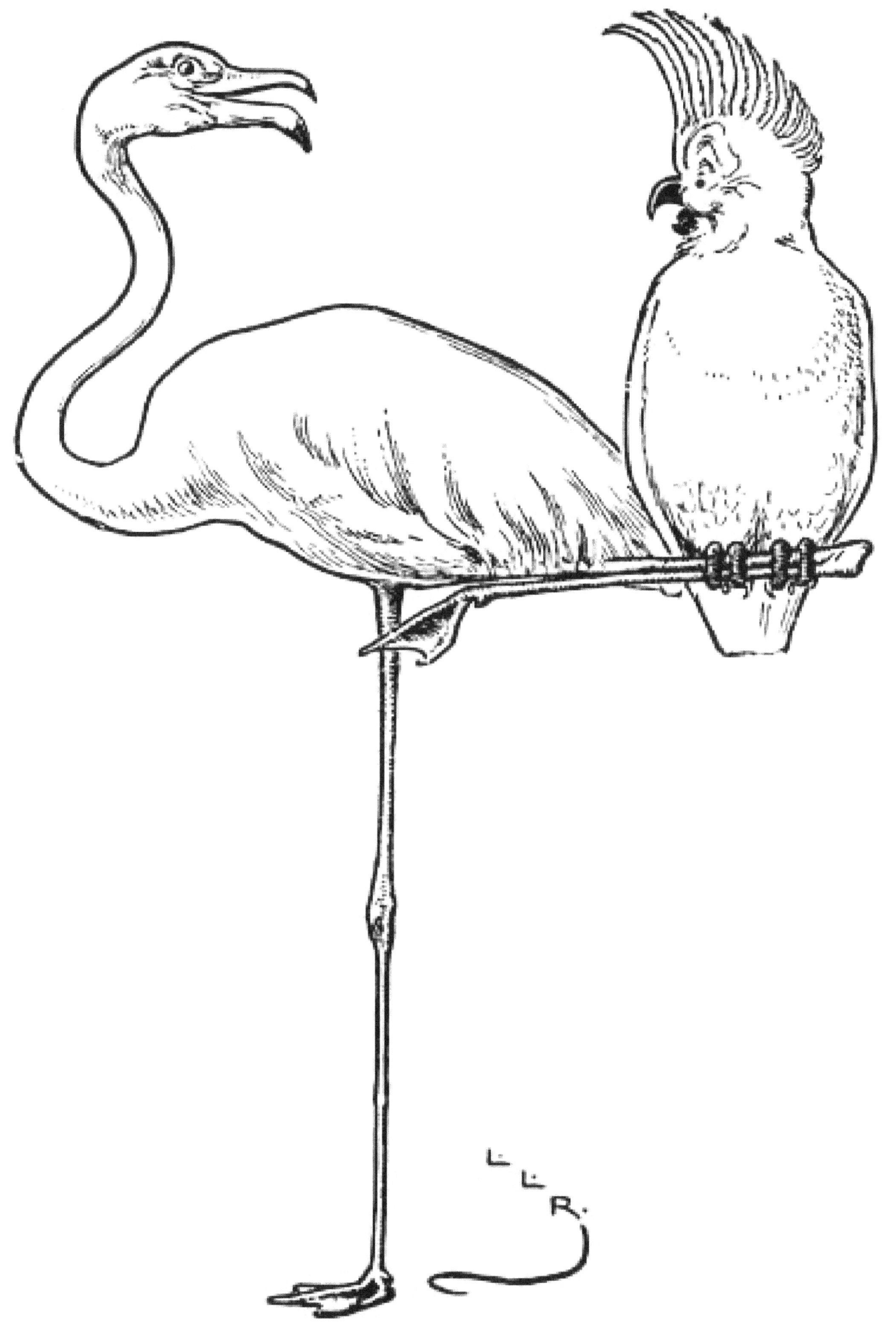

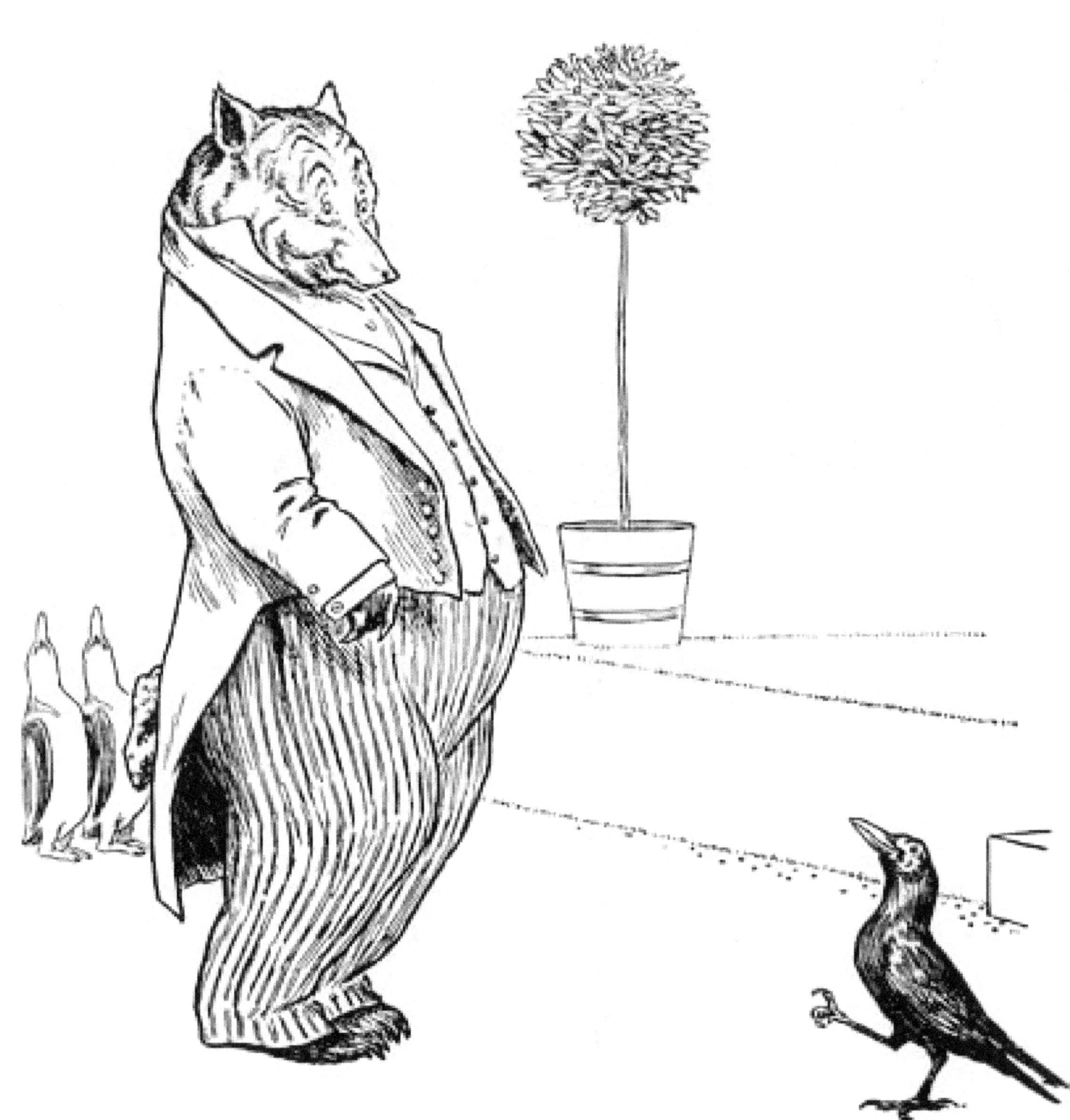

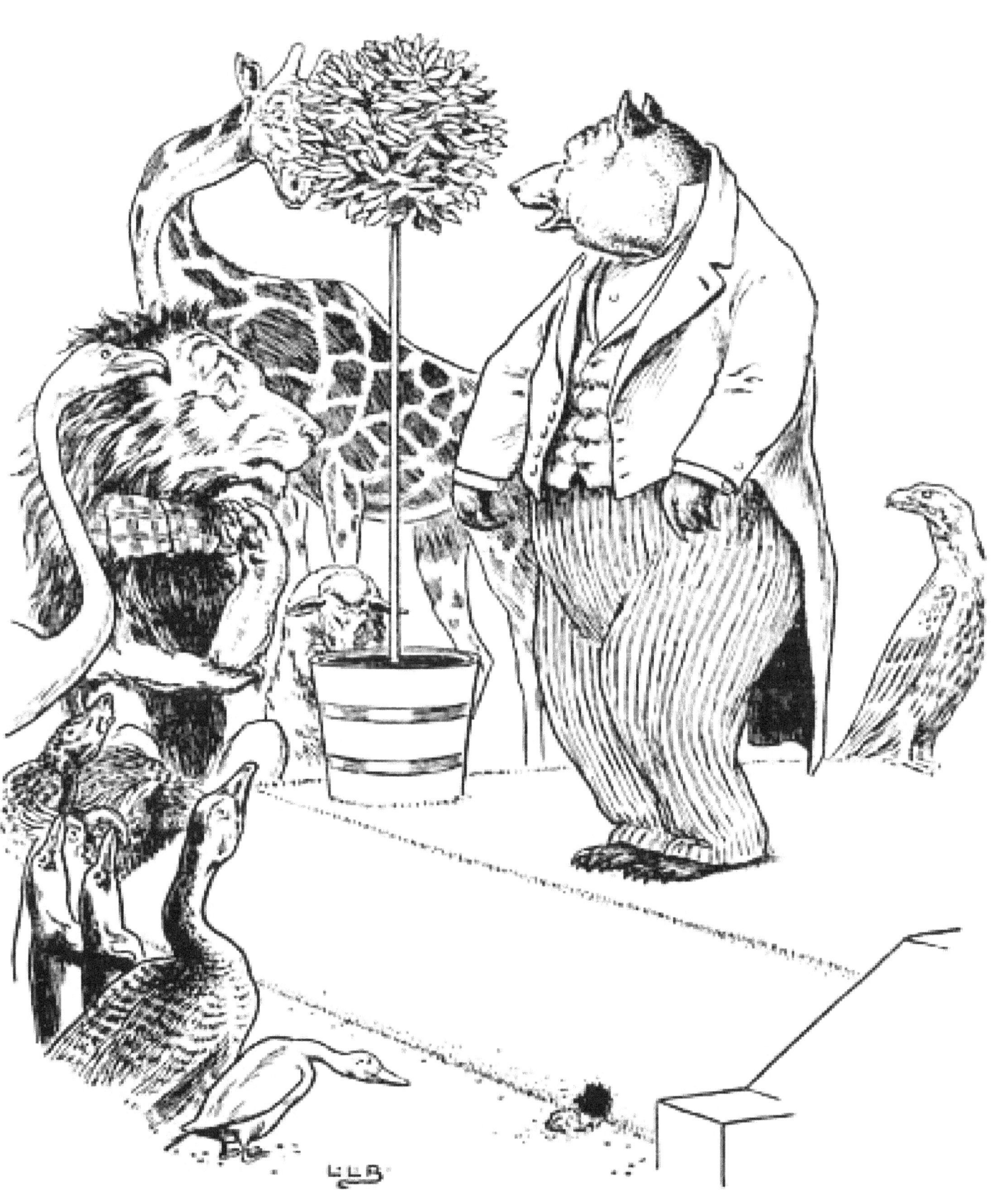

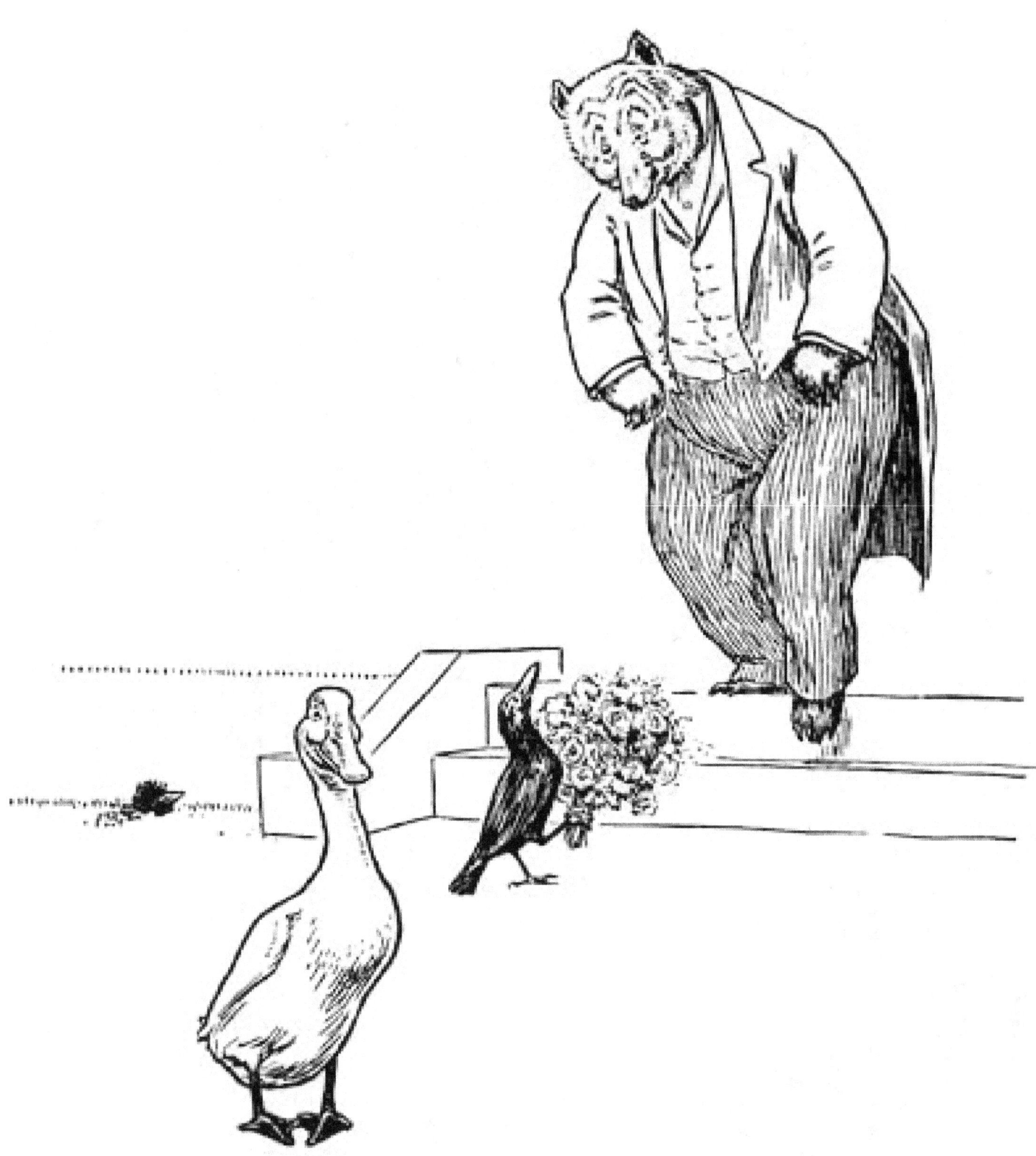

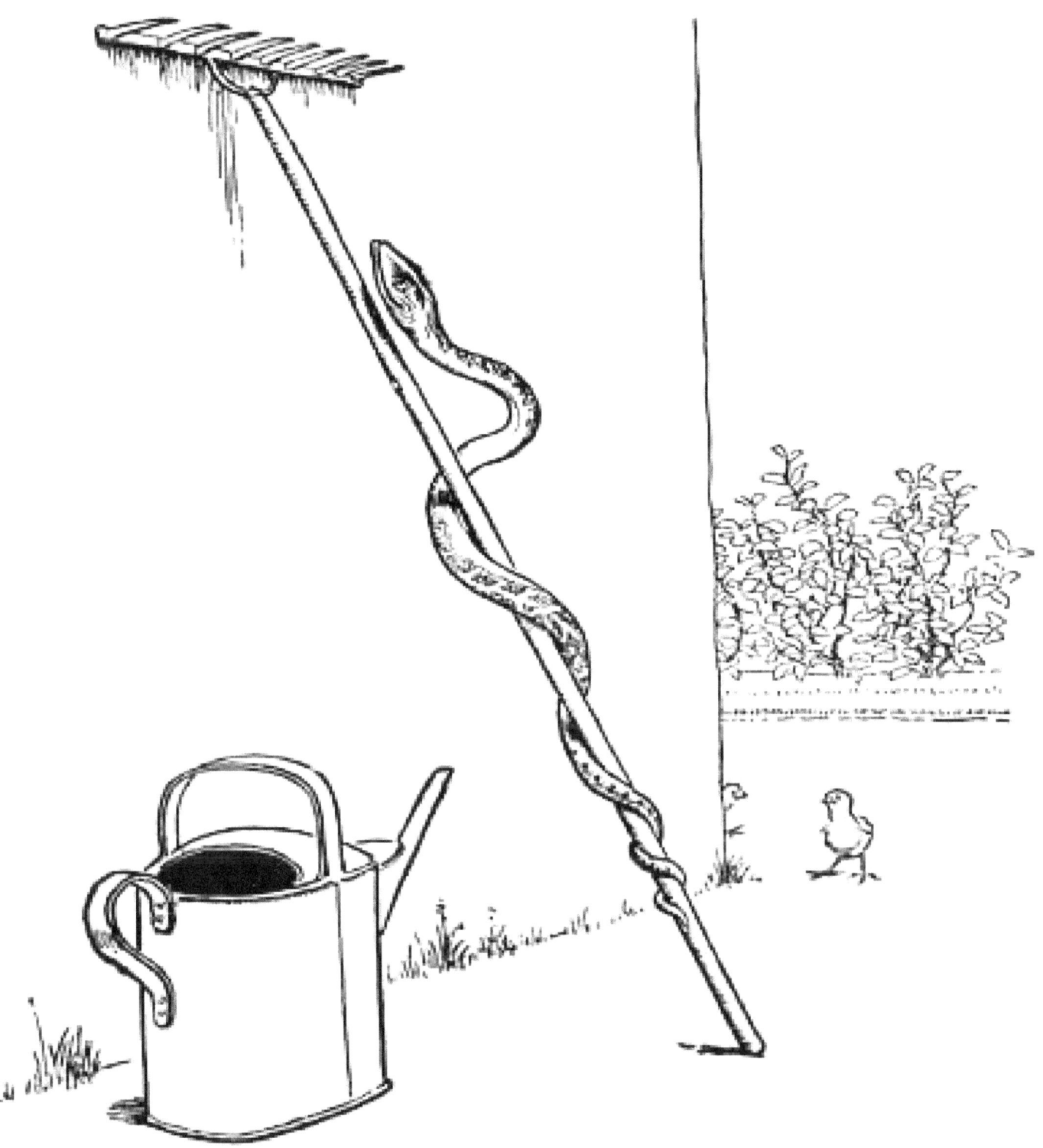

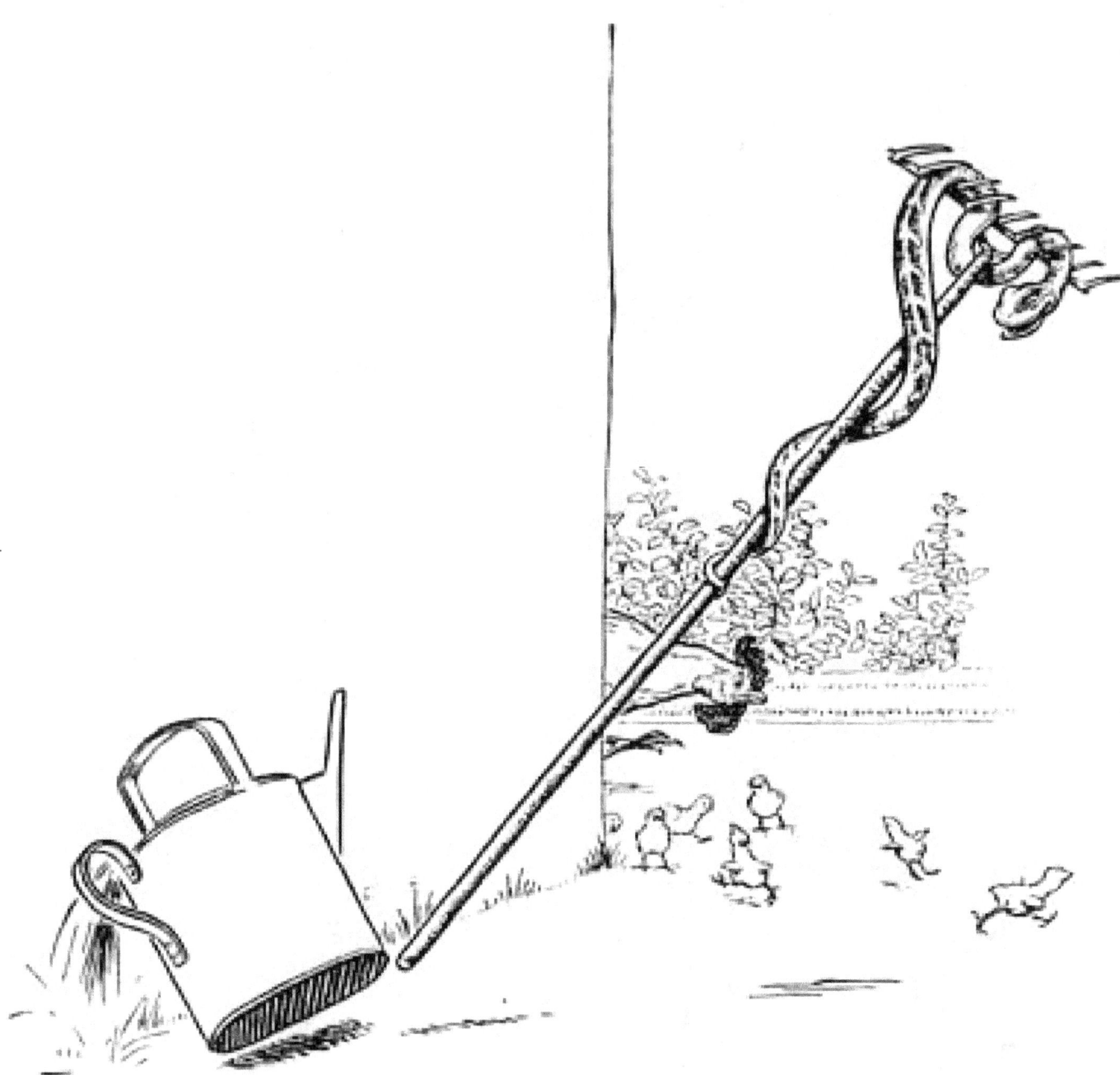

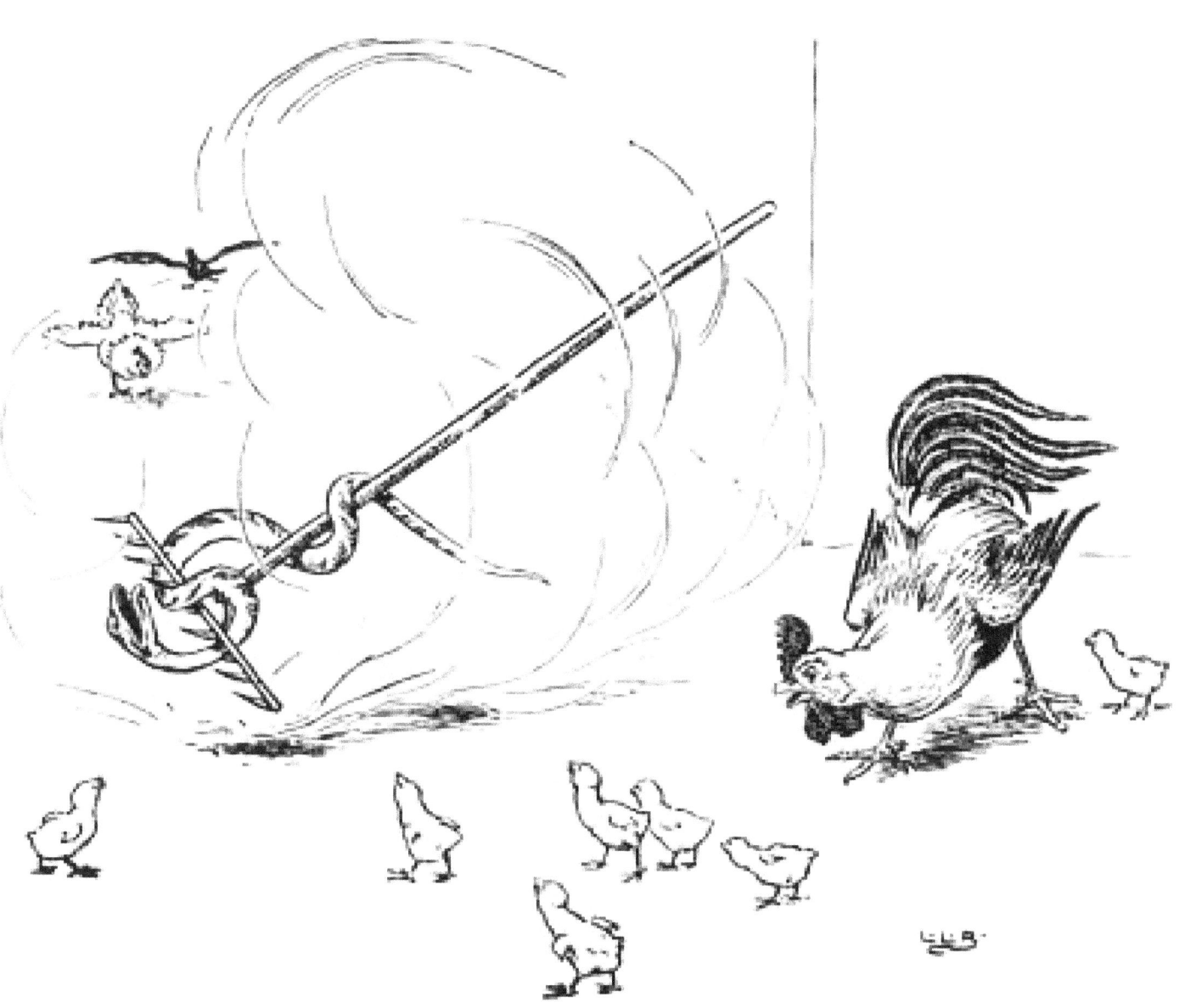

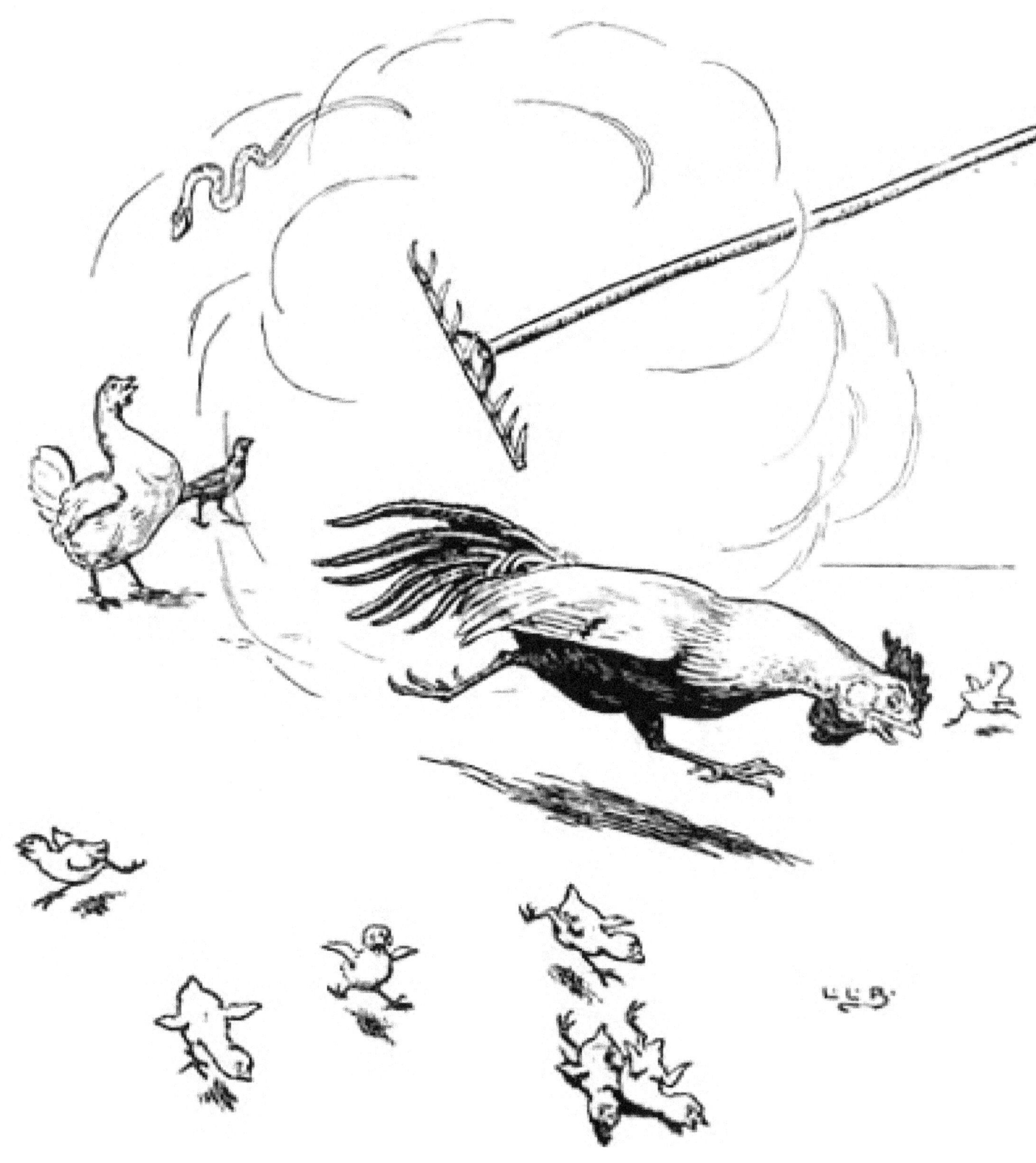

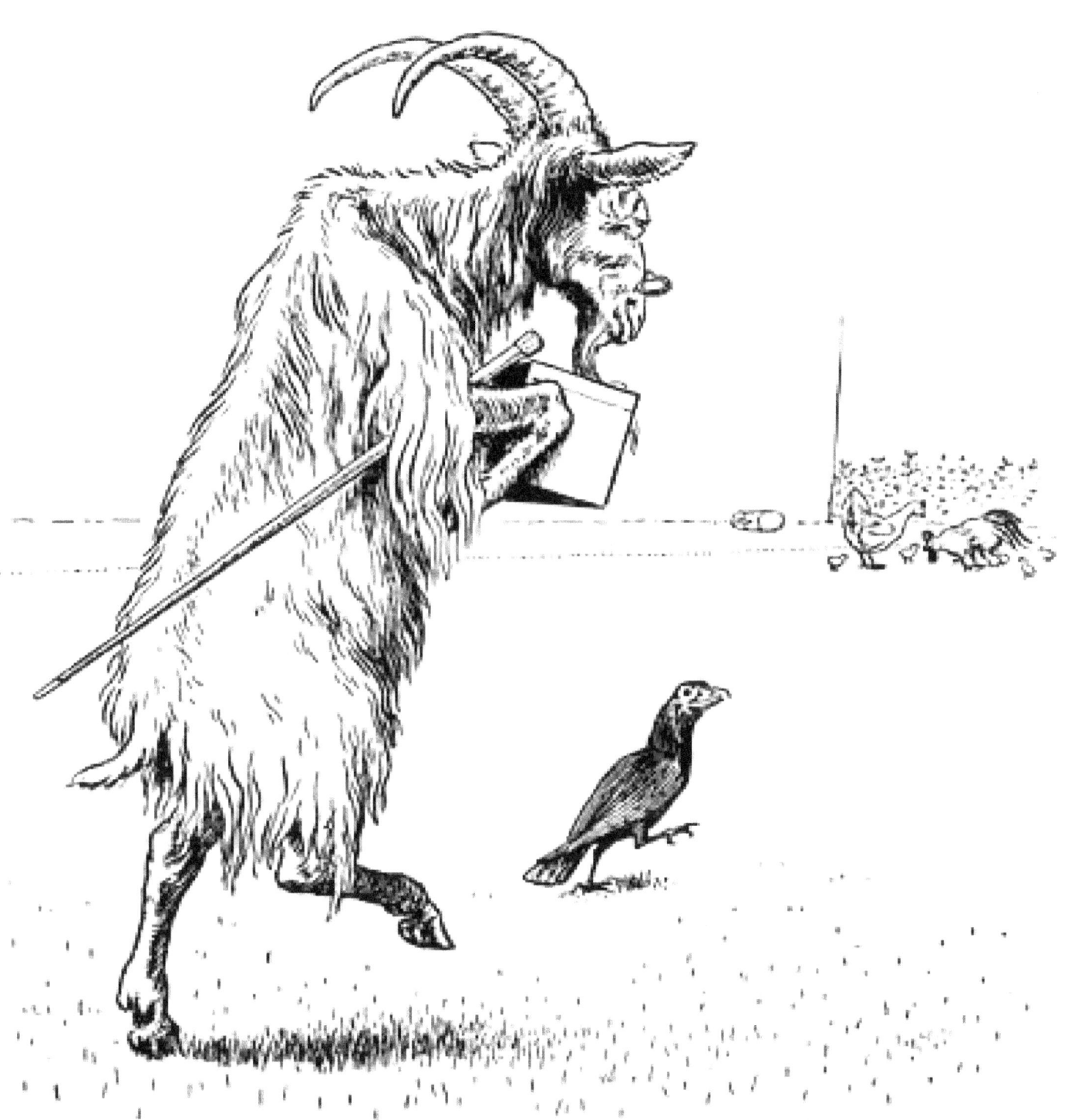

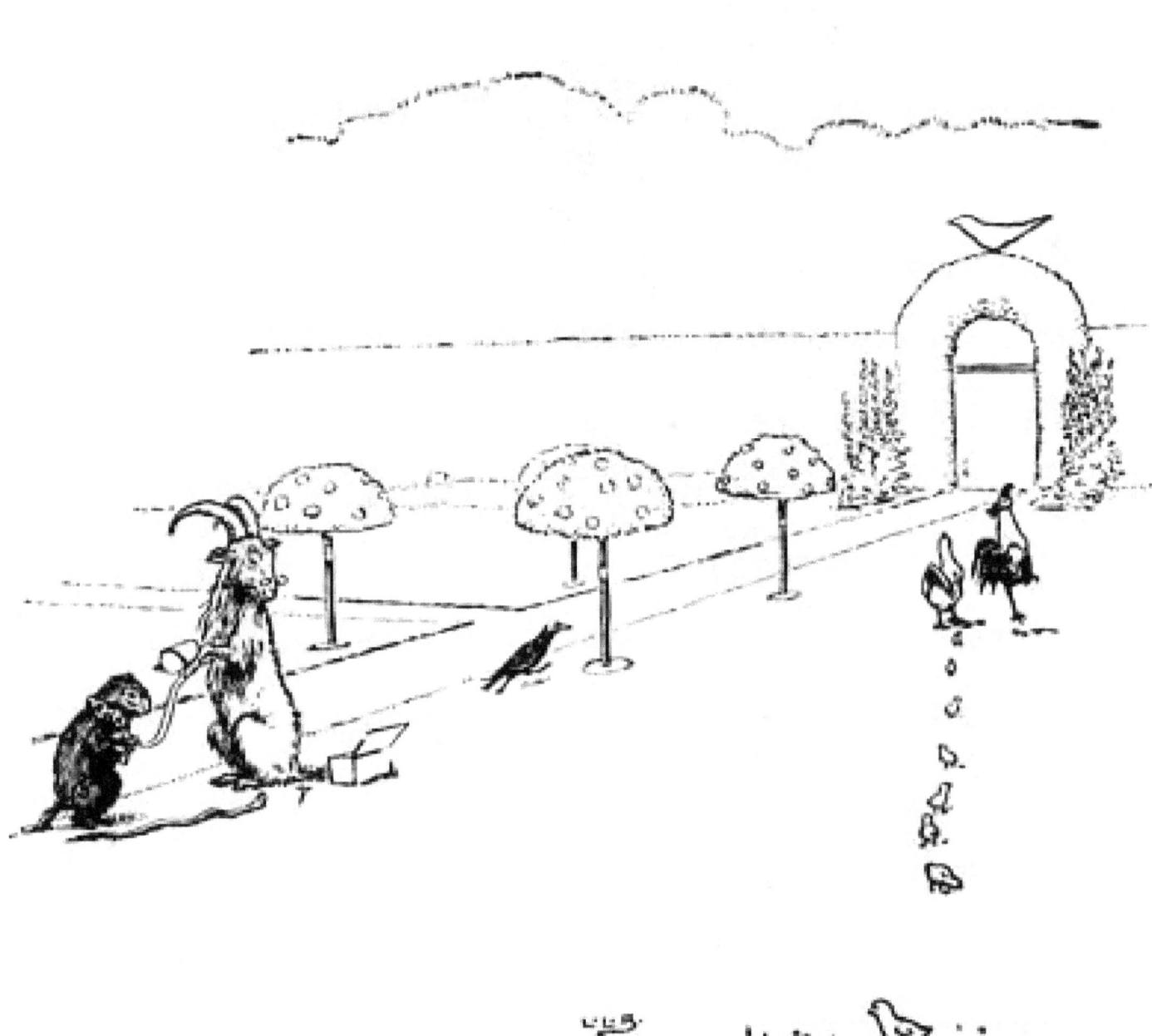

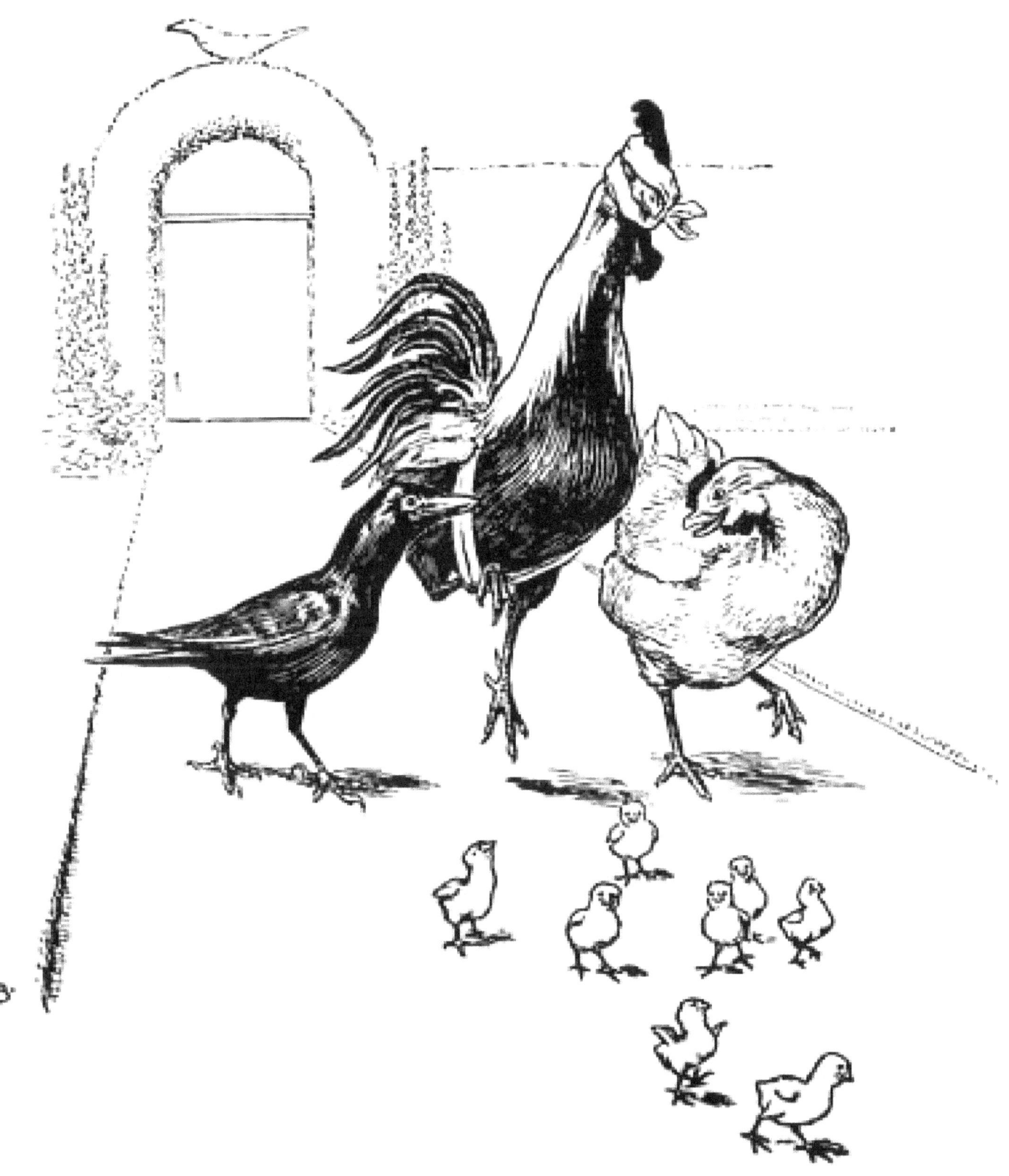

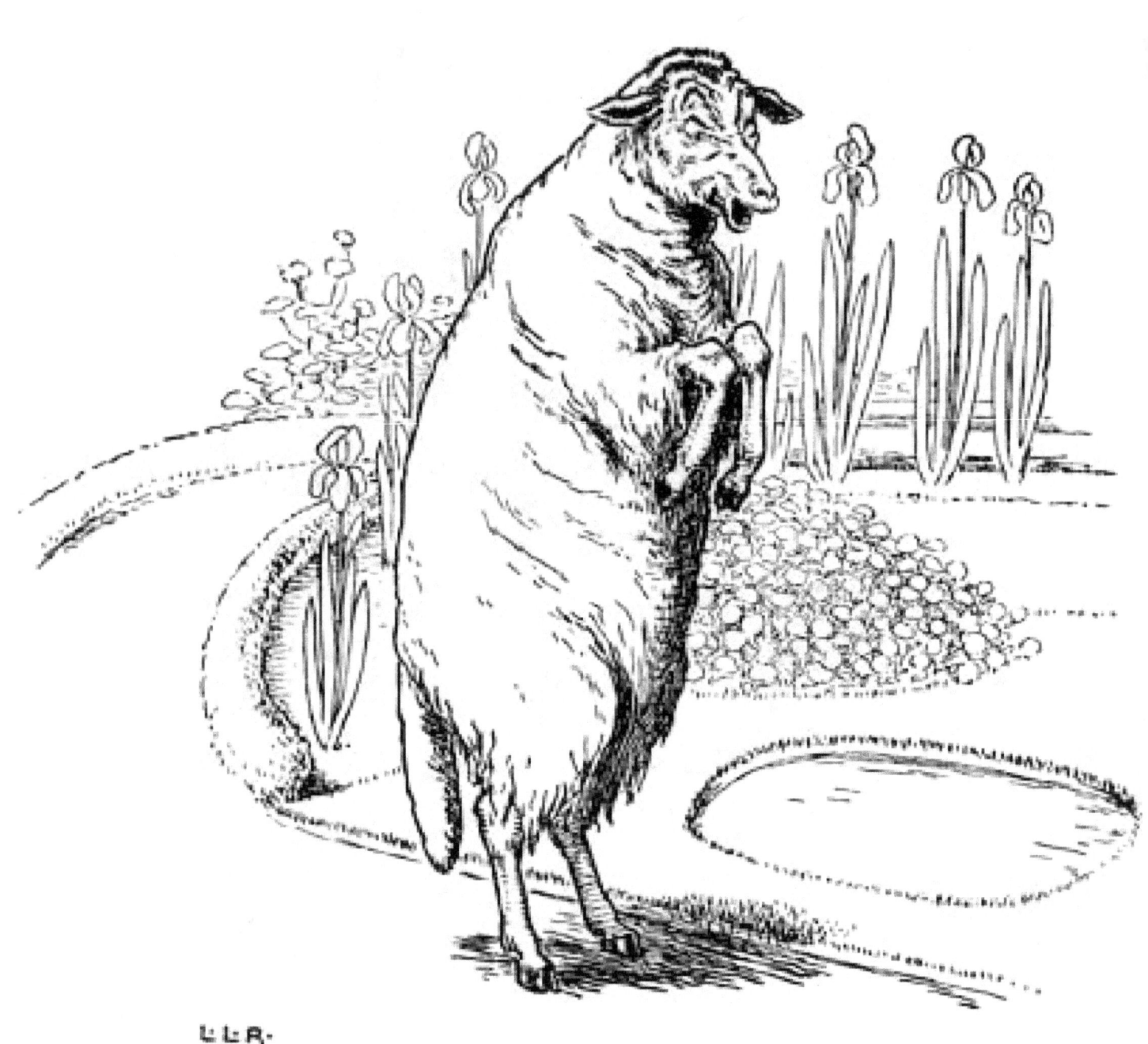

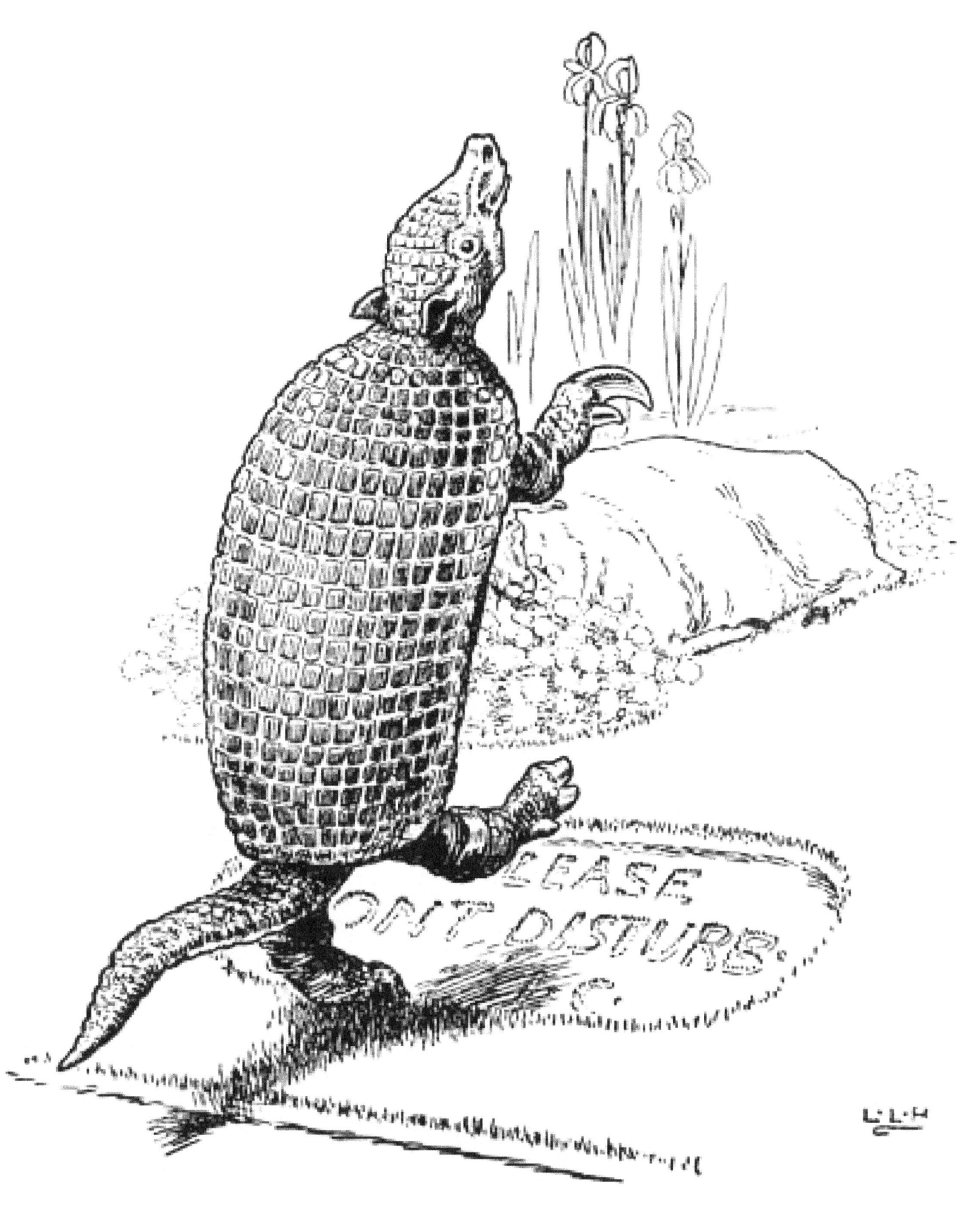

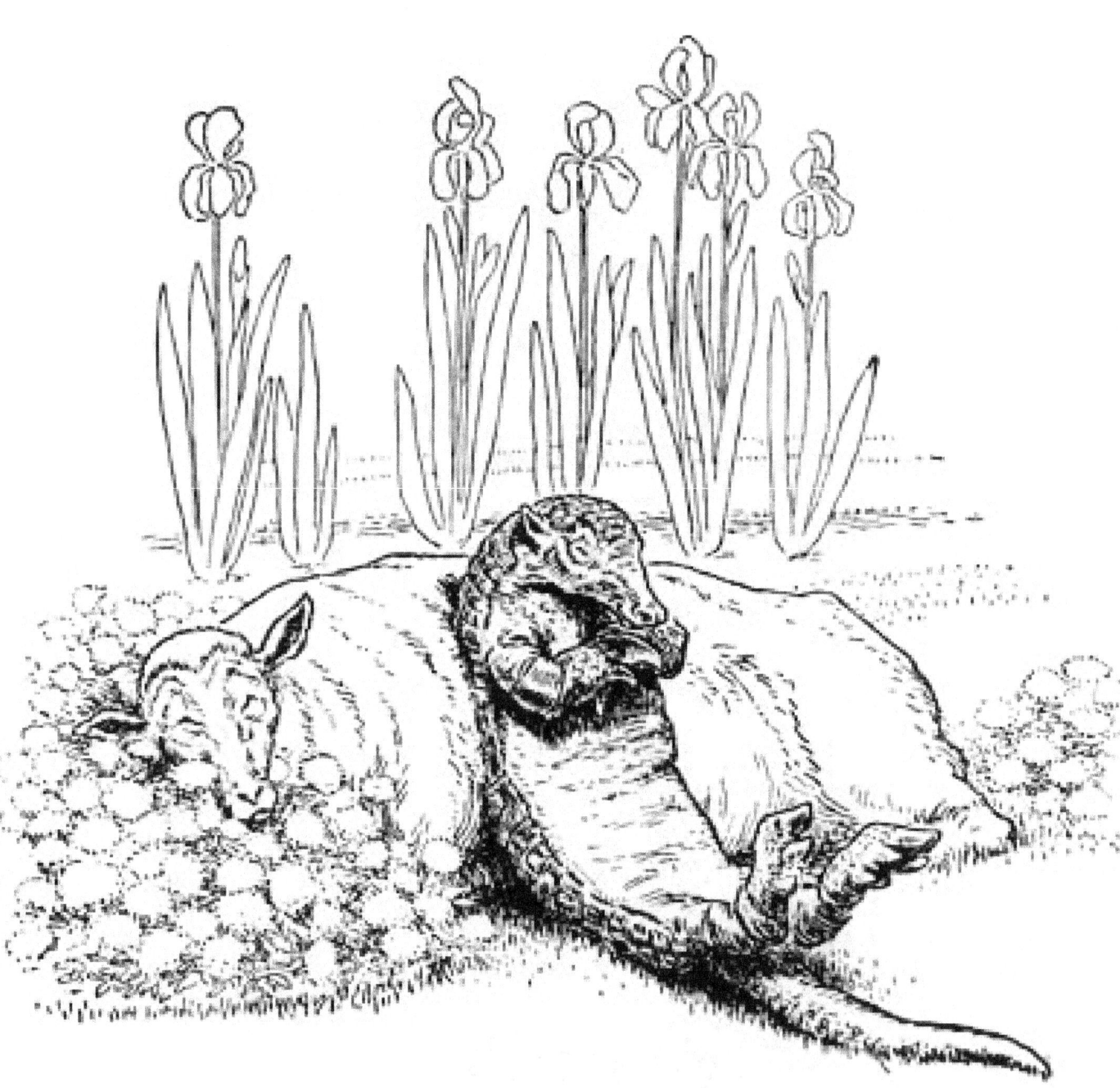

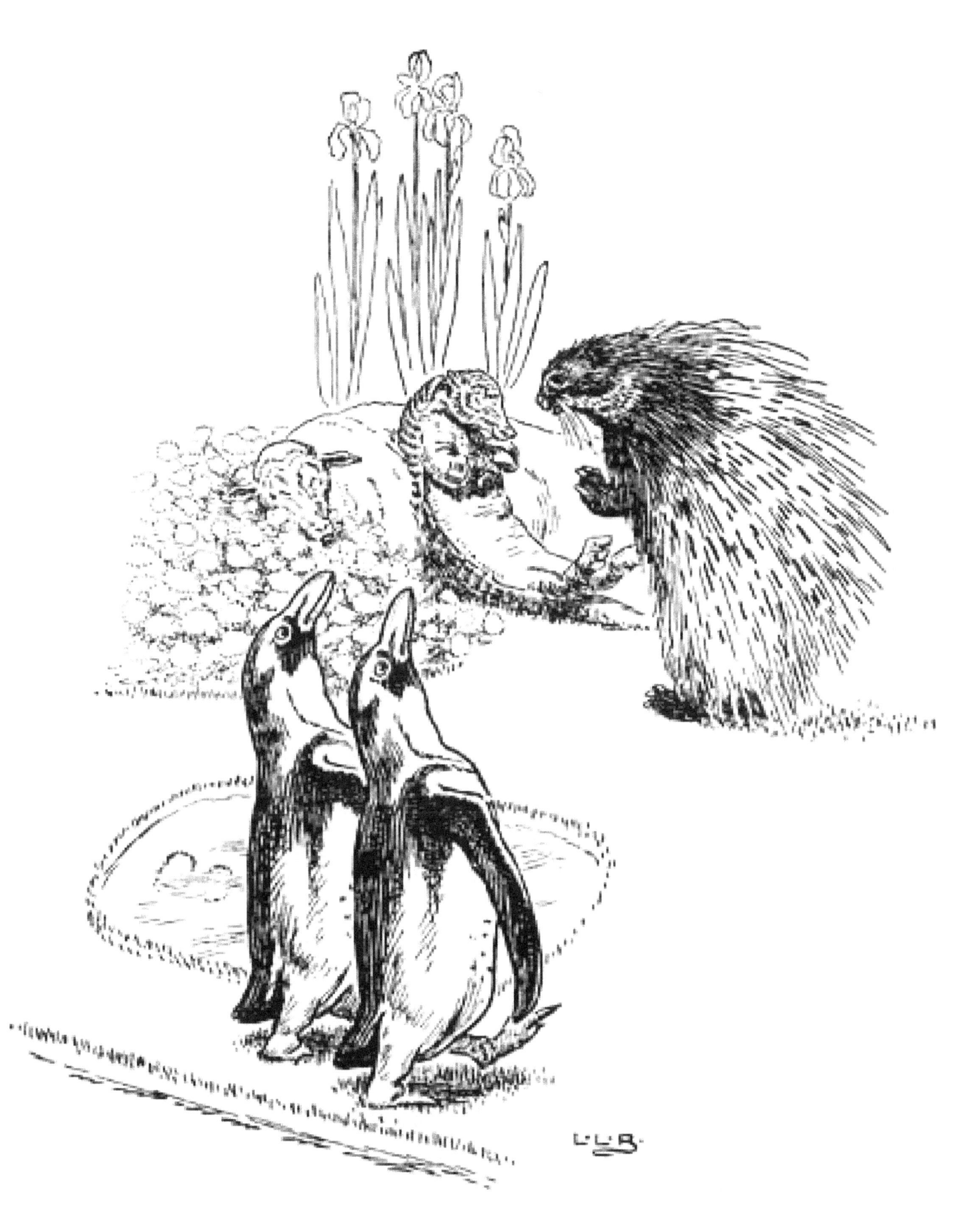

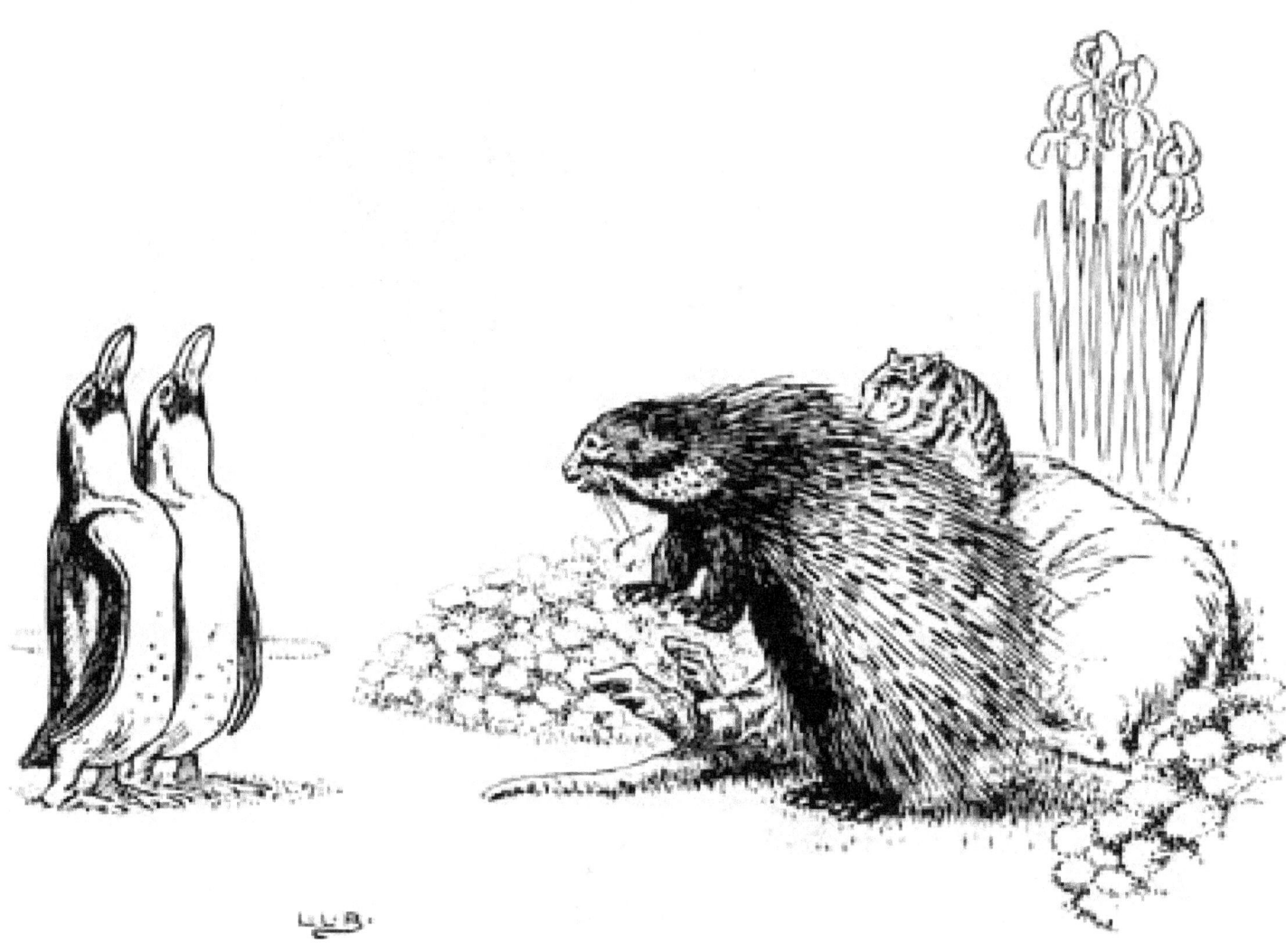

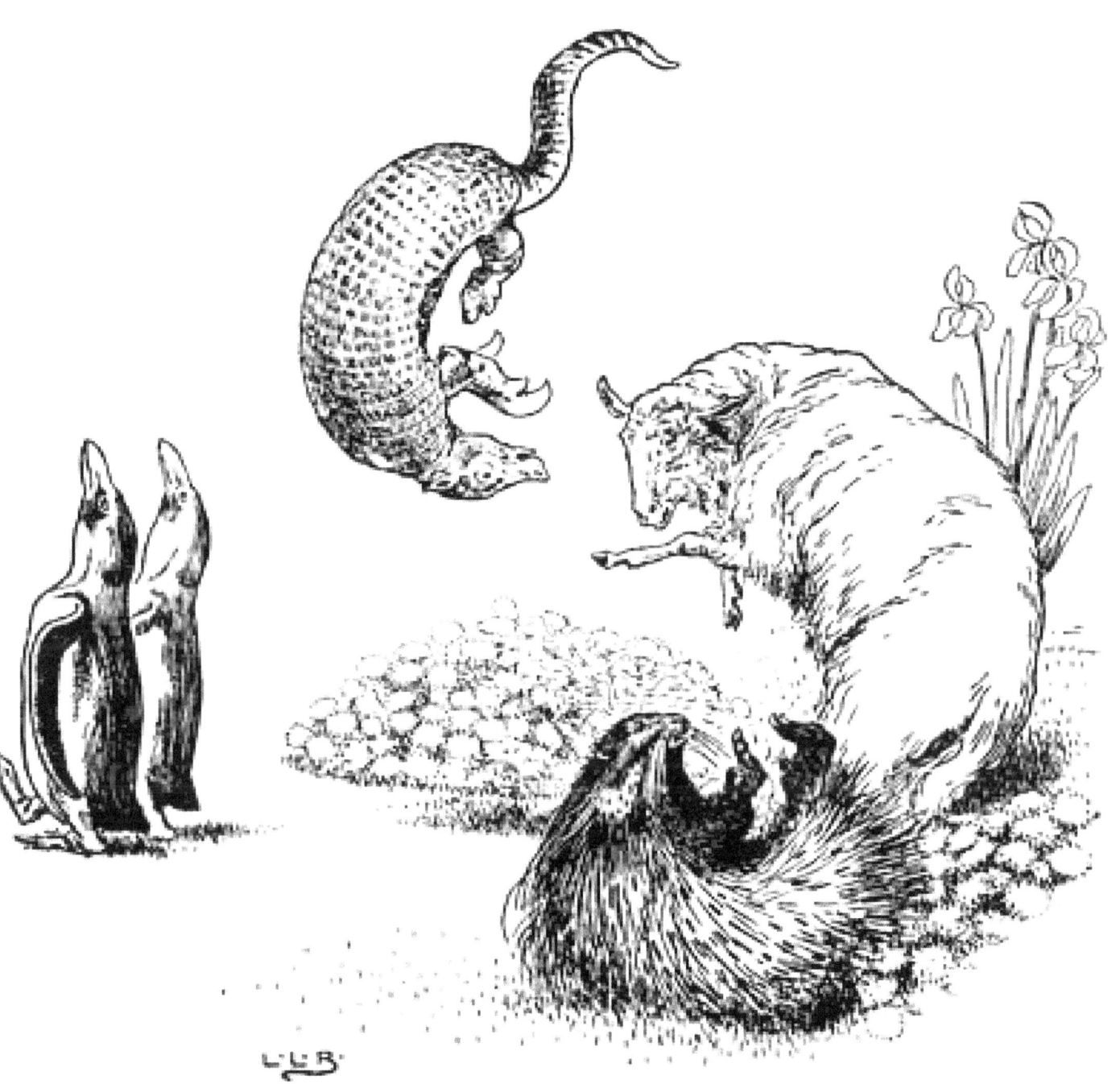

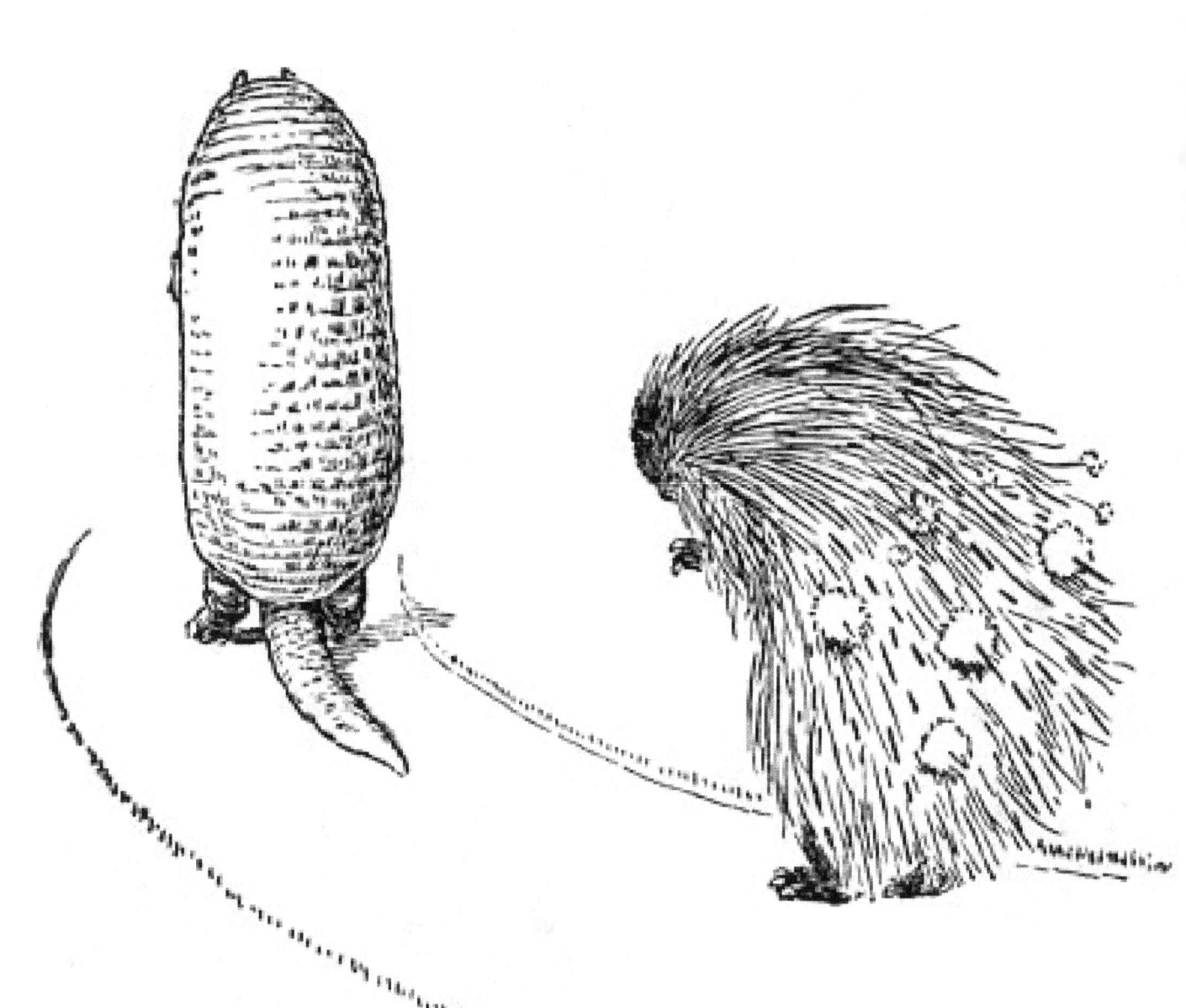

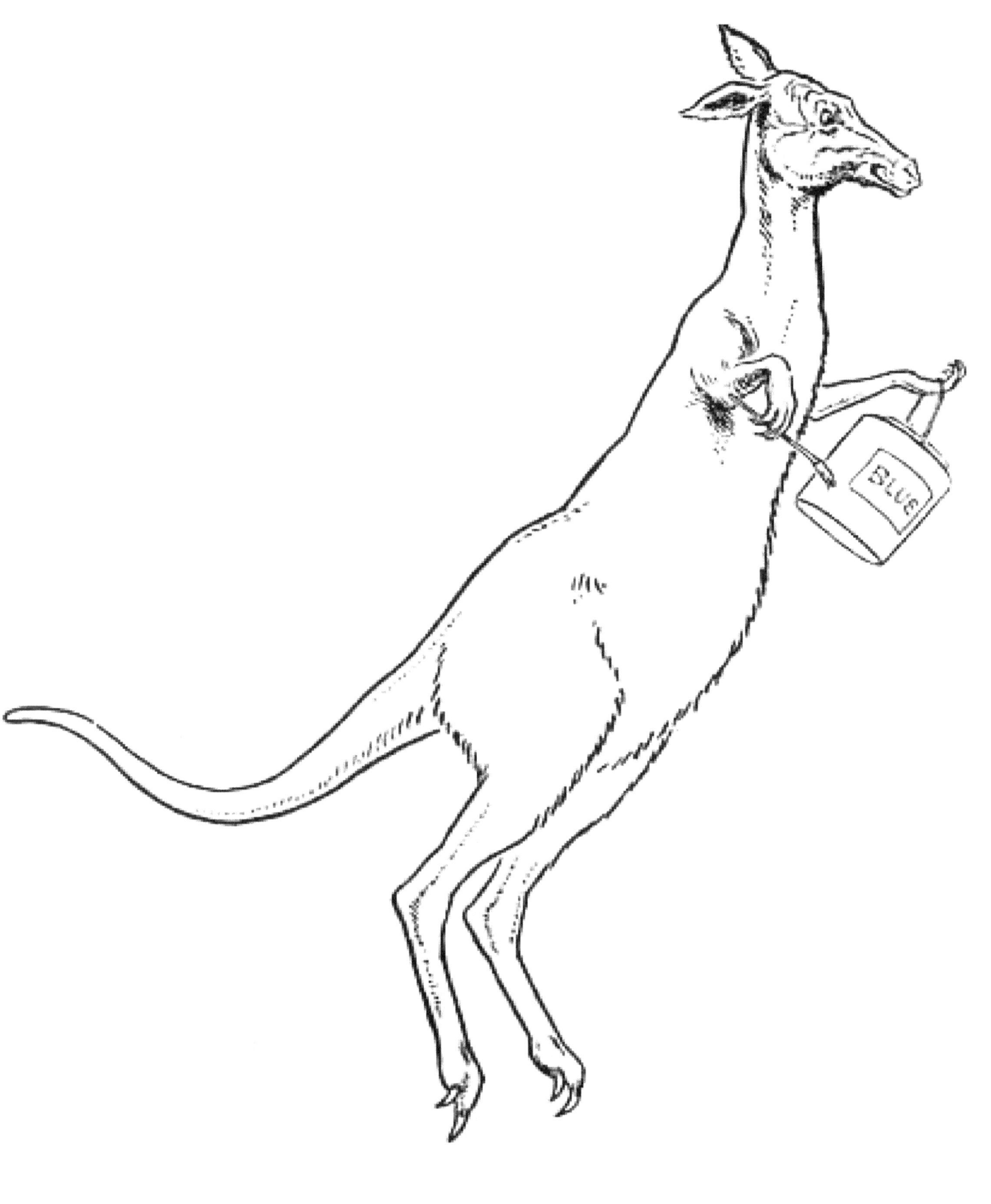

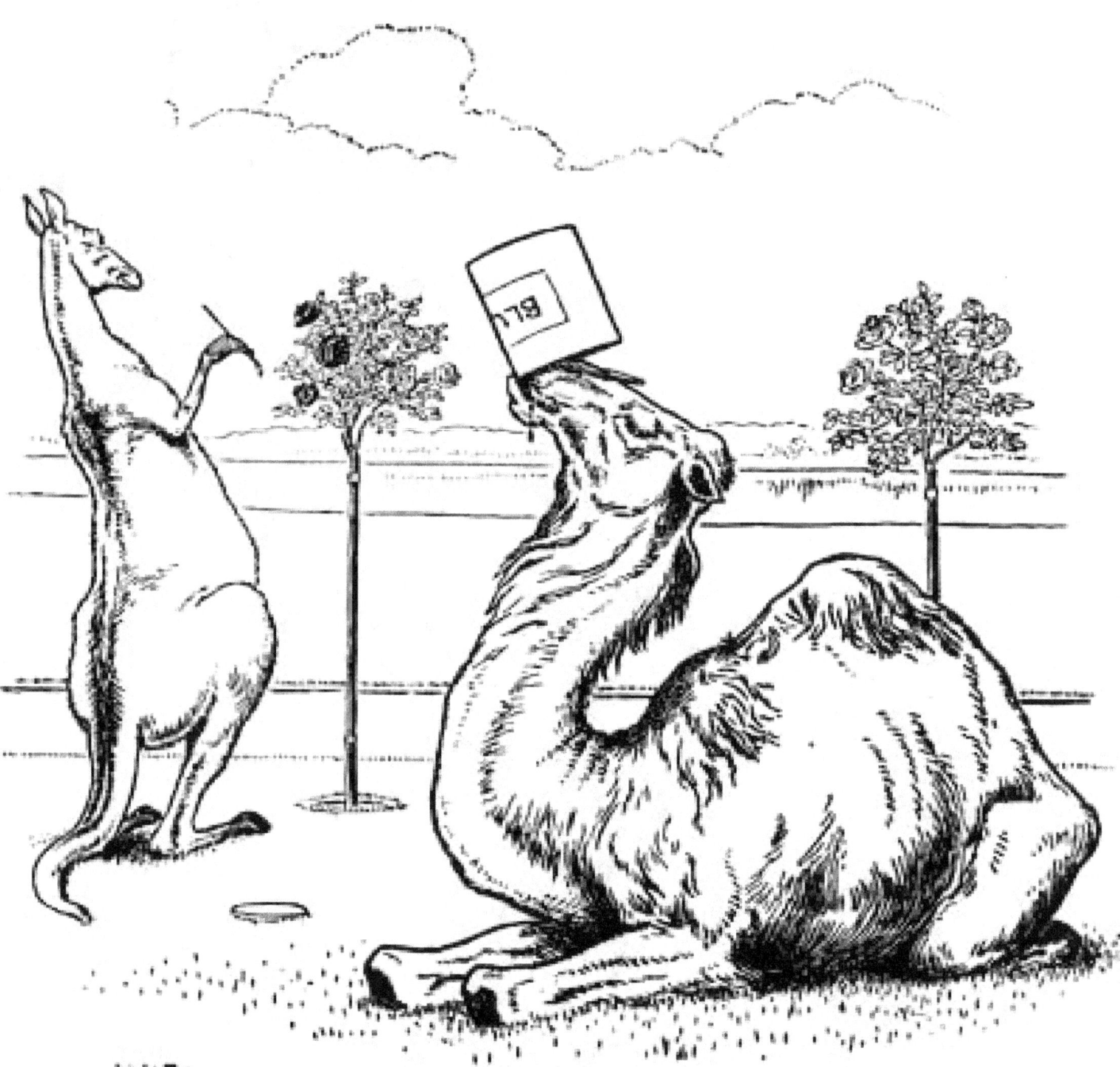

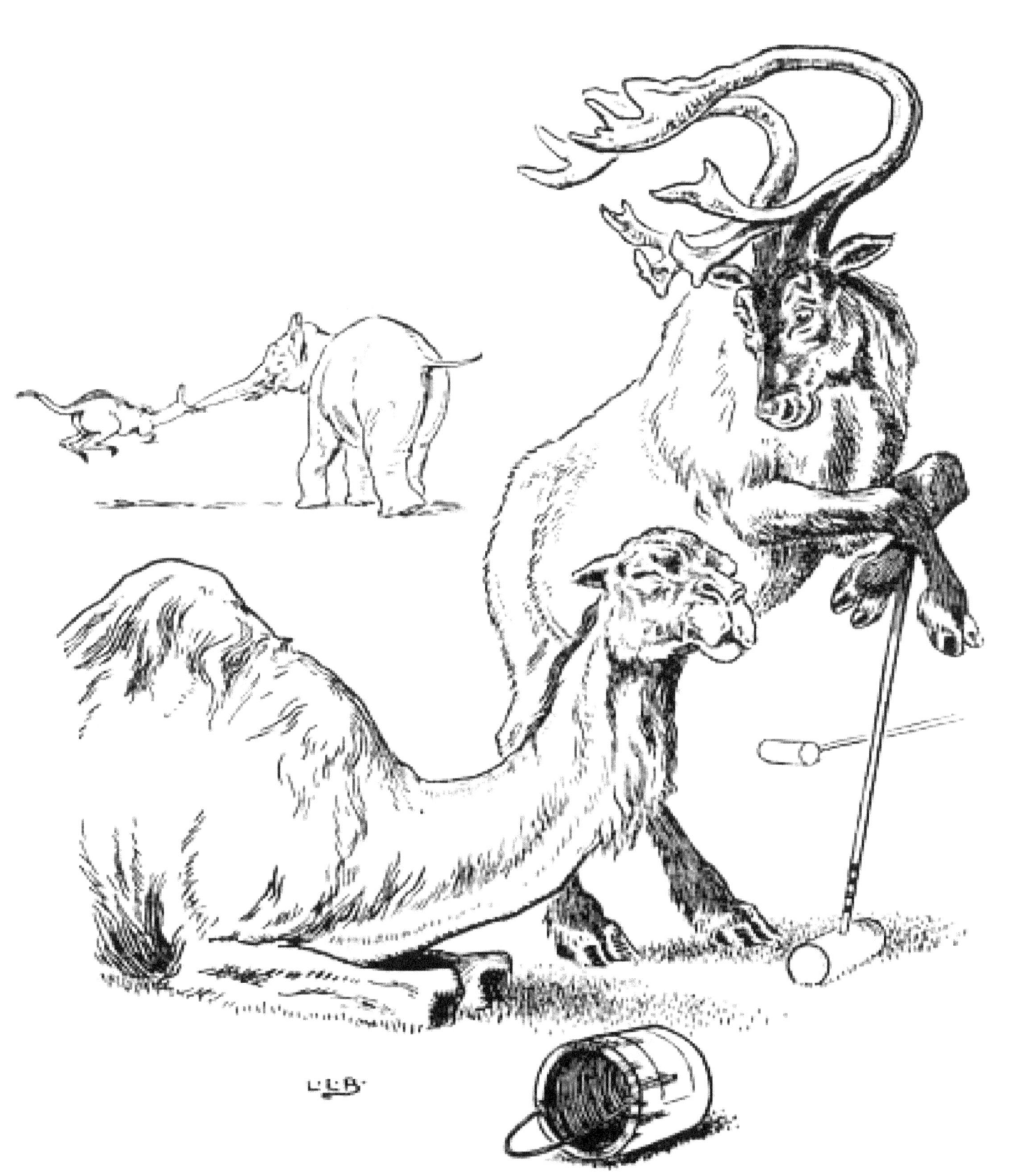

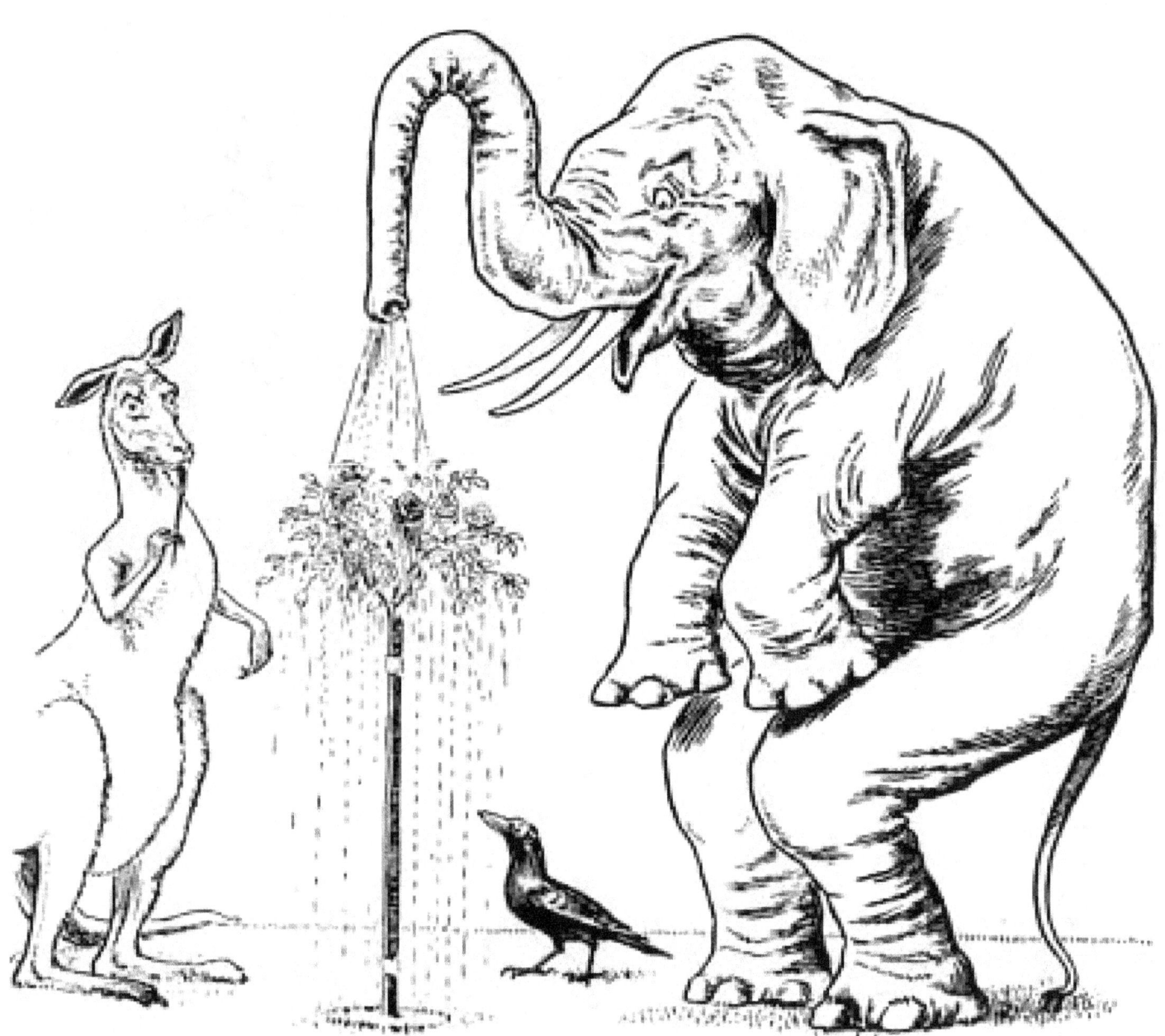

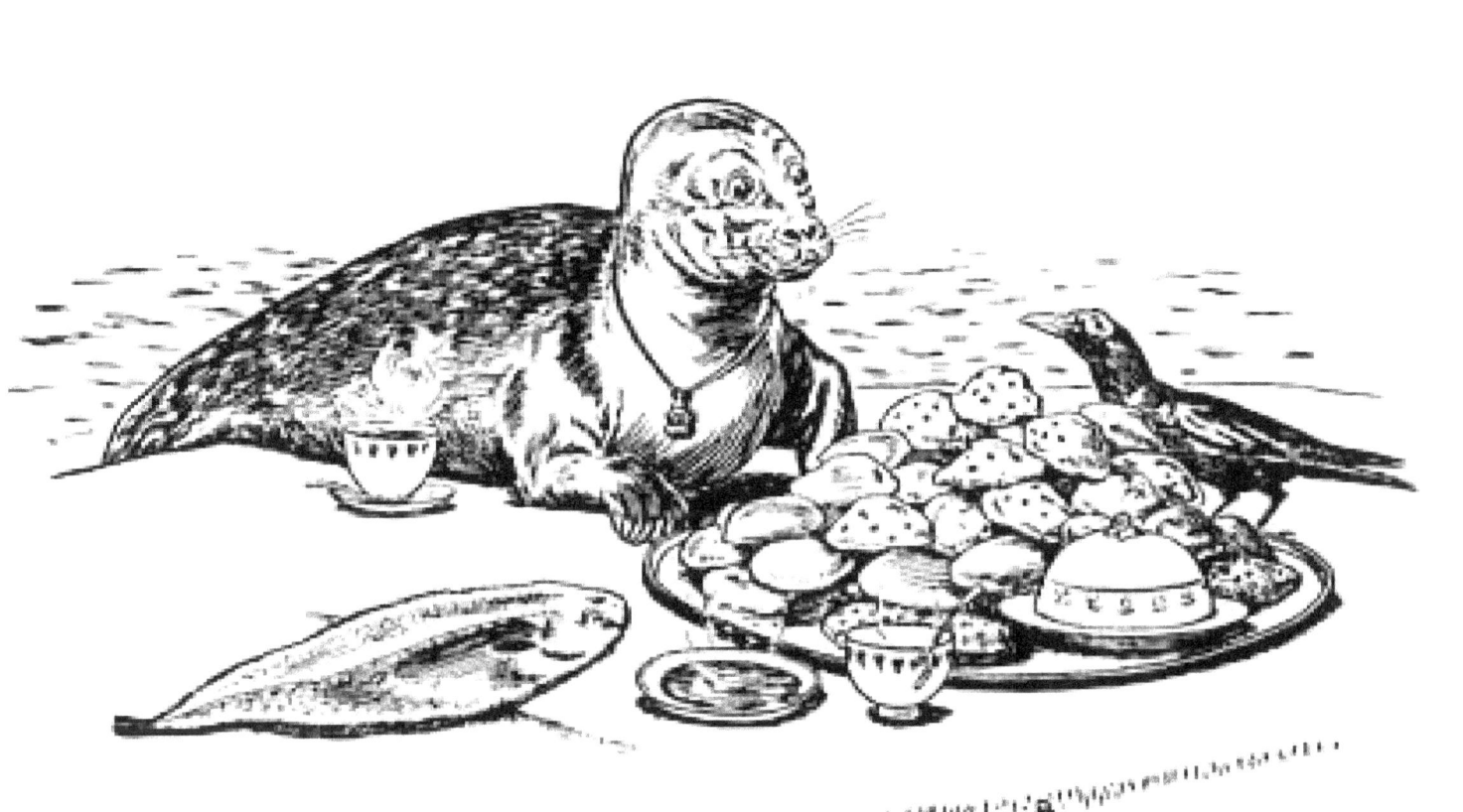

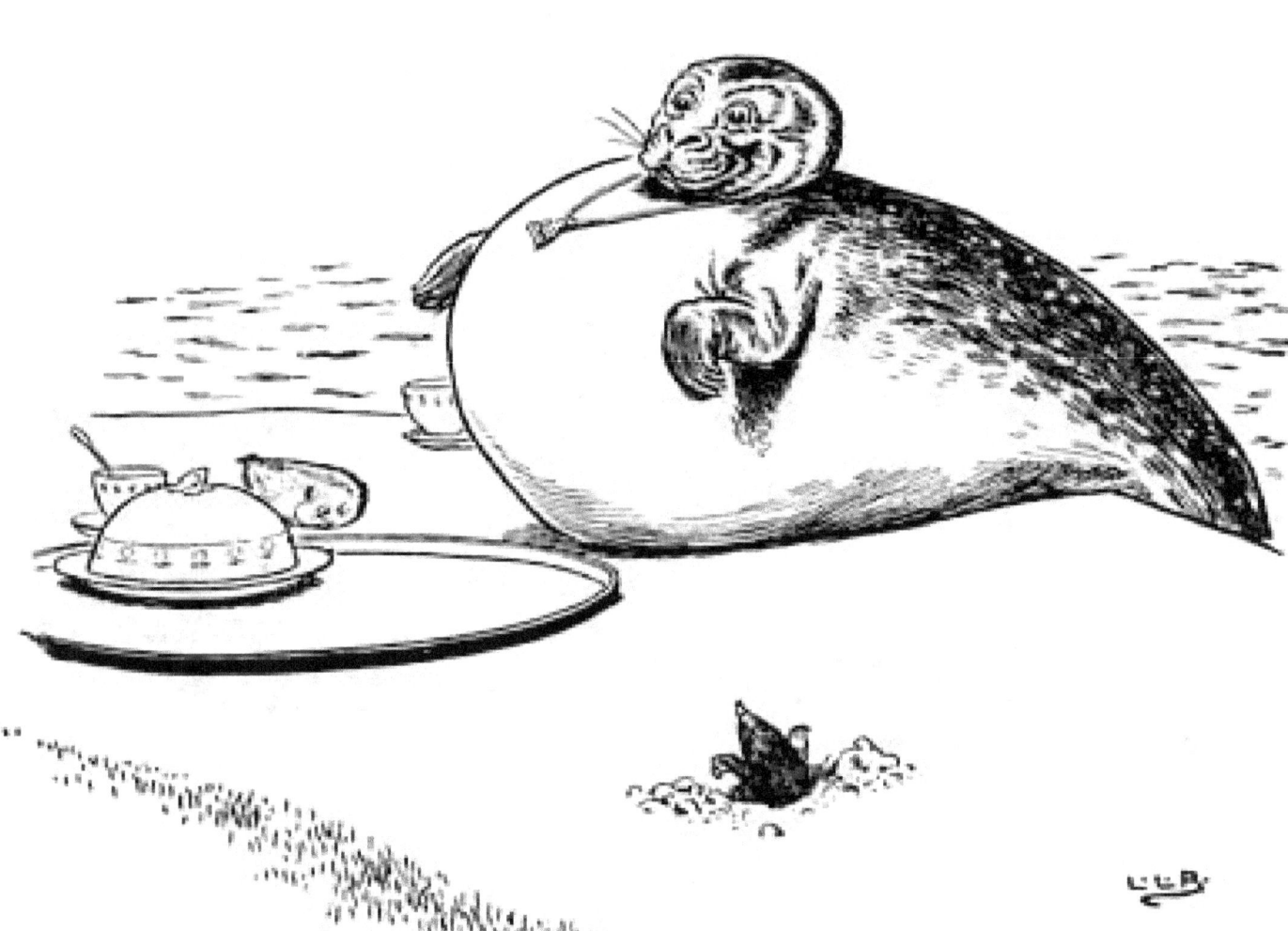

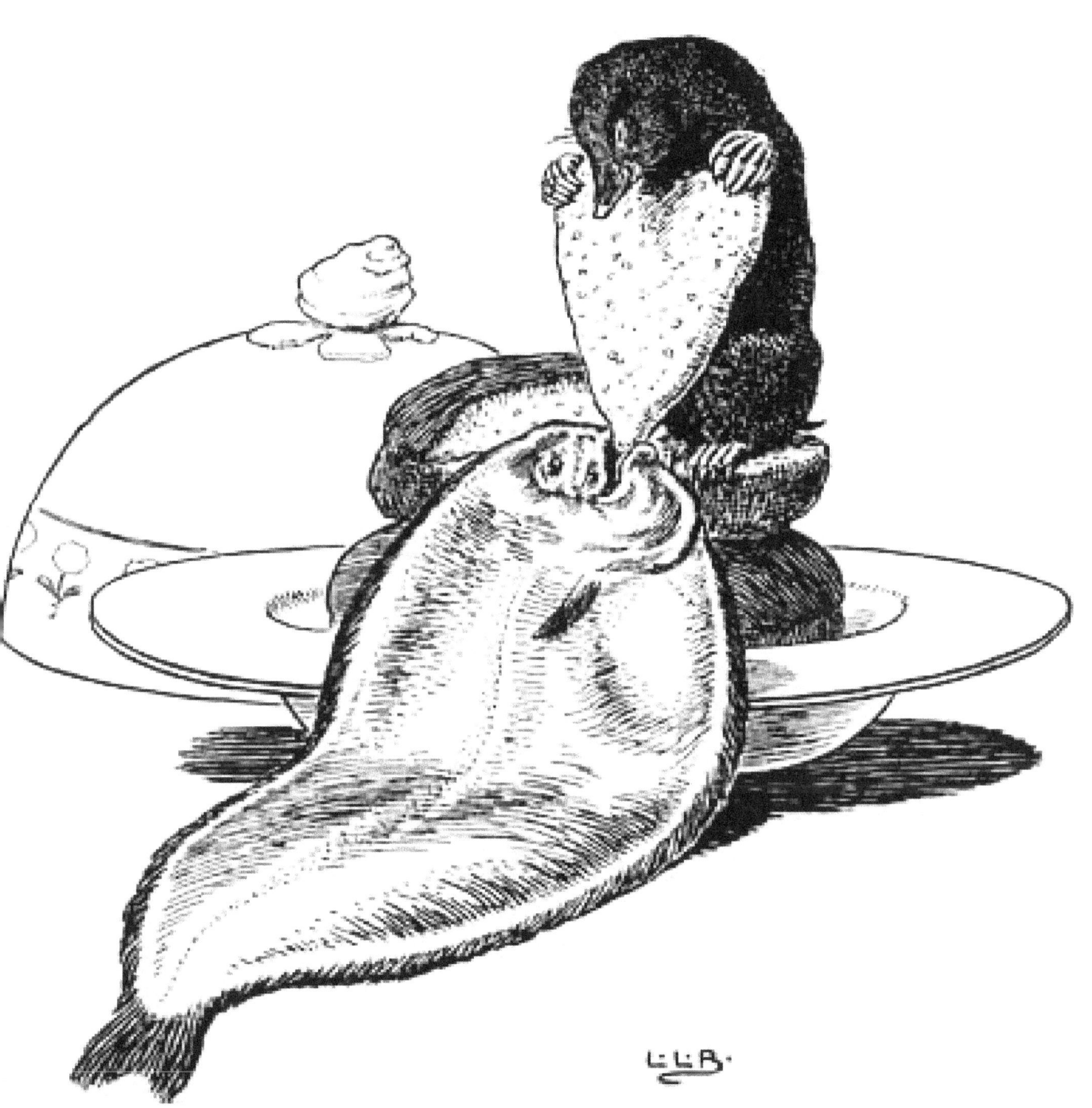

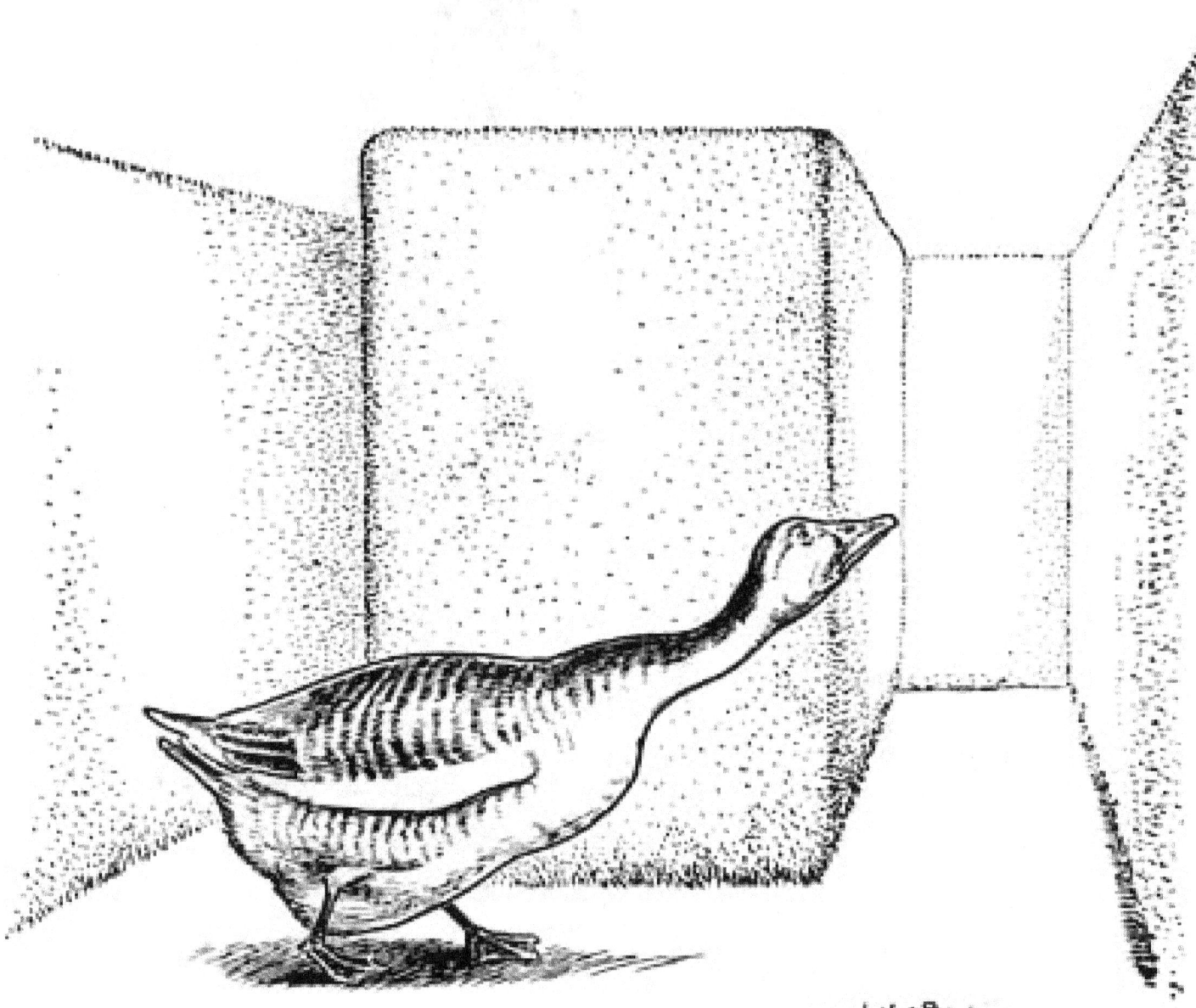

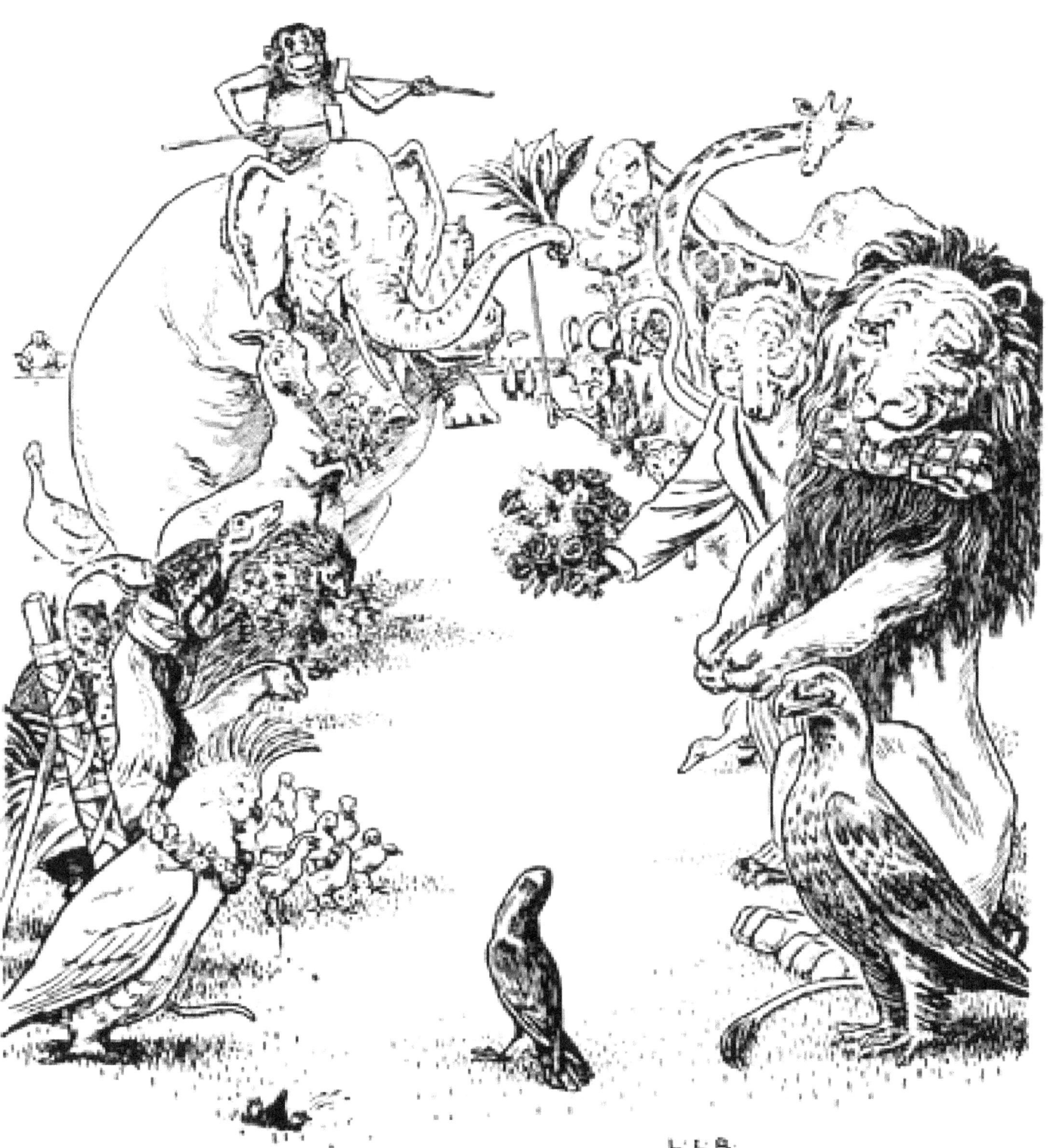

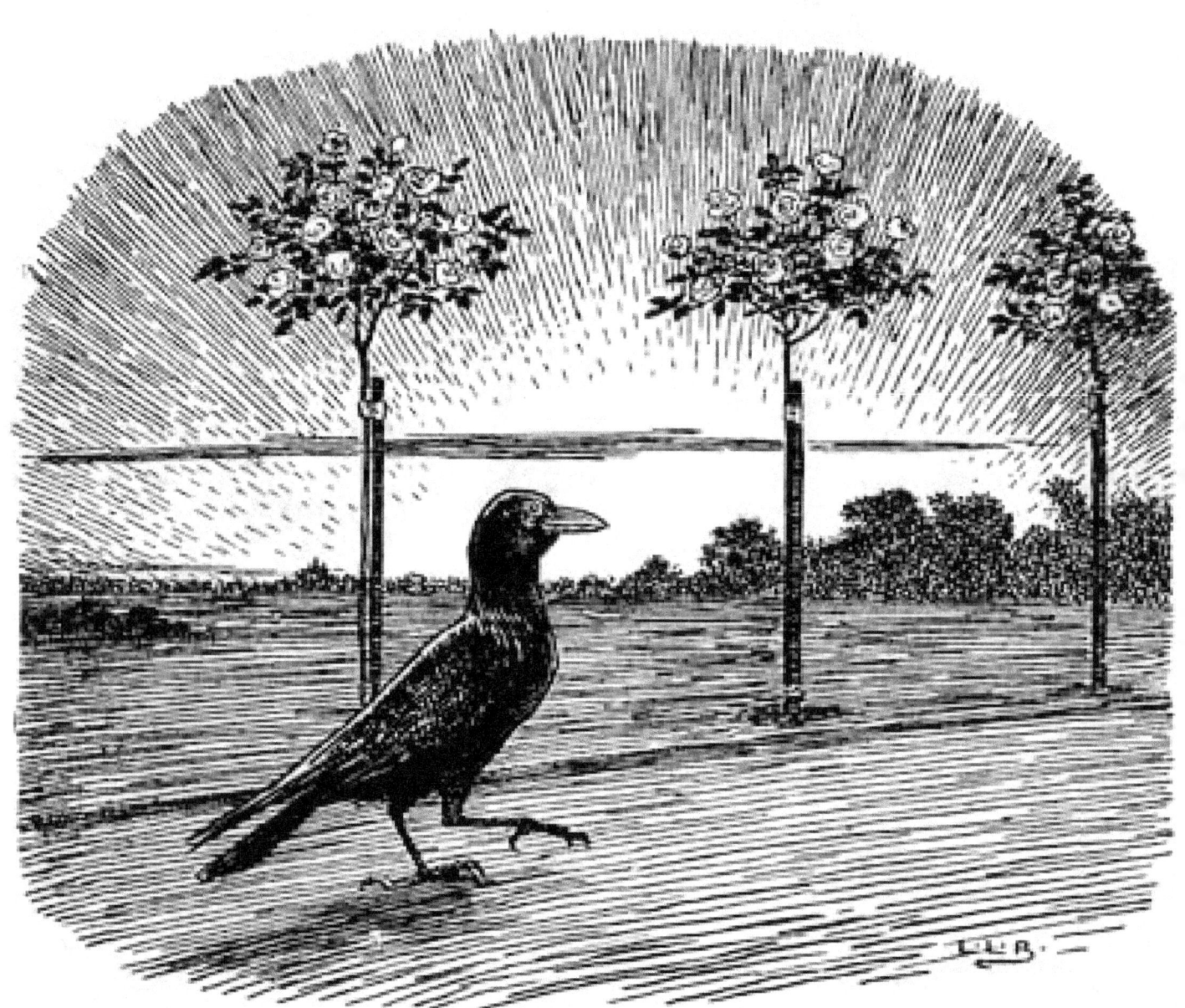

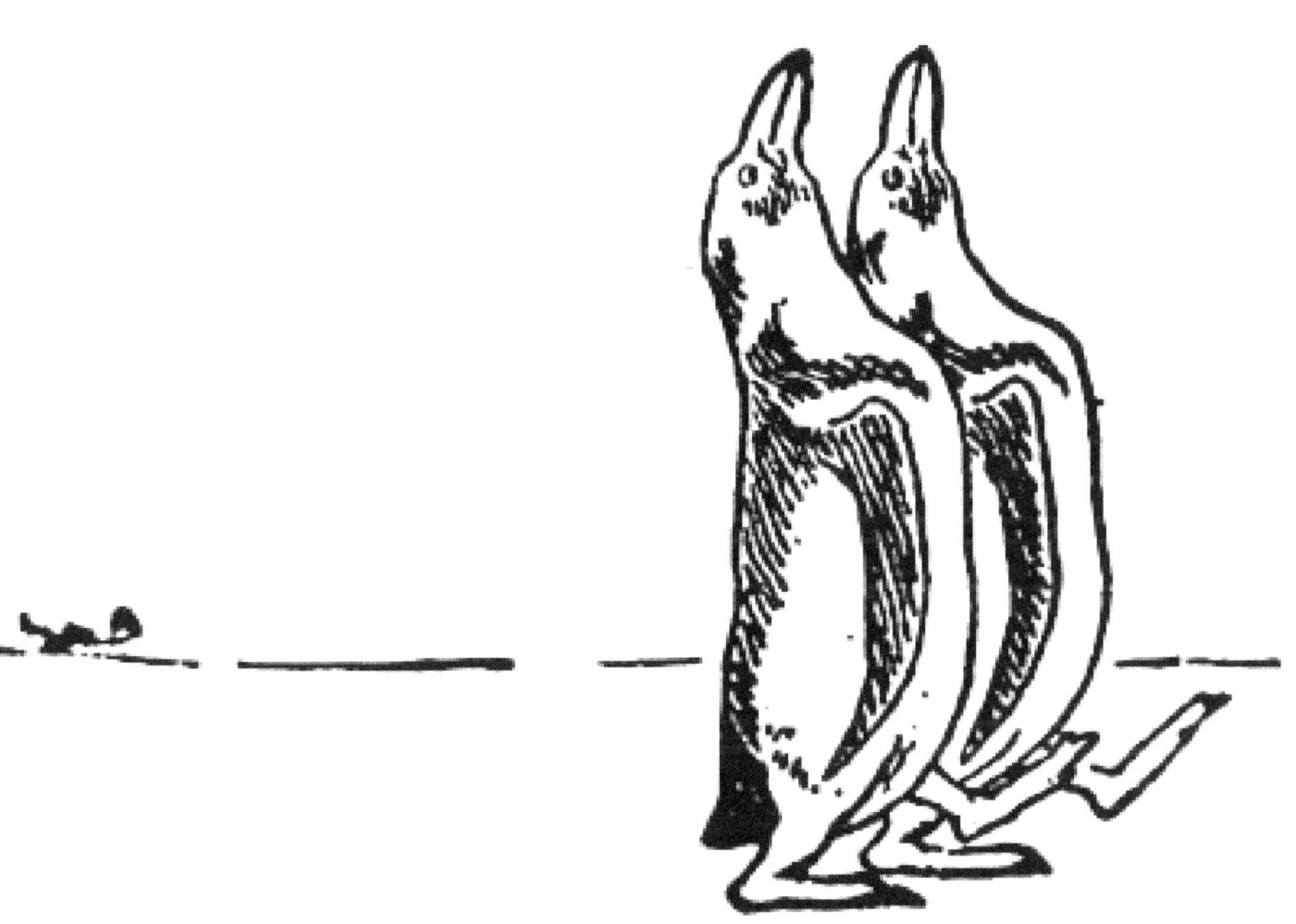

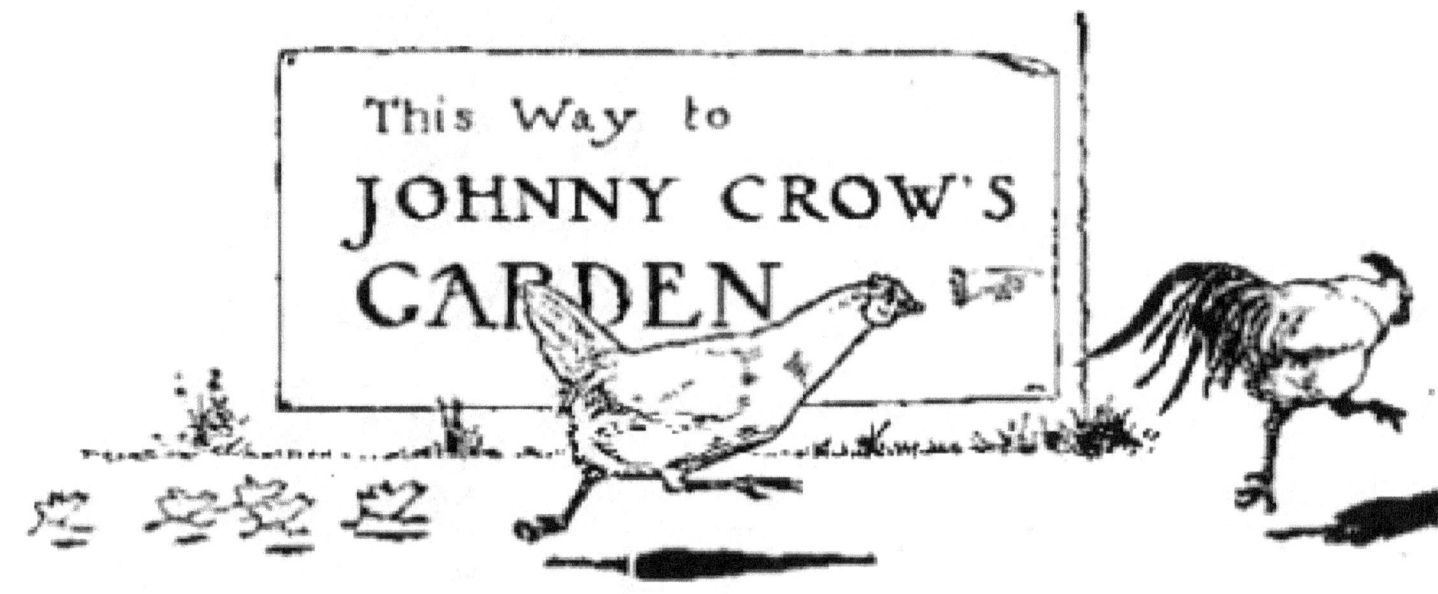

This Way to
JOHNNY CROW'S
GARDEN

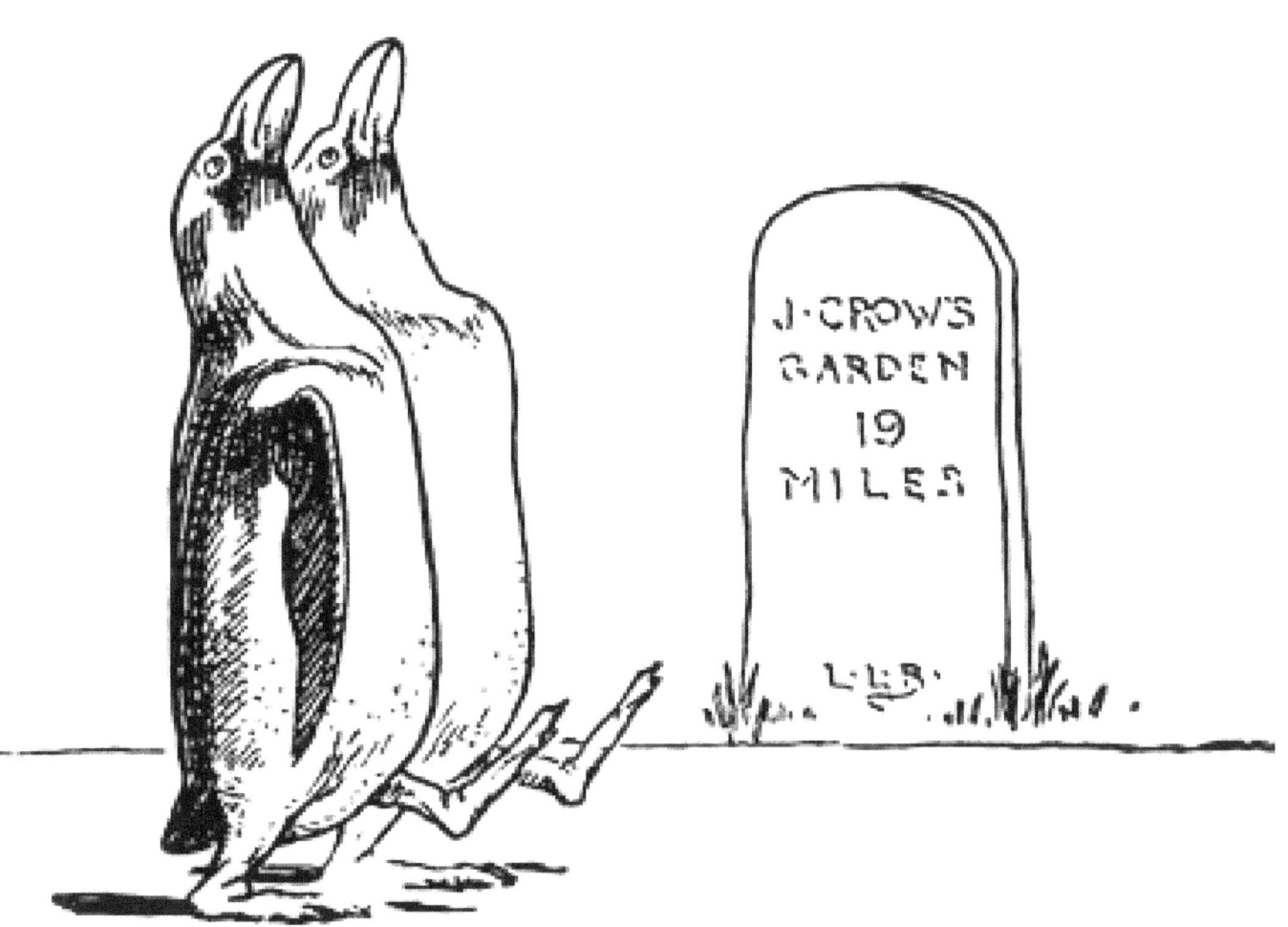

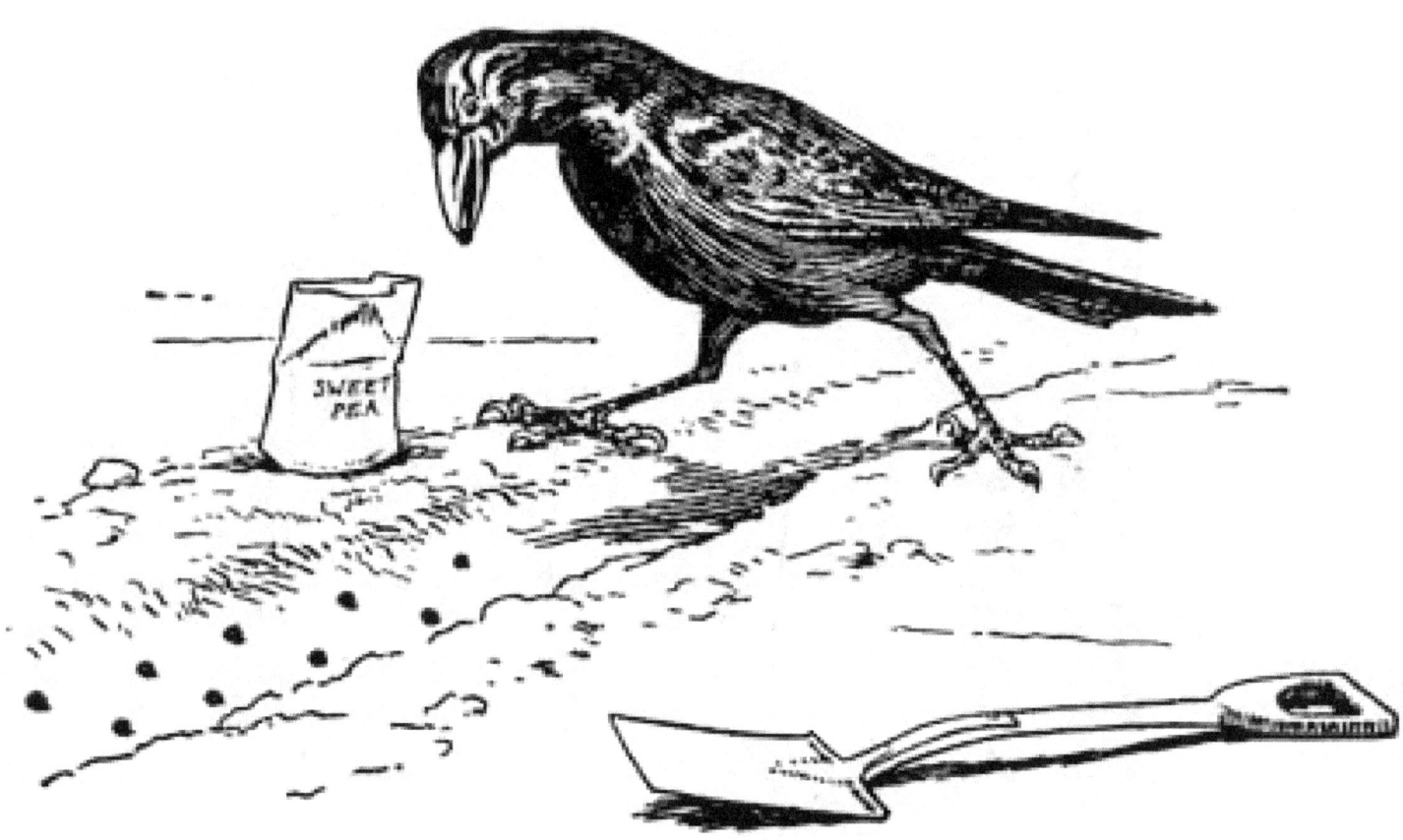

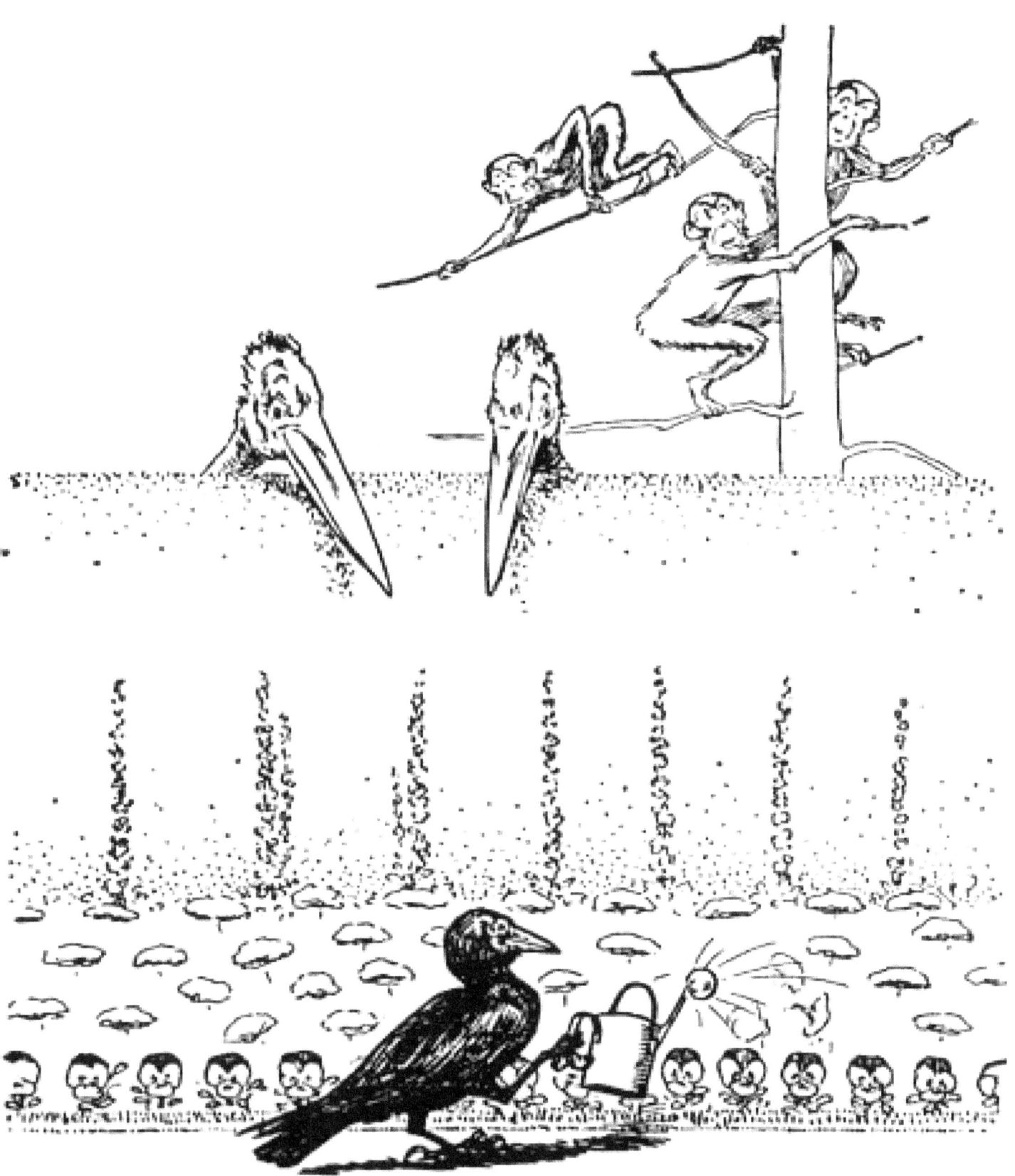

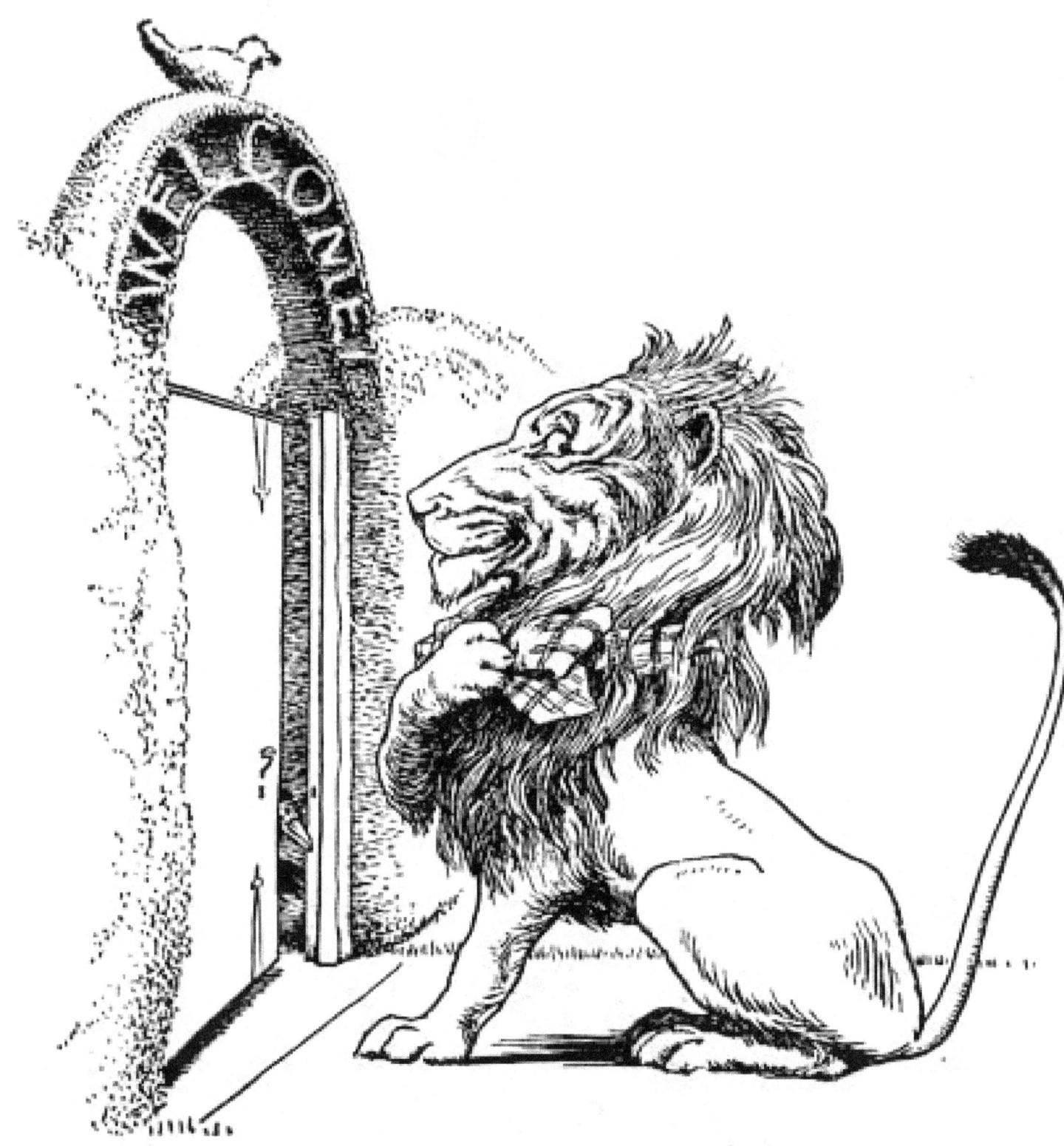

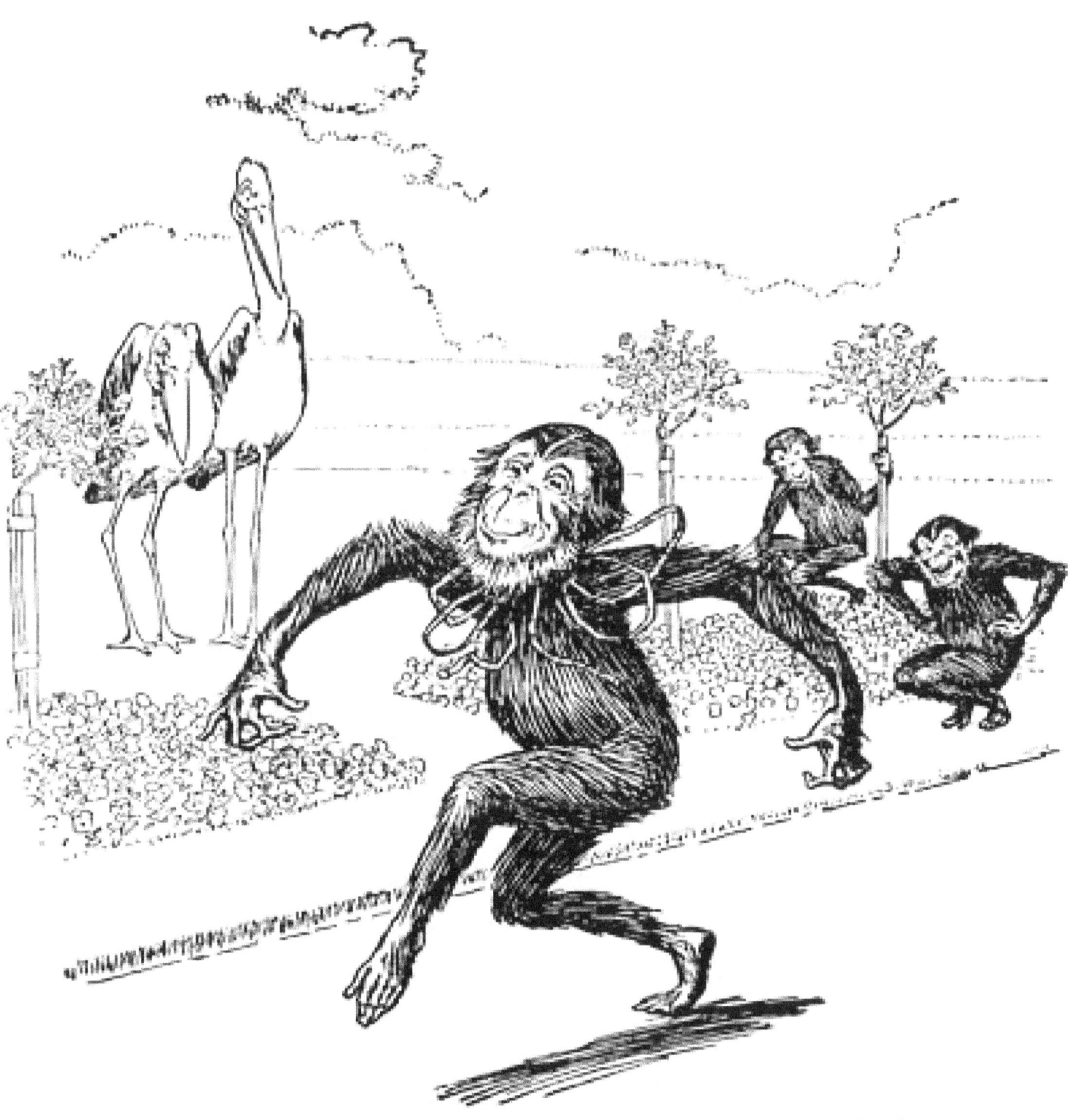

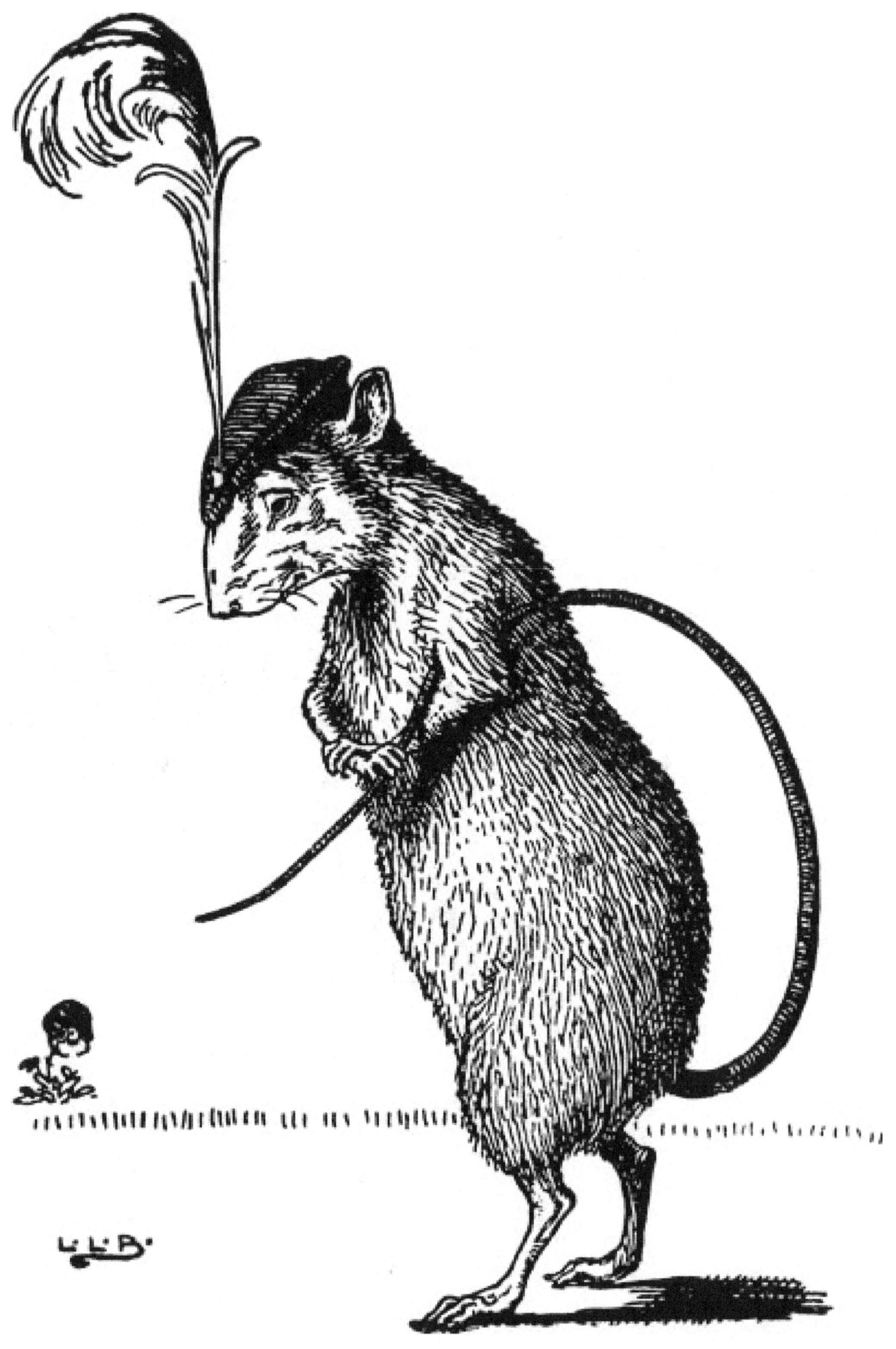

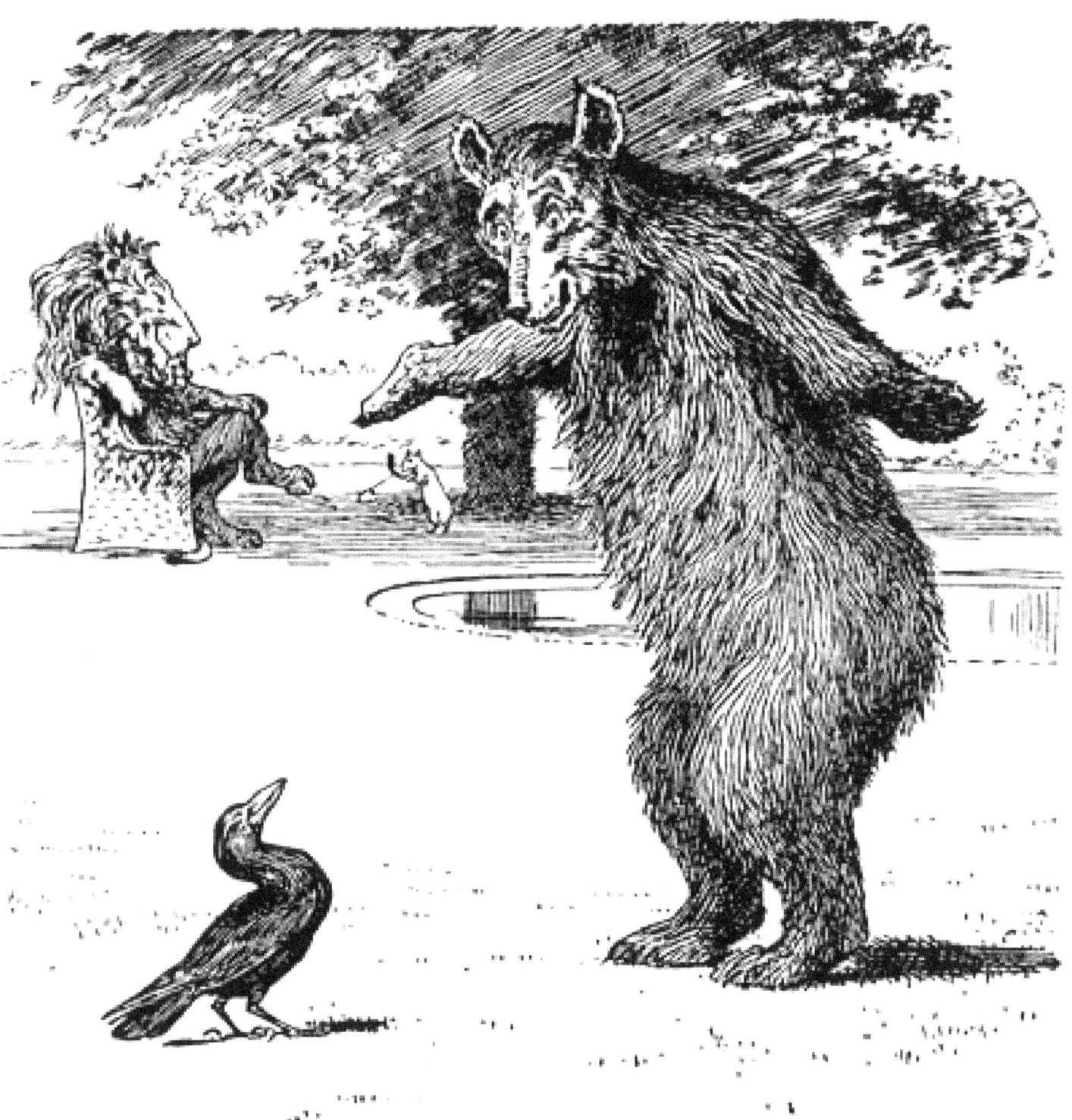

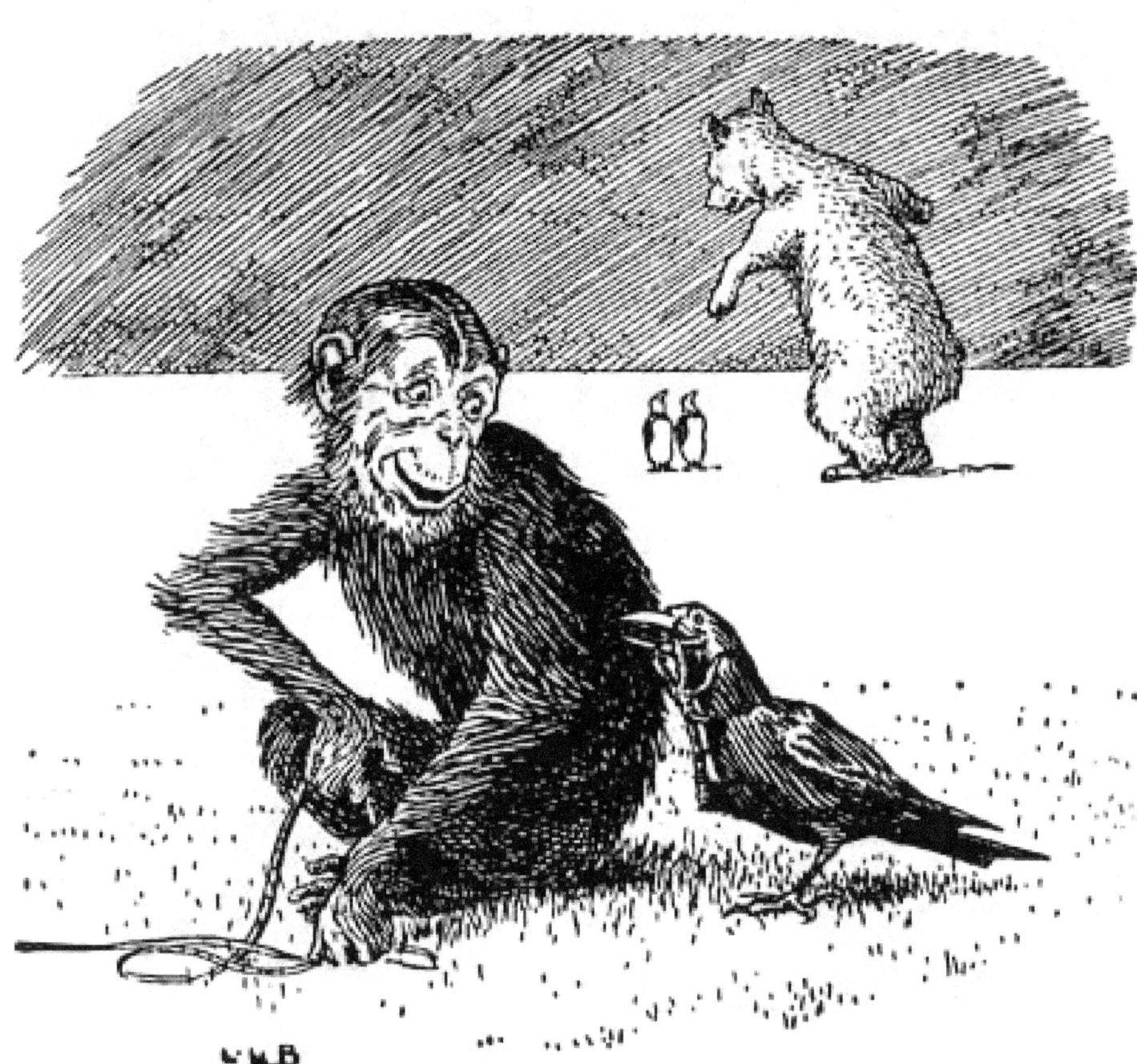

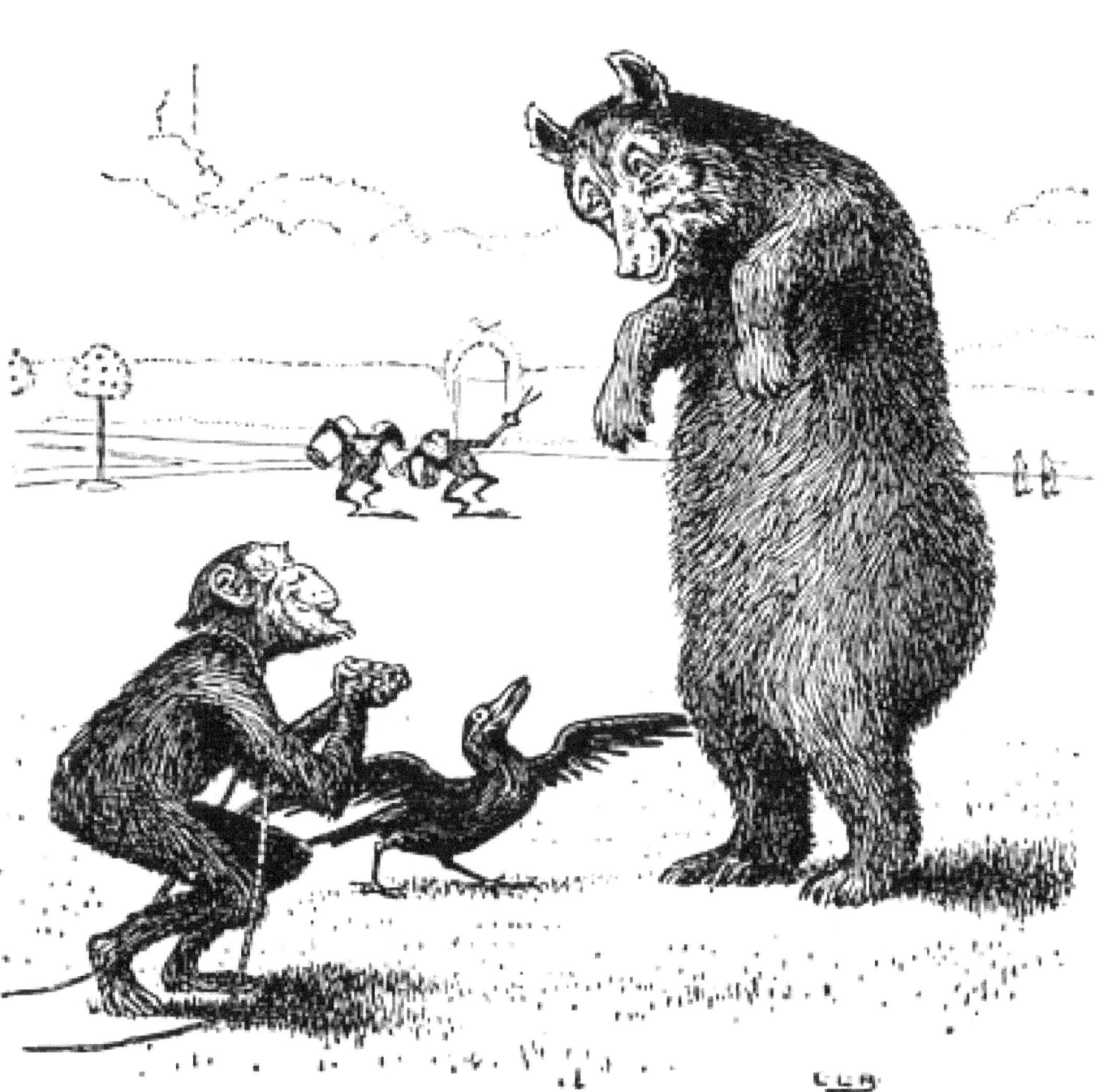

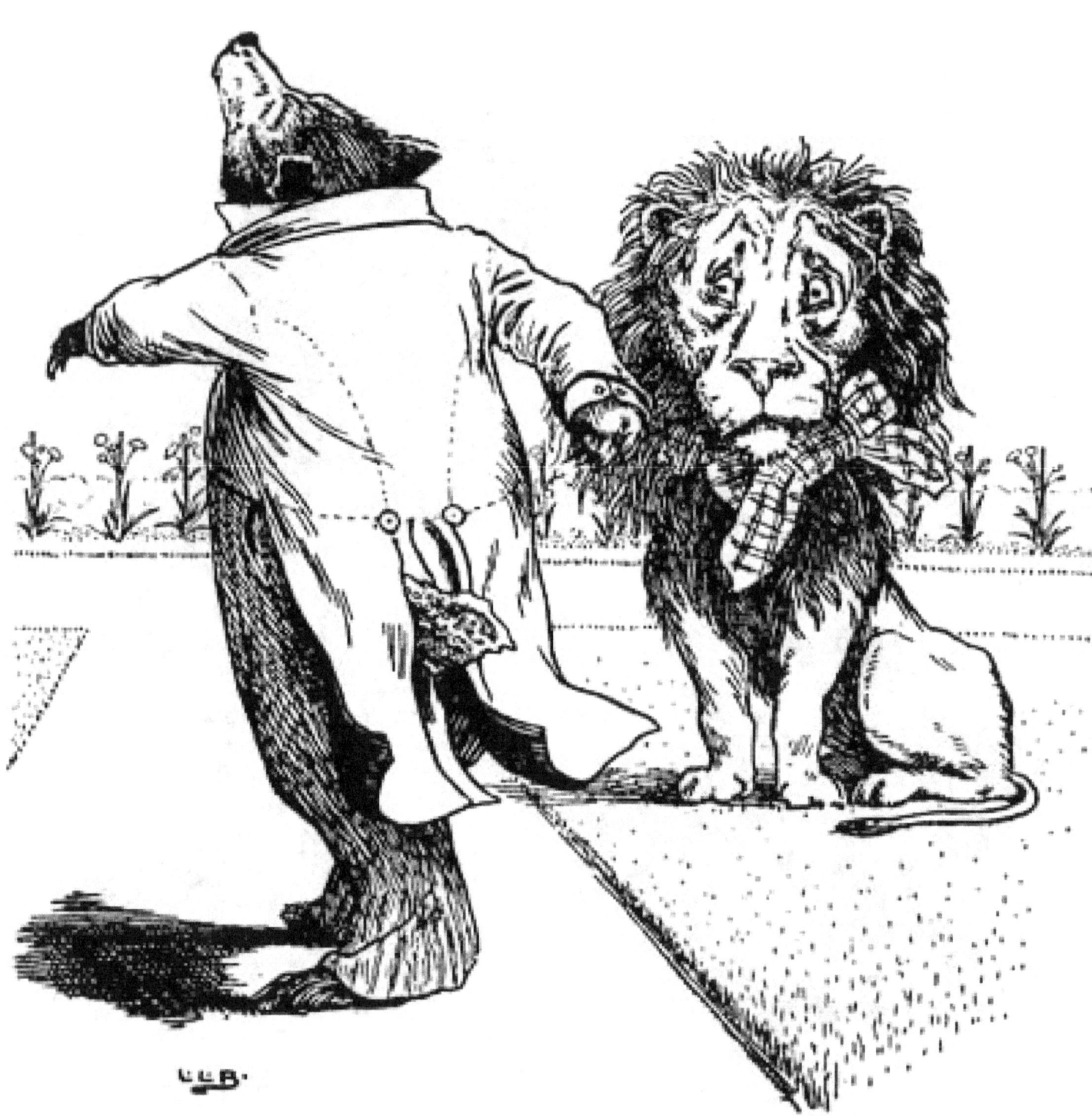

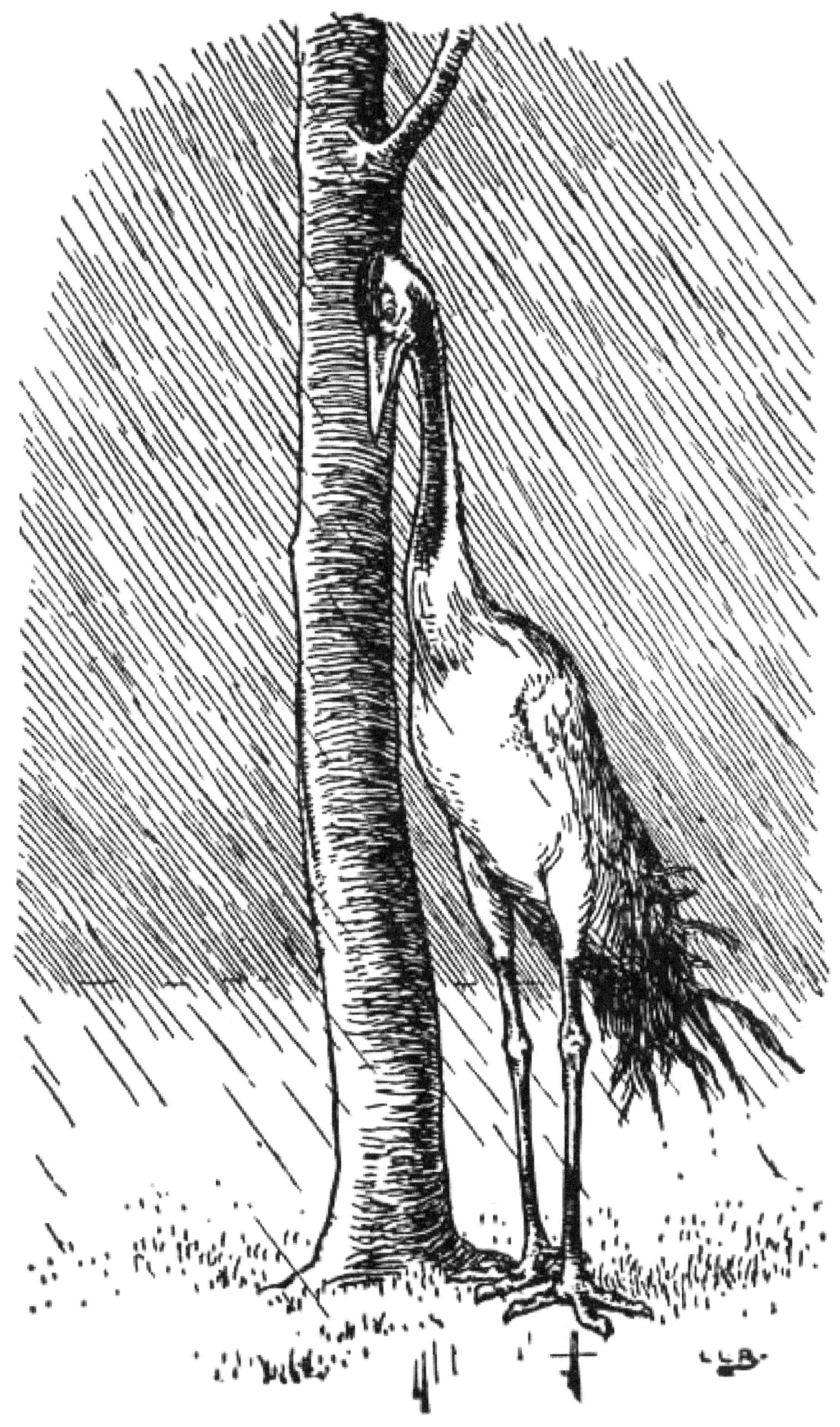

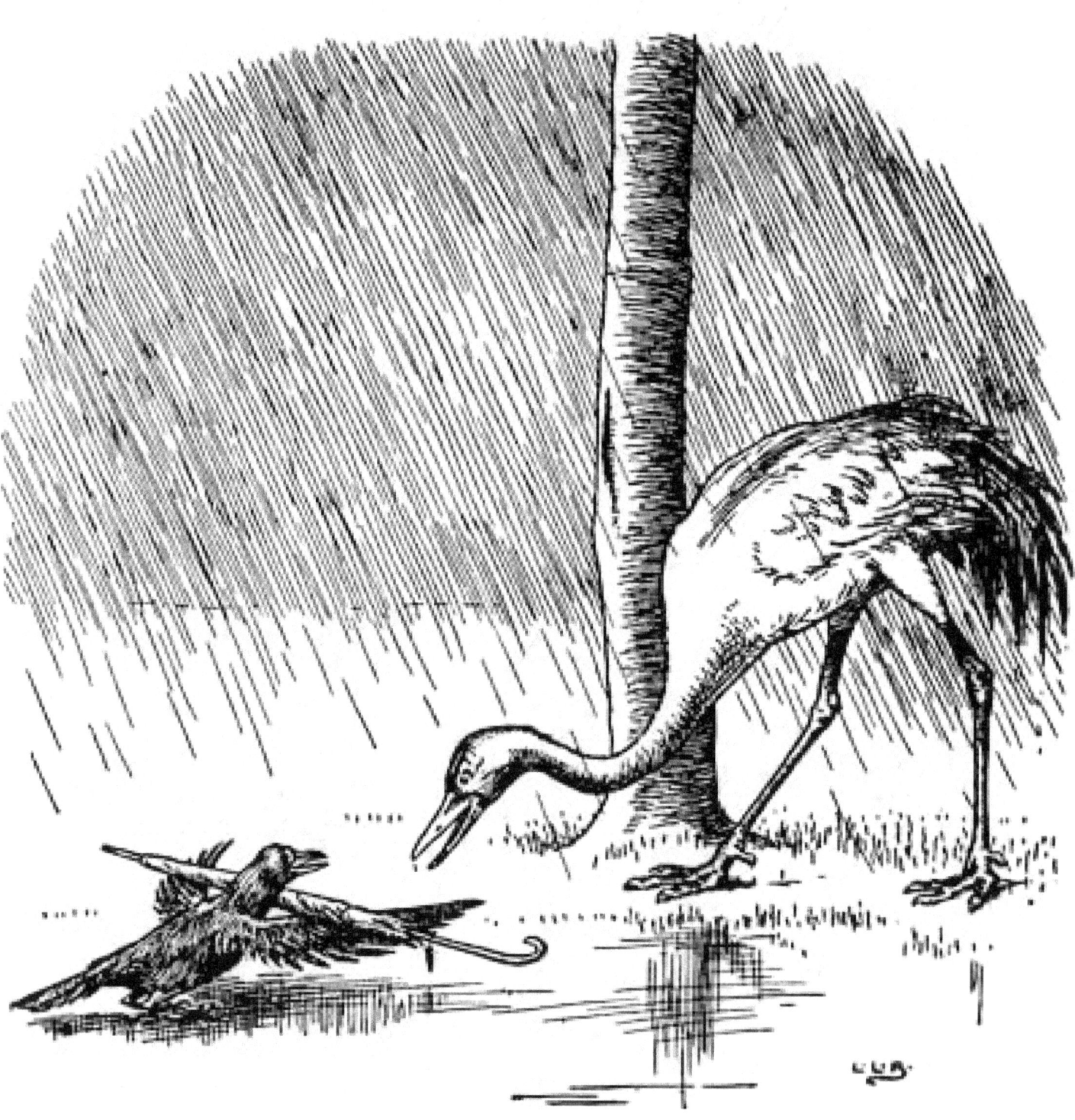

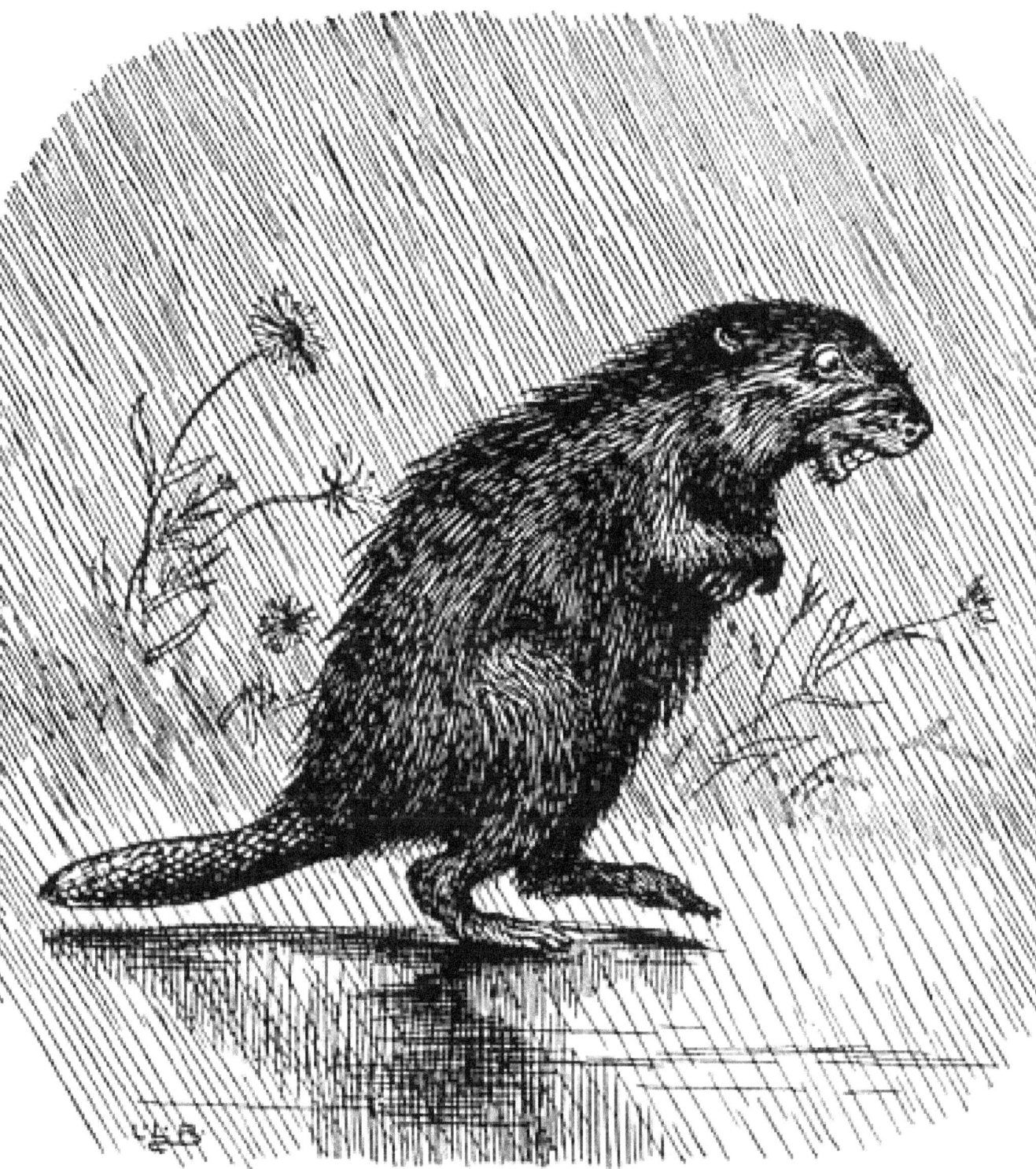

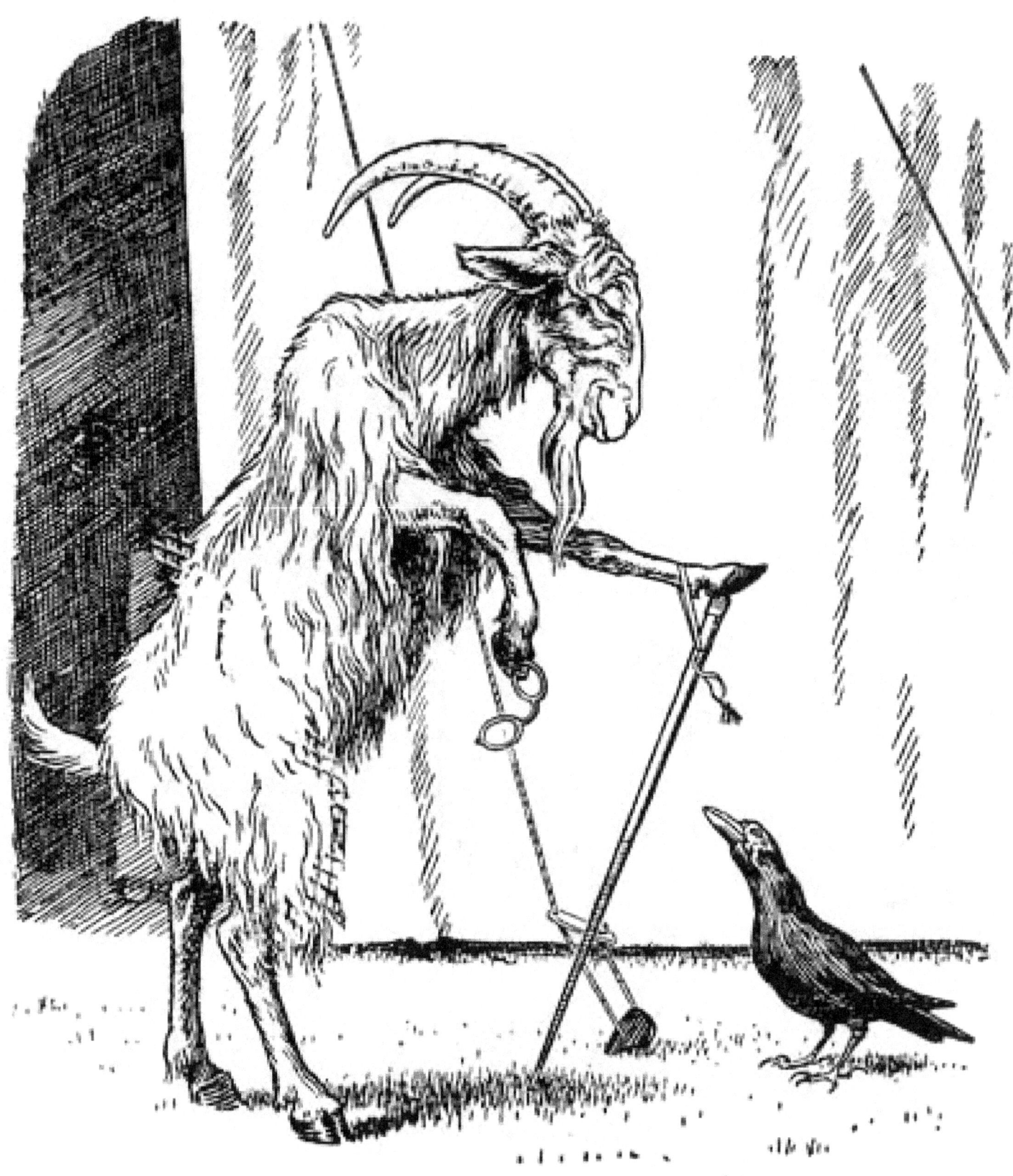

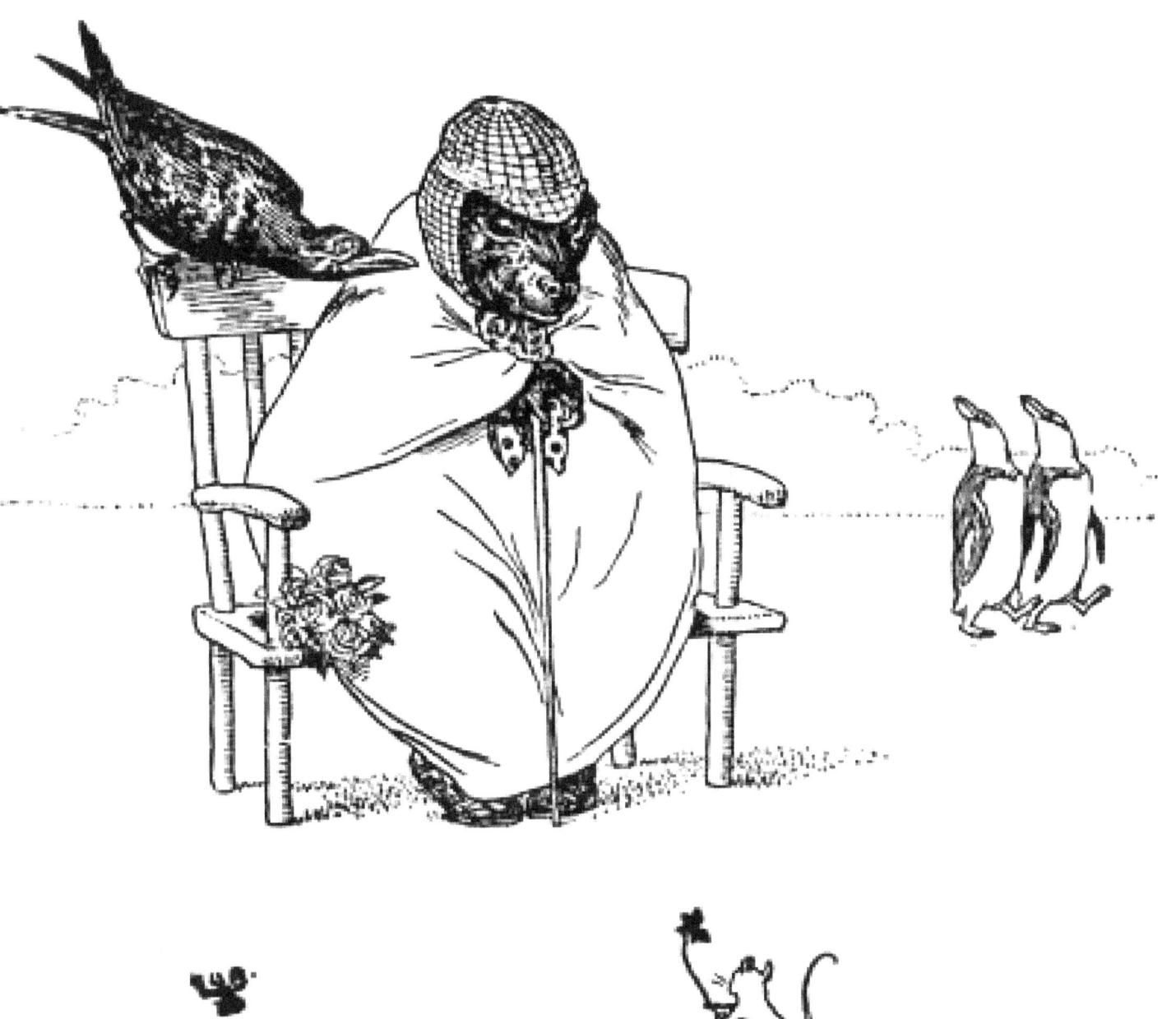

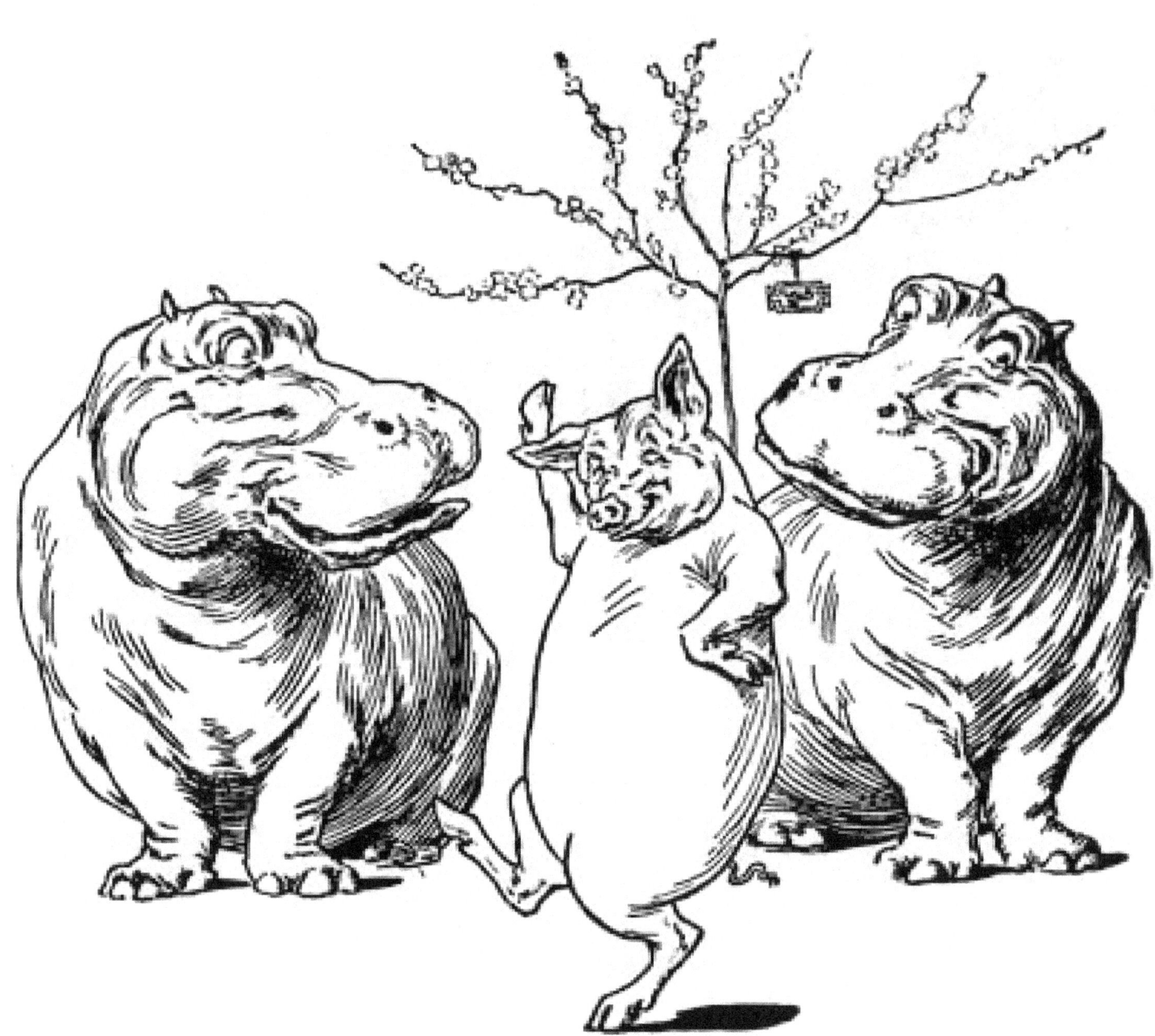

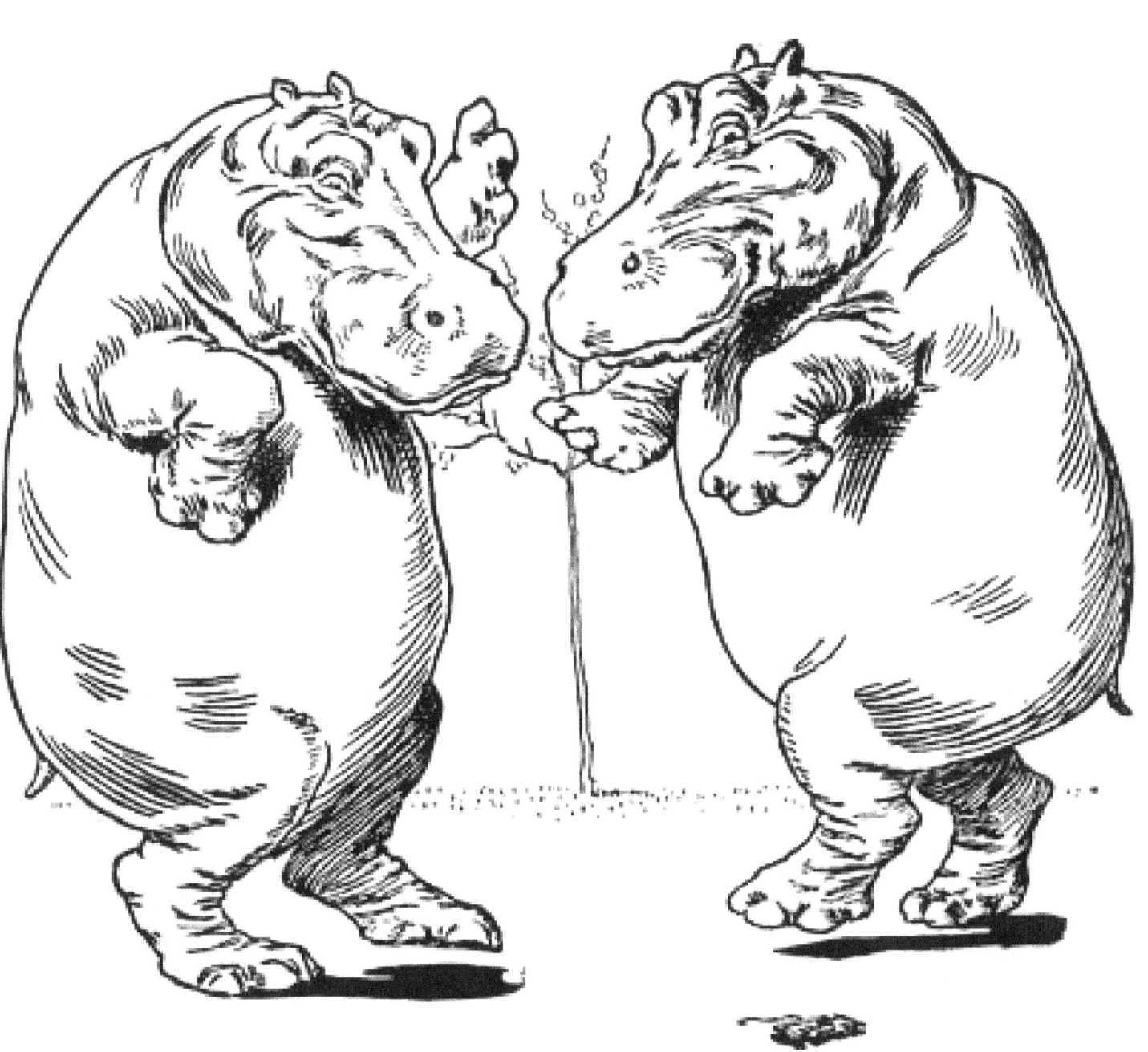

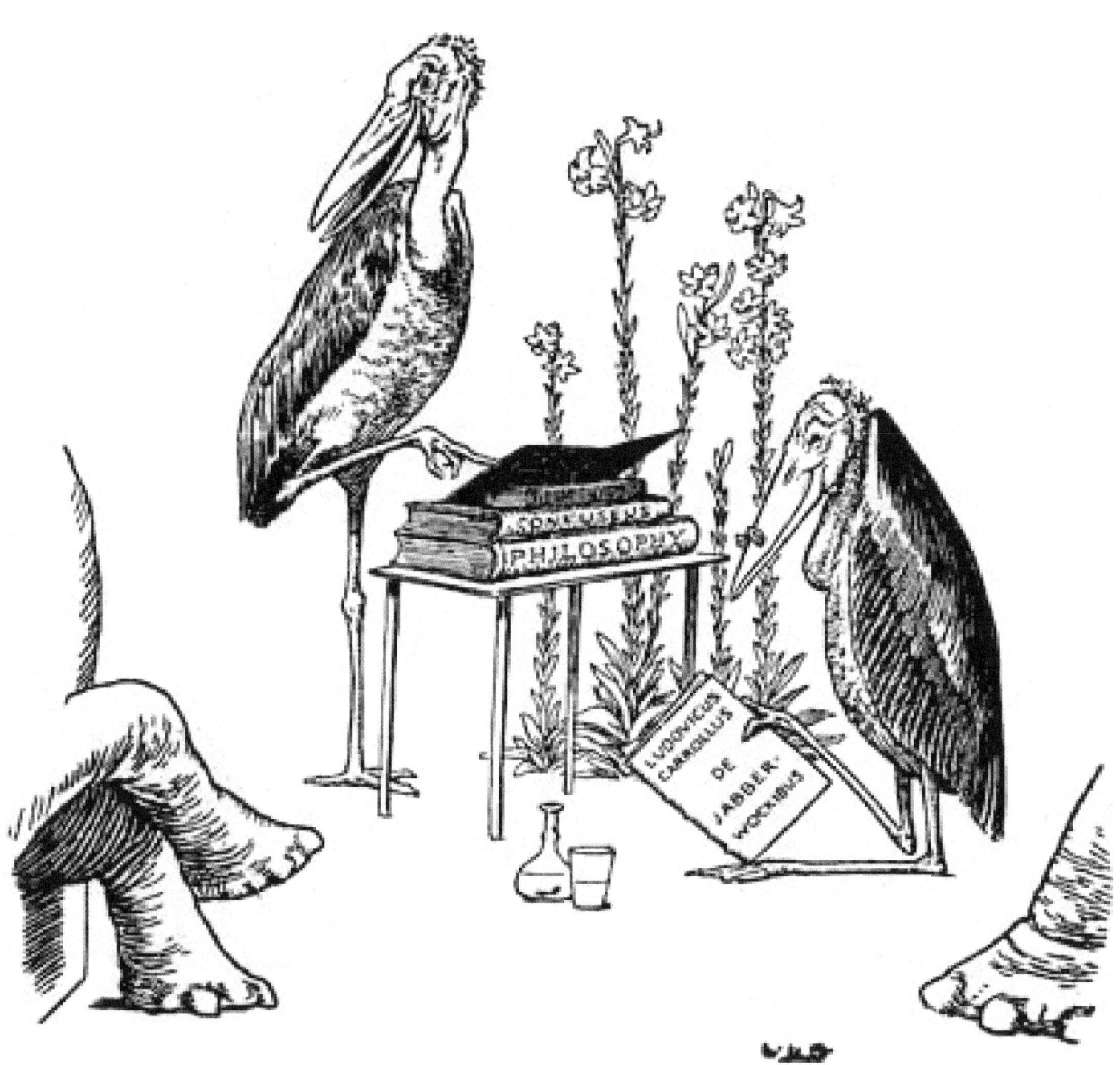

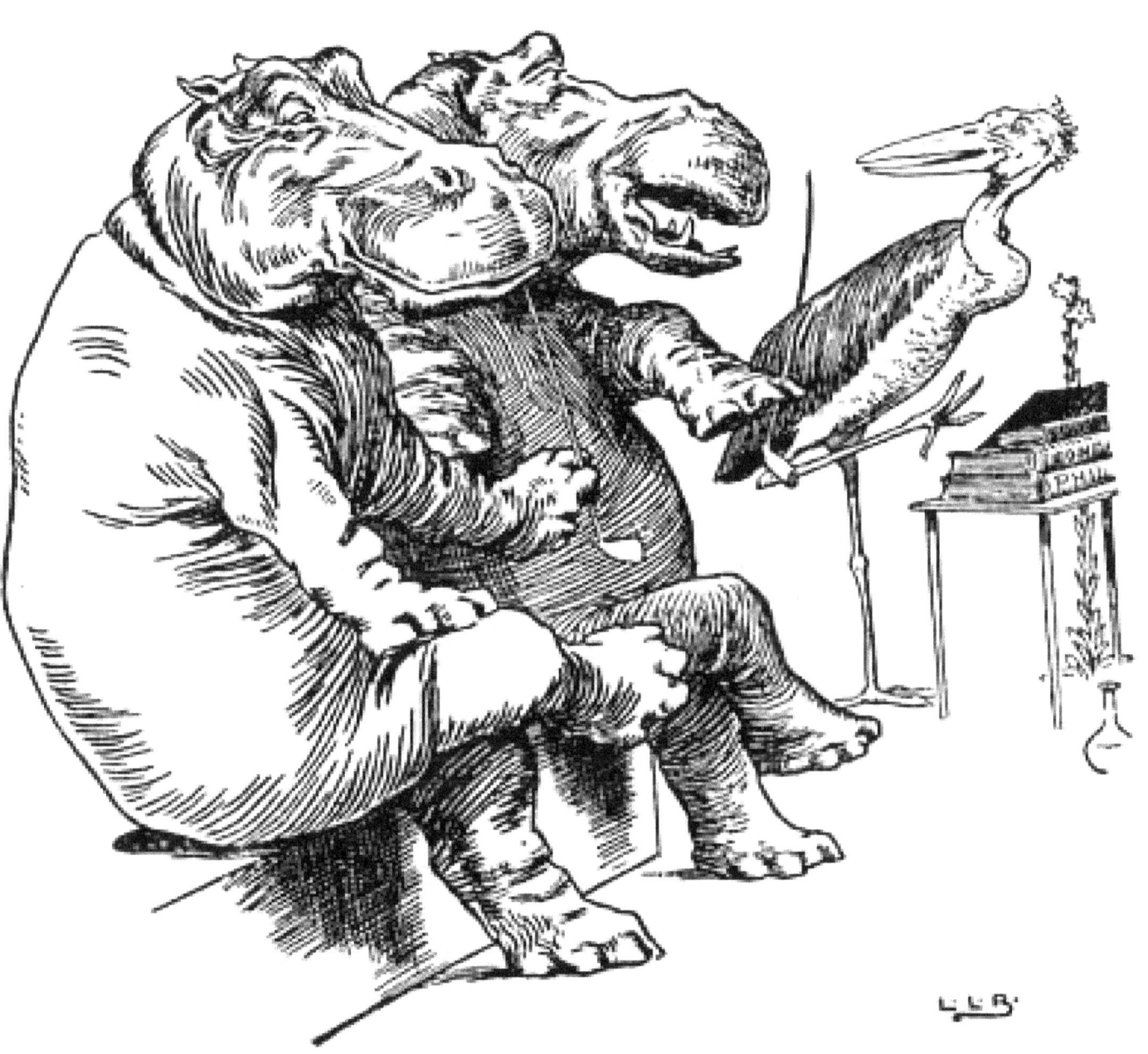

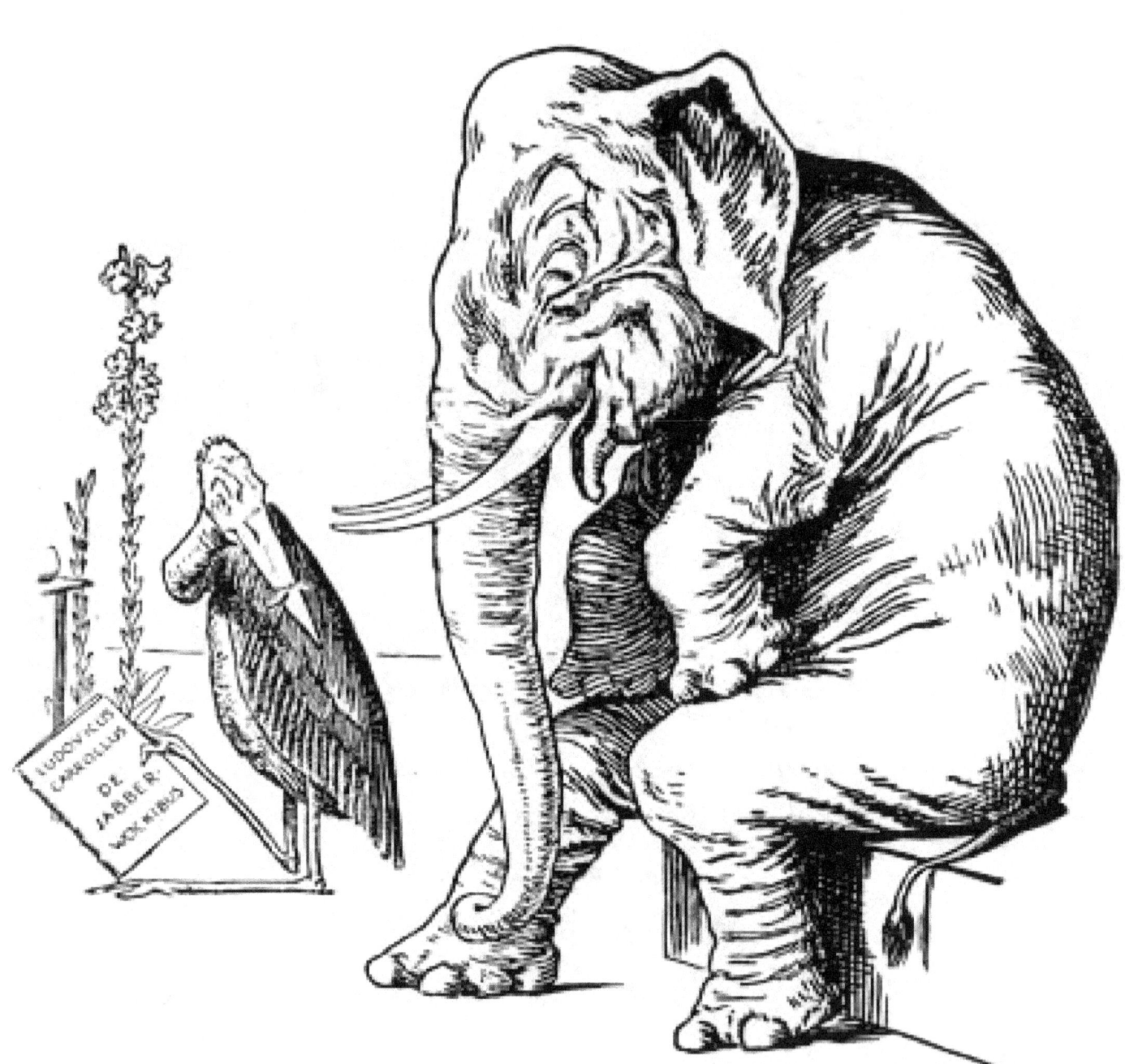

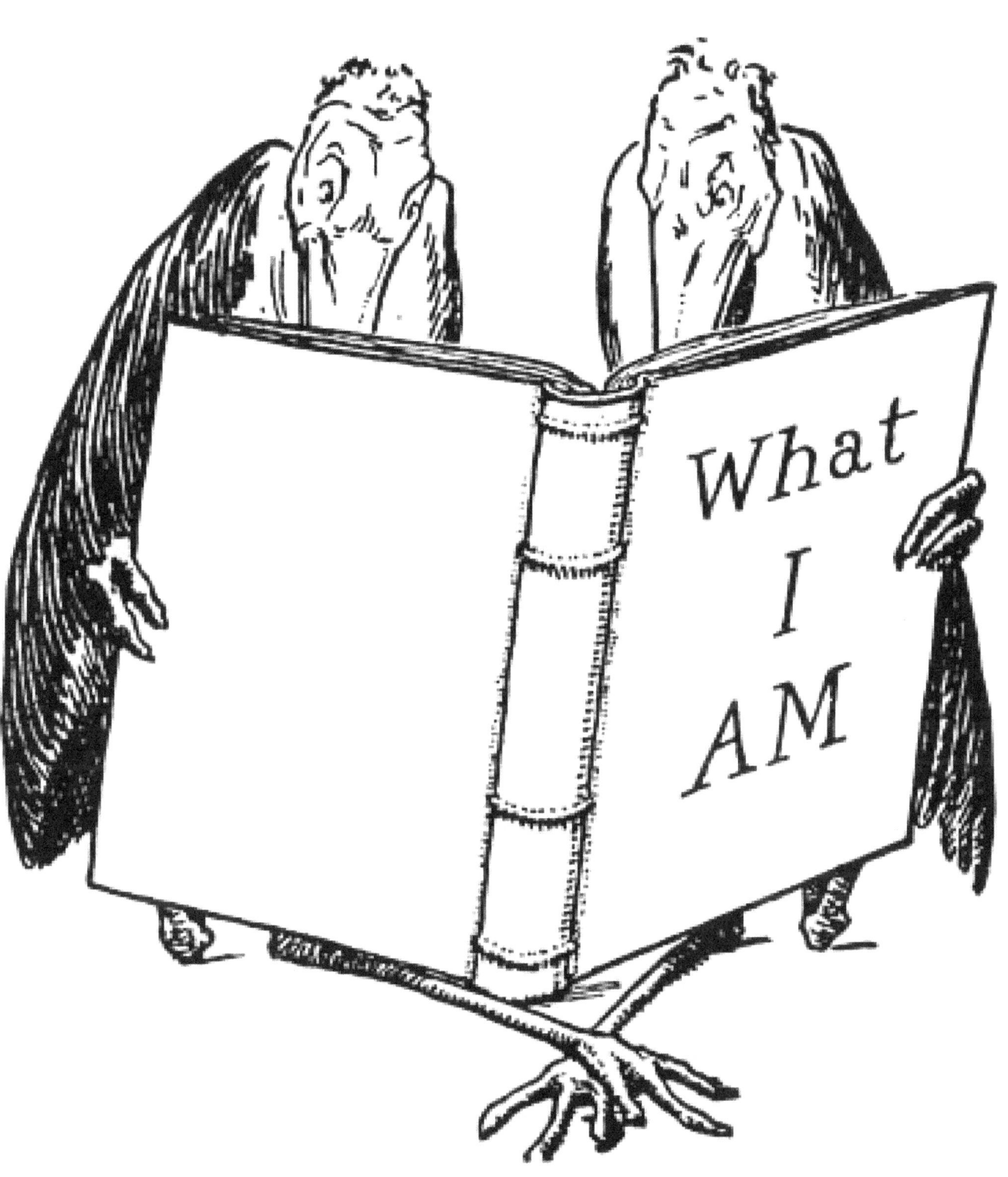

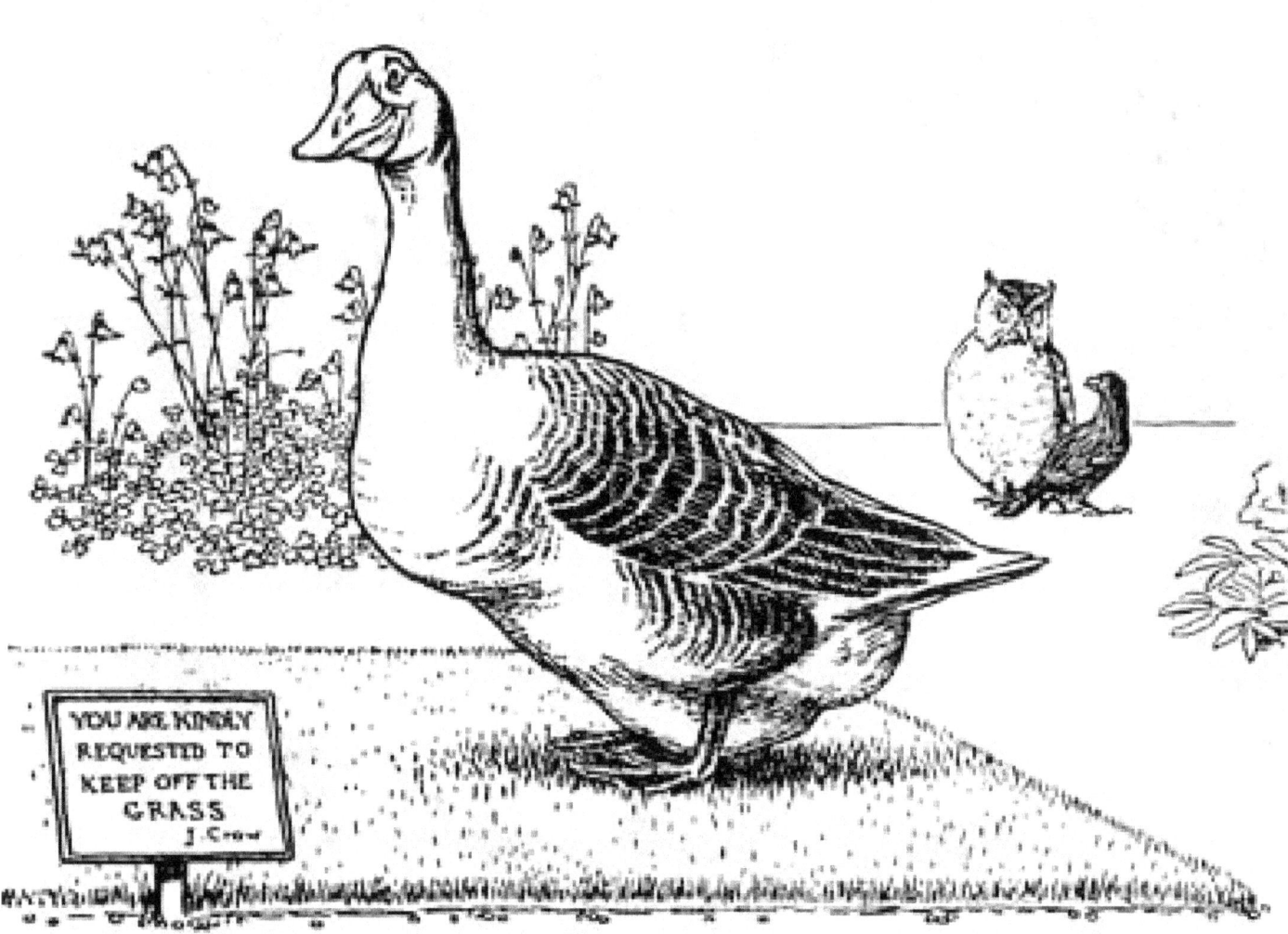

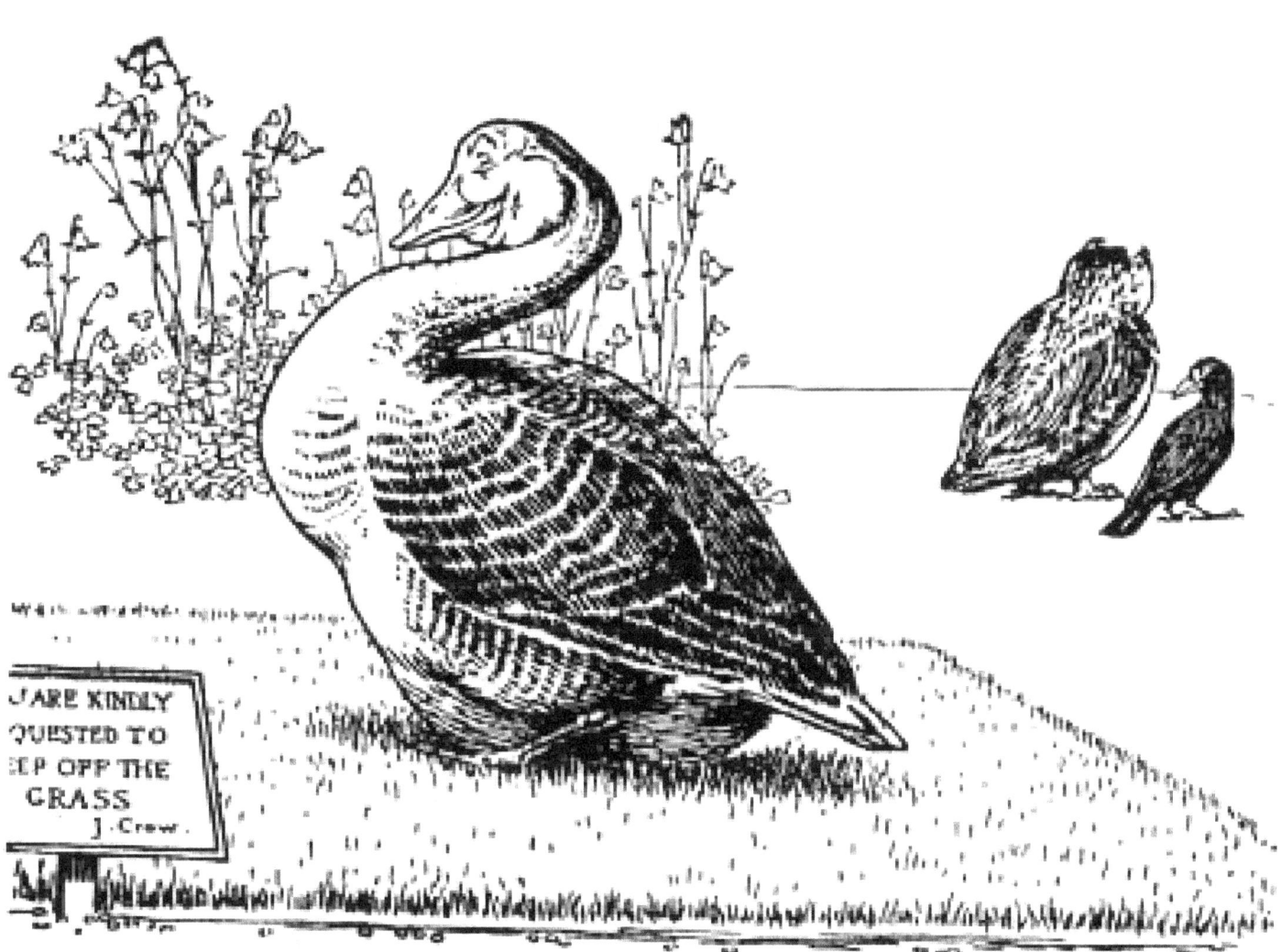

YOU ARE KINDLY
REQUESTED TO
KEEP OFF THE
GRASS
J. Crow.

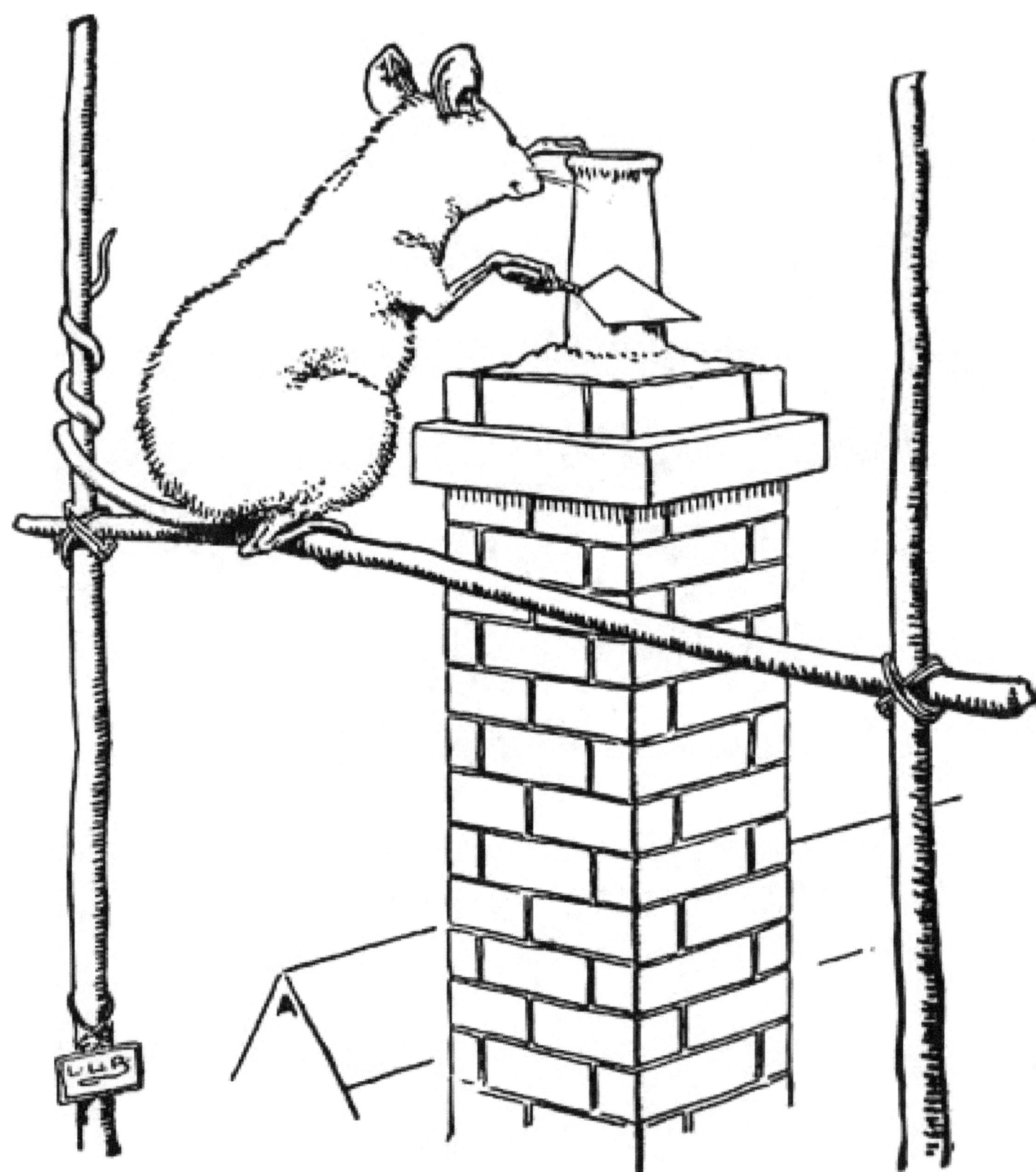

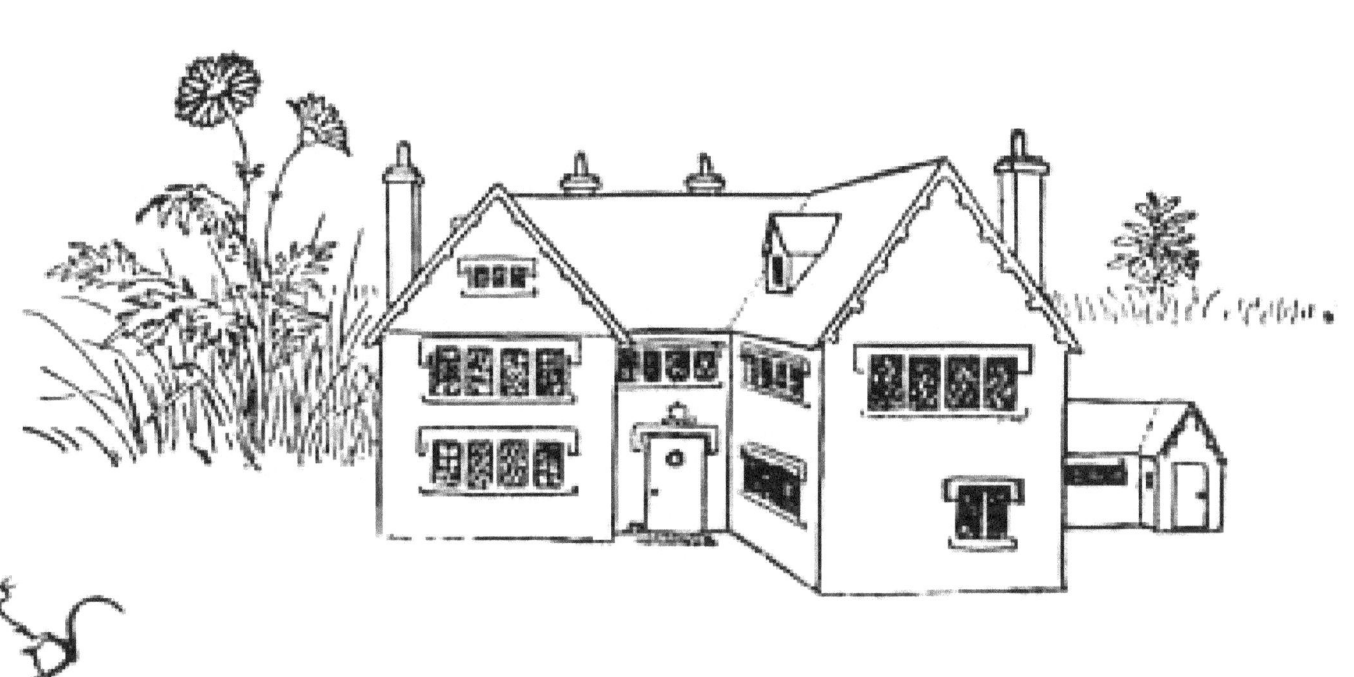

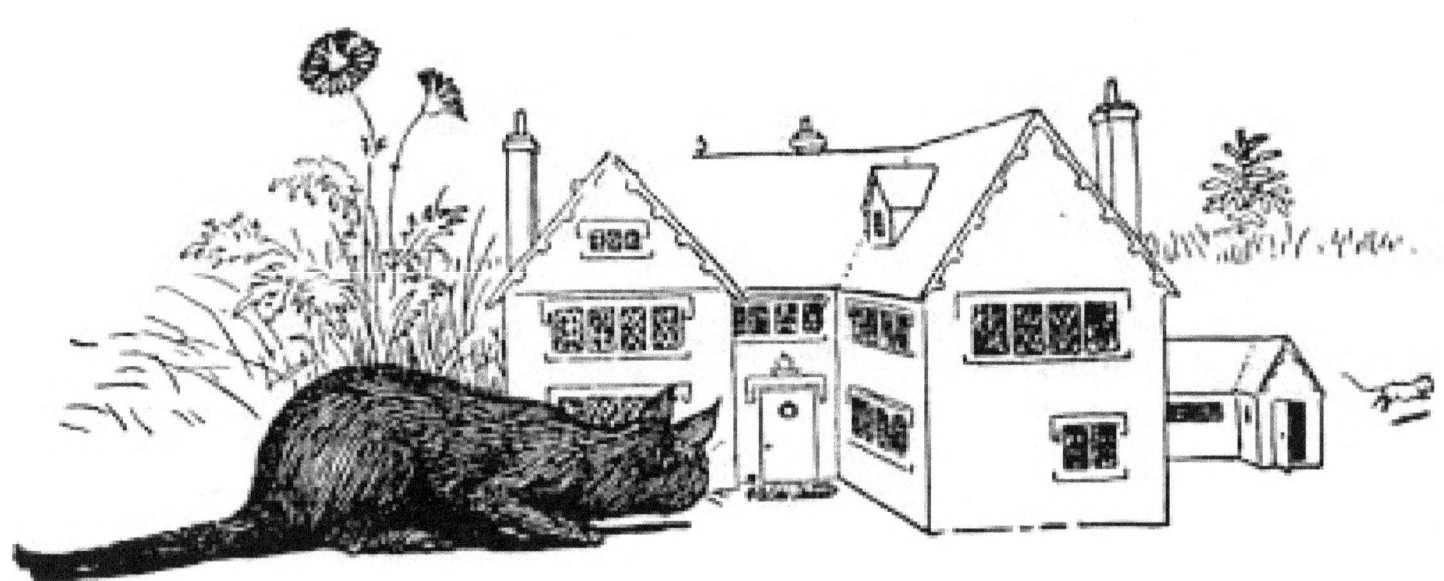

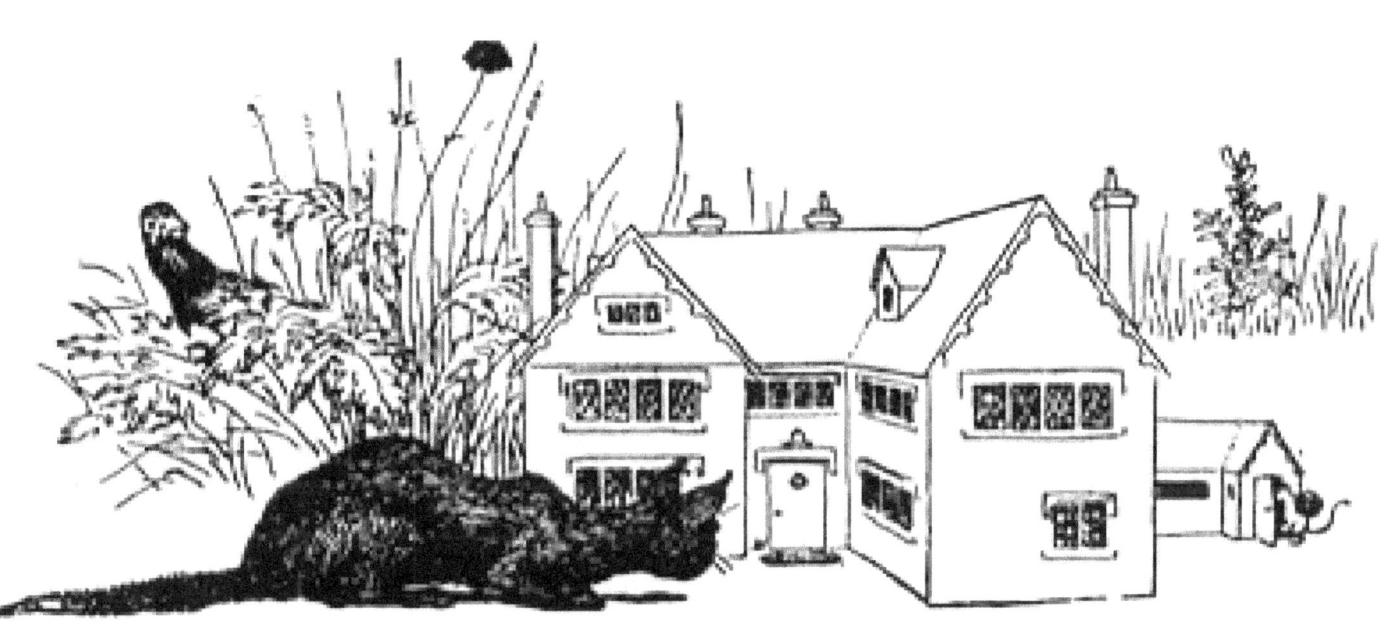

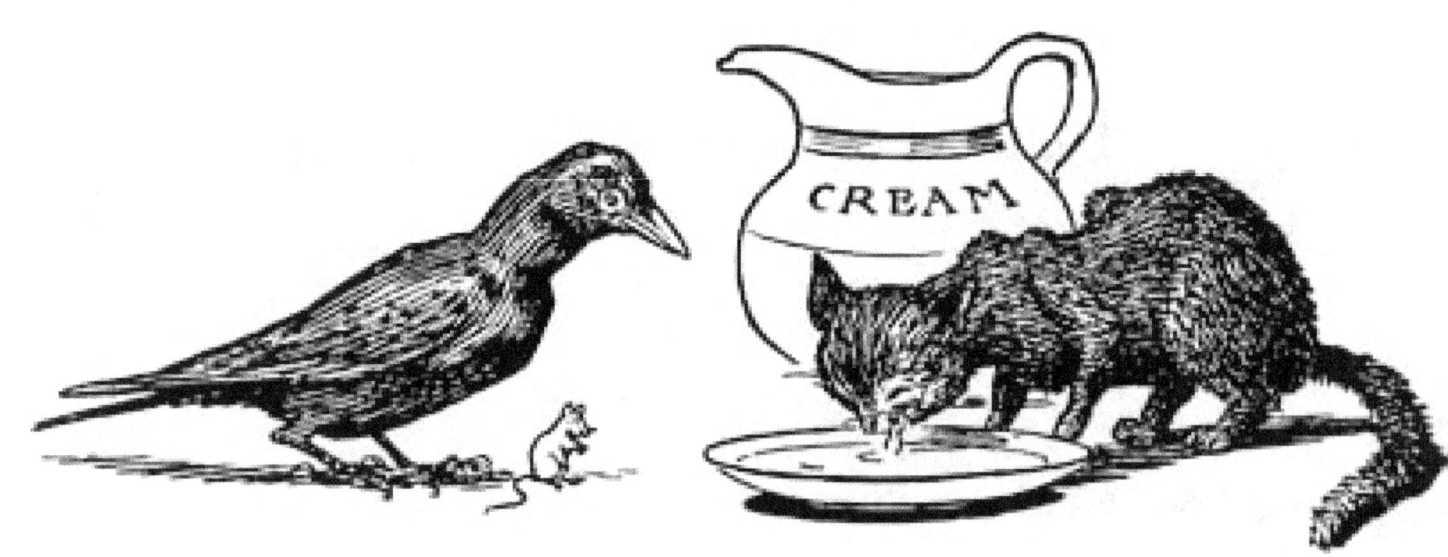

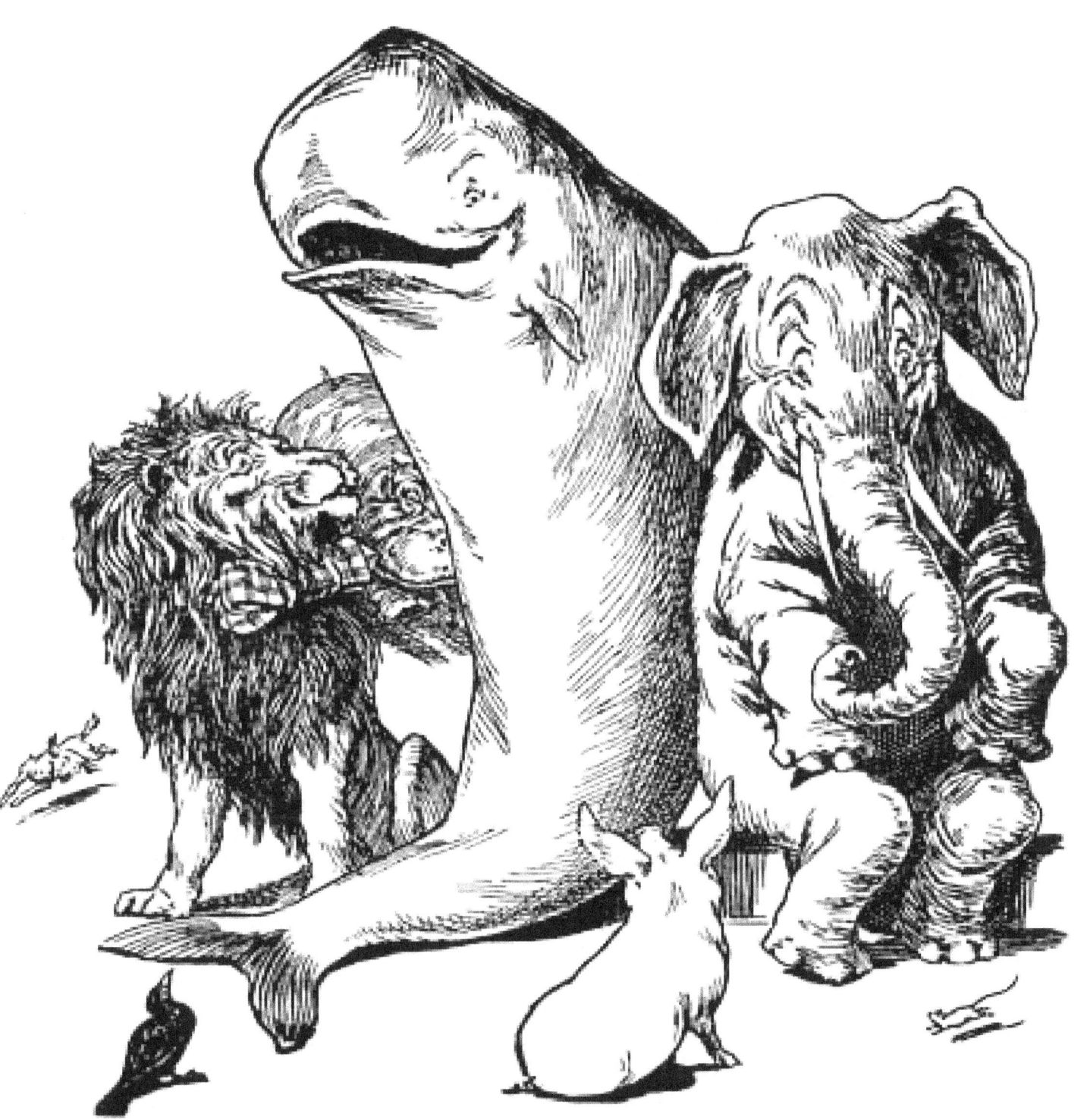

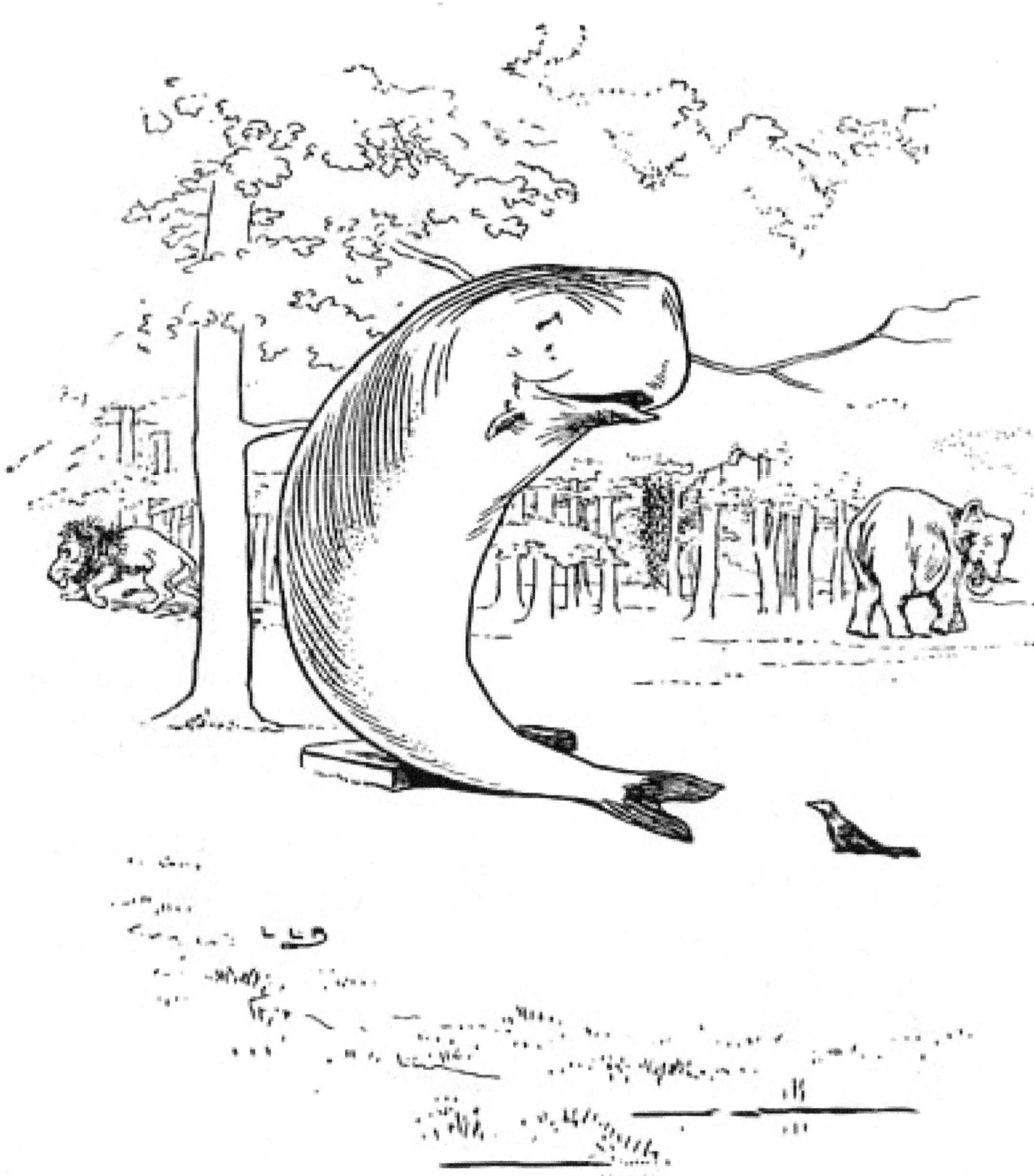

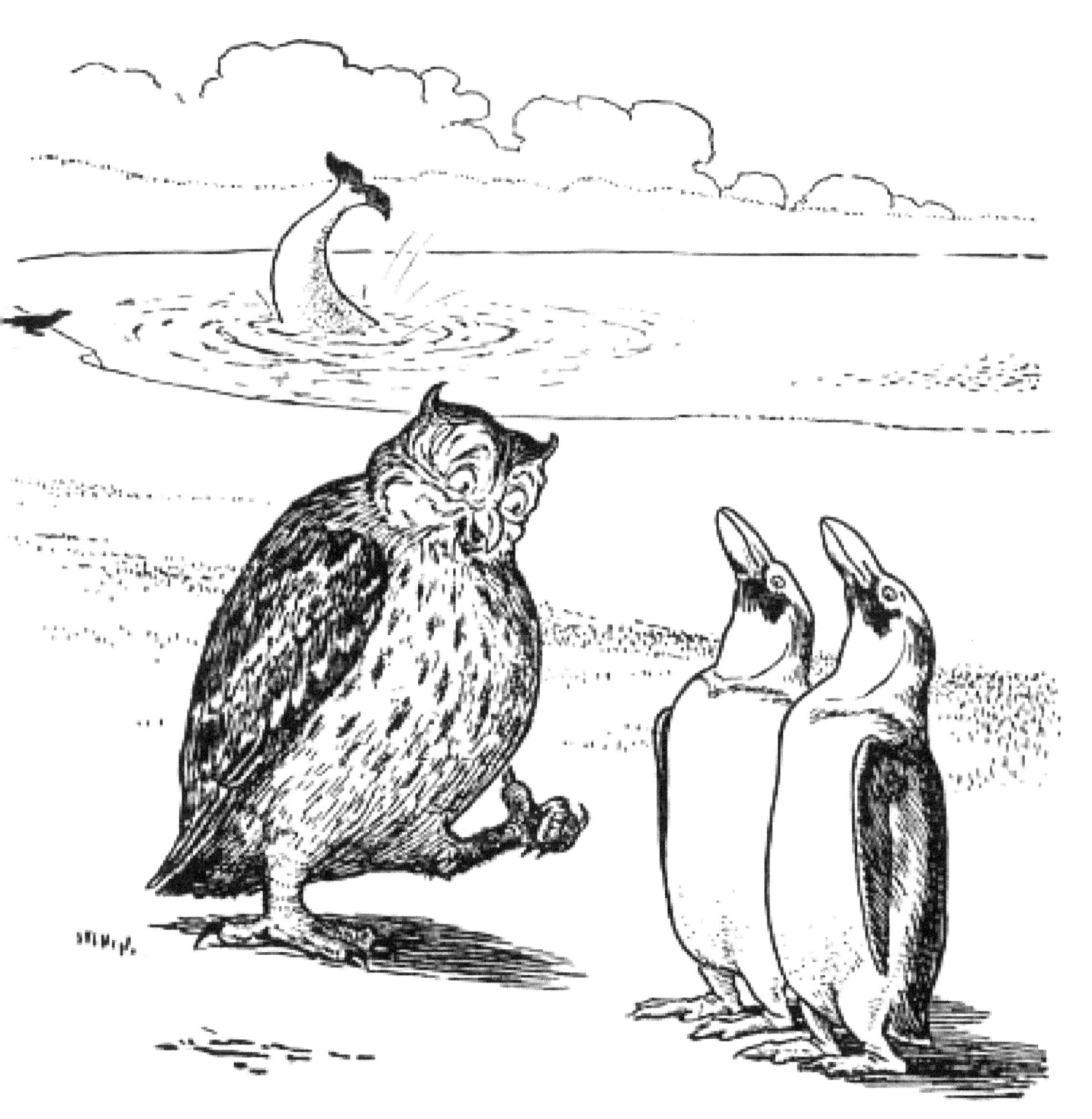

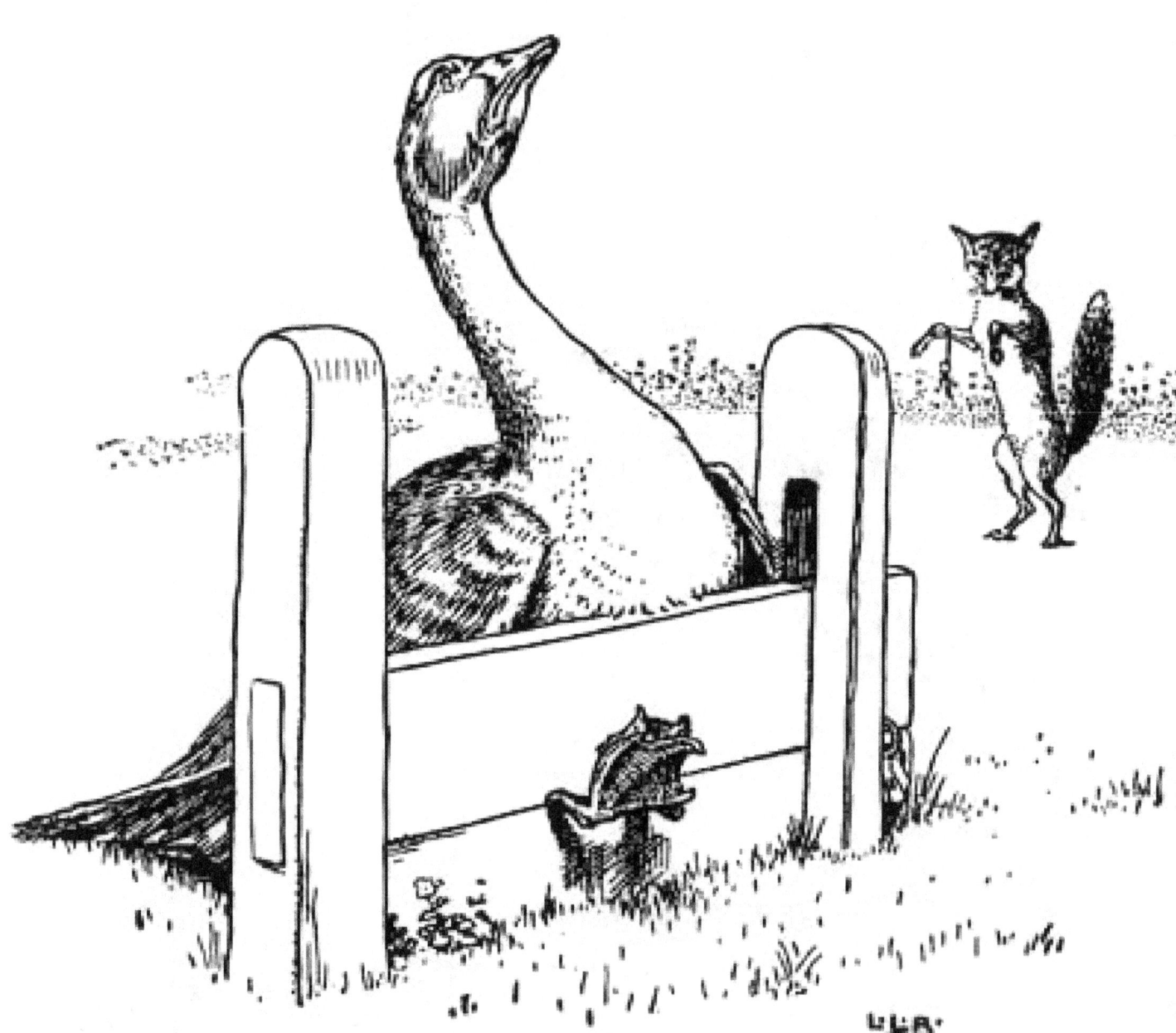

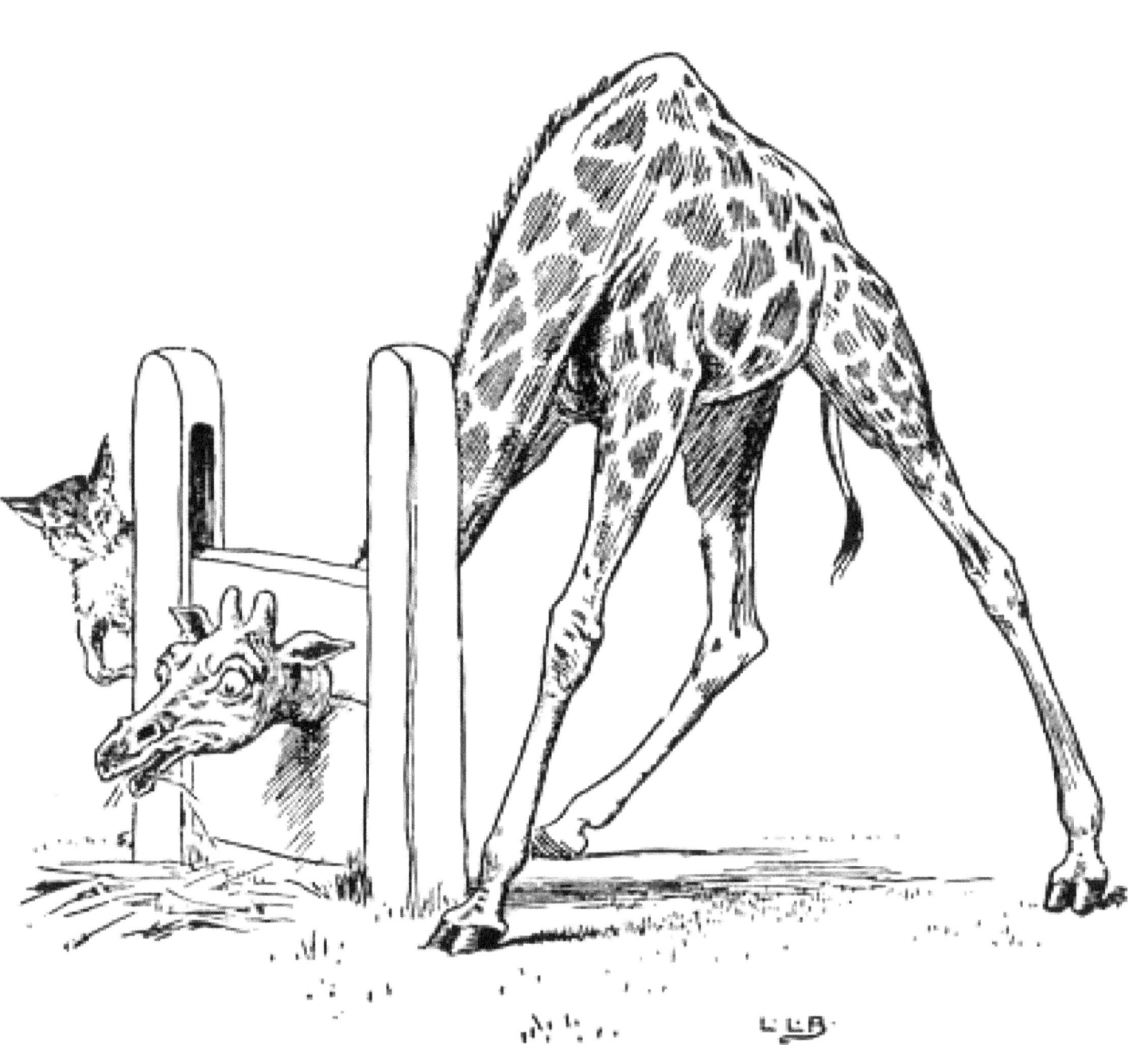

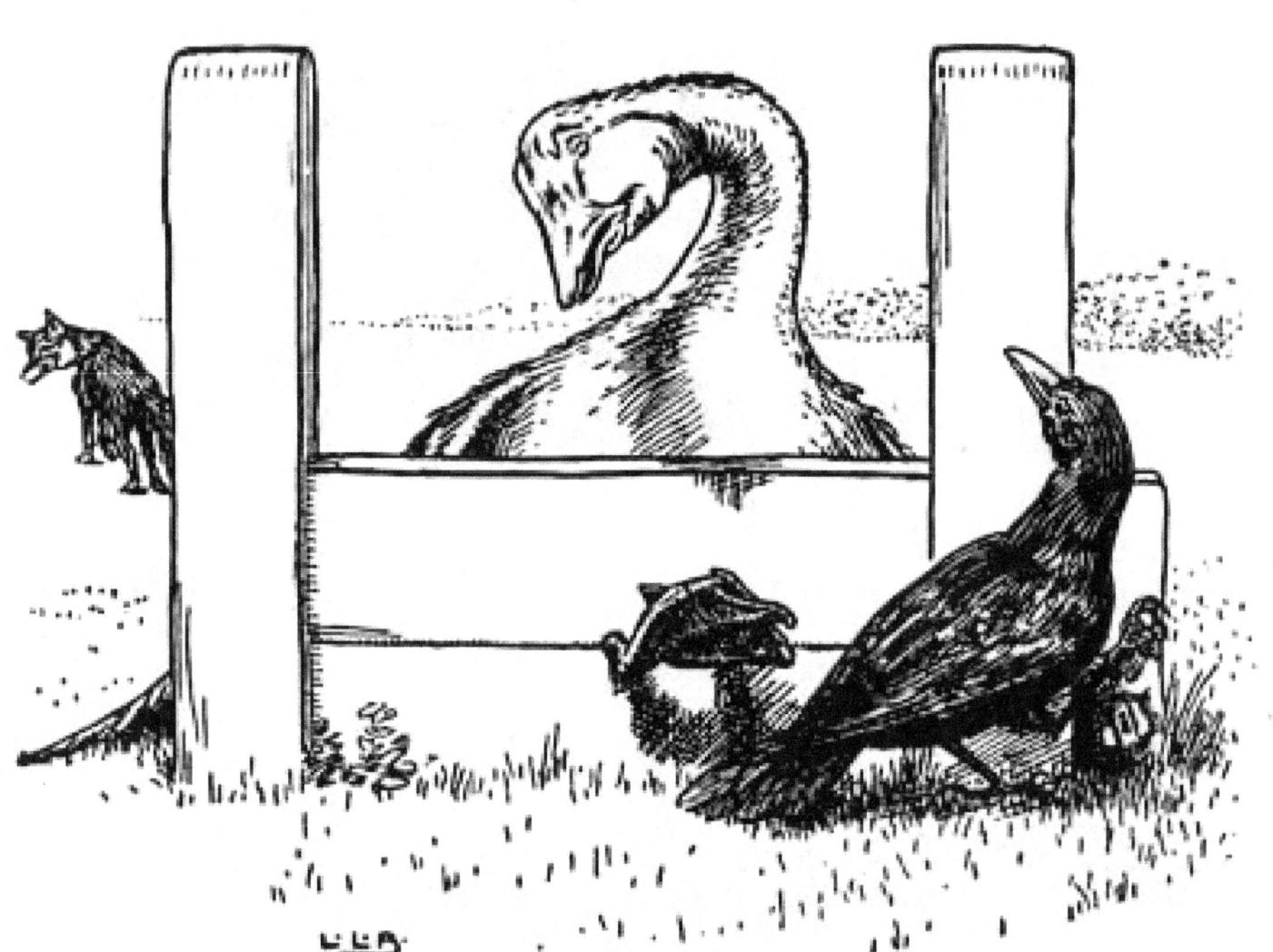

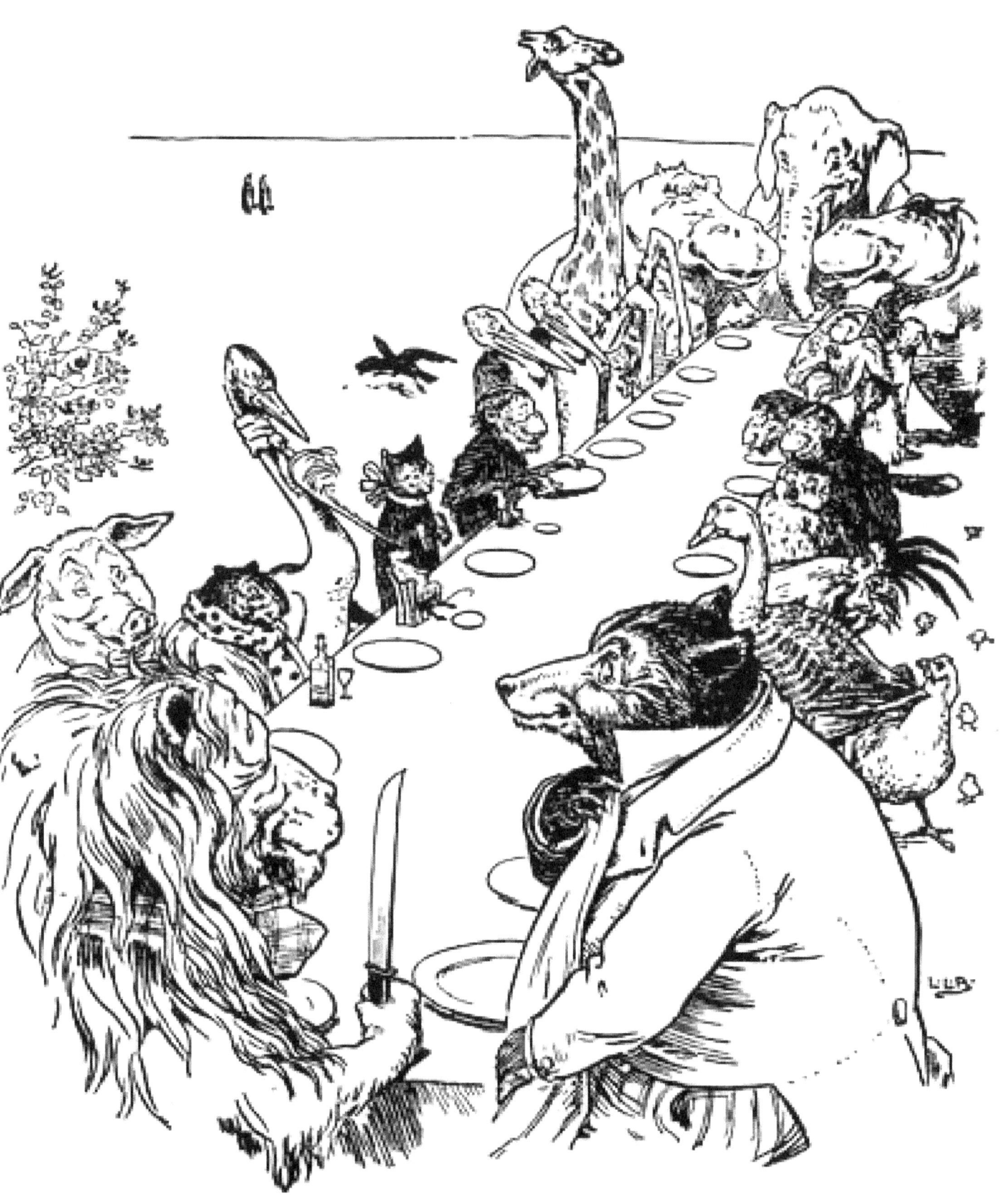

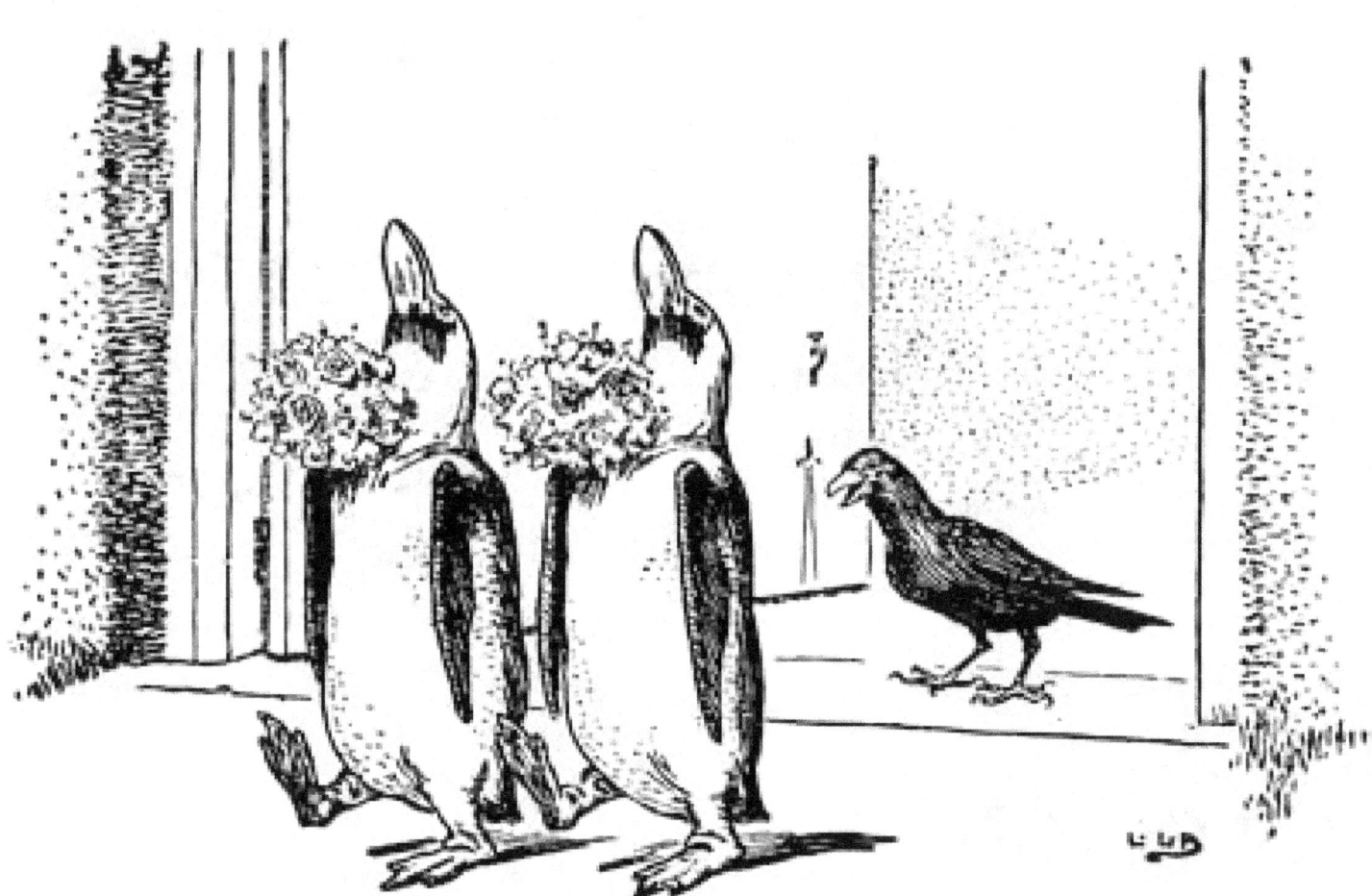

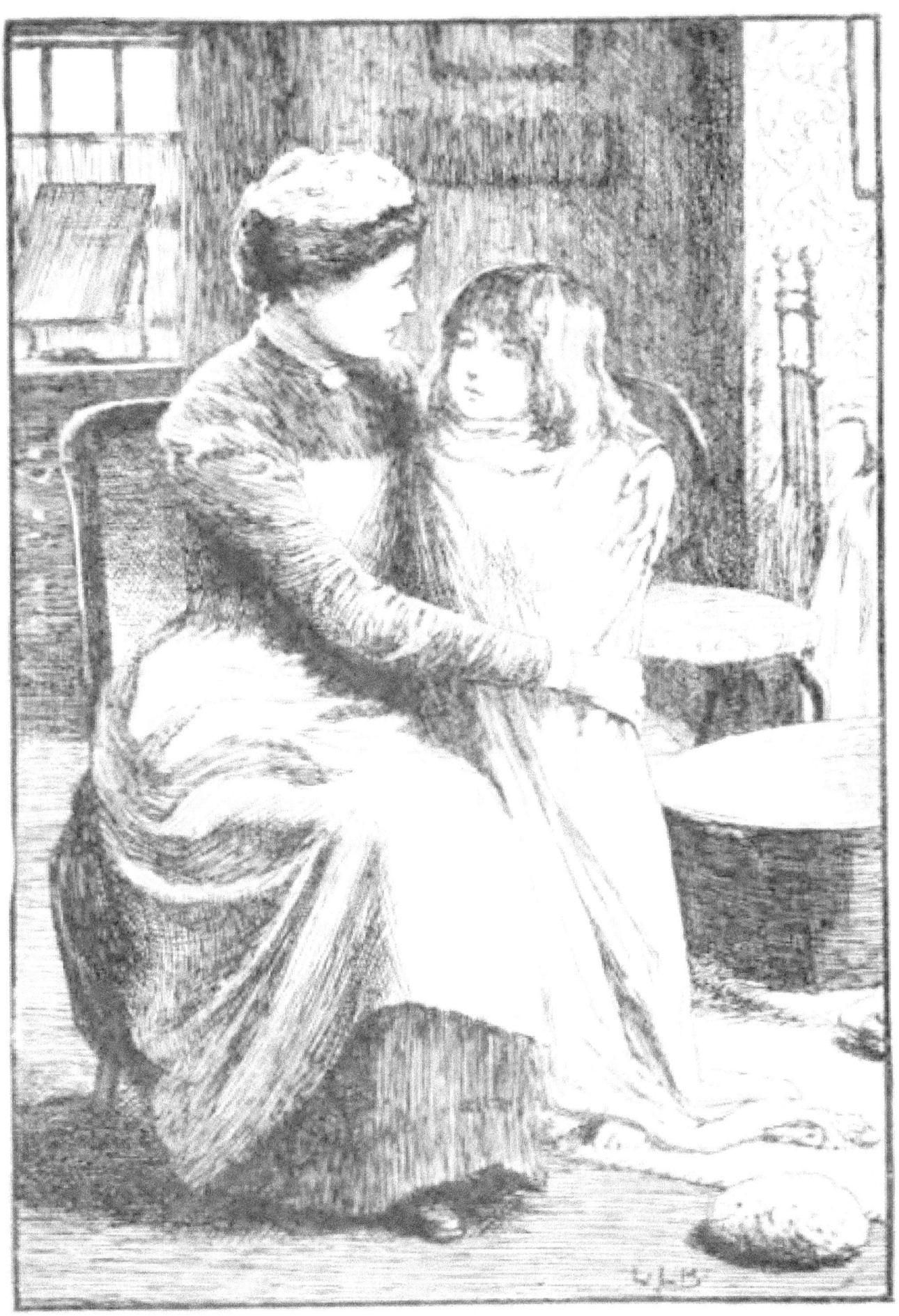

It takes away all the birfday-ness. —P. 13.

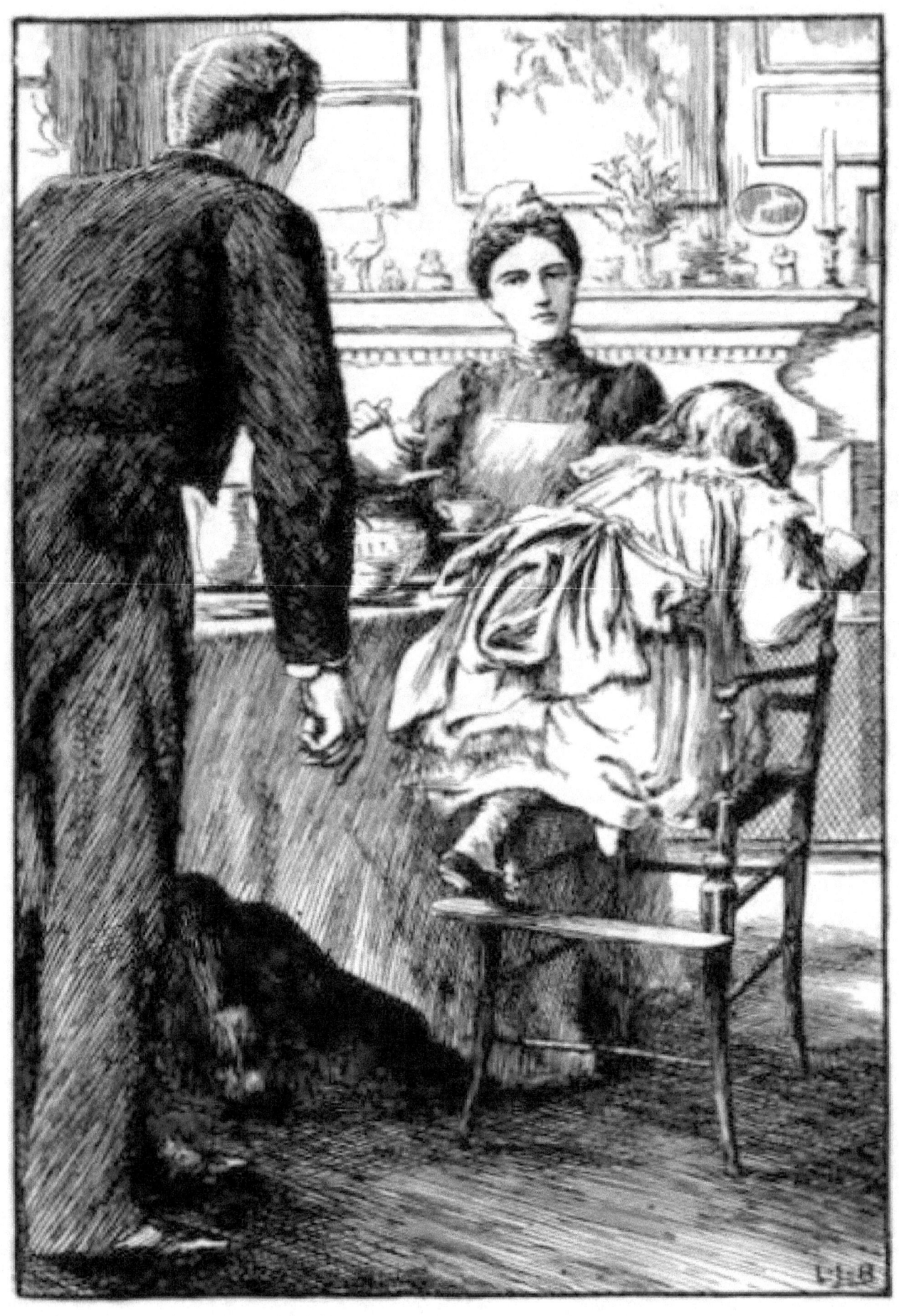

Nothing but a sort of fluff of blue skirts and sash and white muslin pinafore
and shaggy hair, with here and there a shoe or a little pink hand.—P. 22.

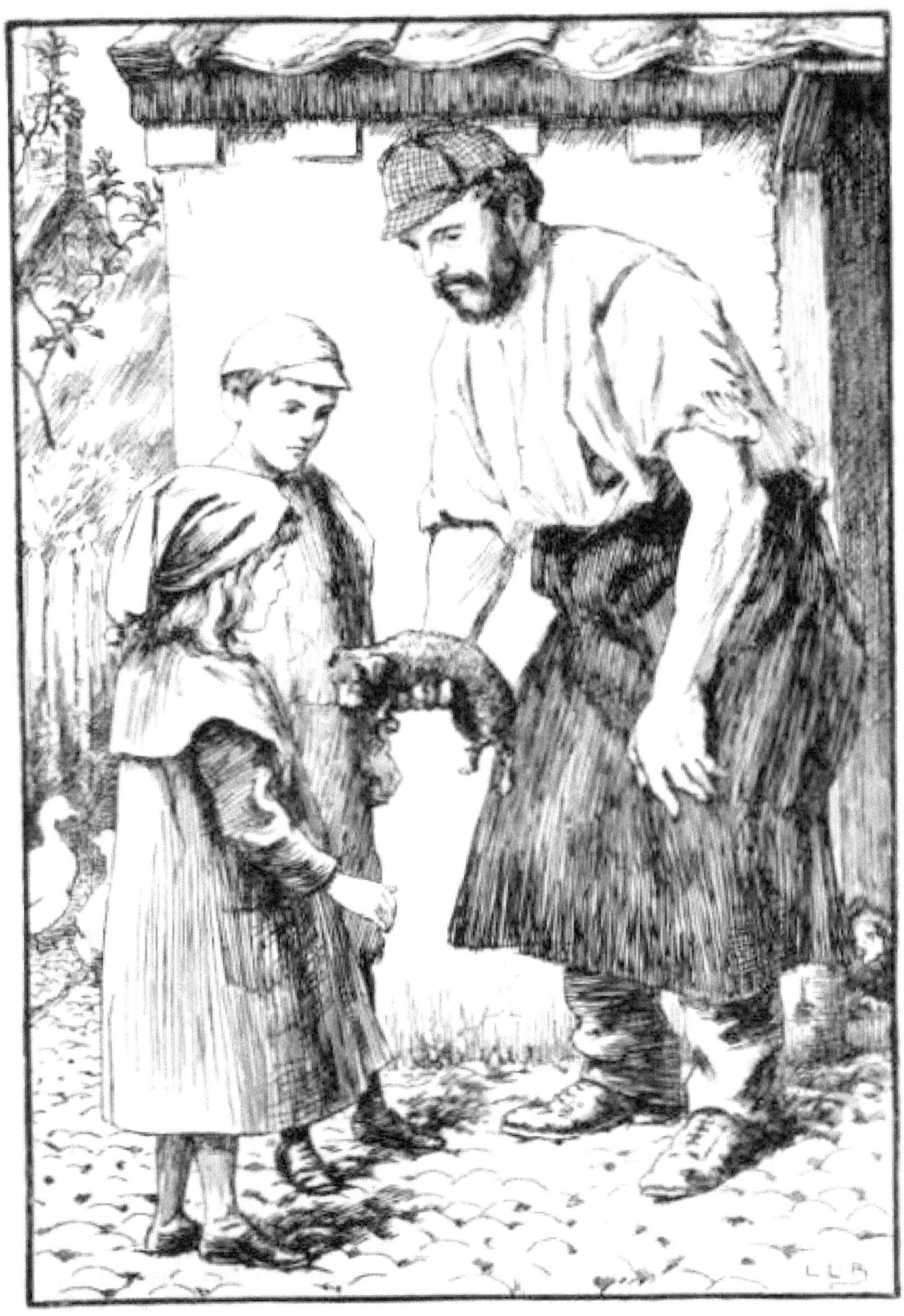

Yakeman stooped down and picked one up with his big hand and held it close to Mary.—P. 54.

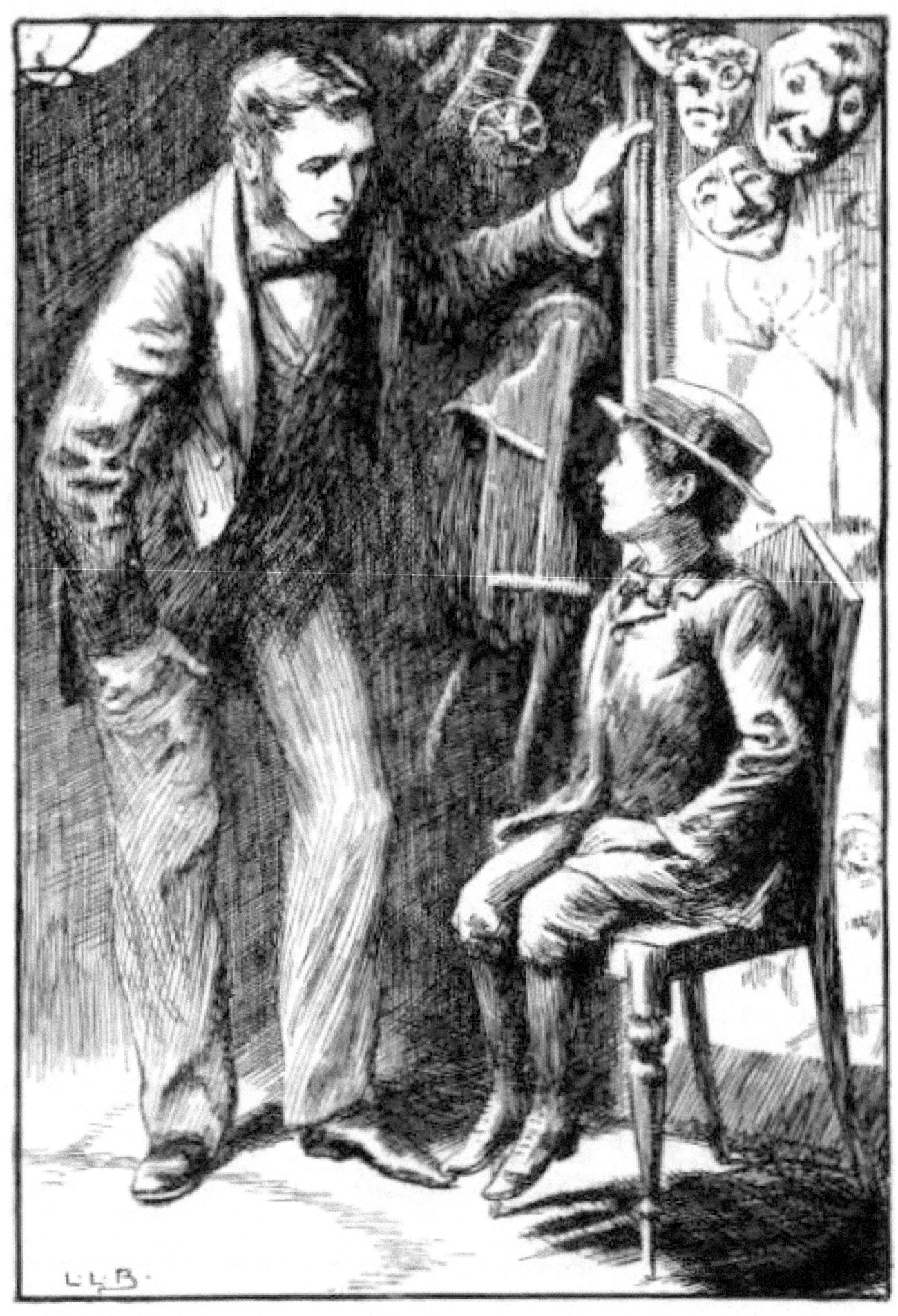

You must see you can't sit there the whole night. — p. 99.

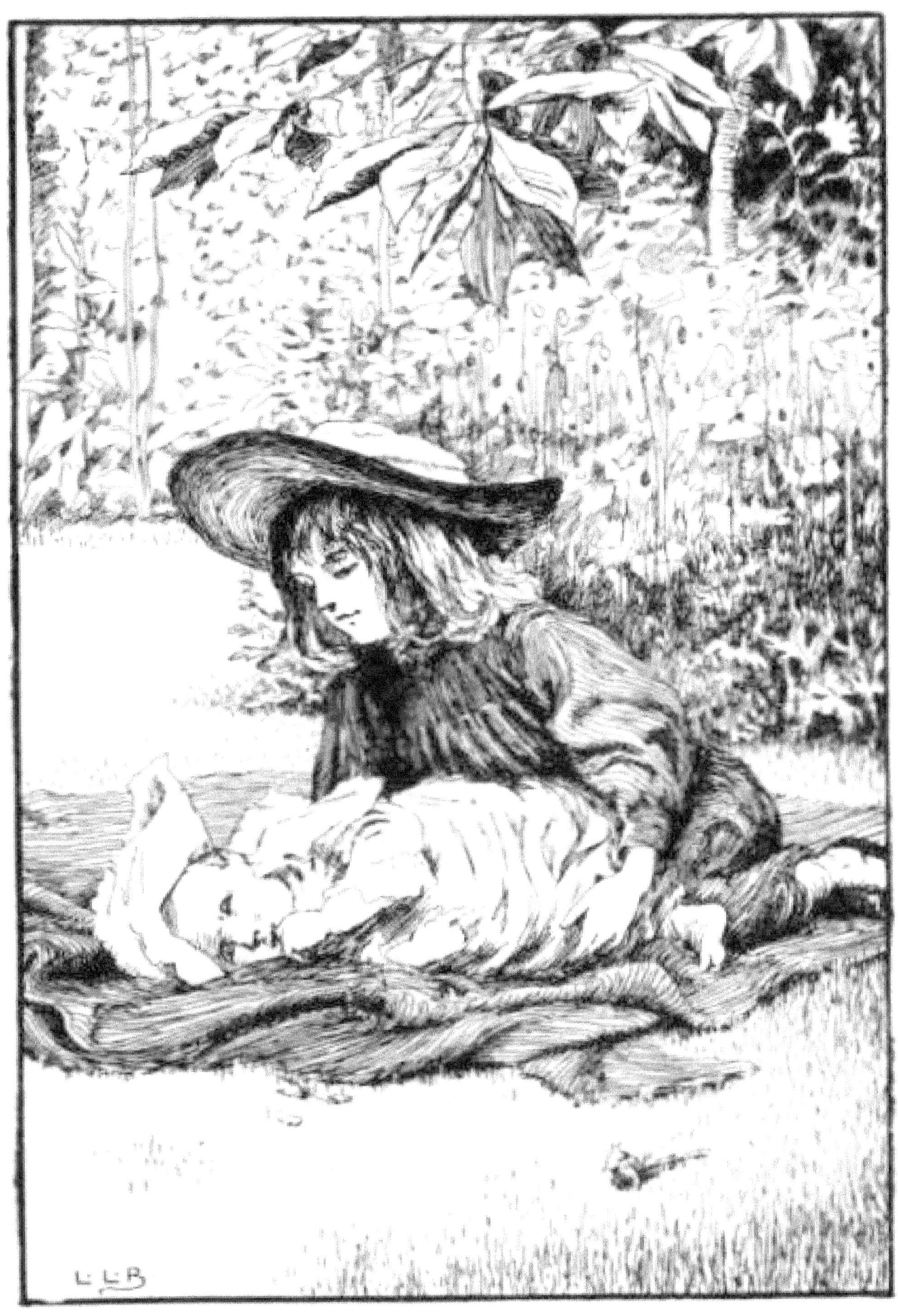

Baby was lying on the ground out on the lawn . . . and Mary was sitting beside her, taking care of her for a minute or two all by herself. —r. 108.

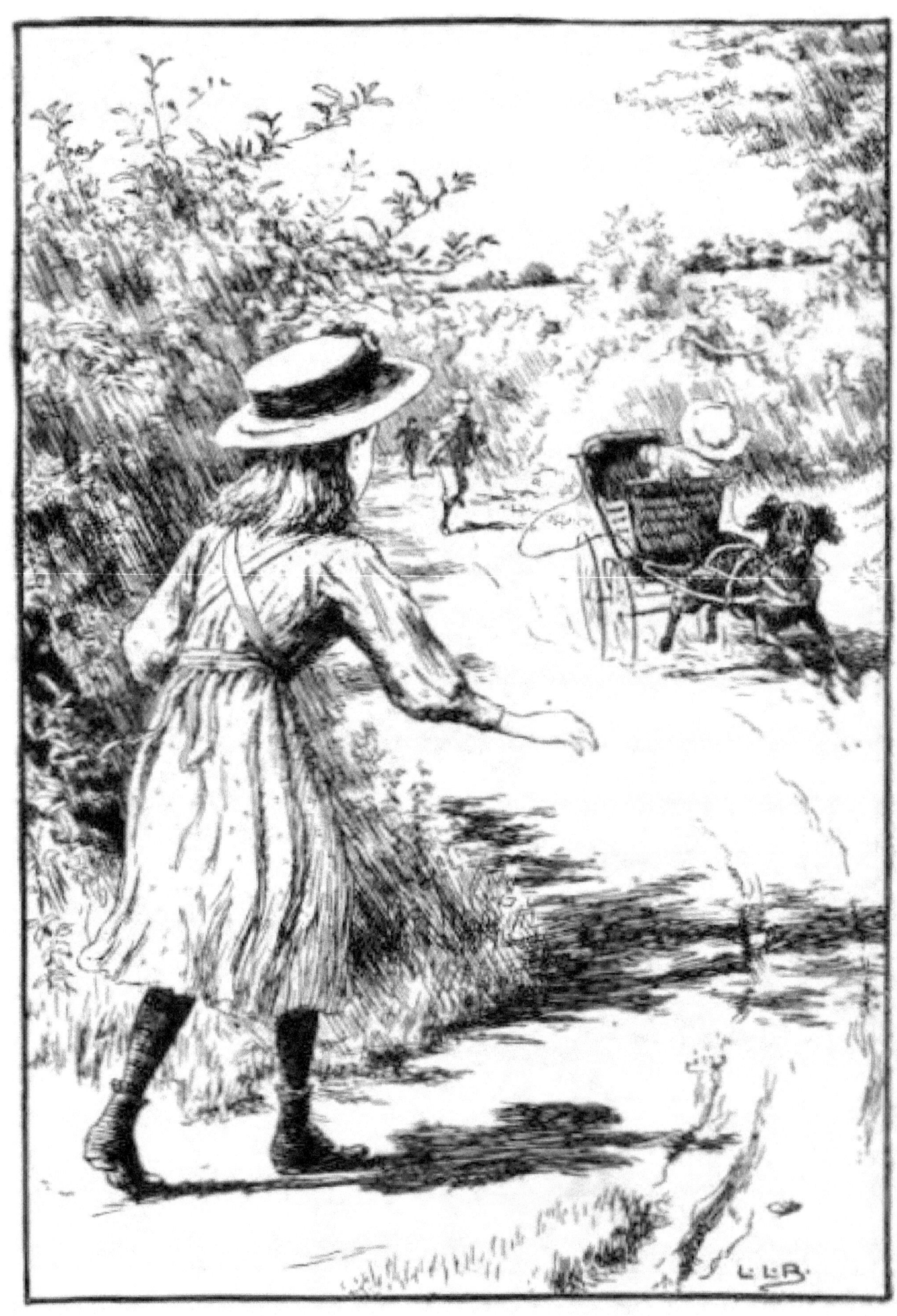

Coming nearer every instant.—p. 178.

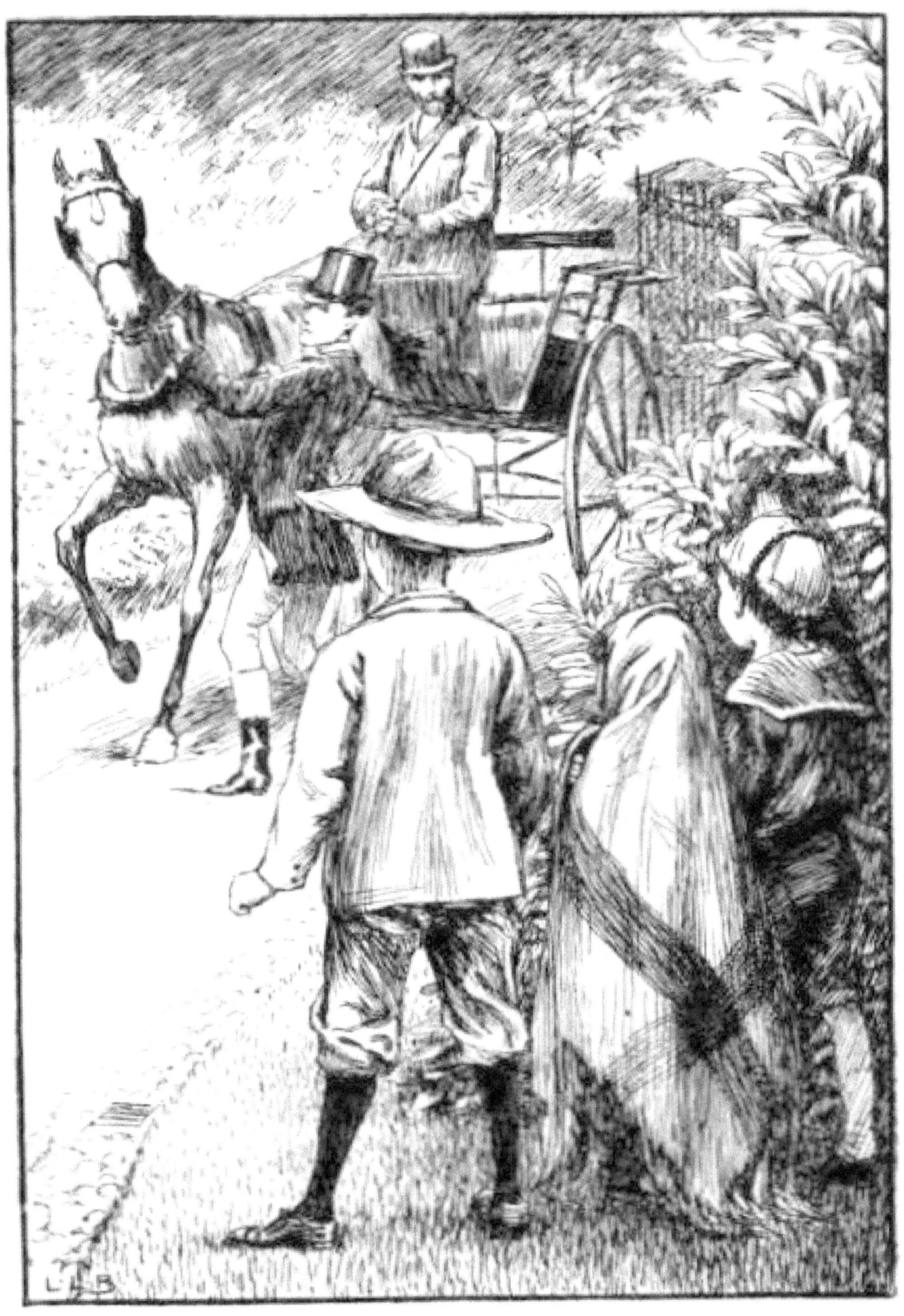

Mr. Wiseman, Mr. Wiseman, please stop.—P. 196.

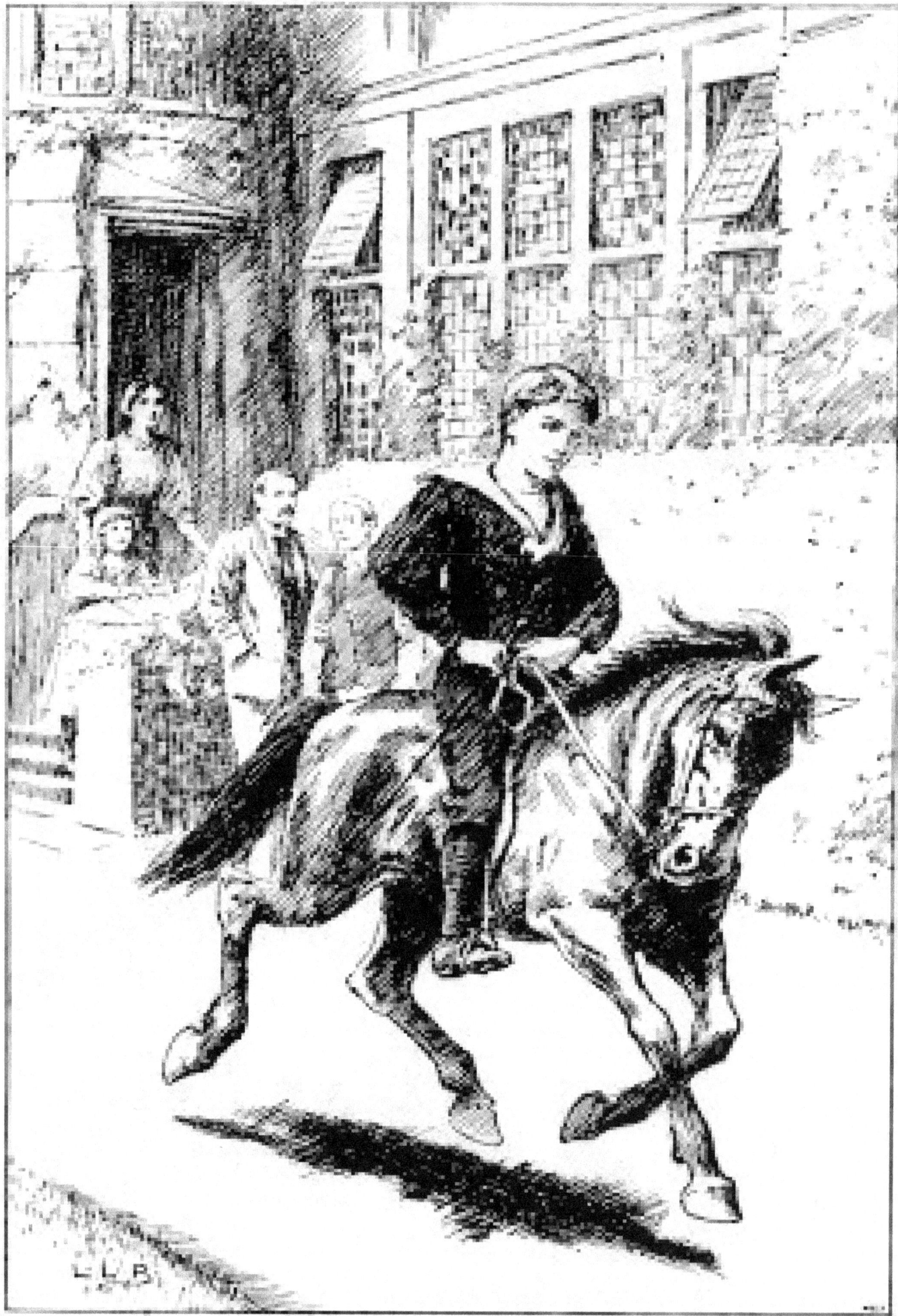

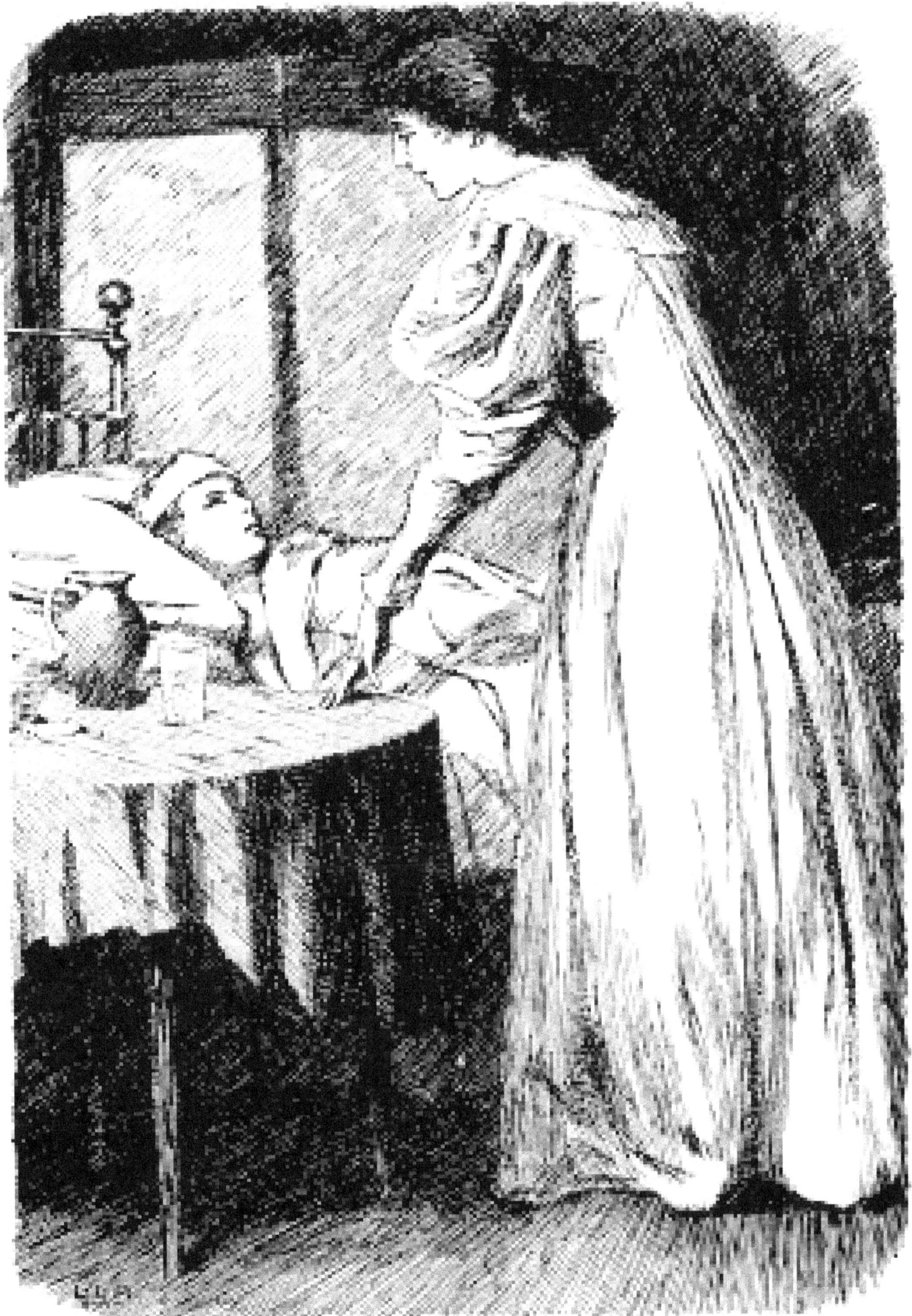

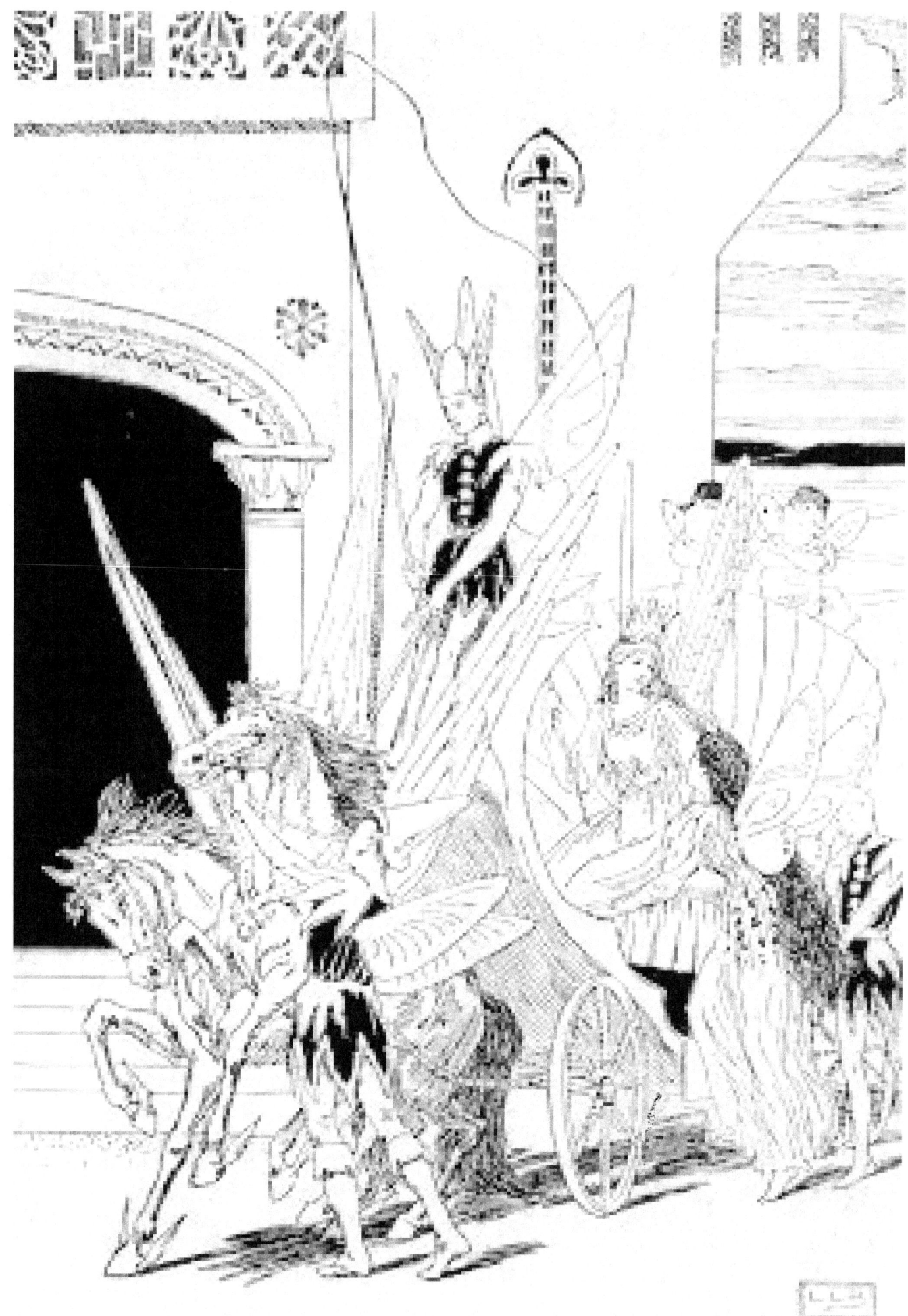

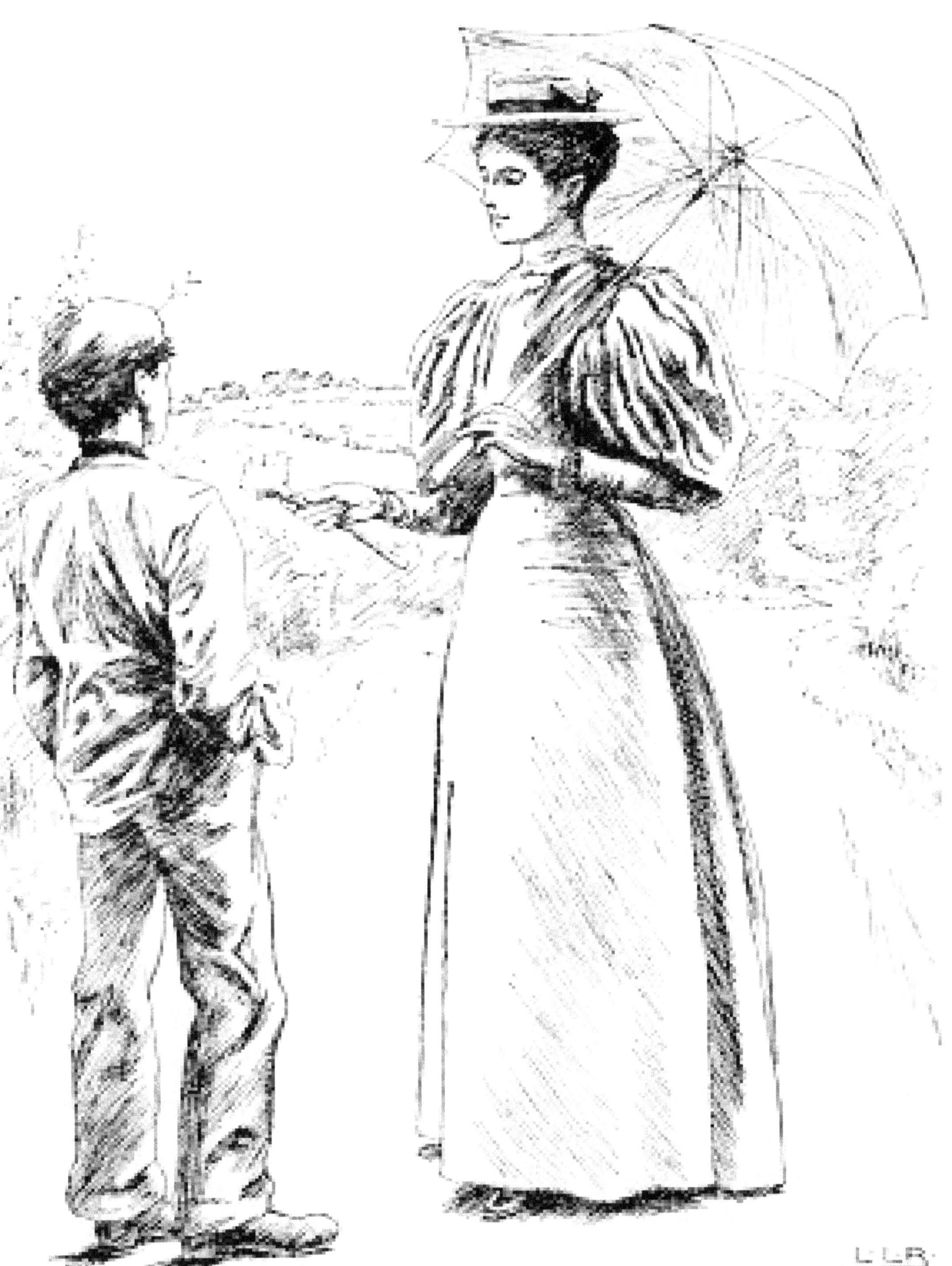

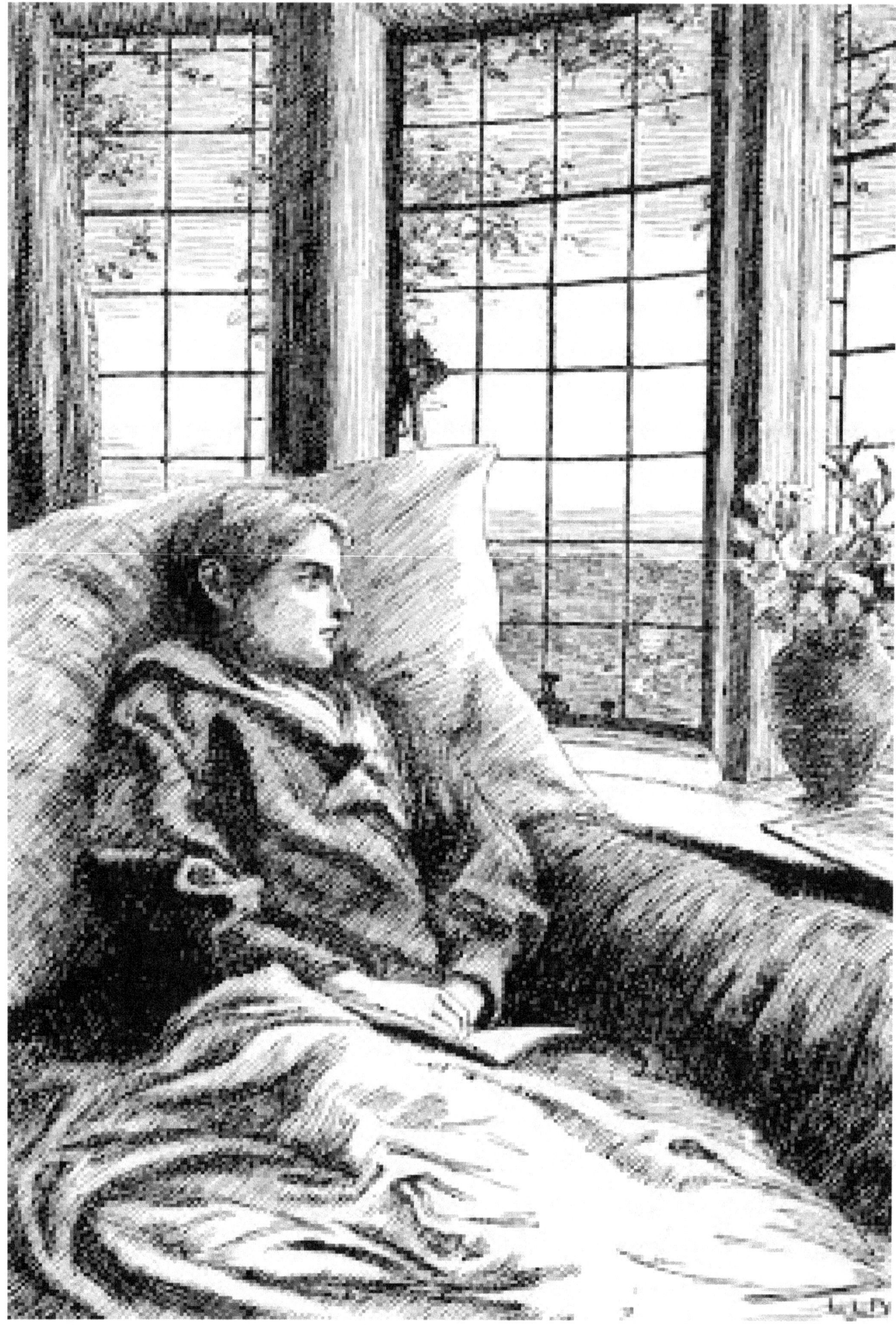

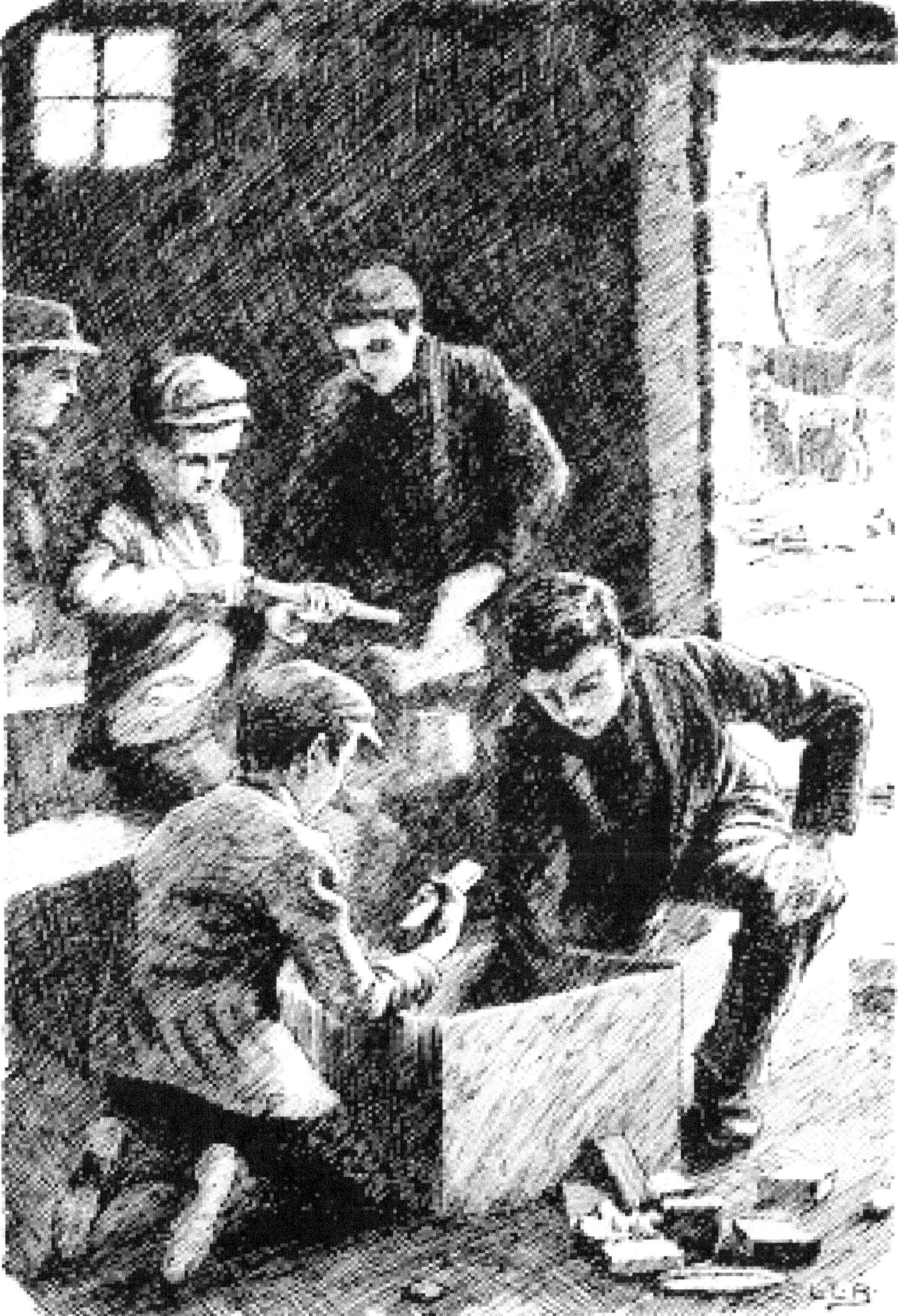

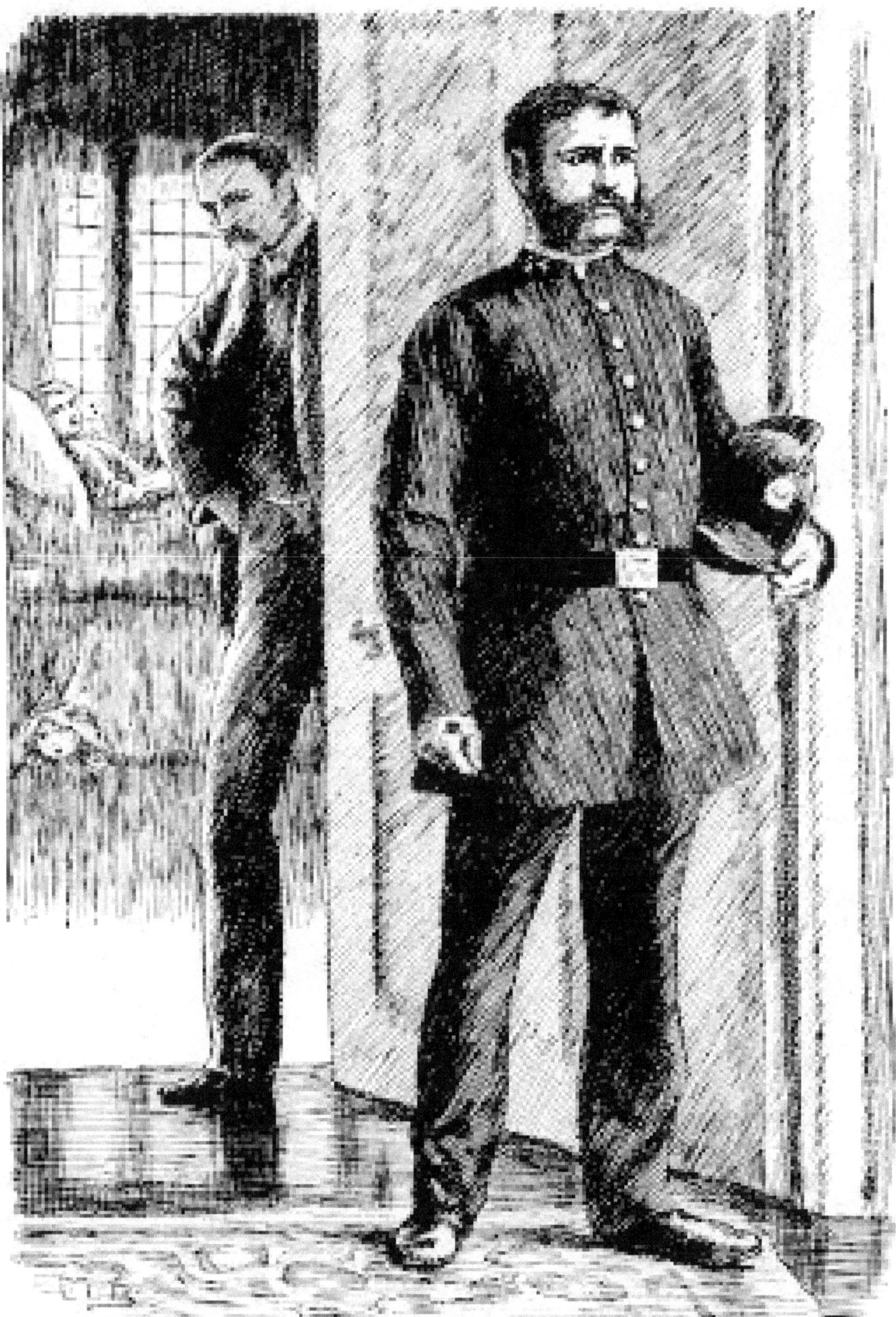

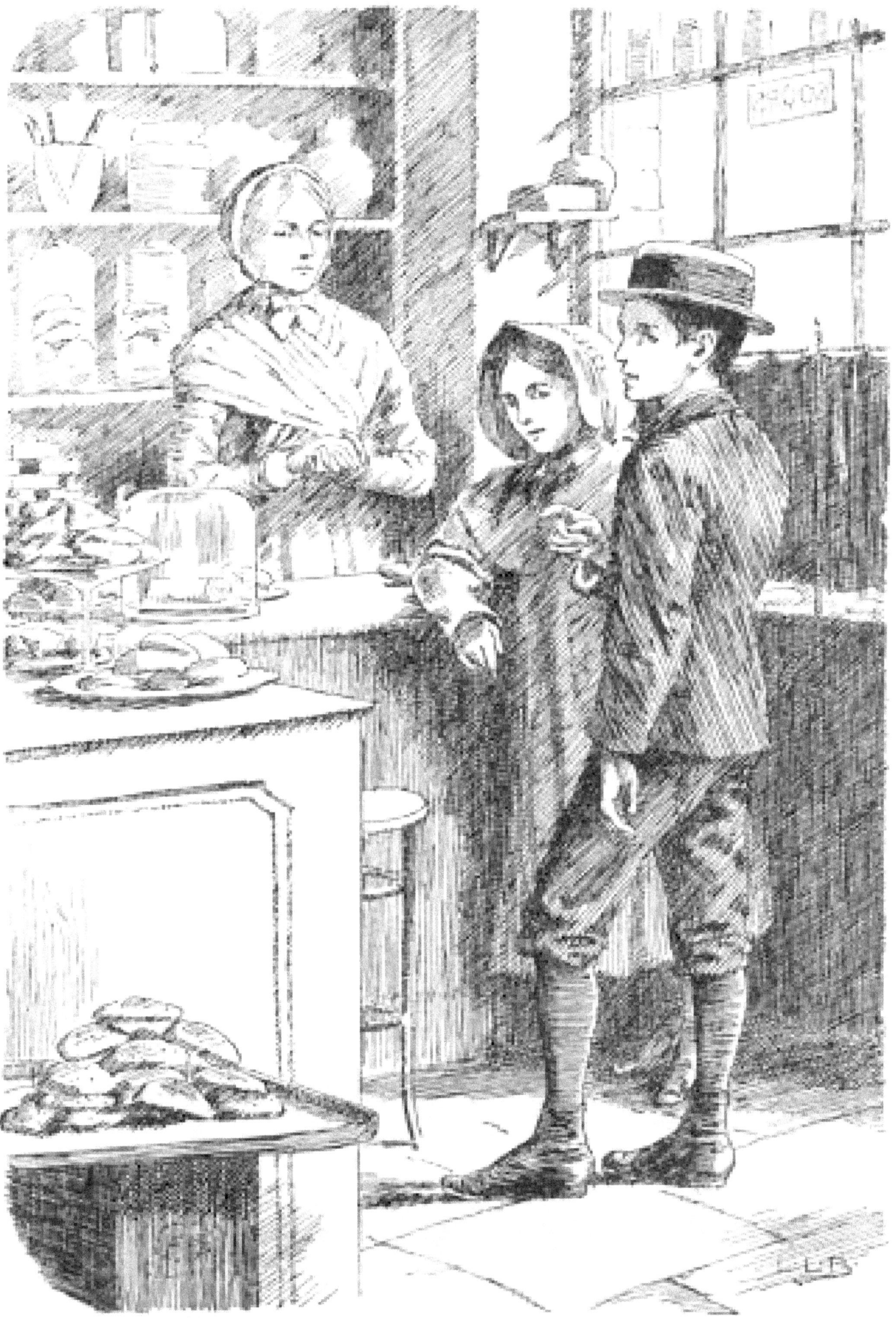

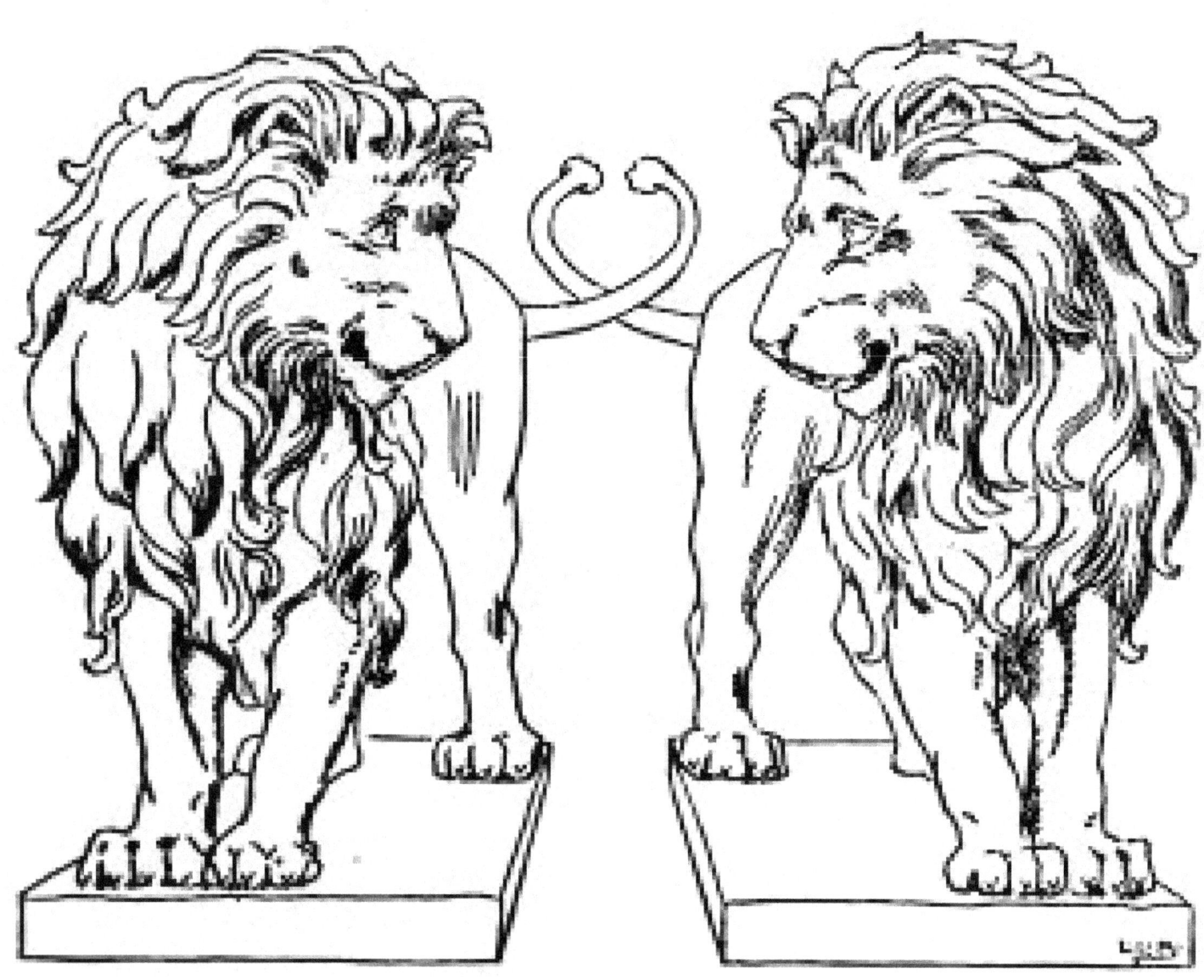

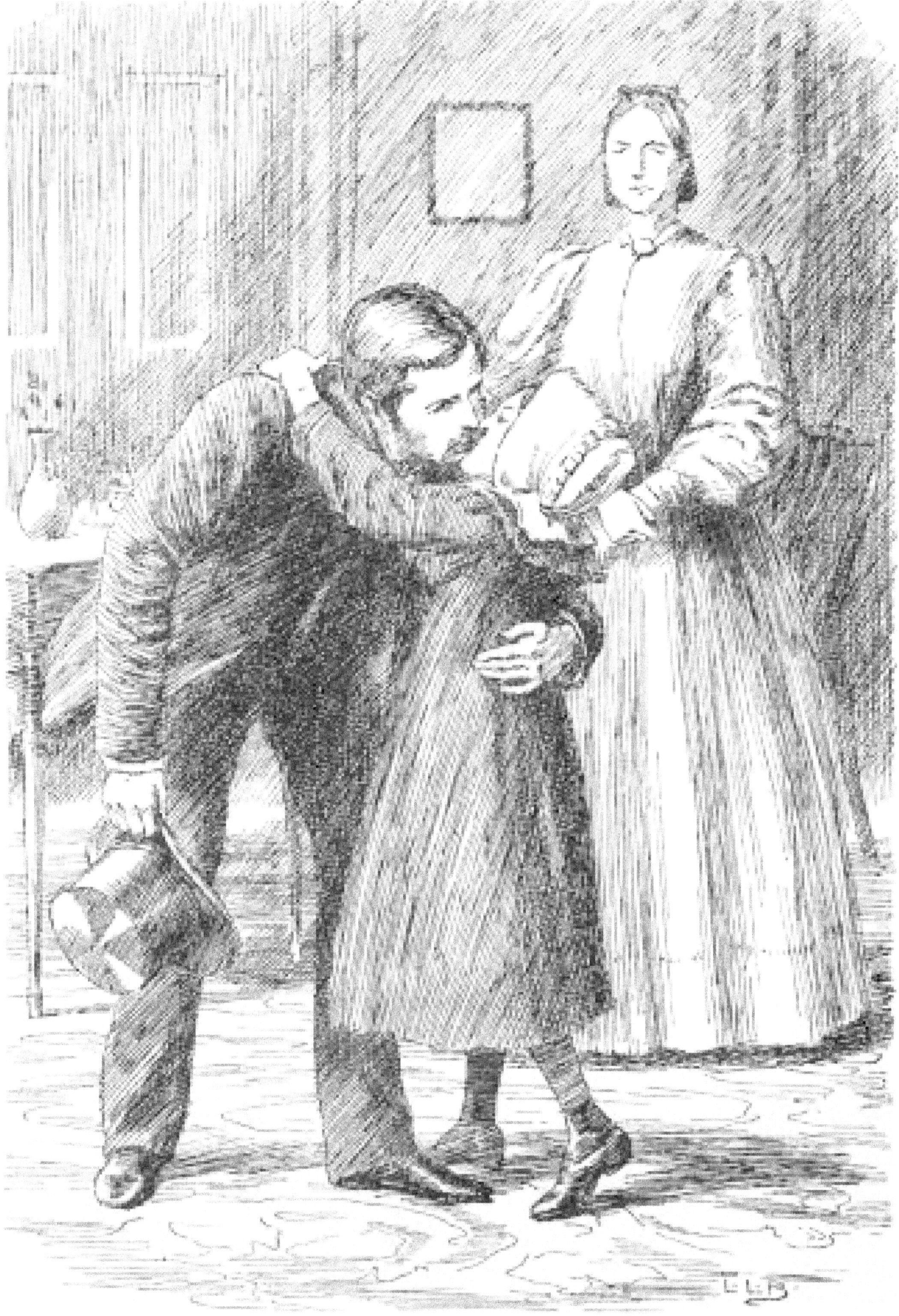

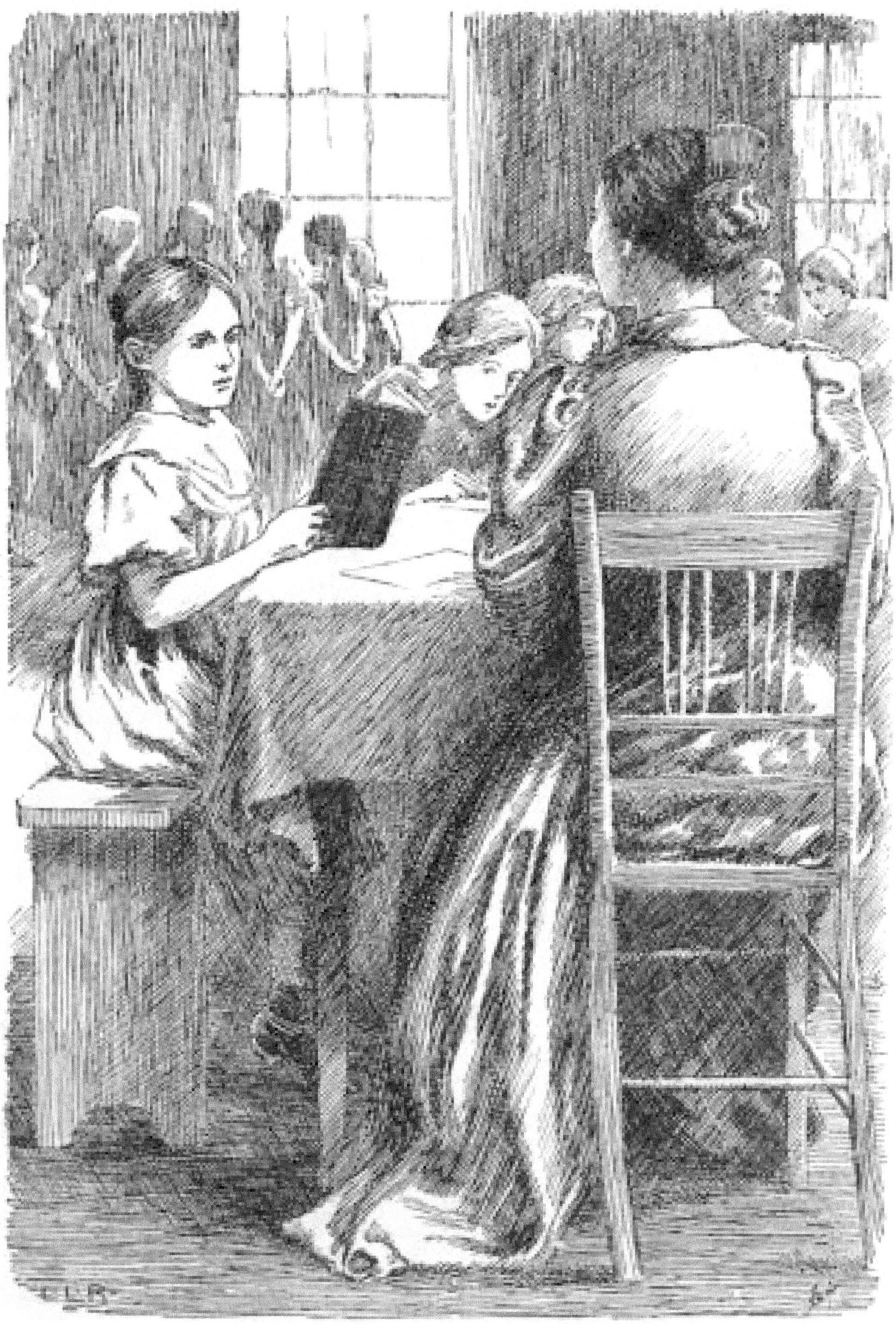

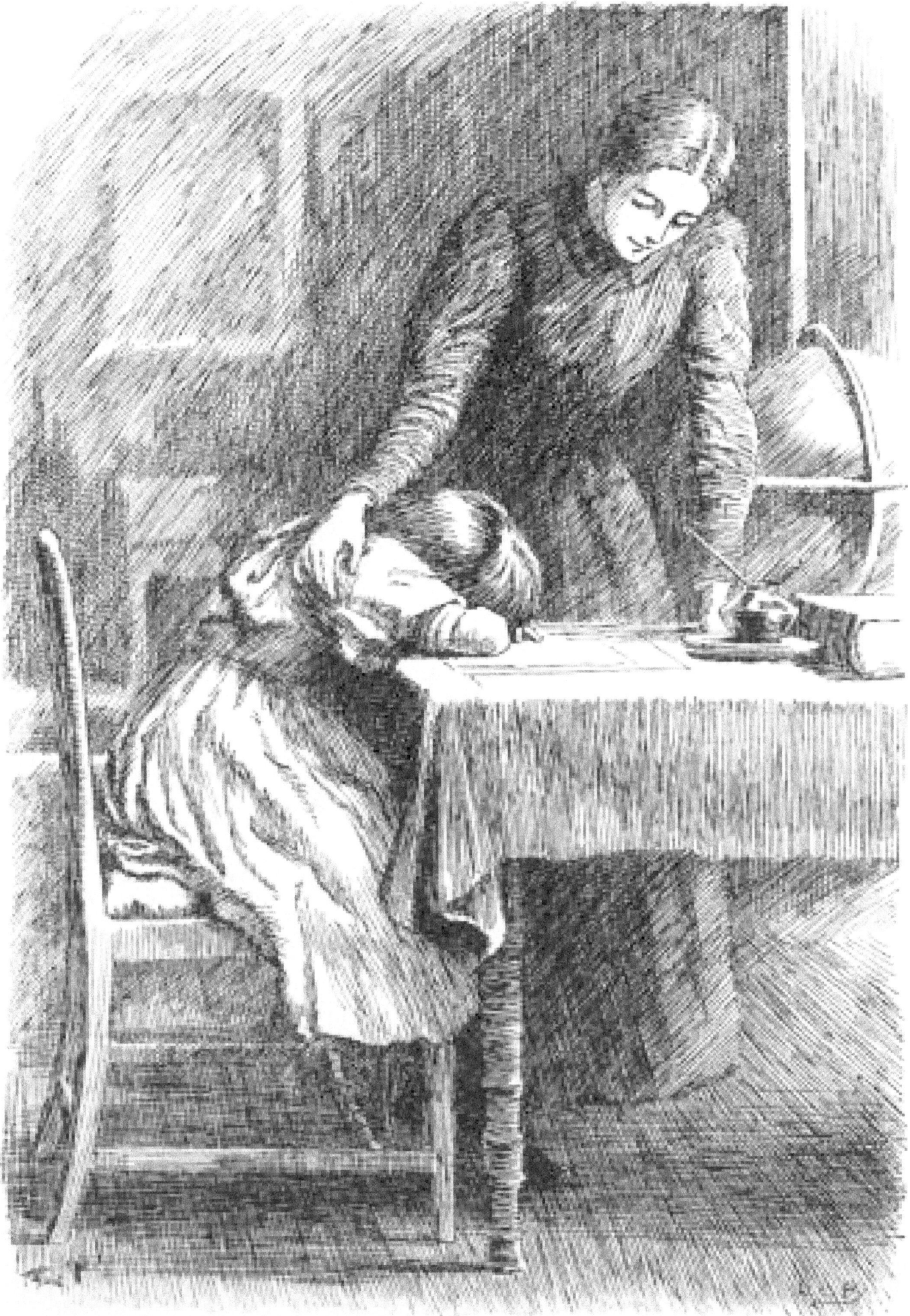

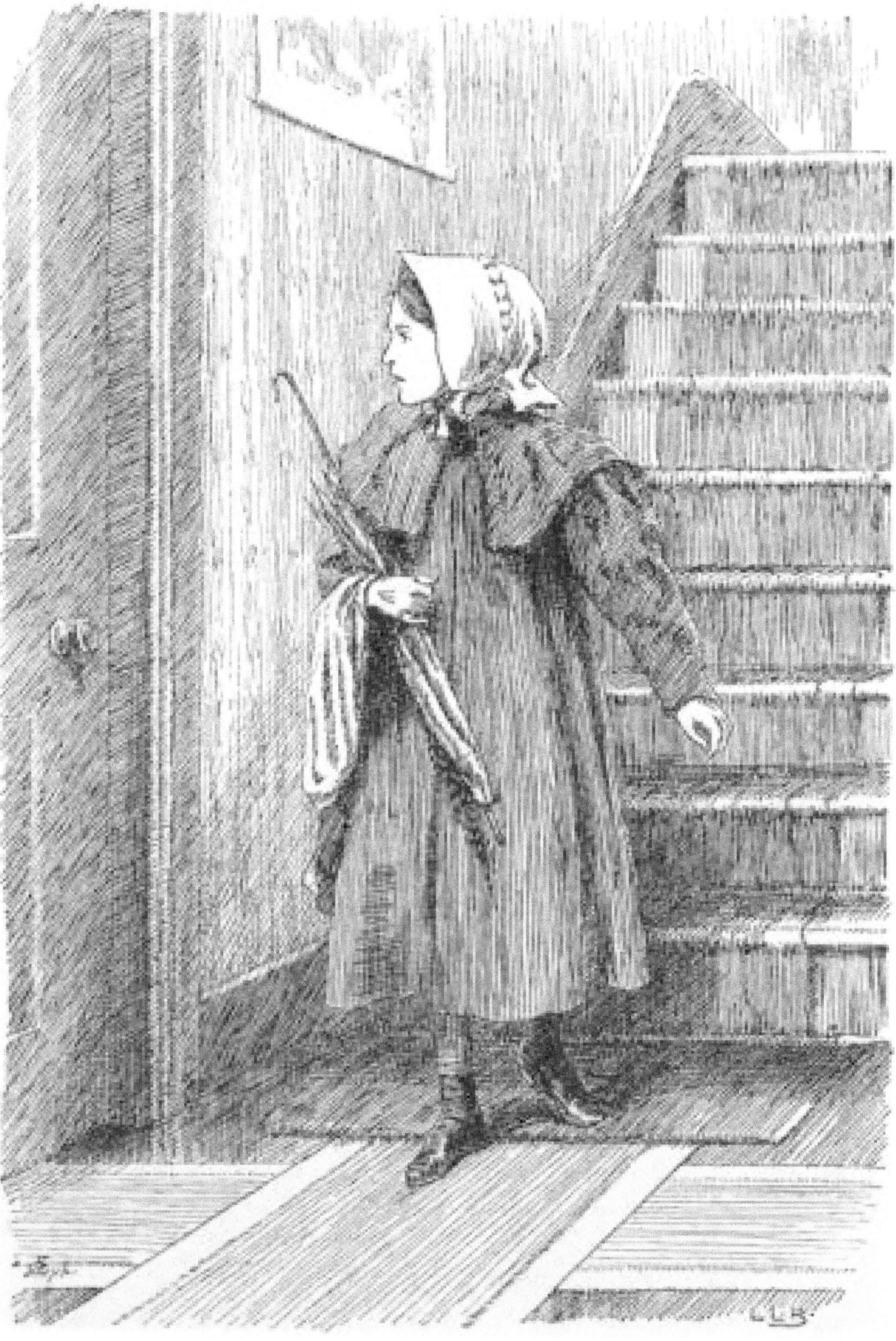

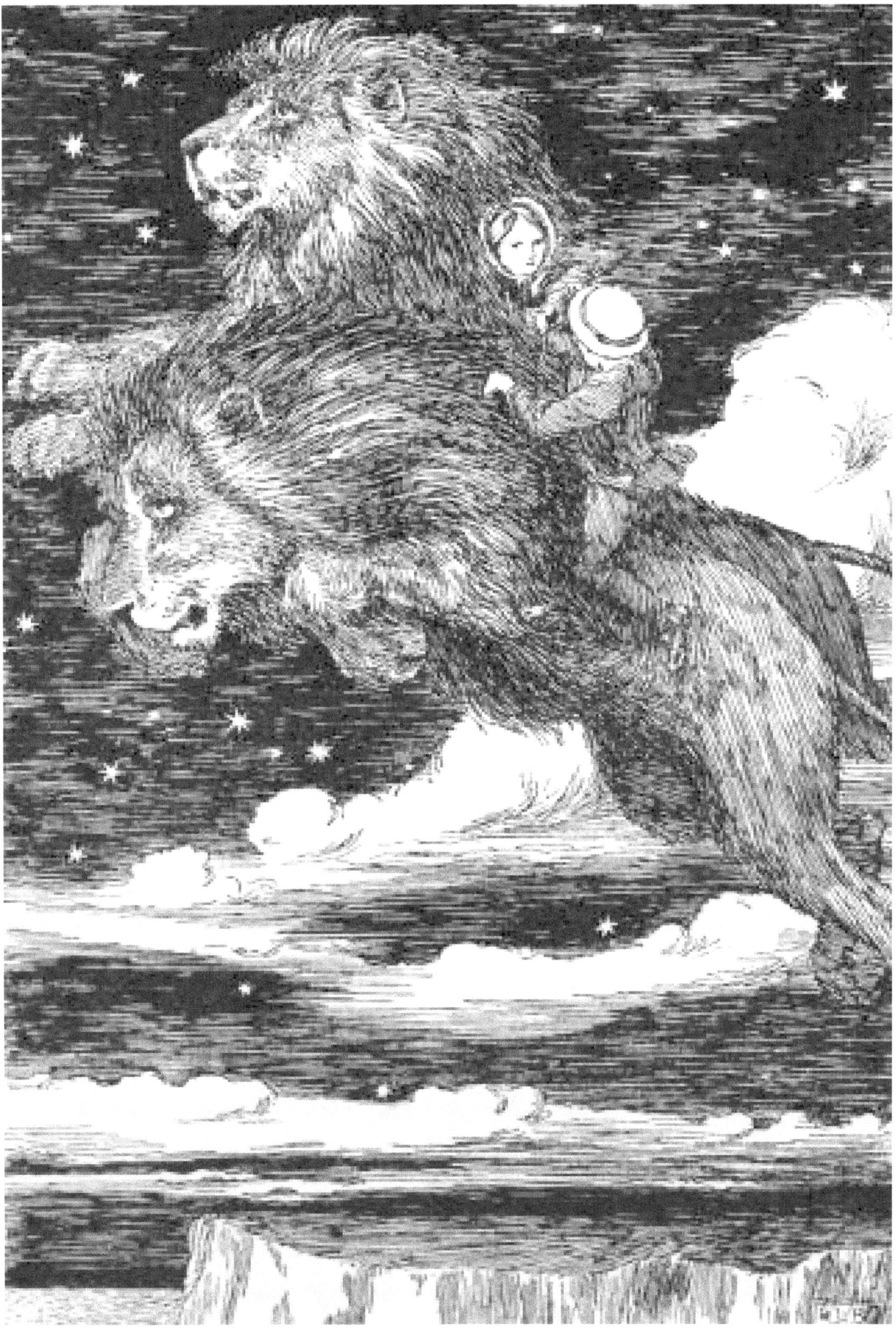

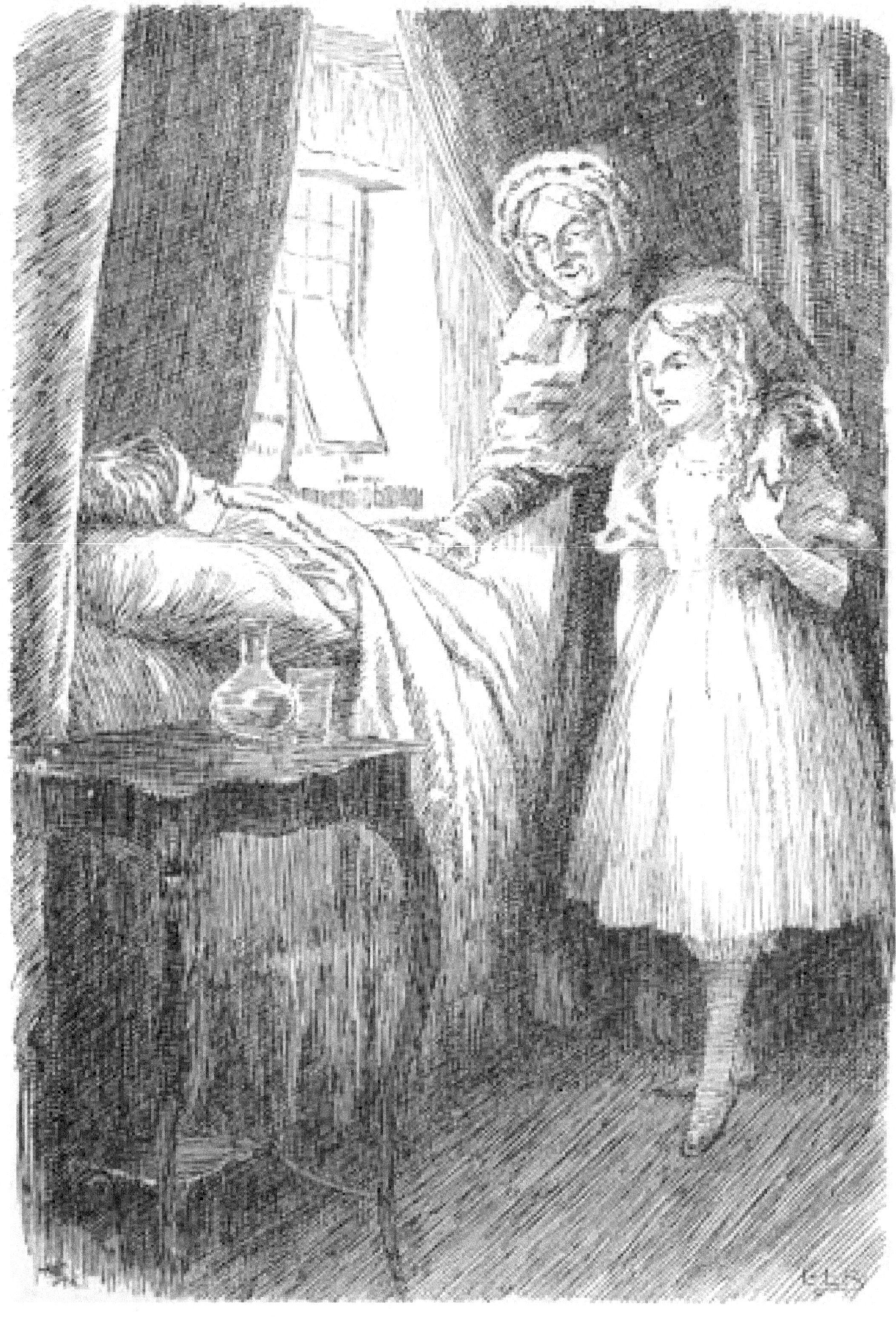

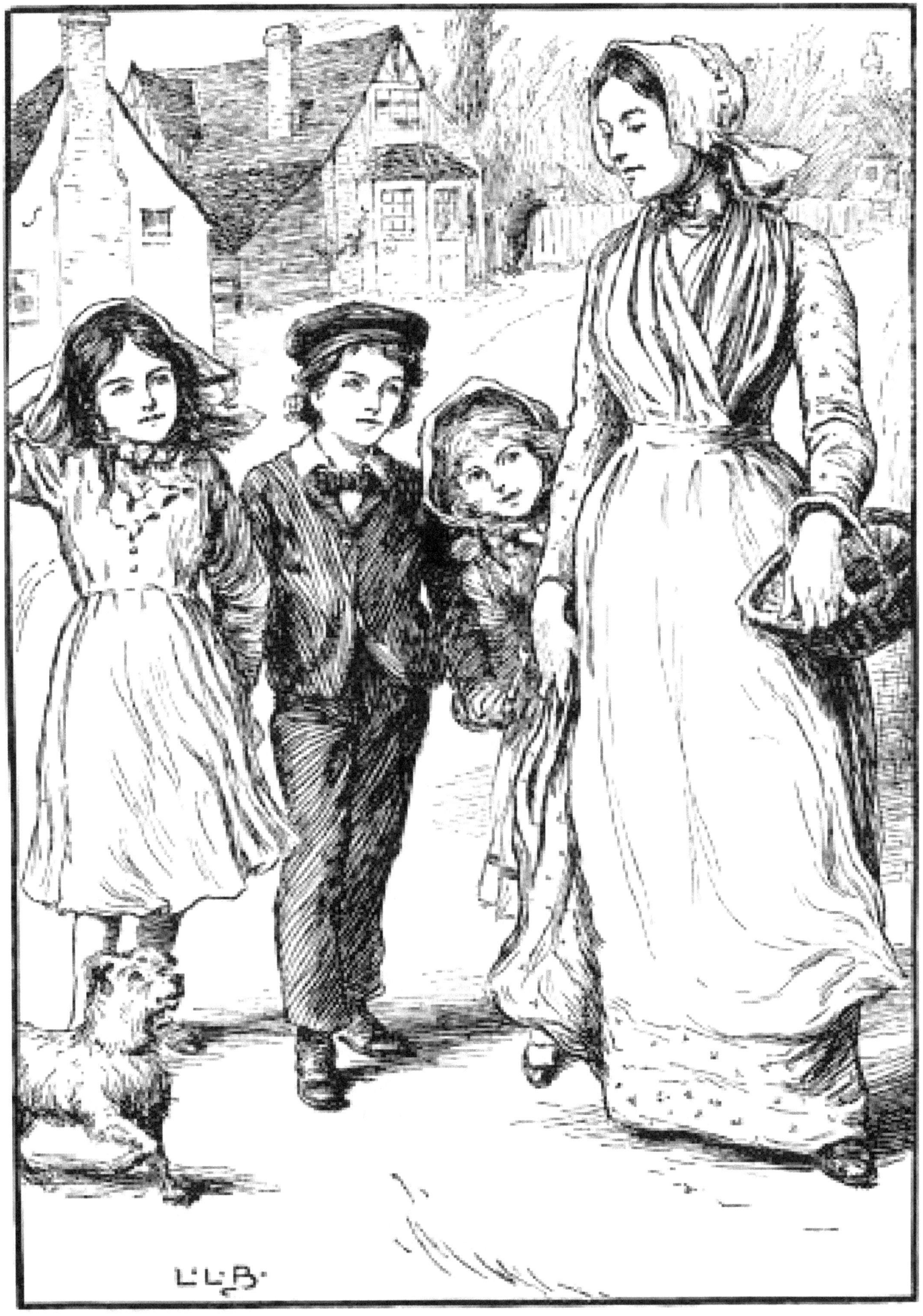

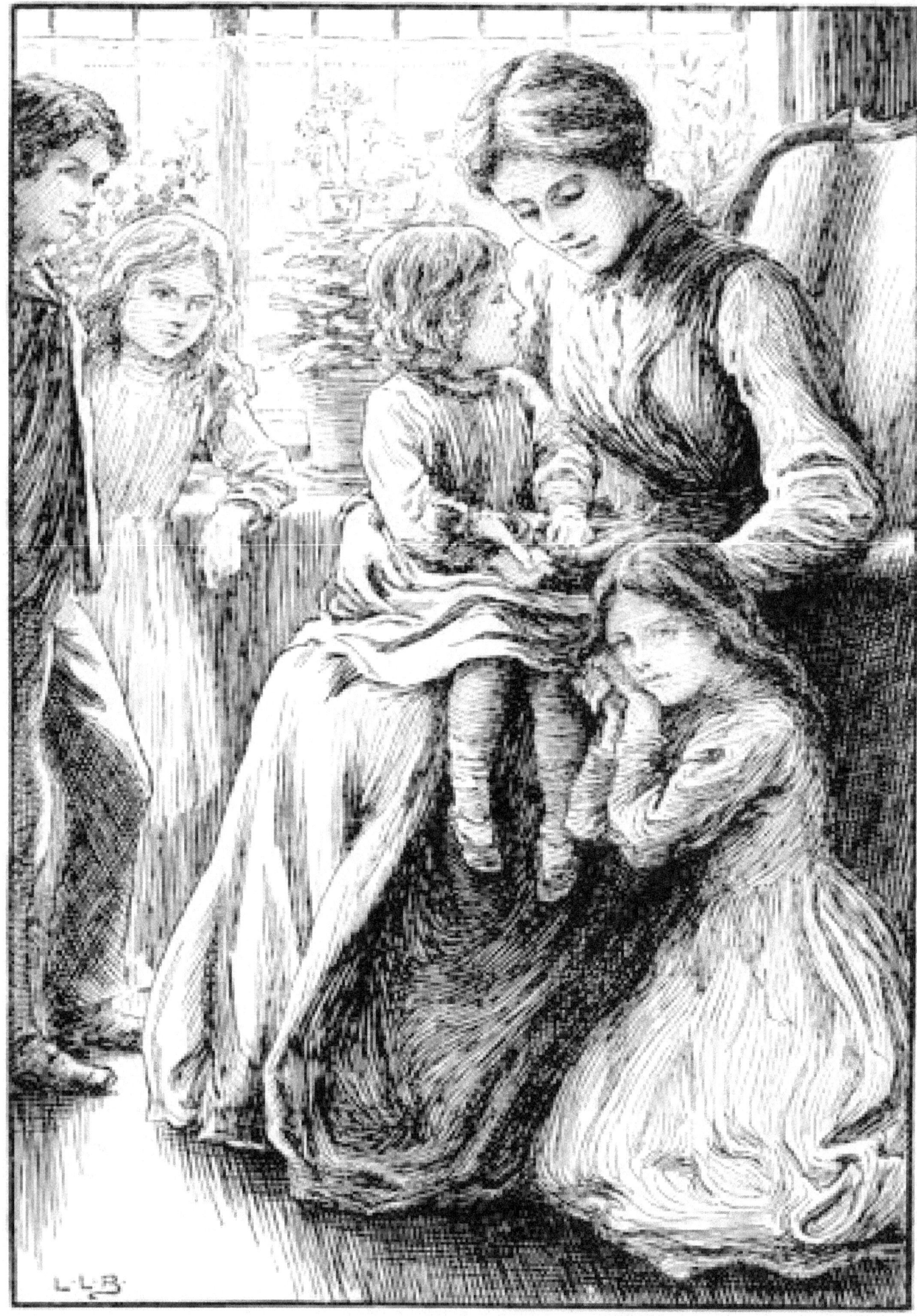

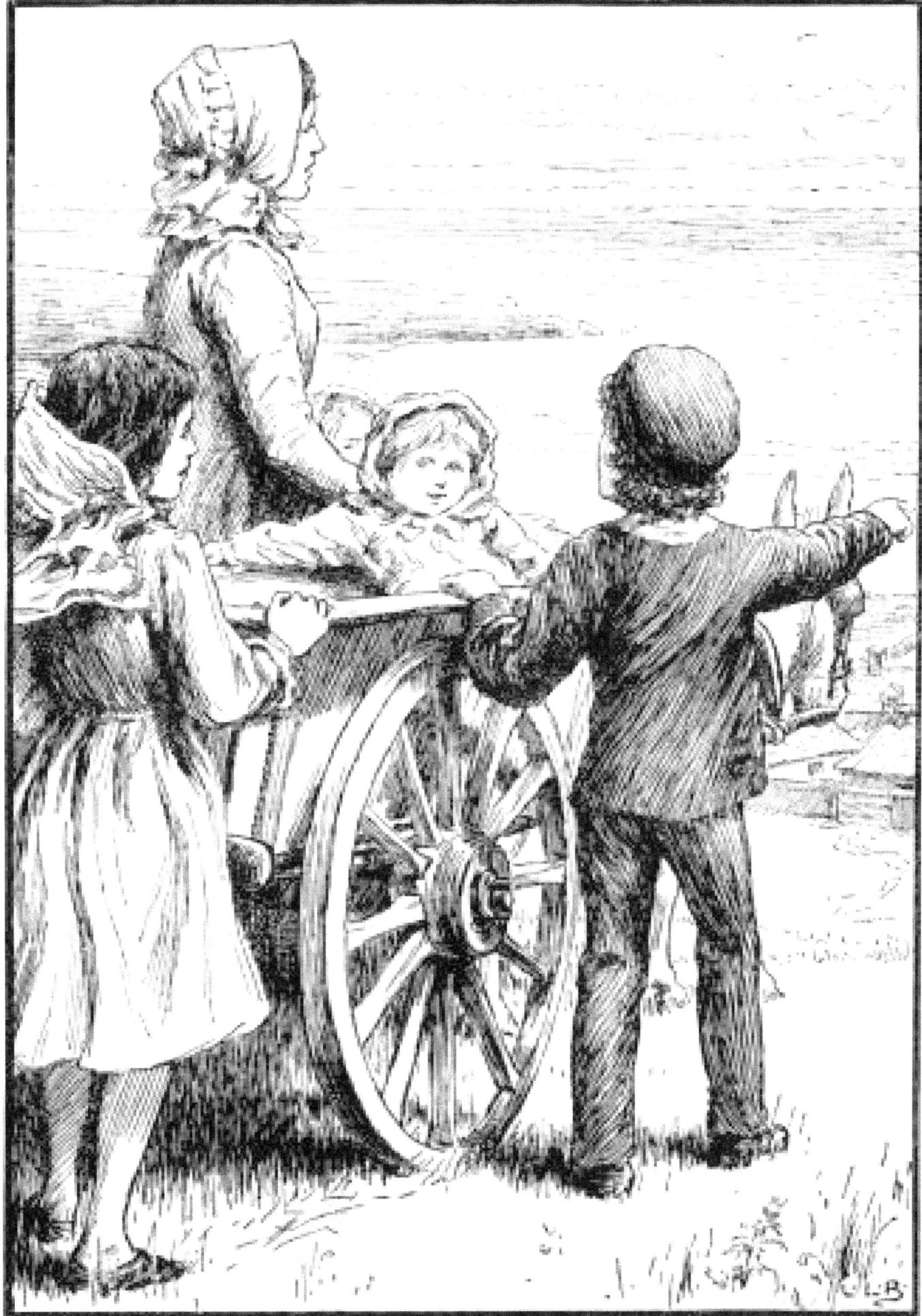

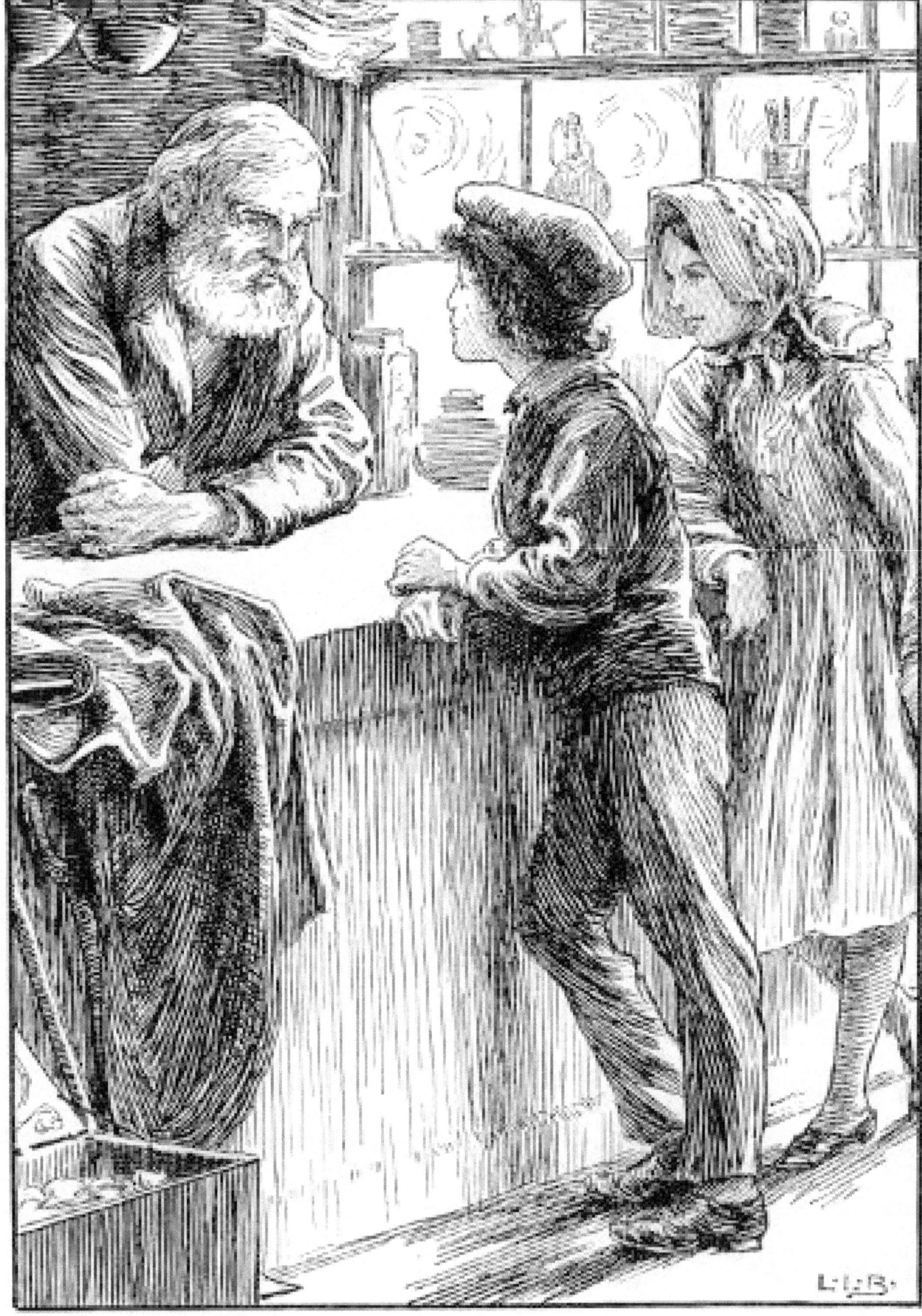

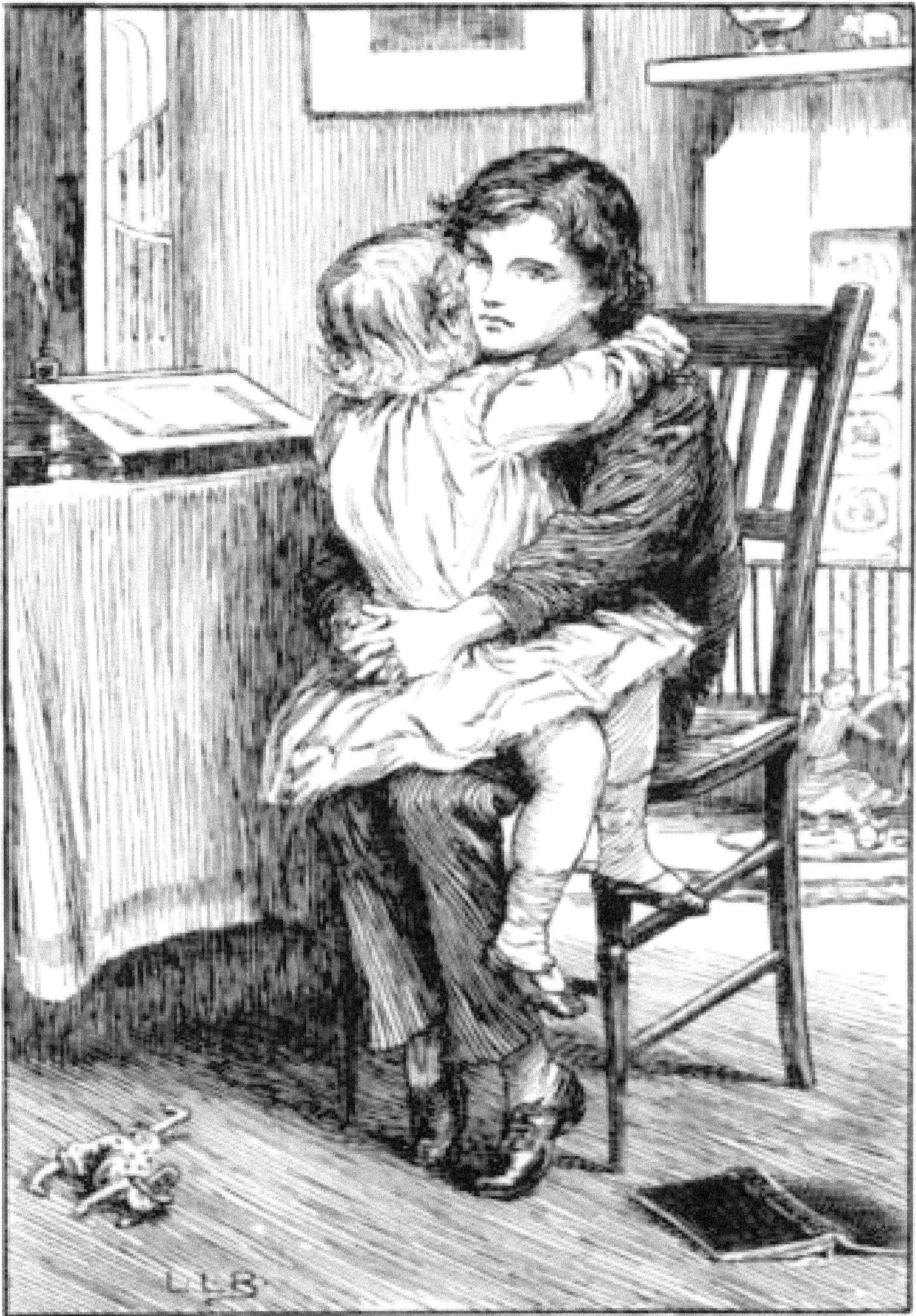

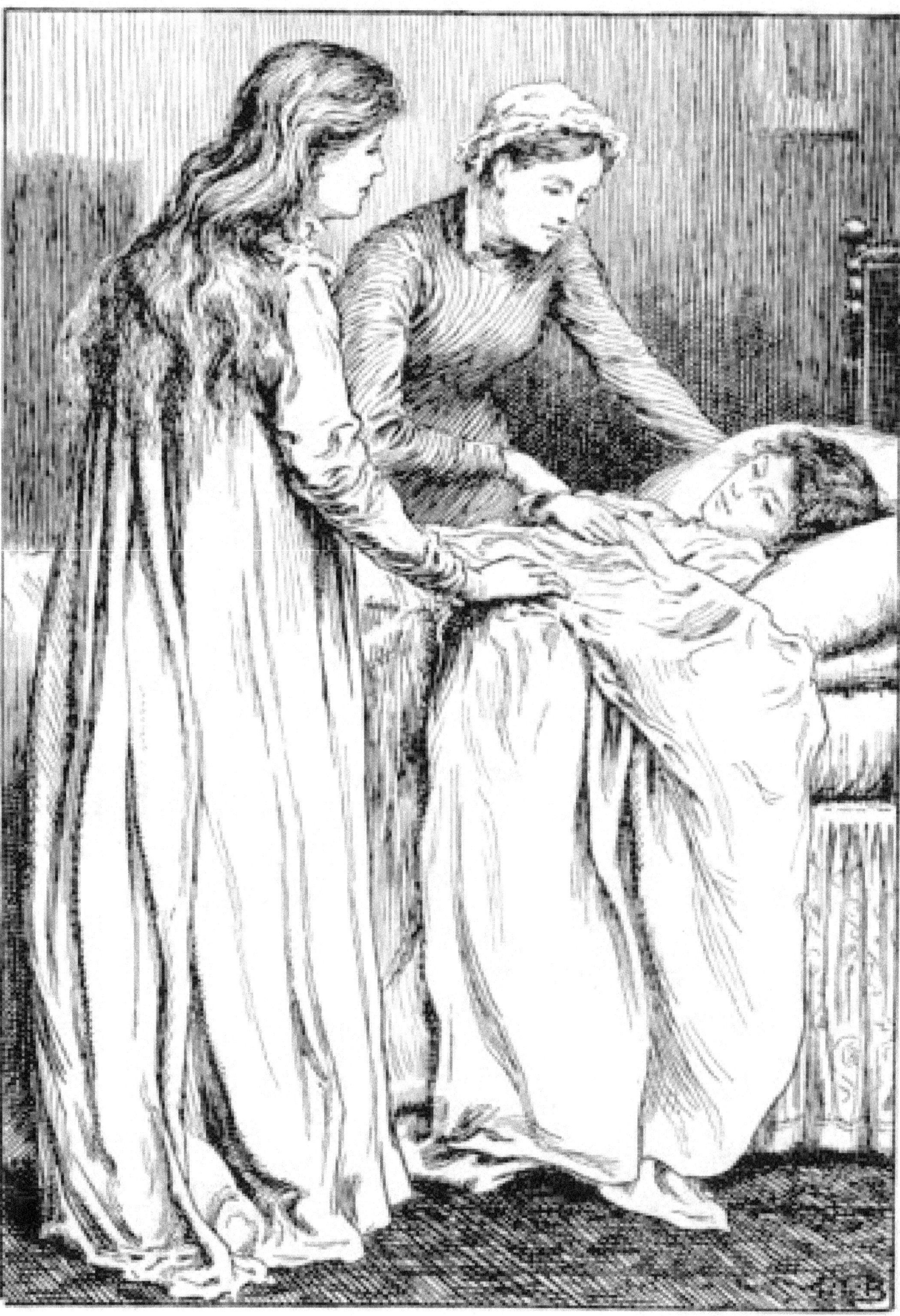

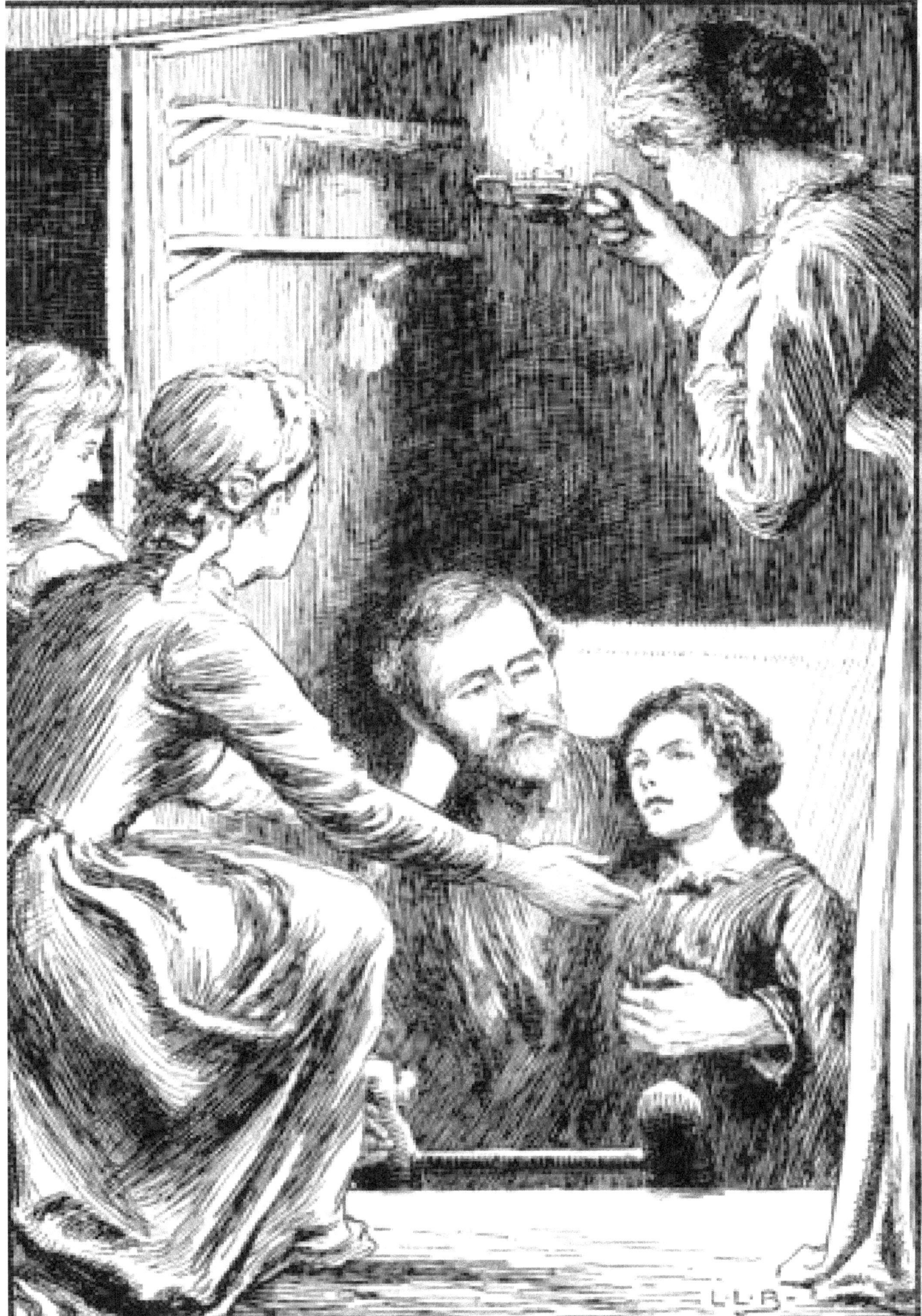

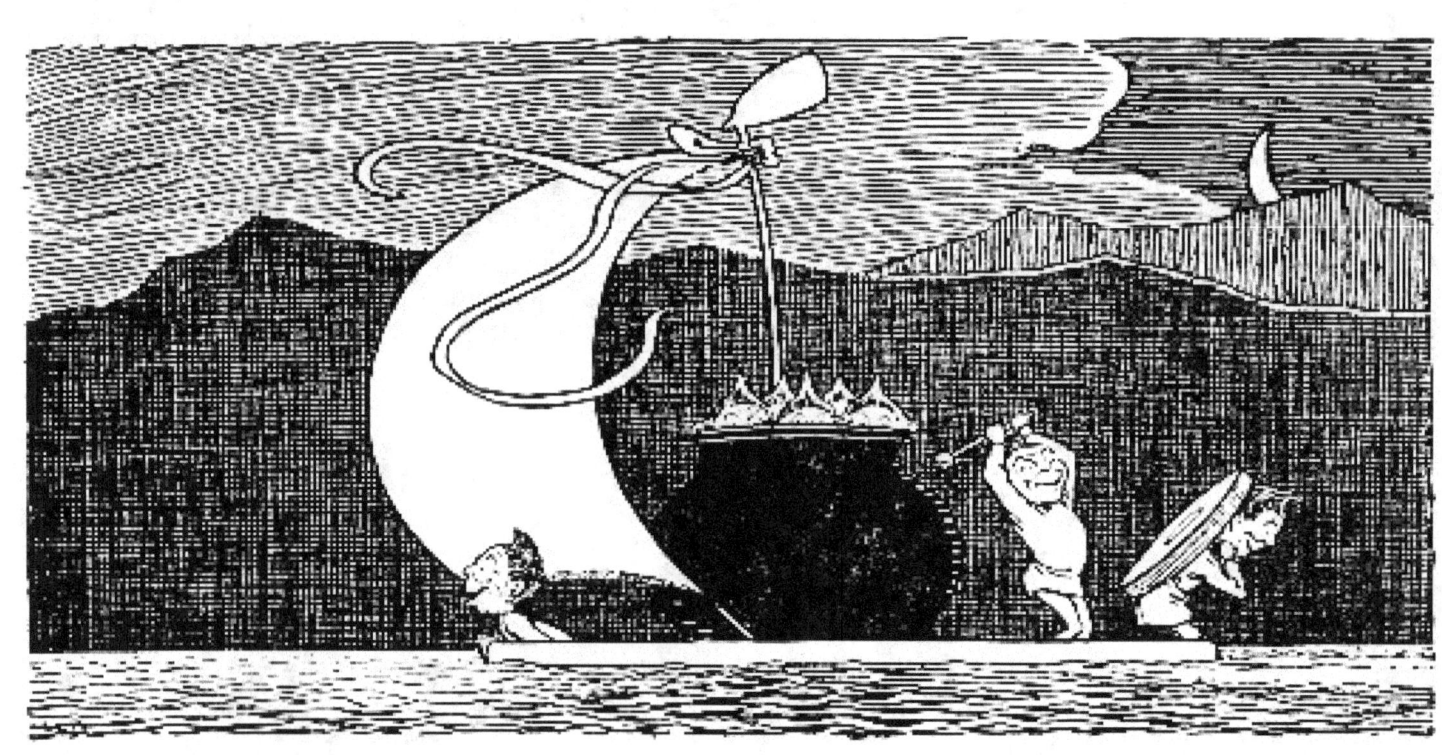

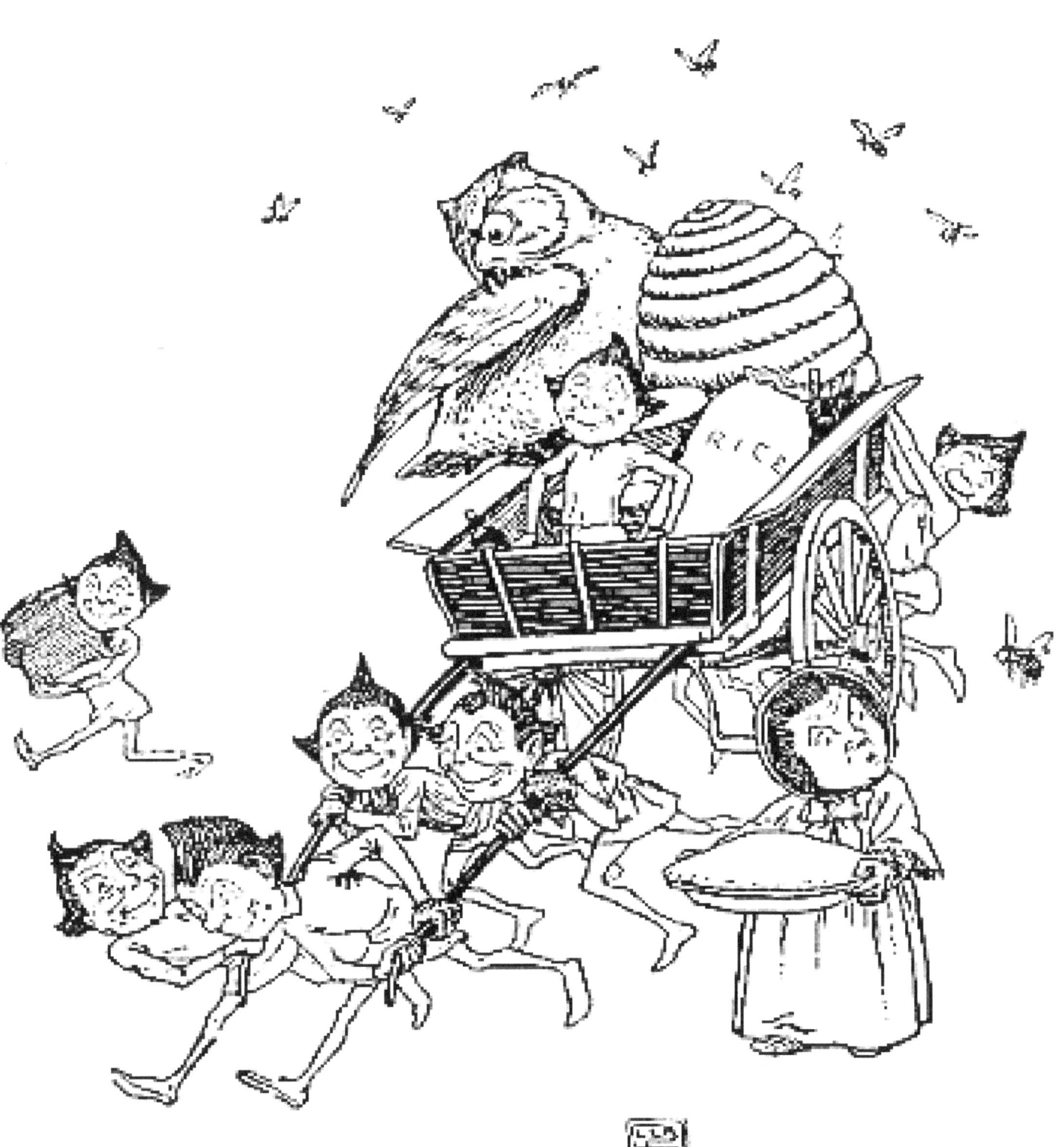

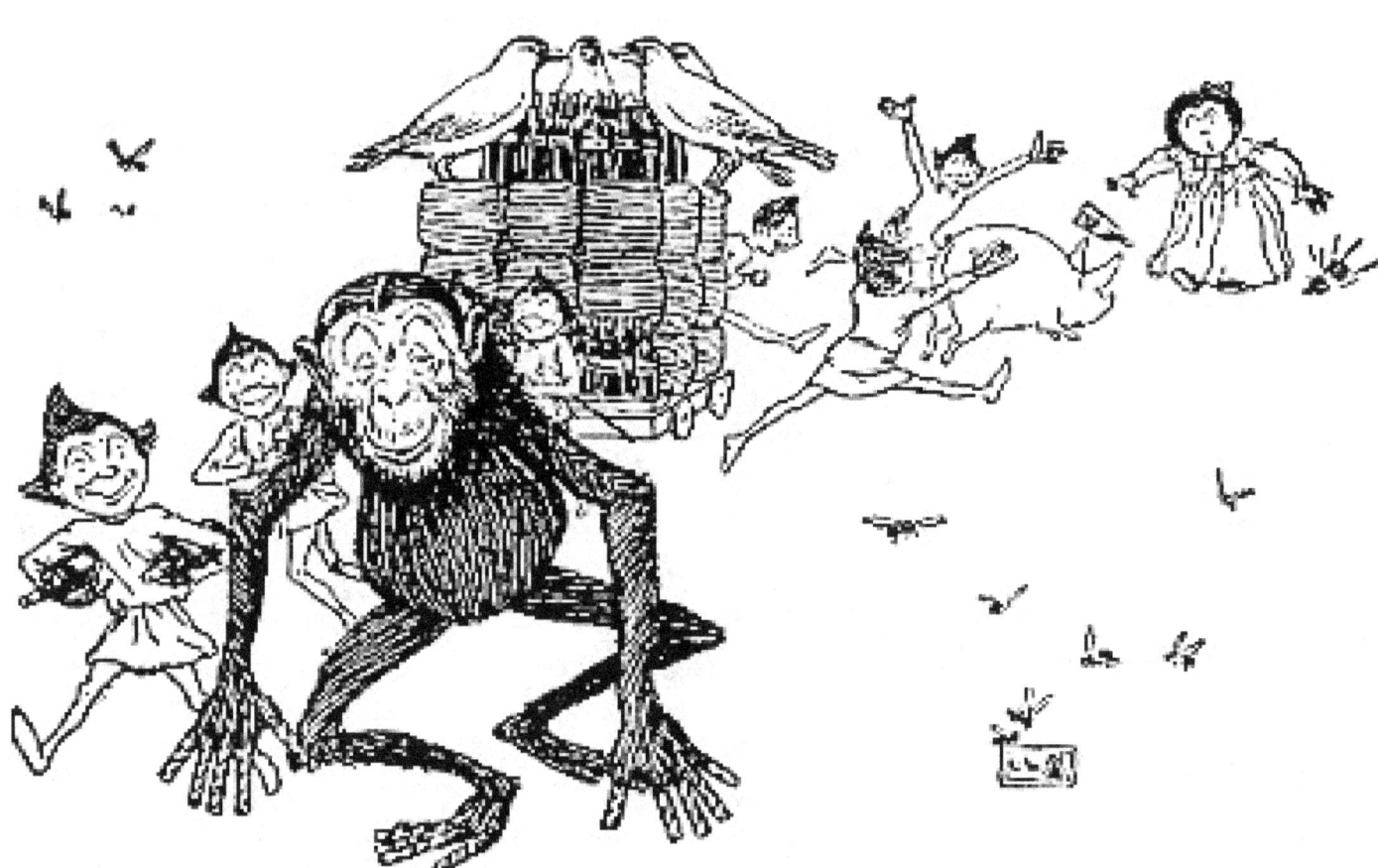

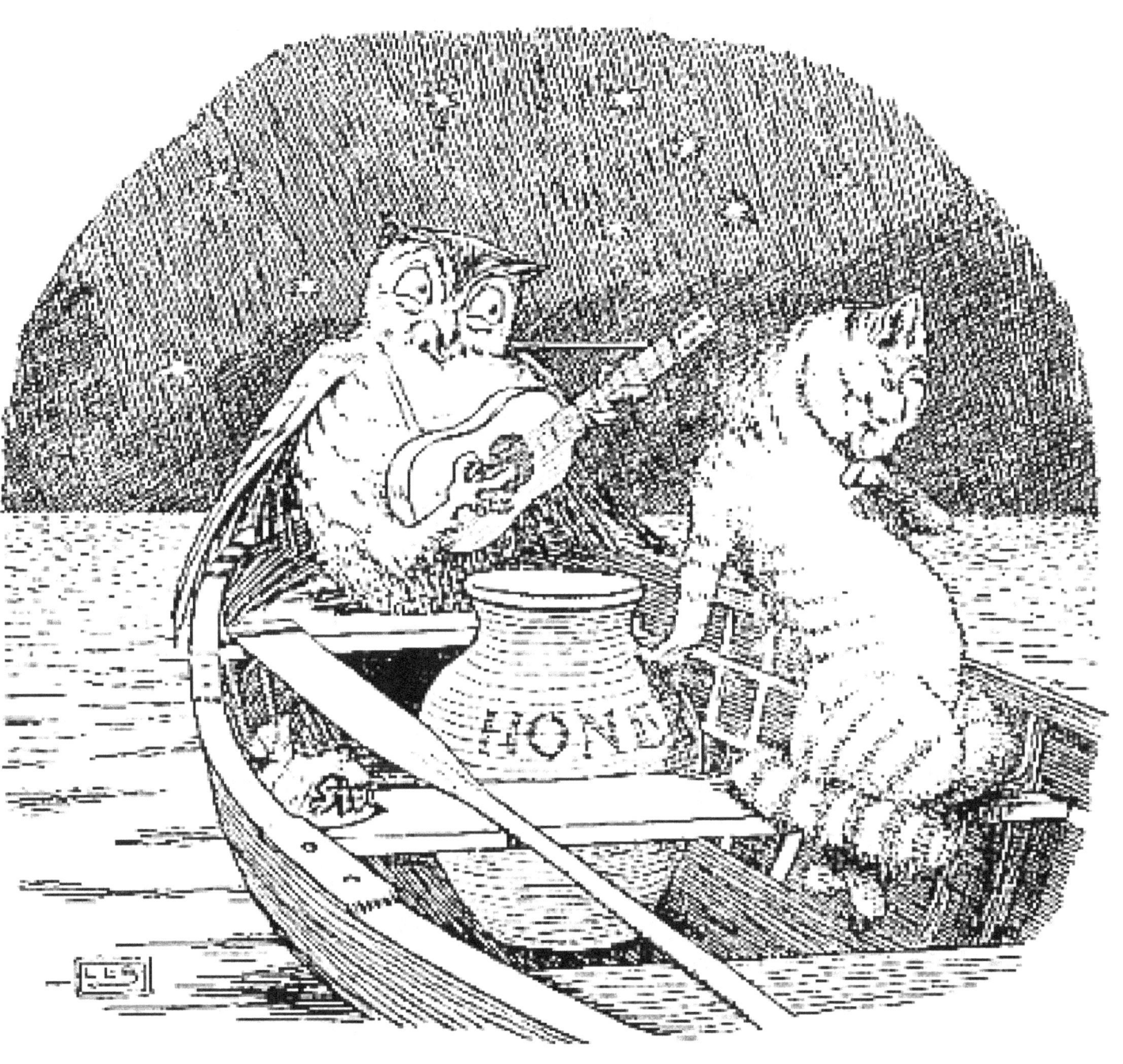

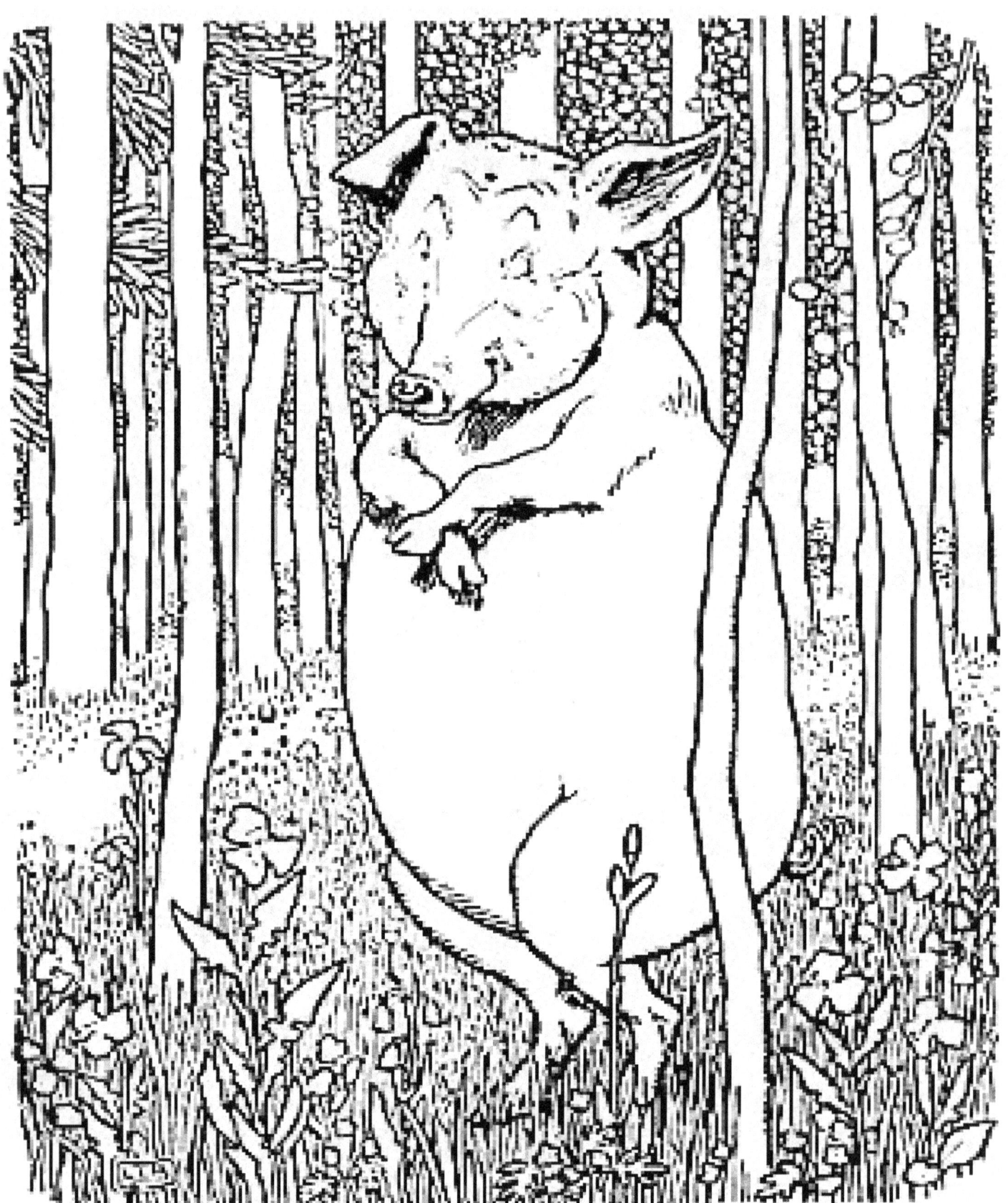

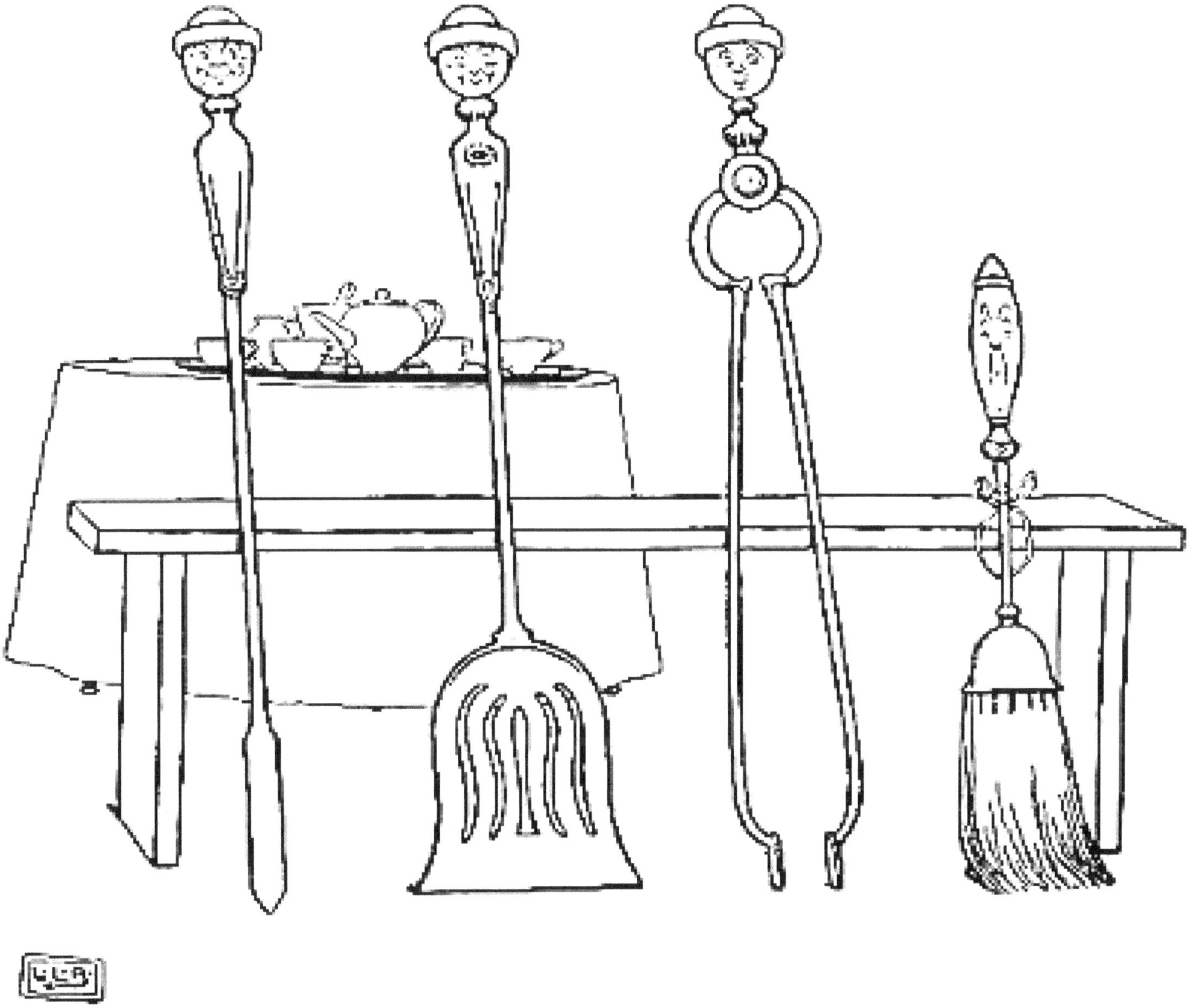

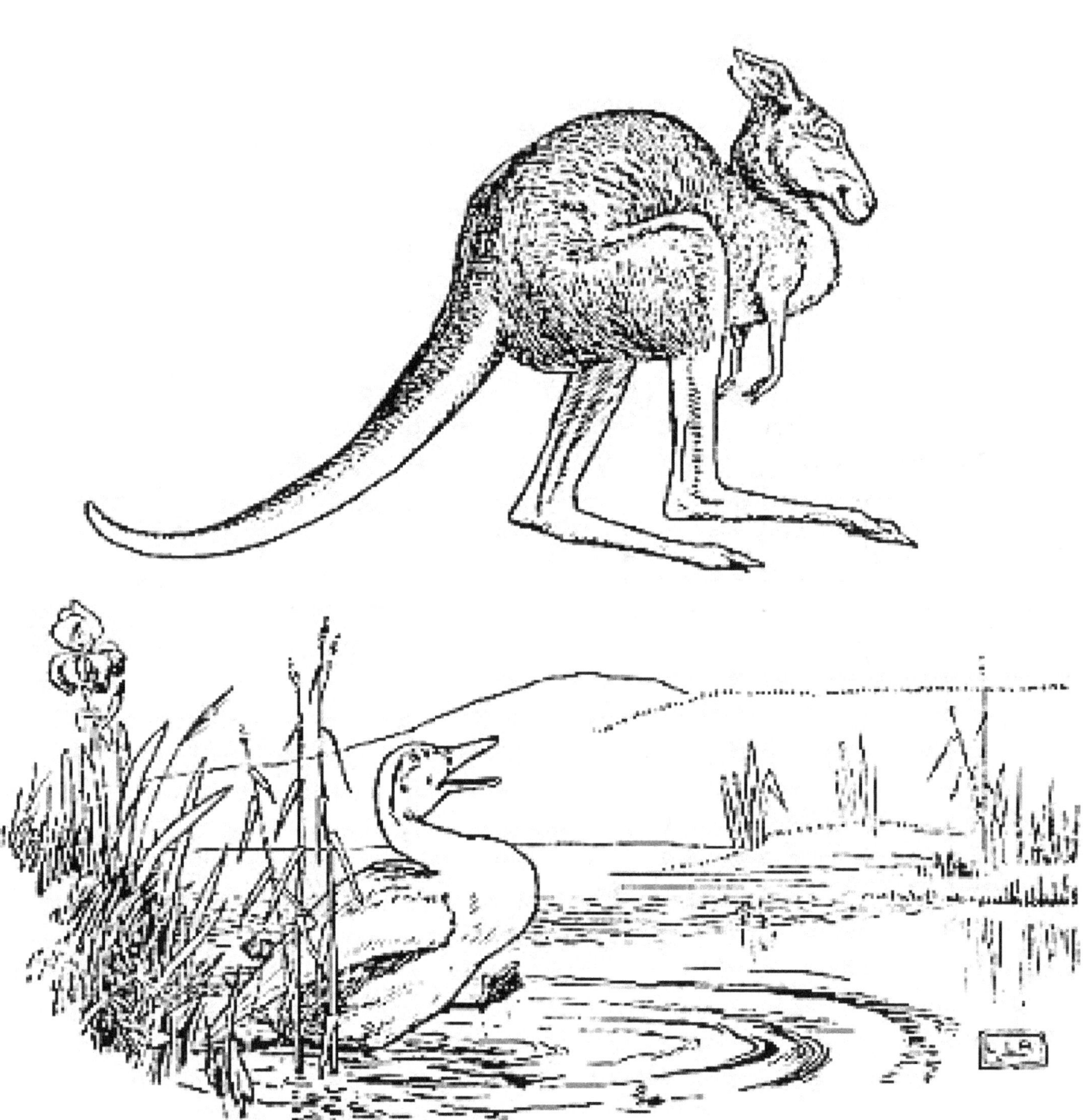

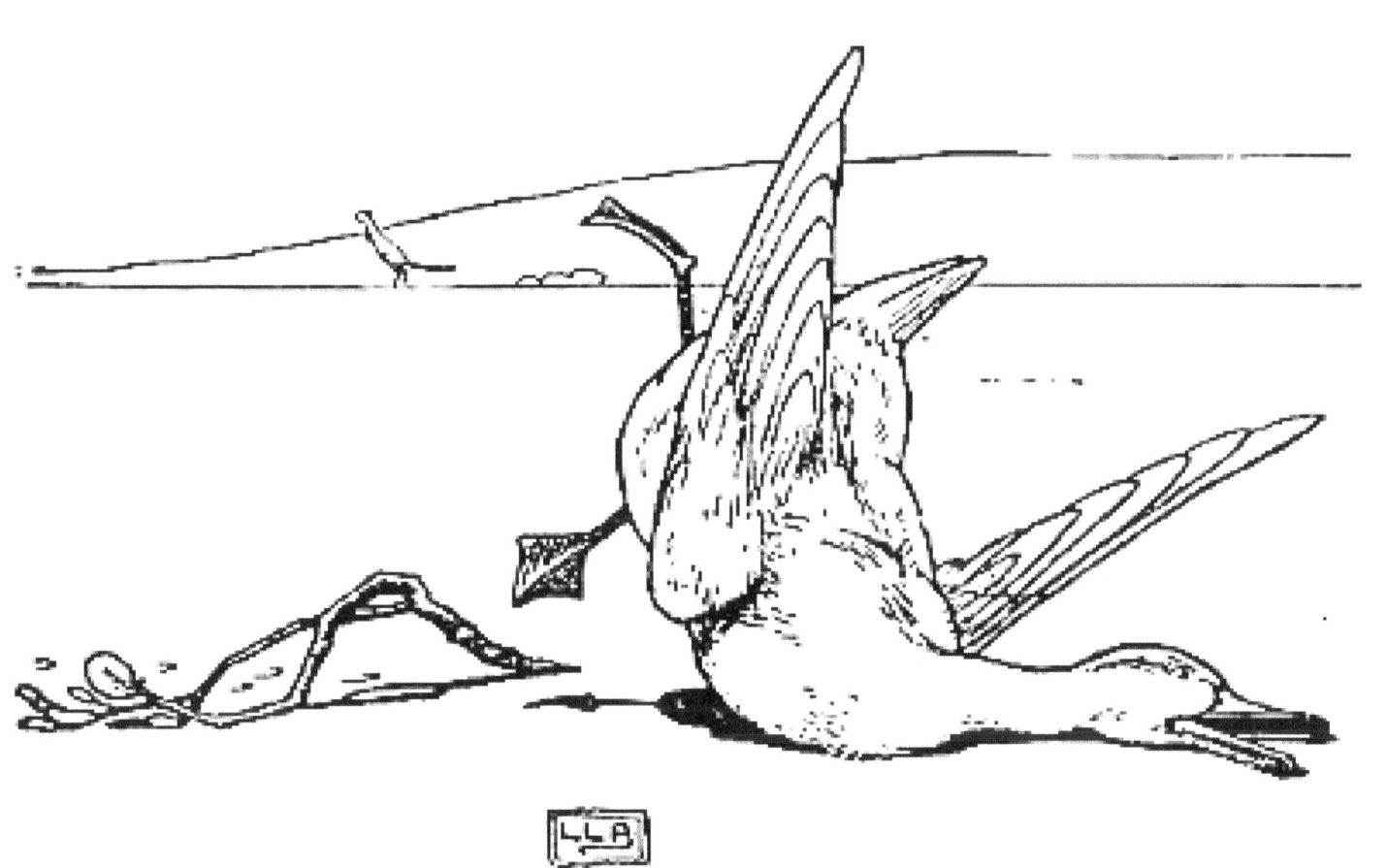

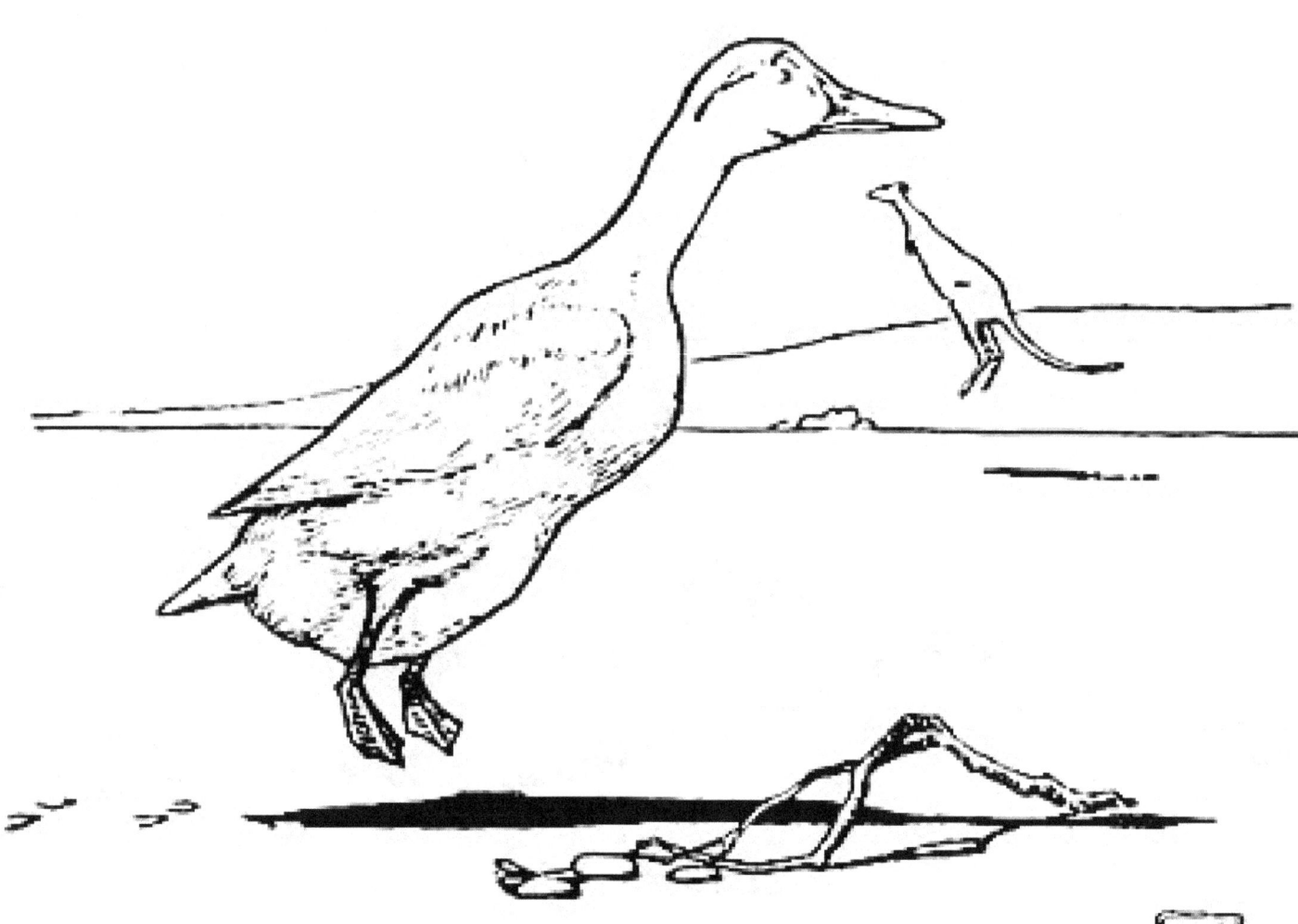

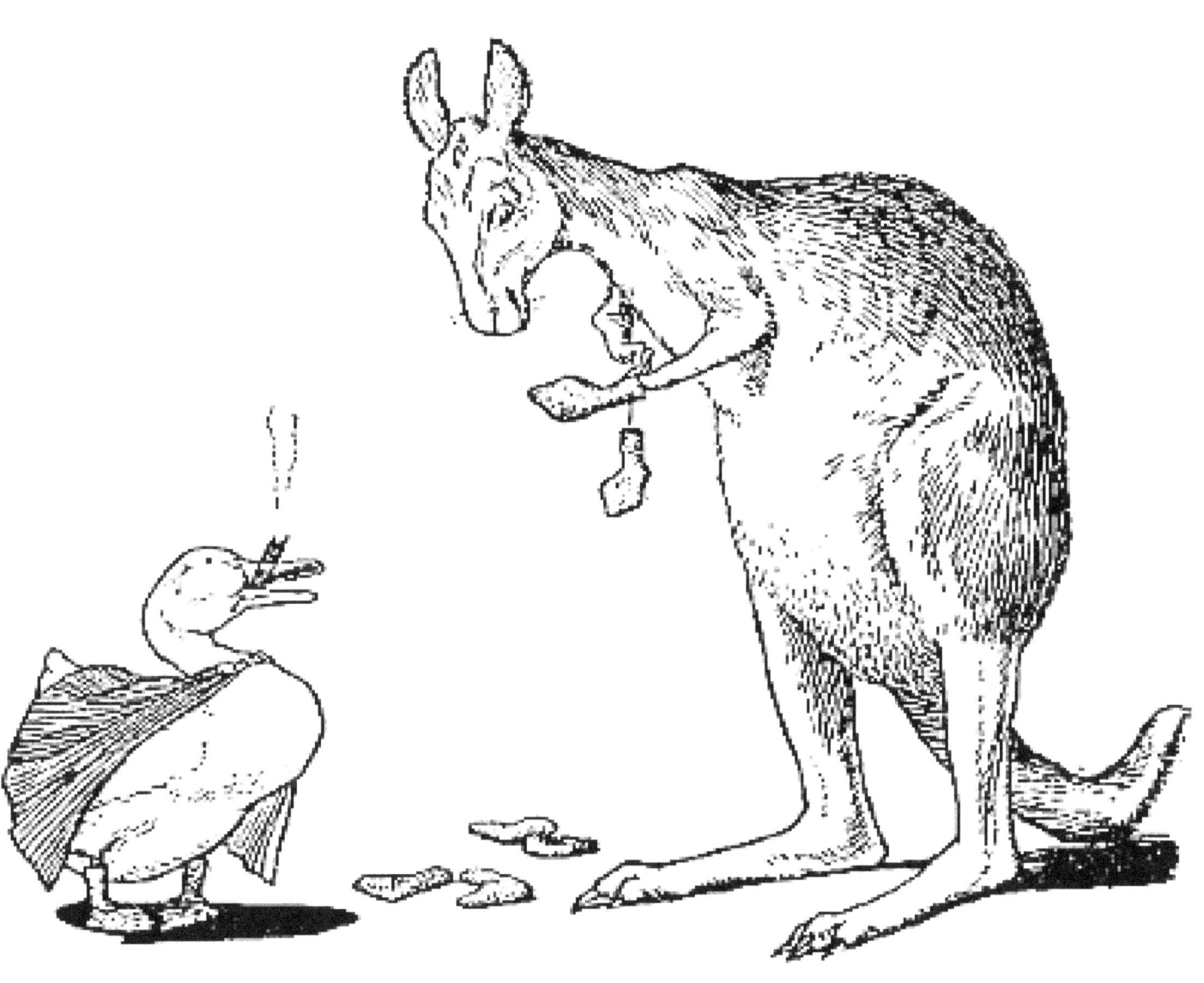

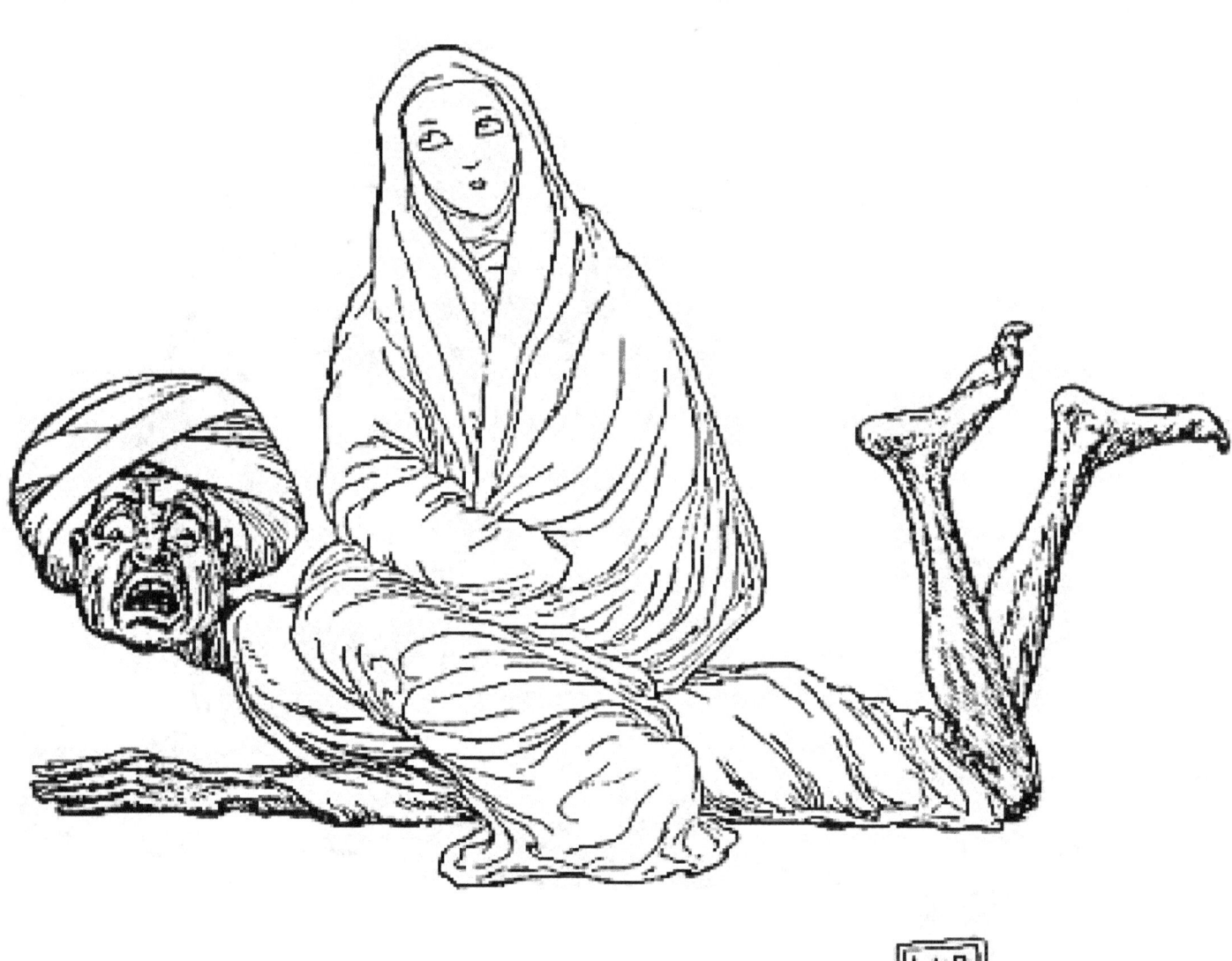

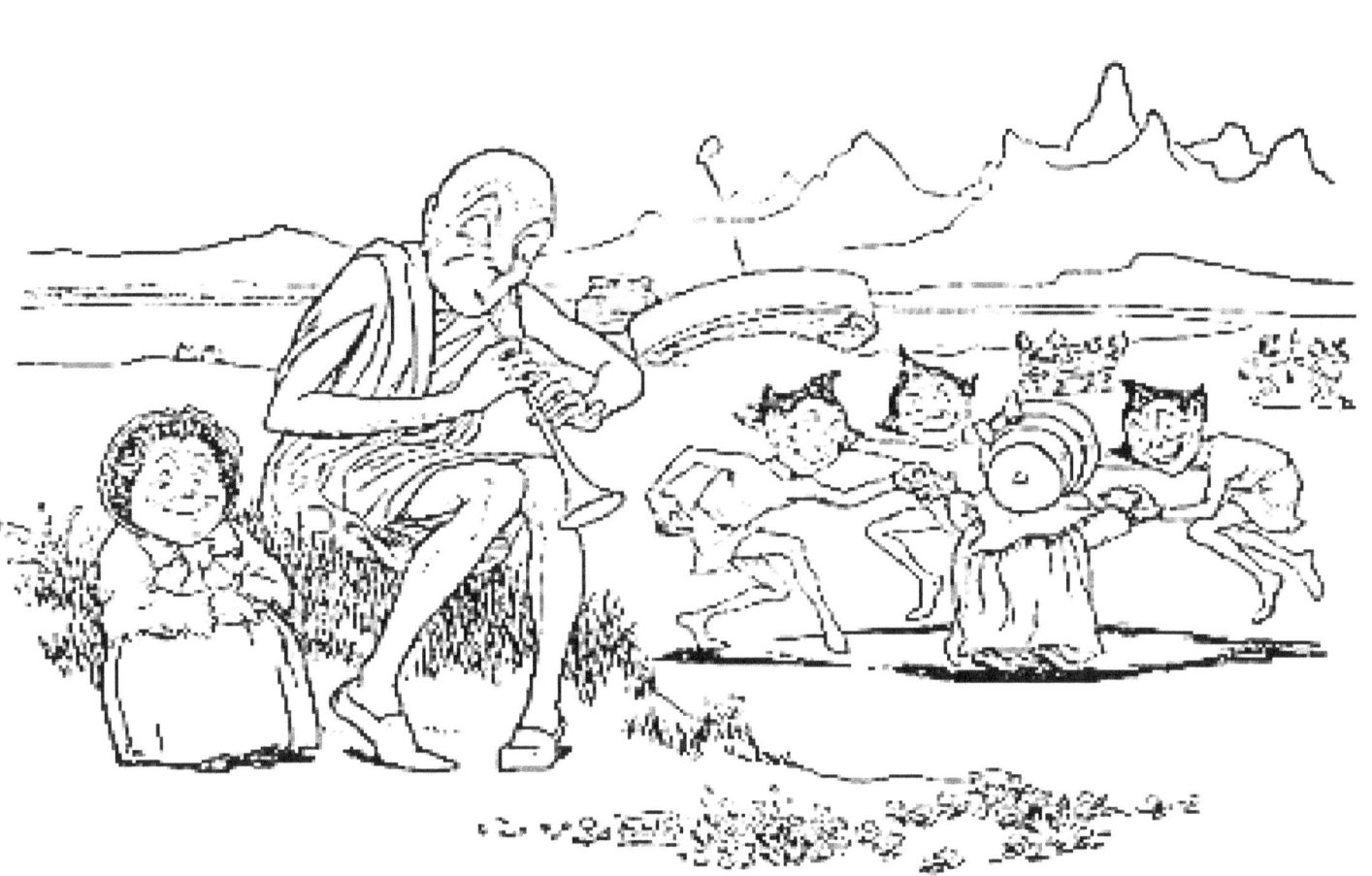

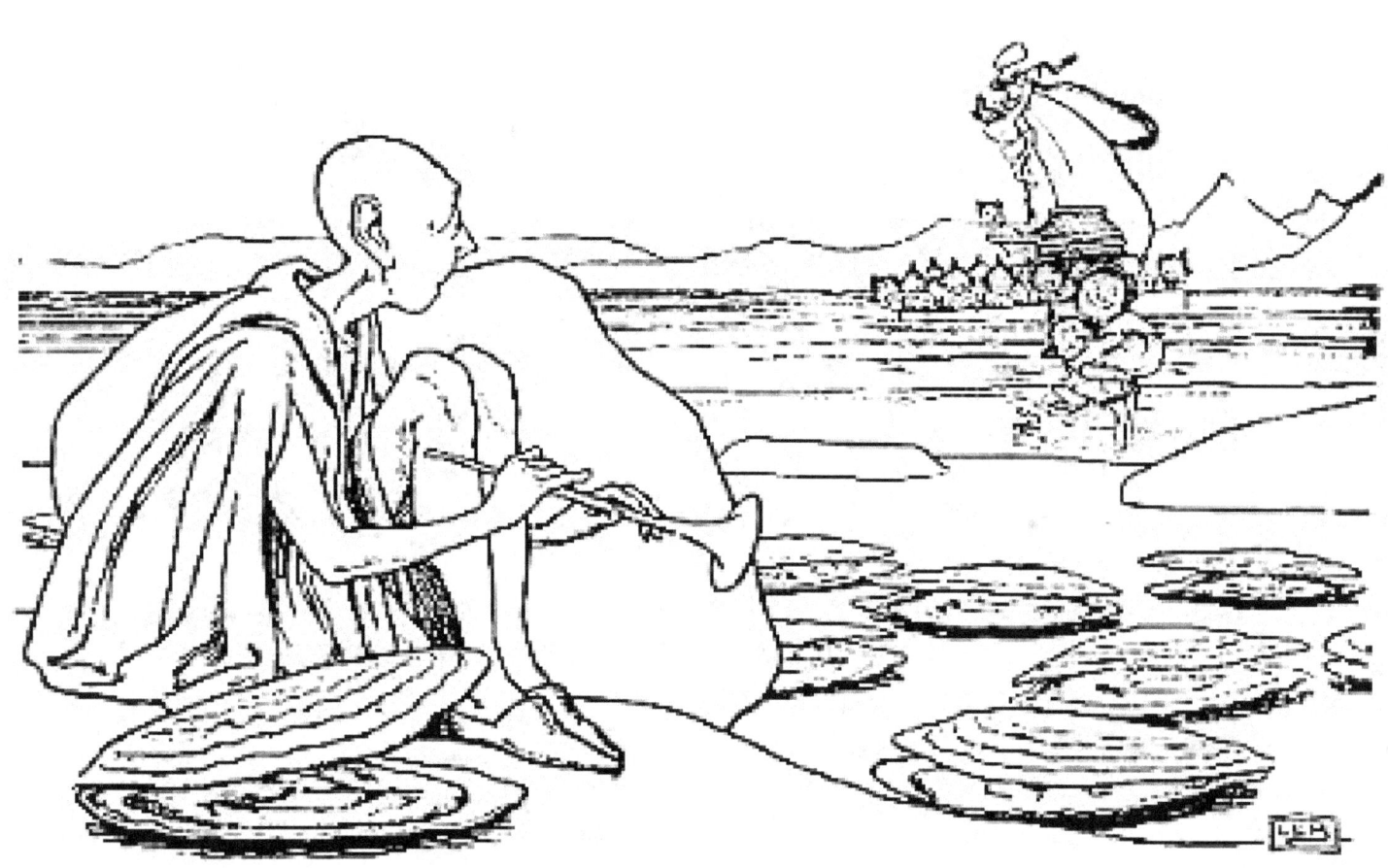

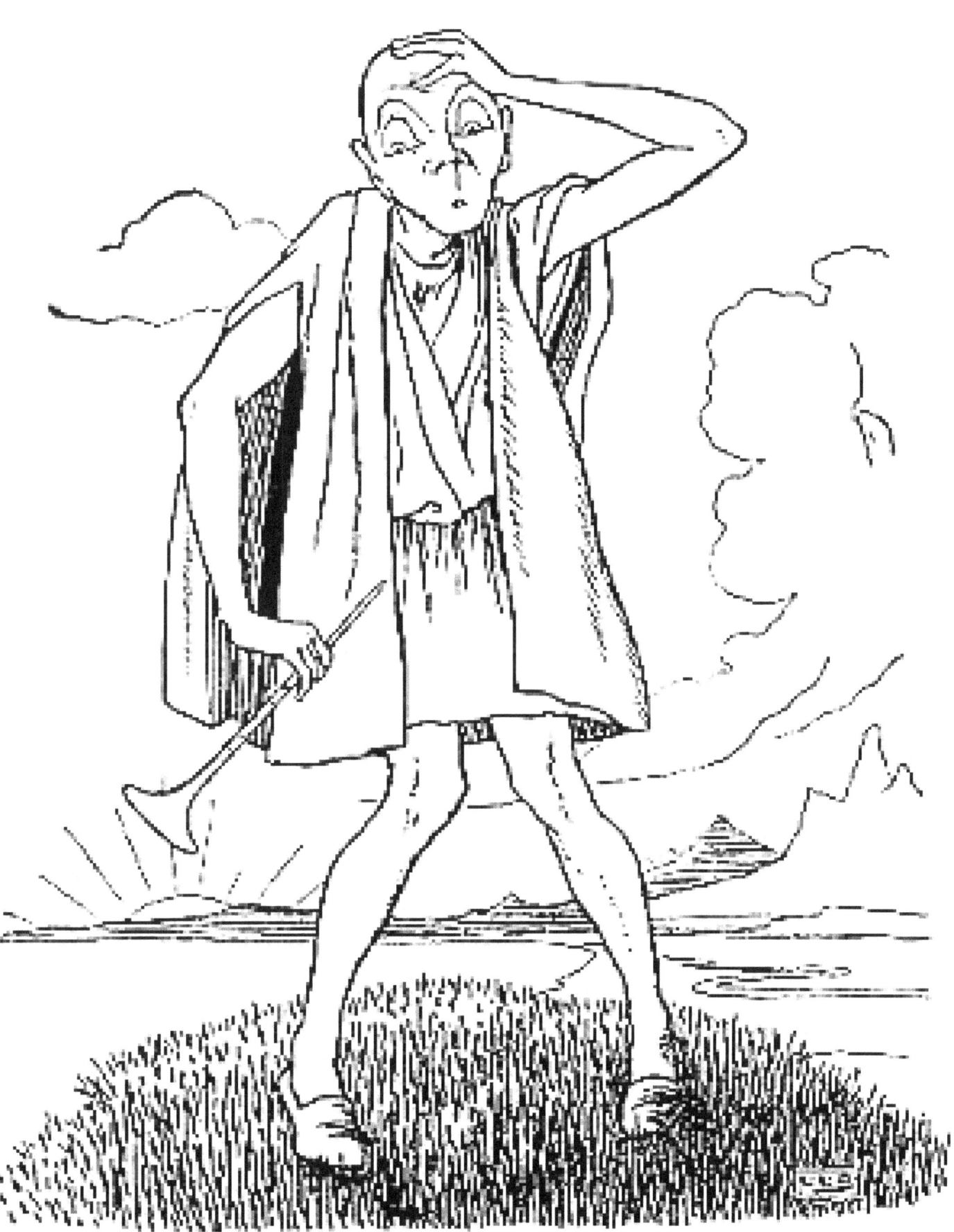

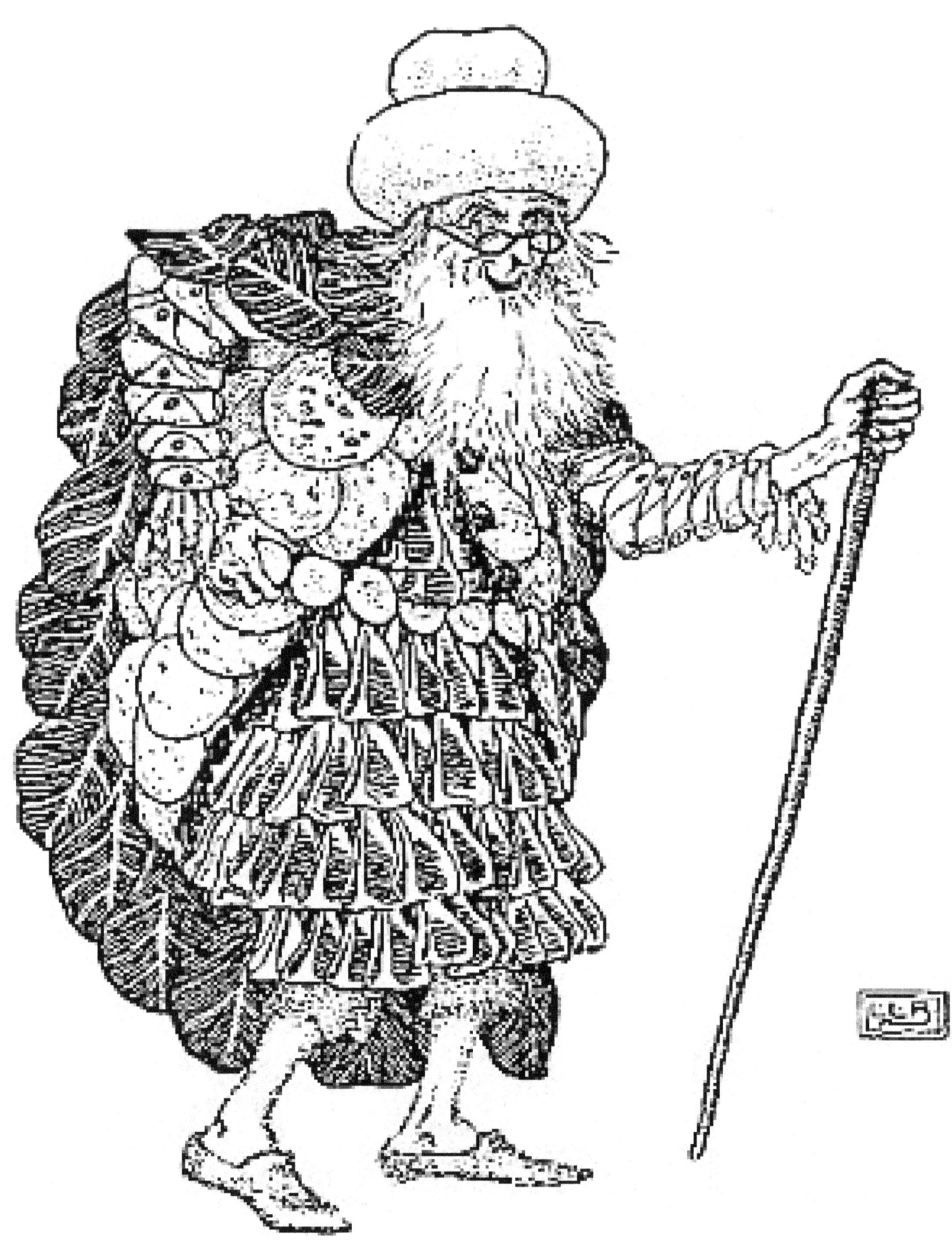

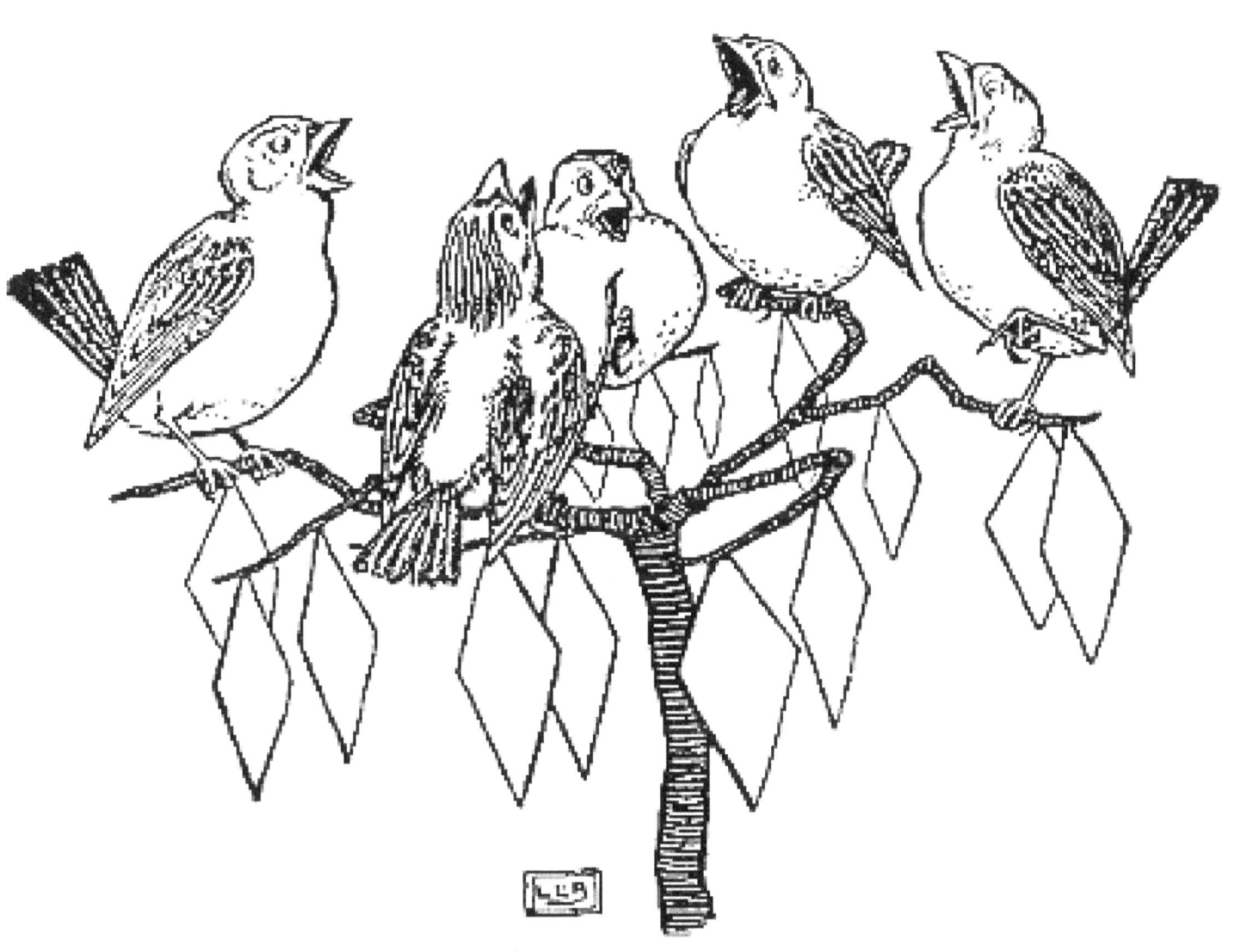

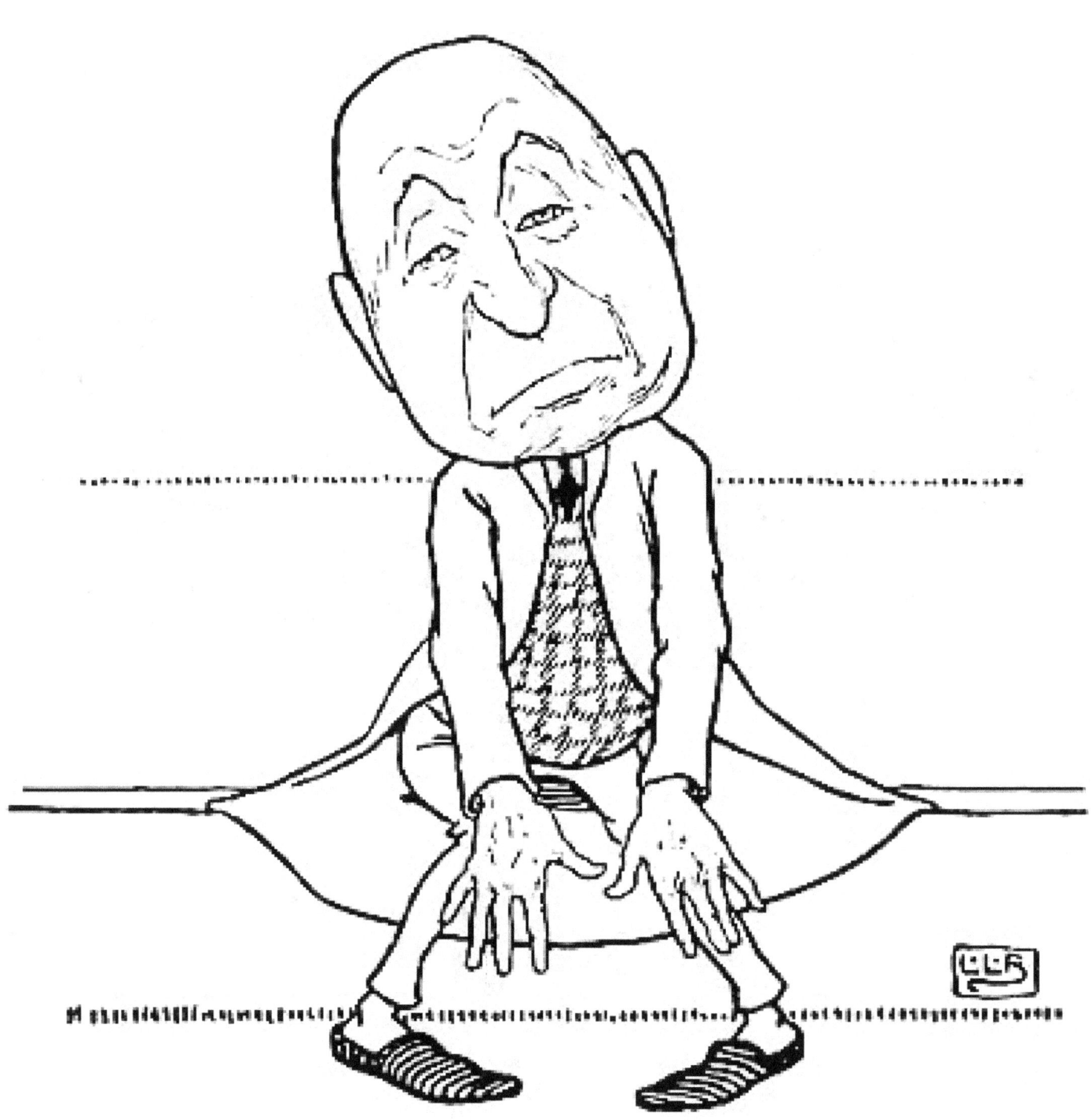

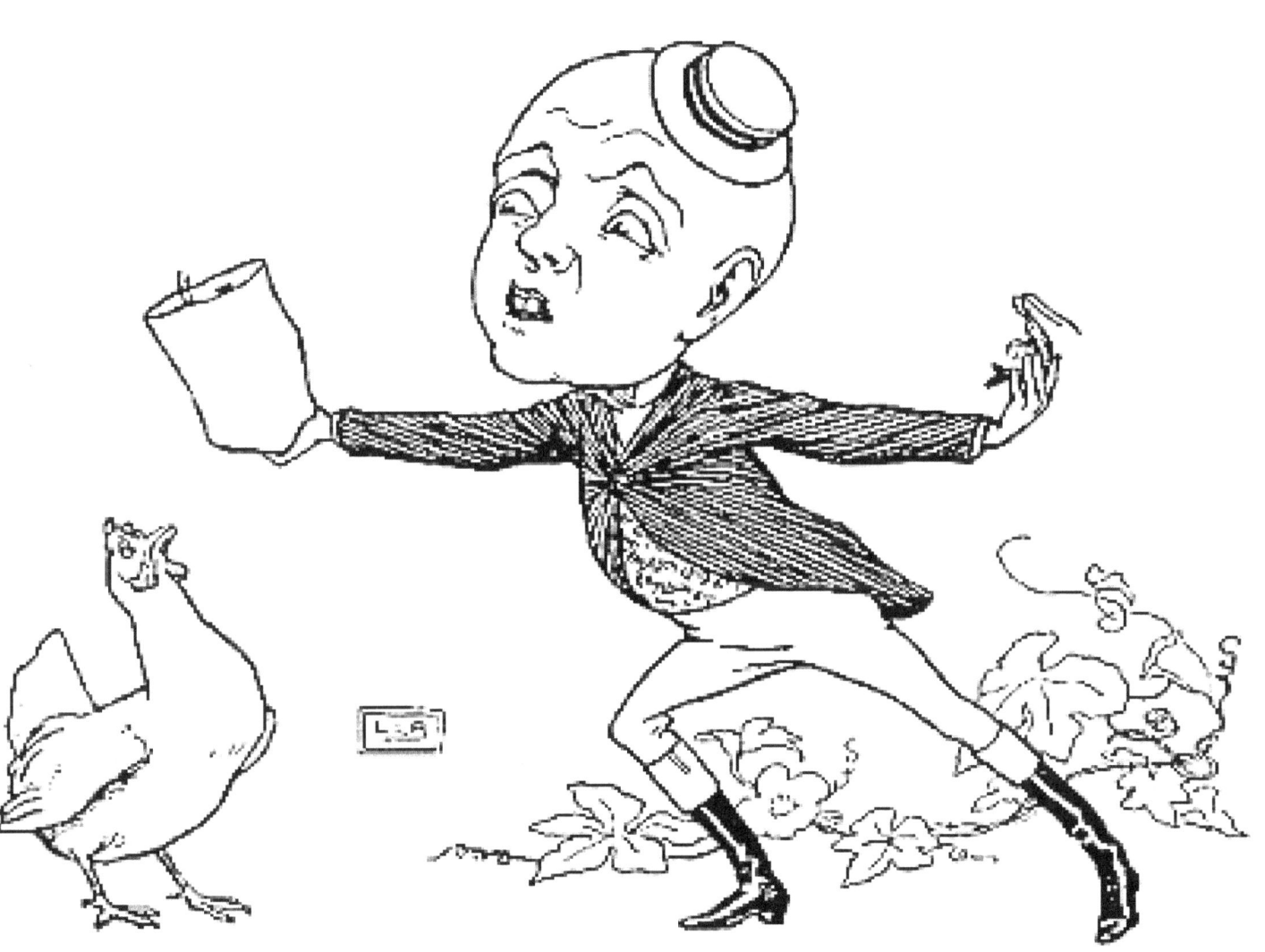

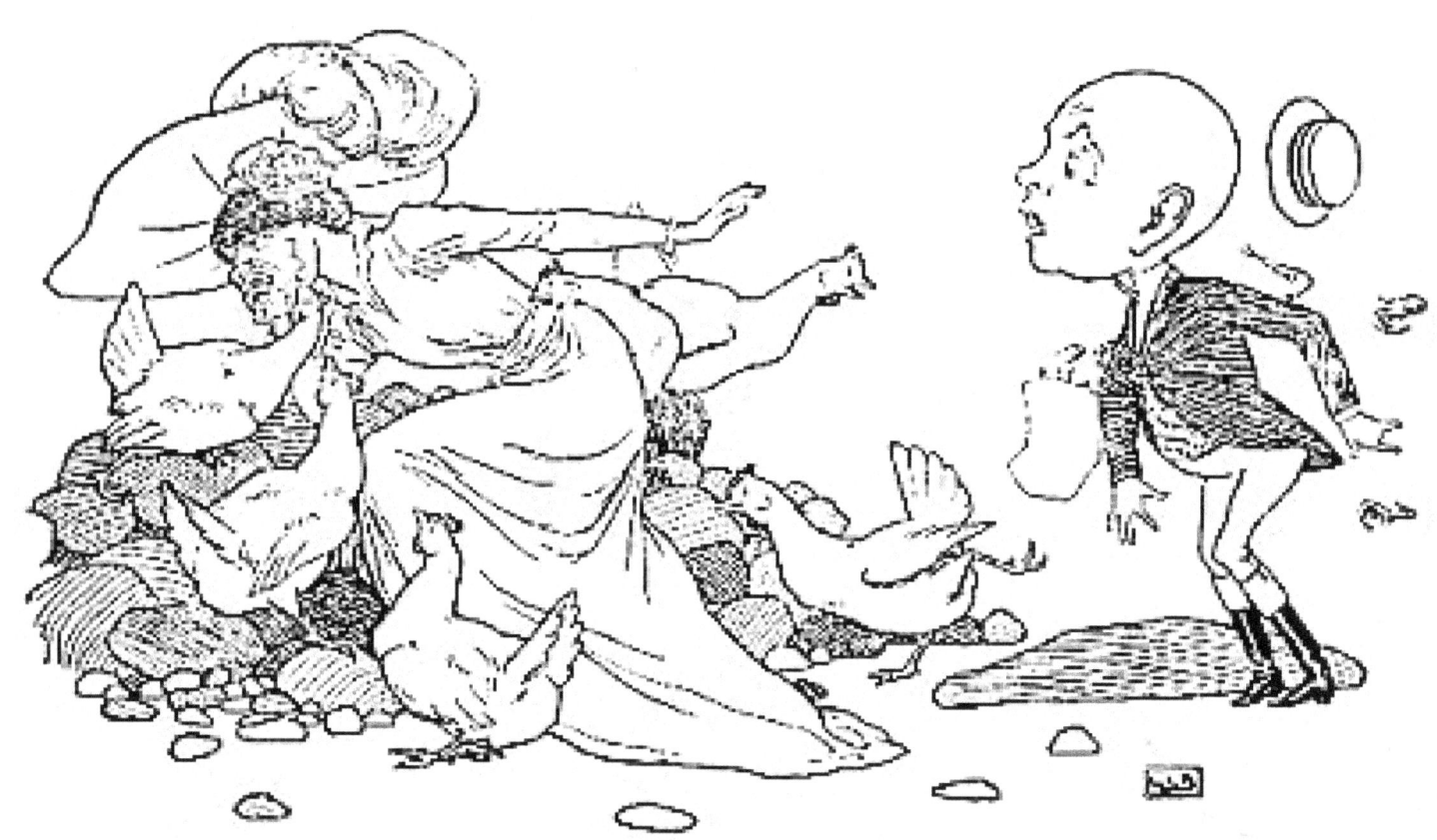

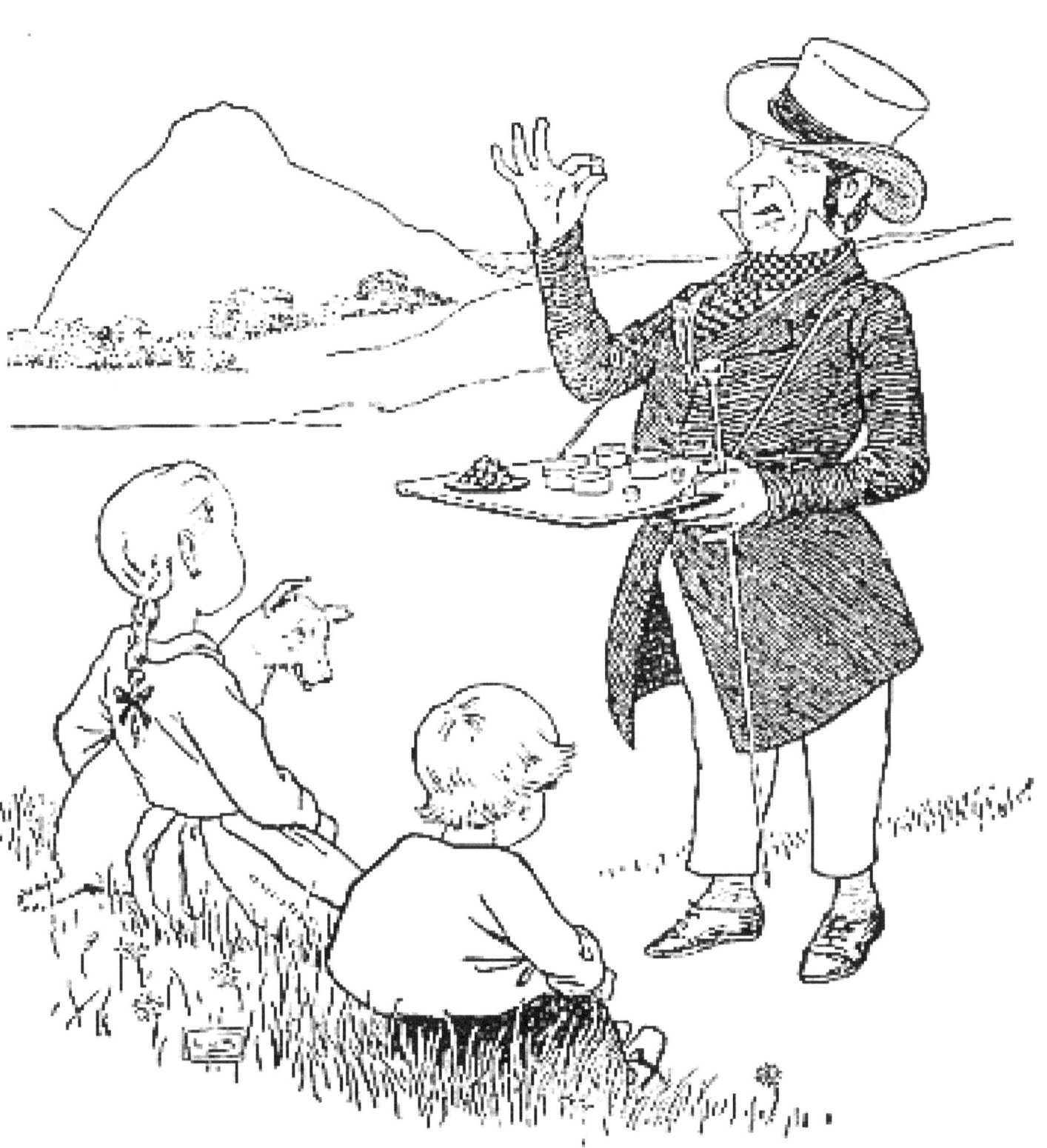

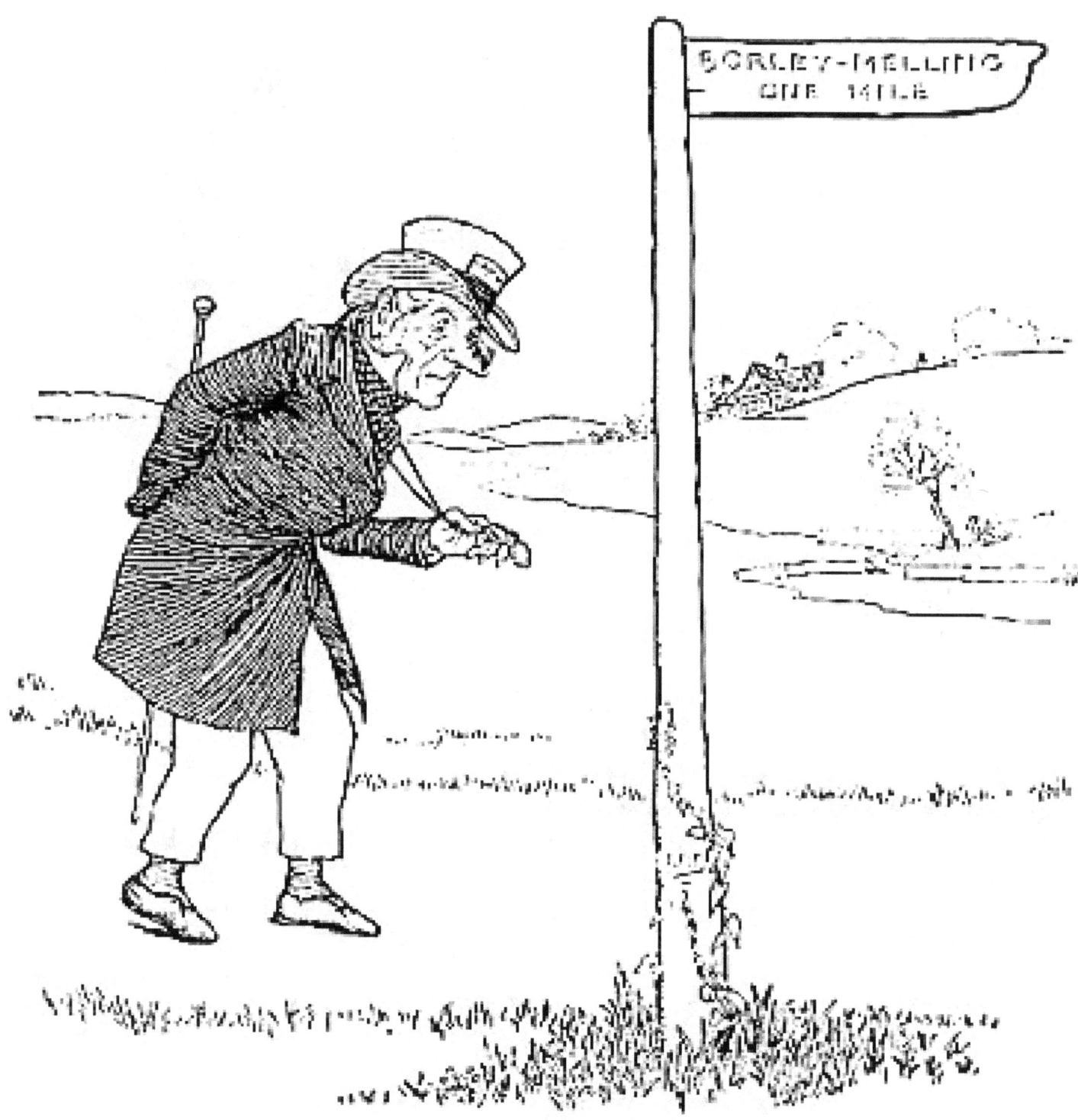

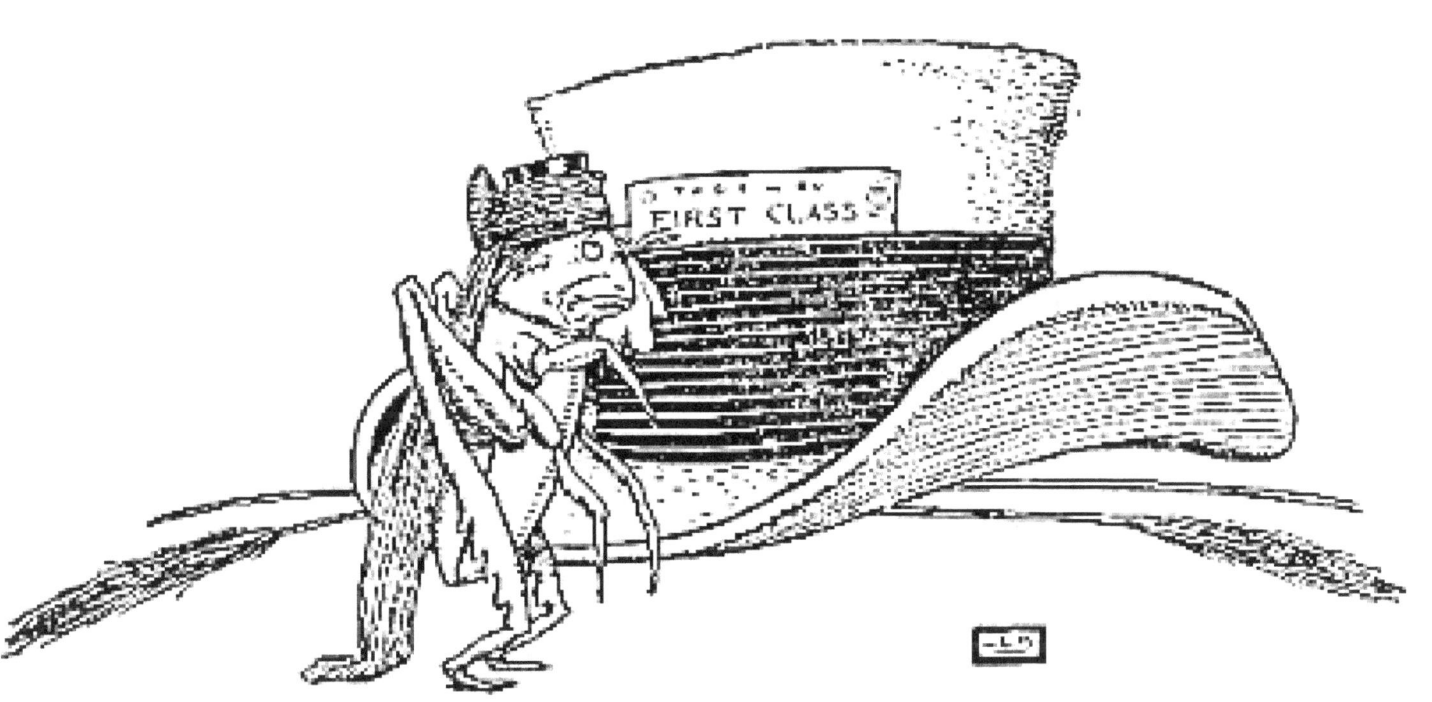

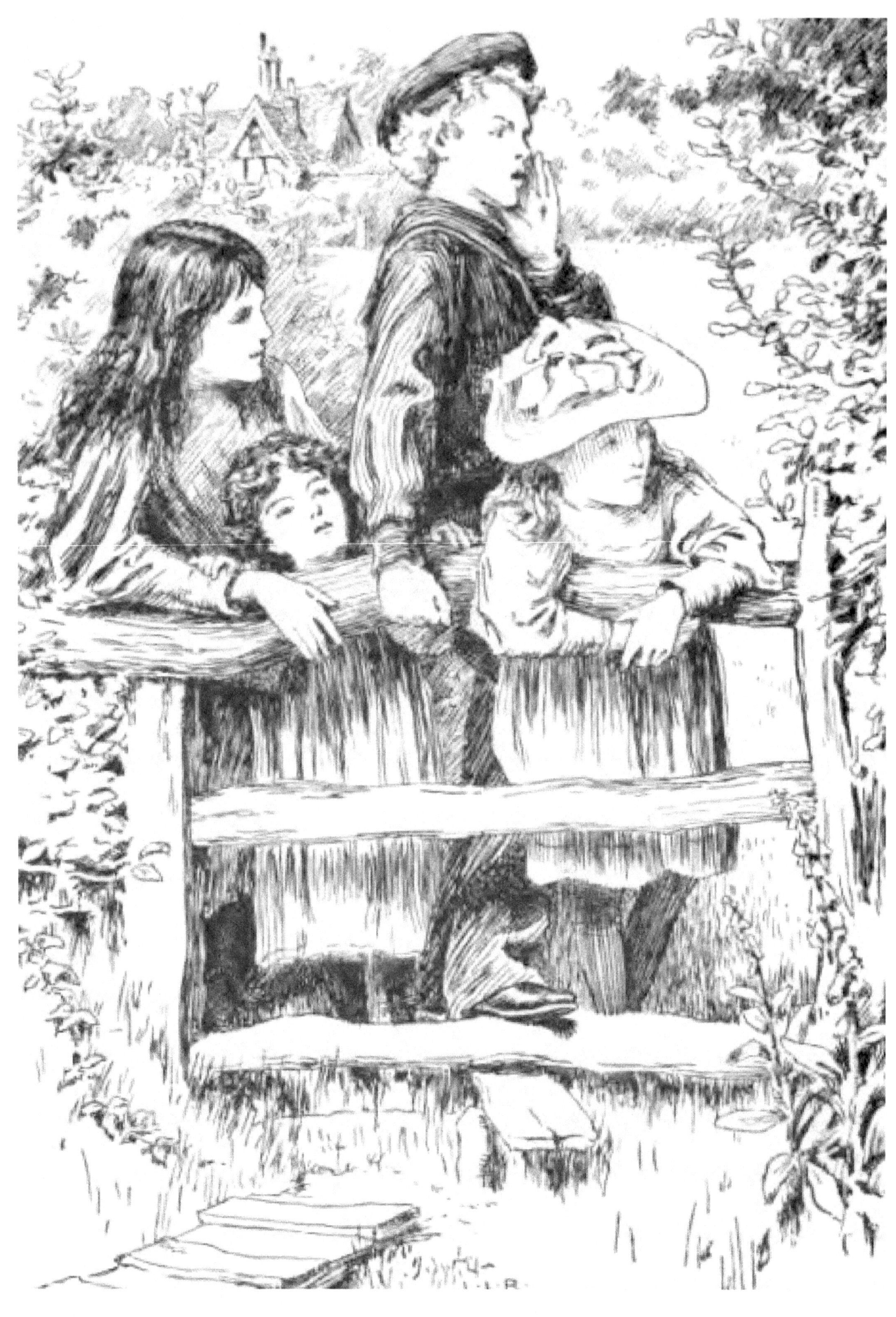

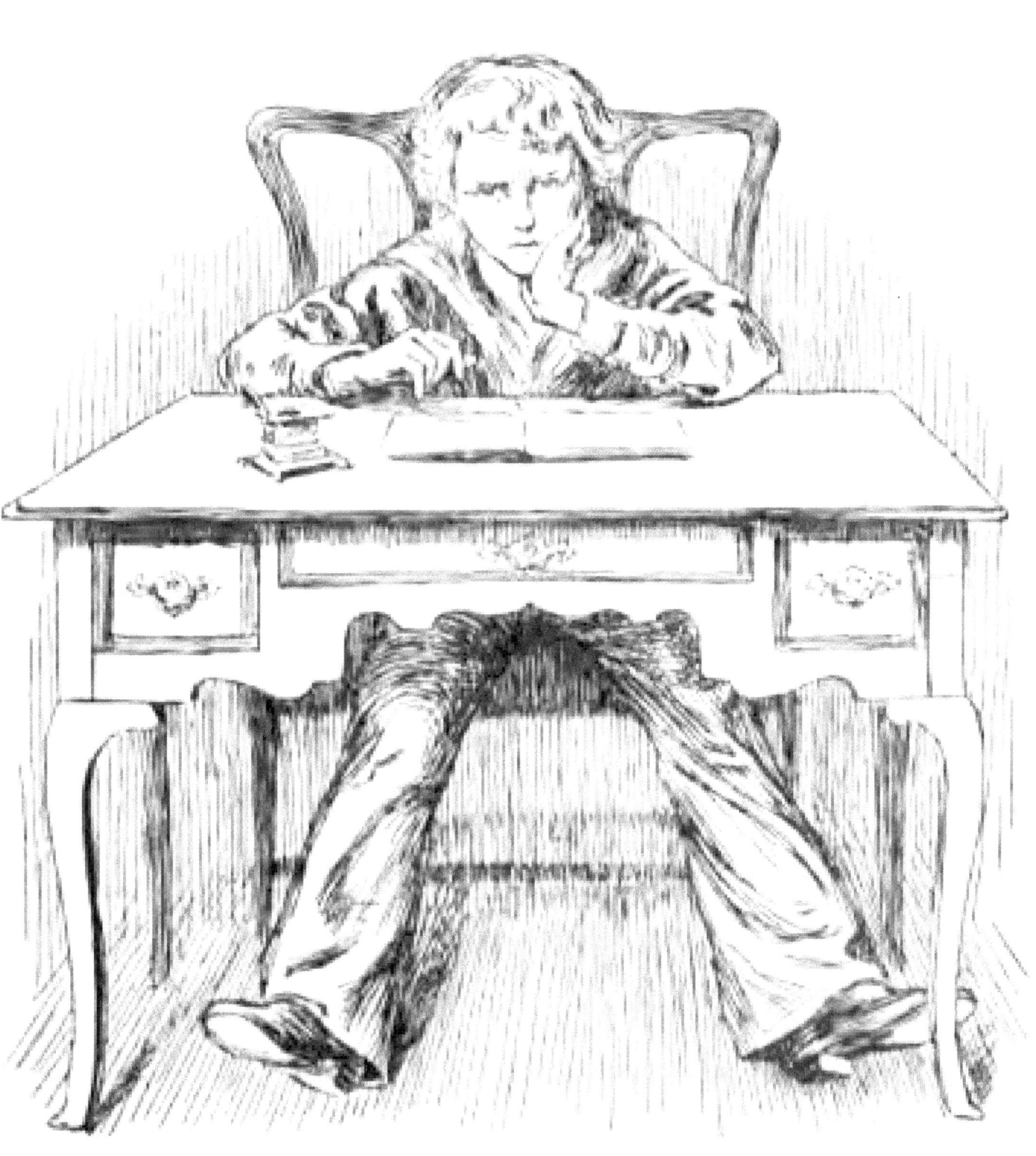

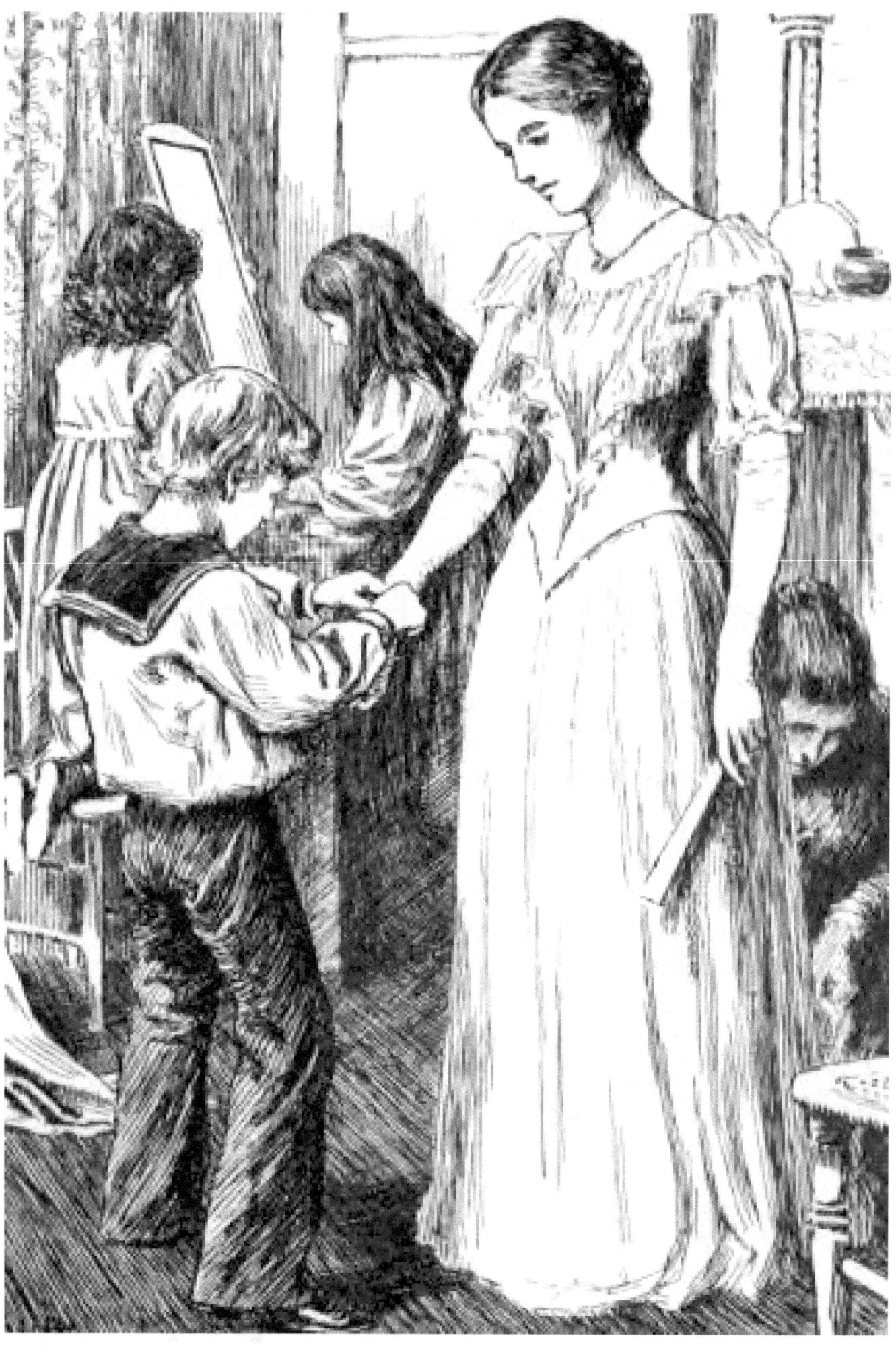

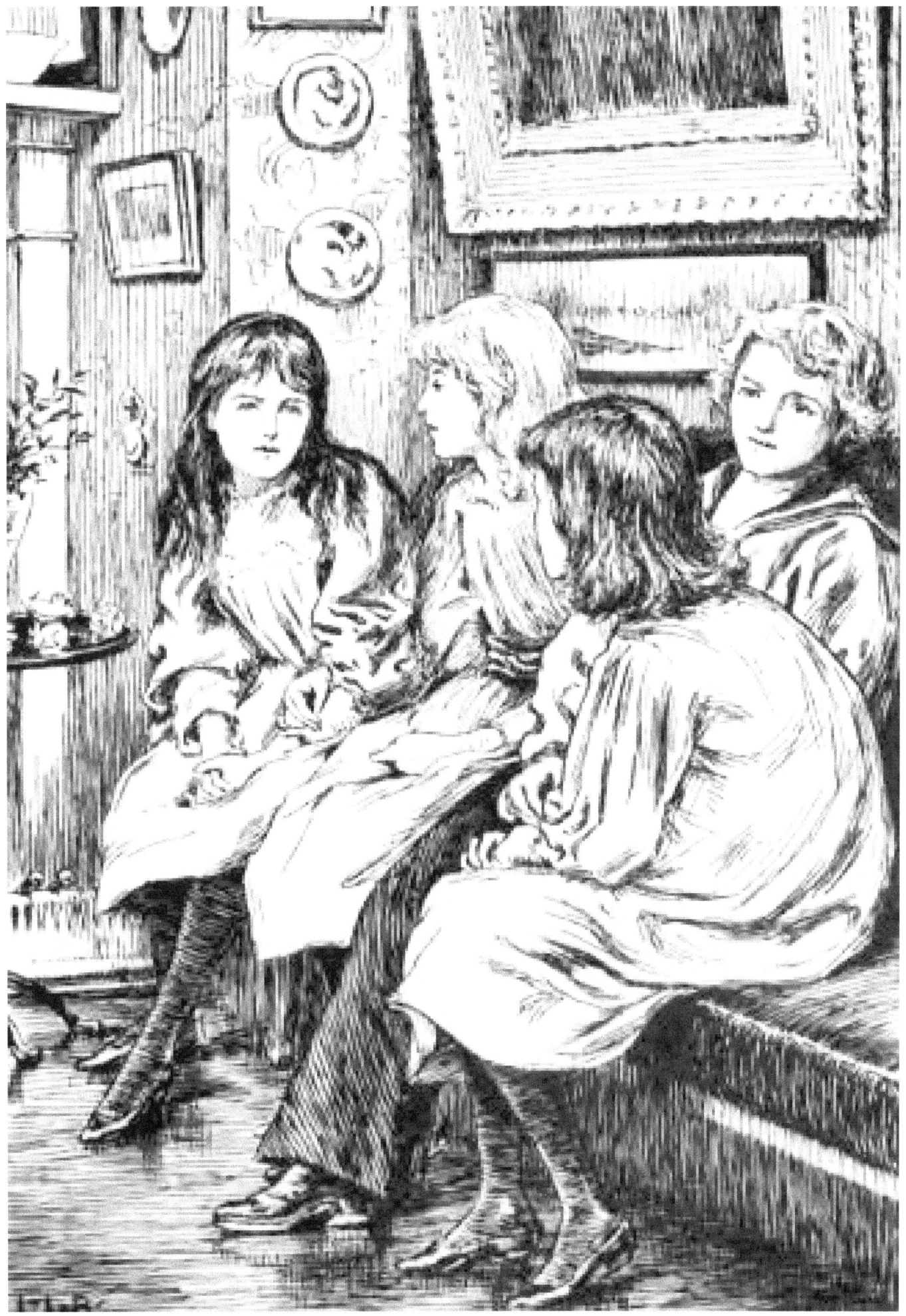

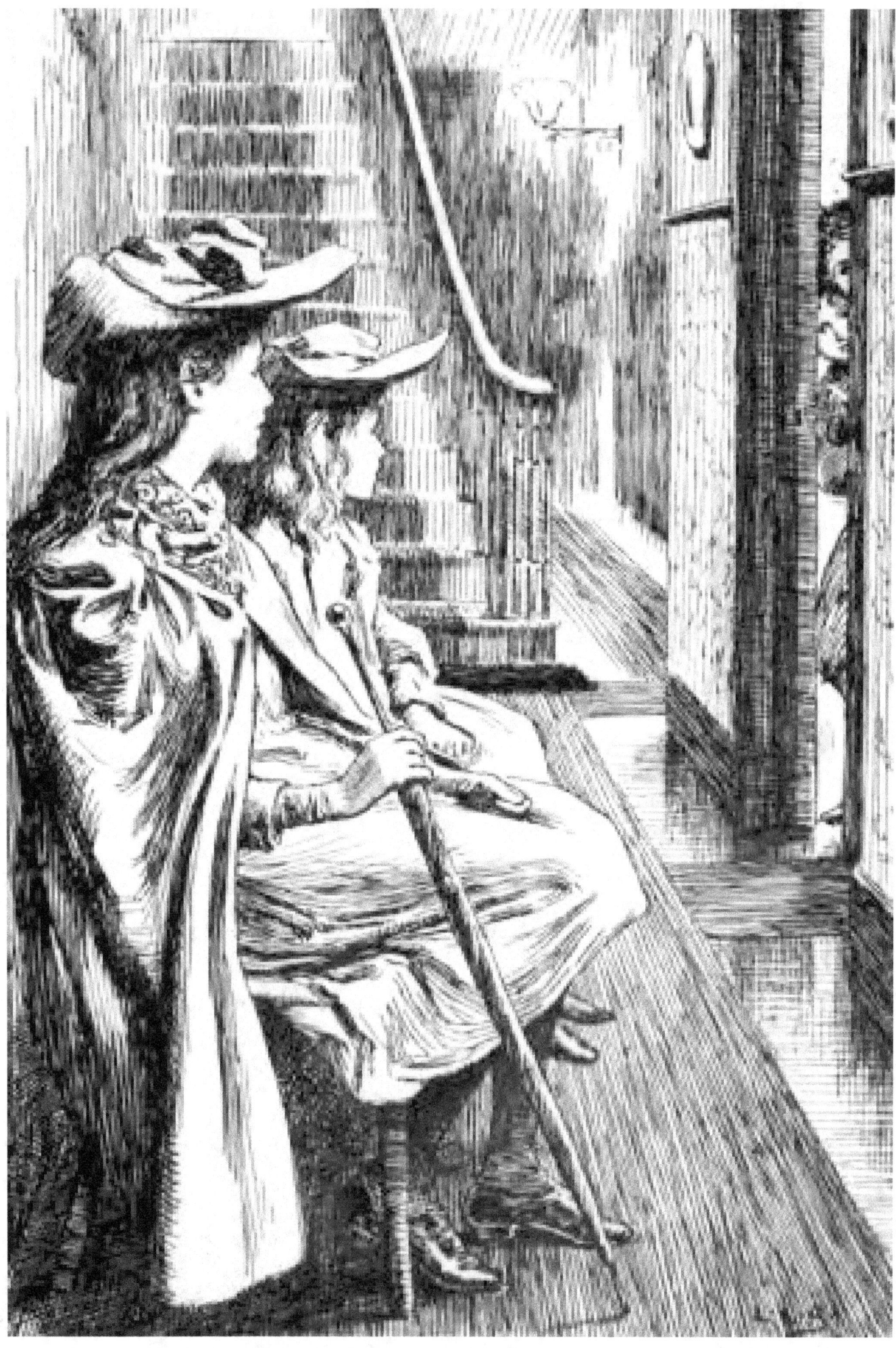

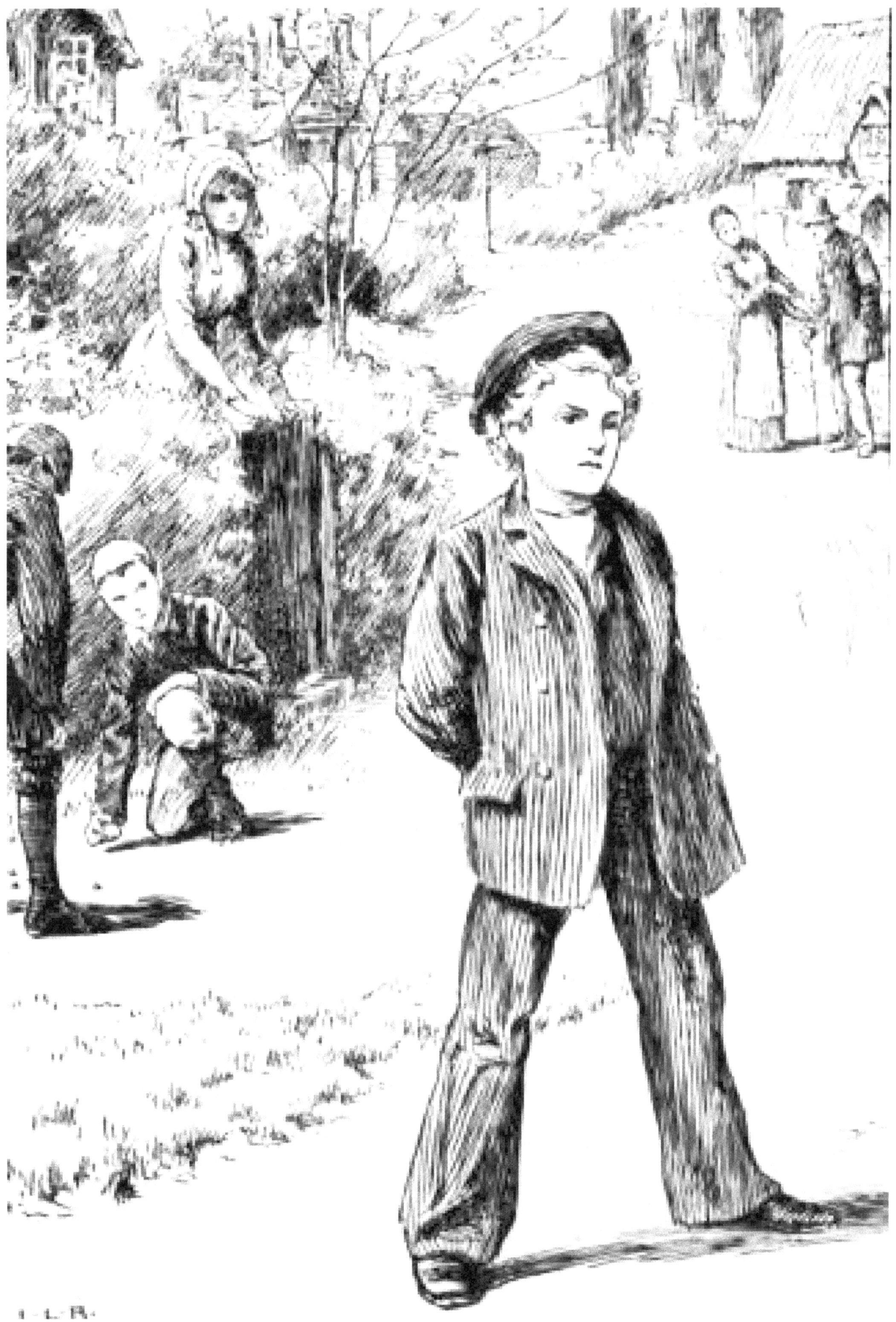

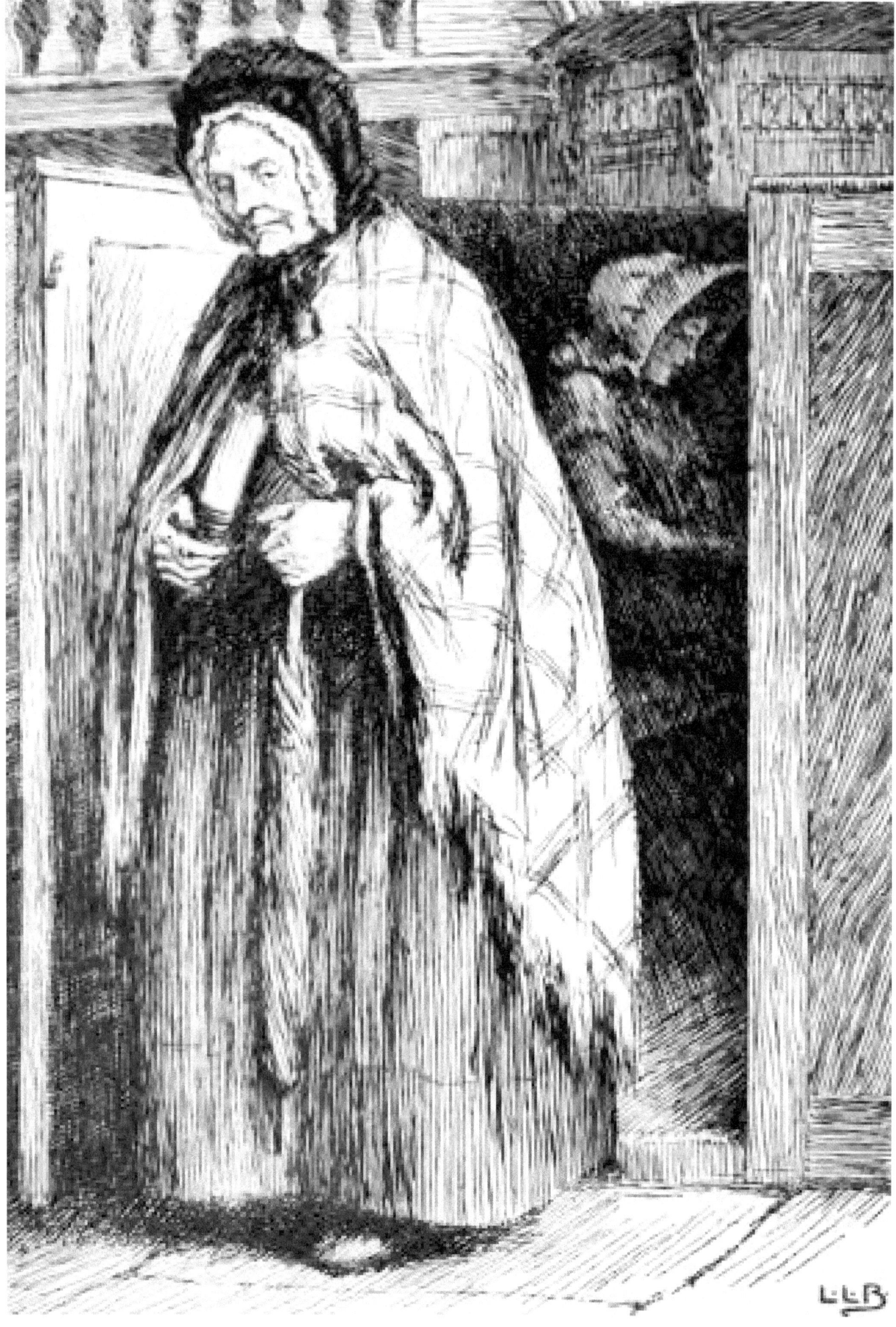

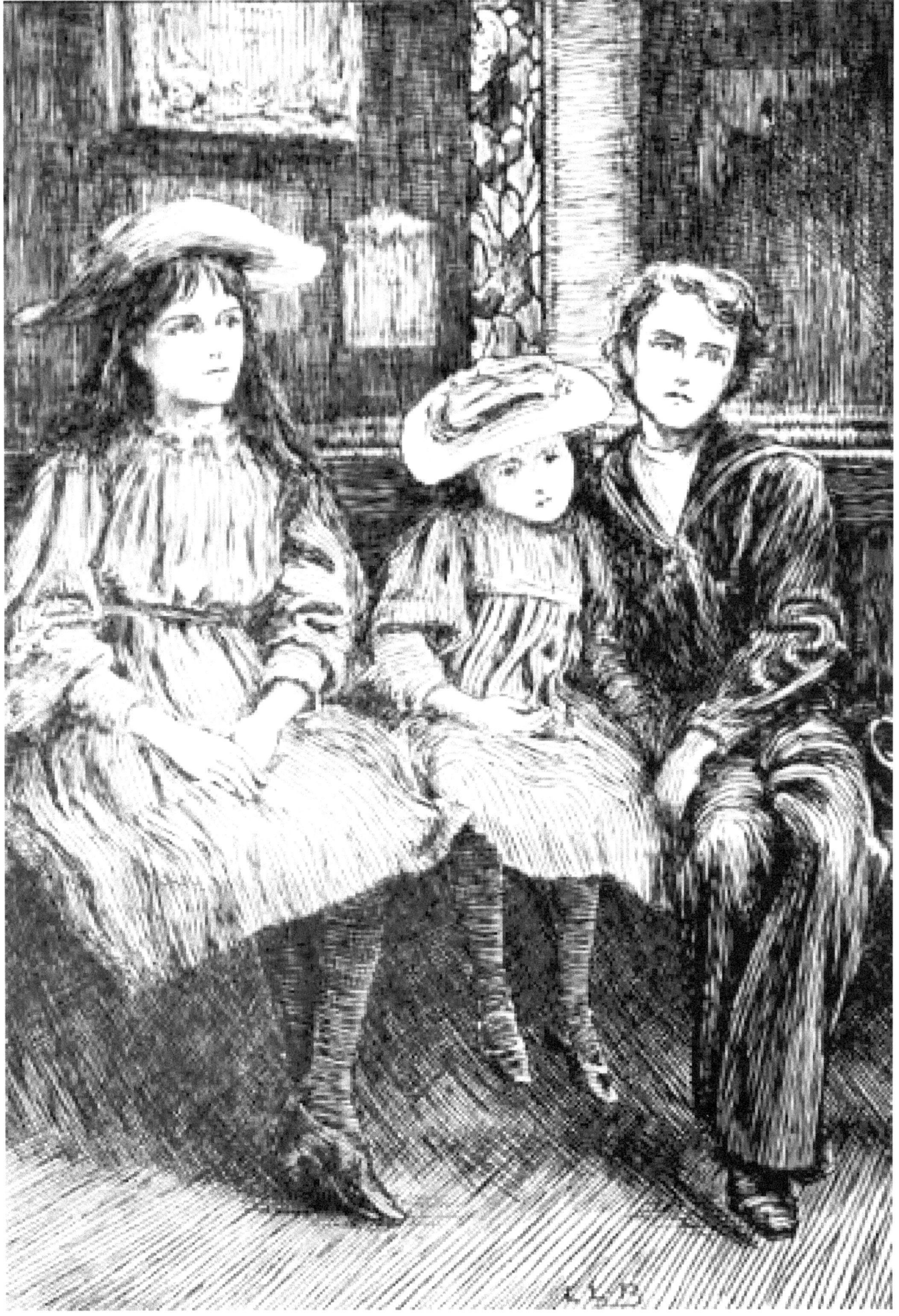

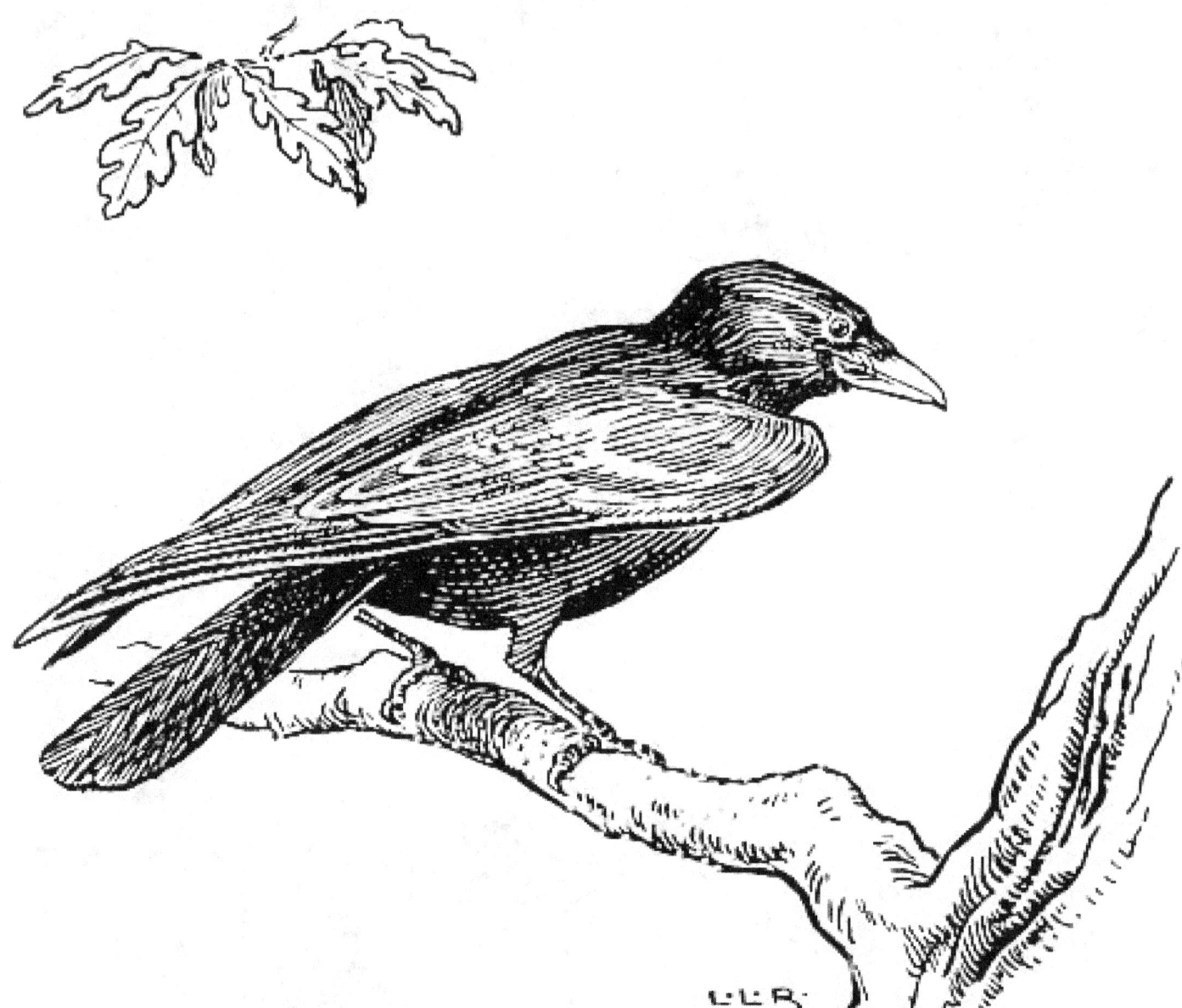

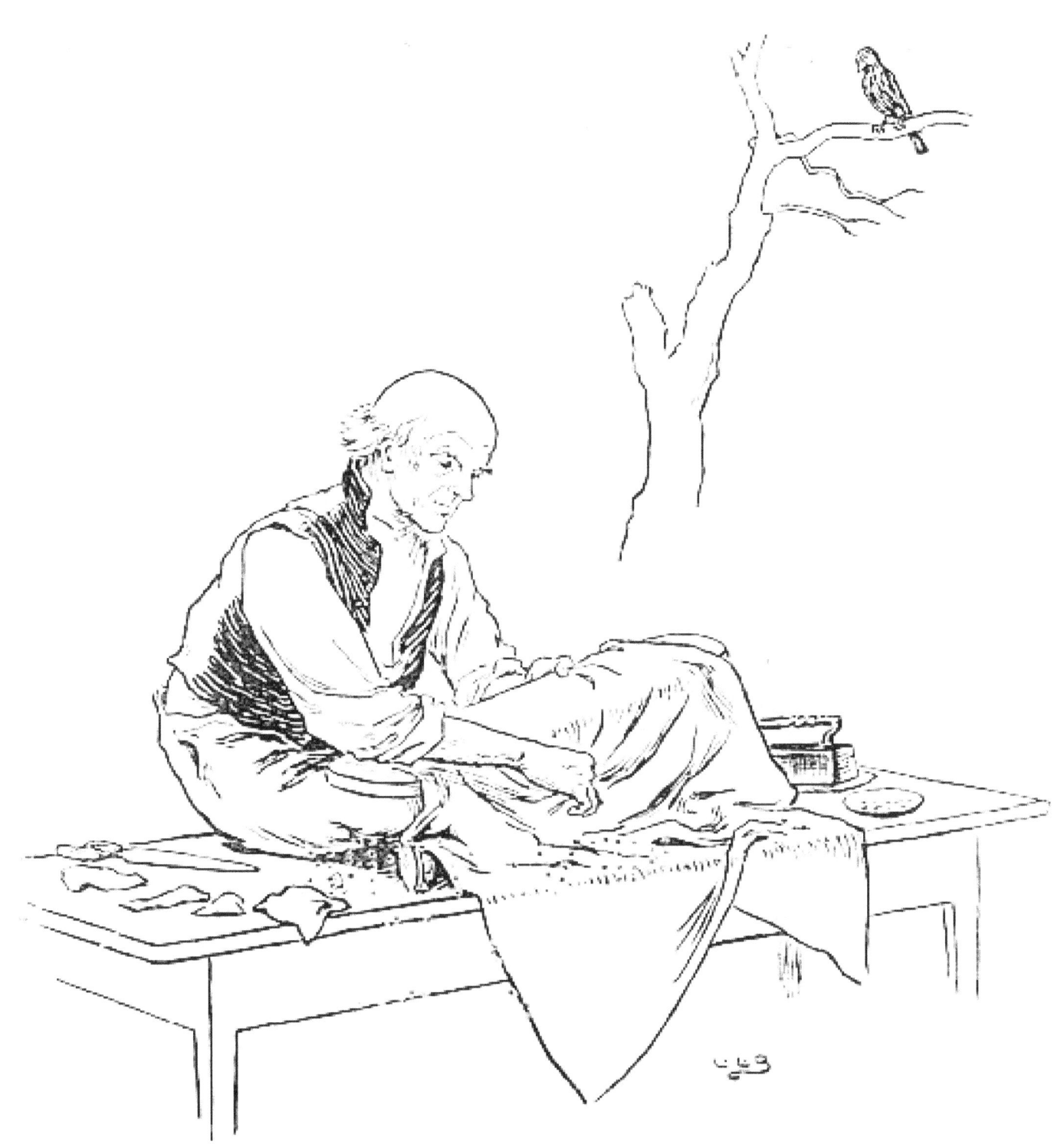

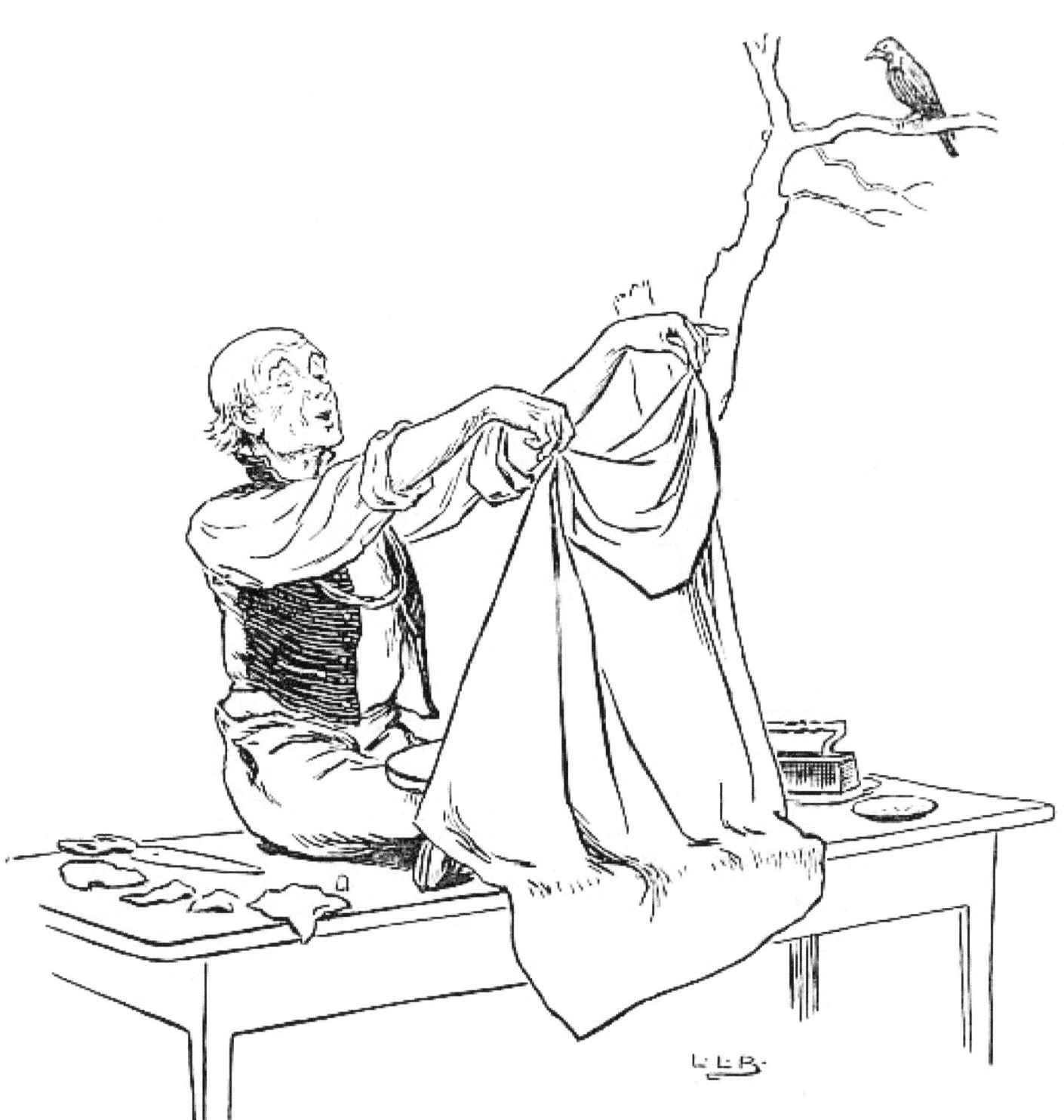

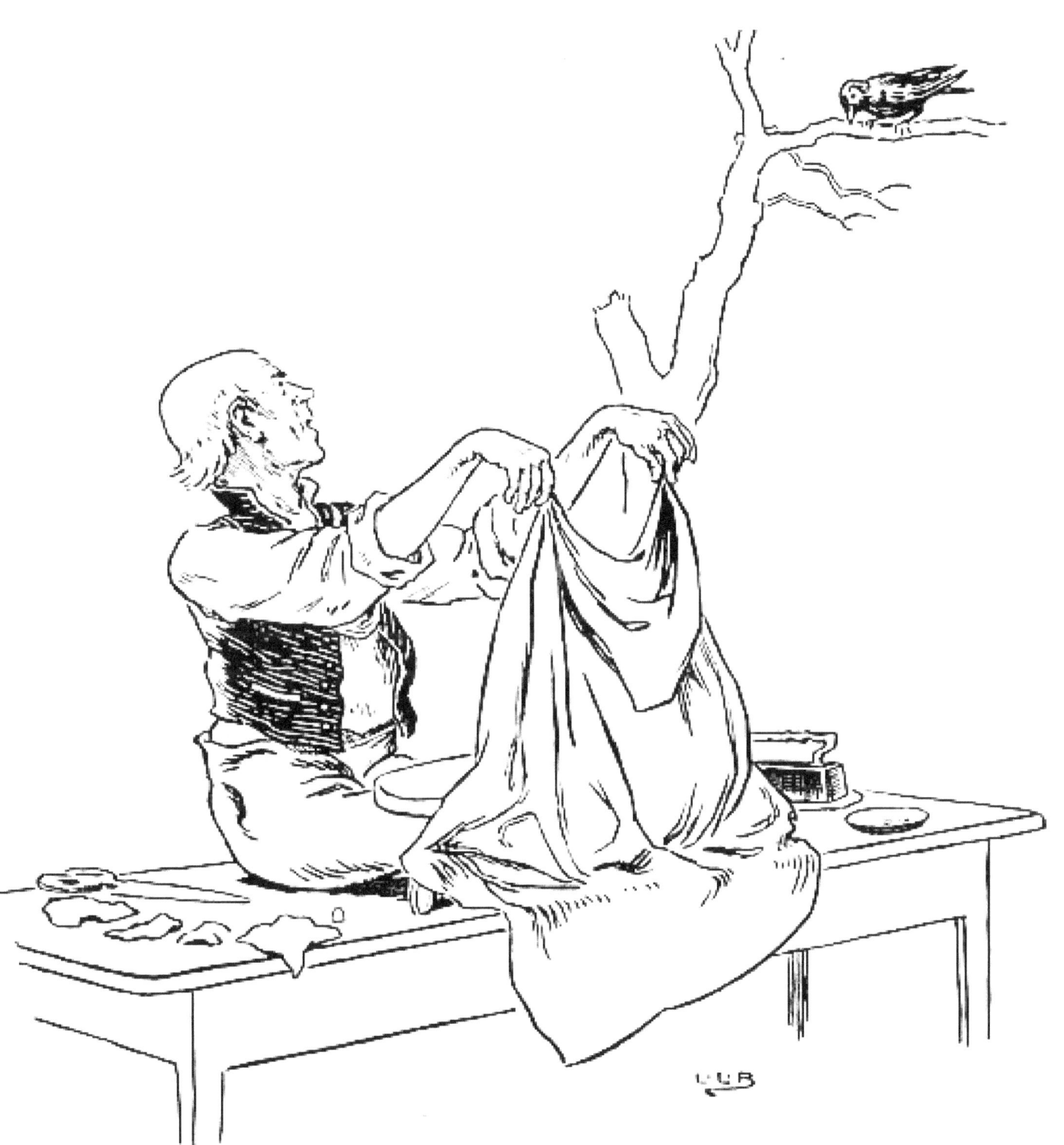

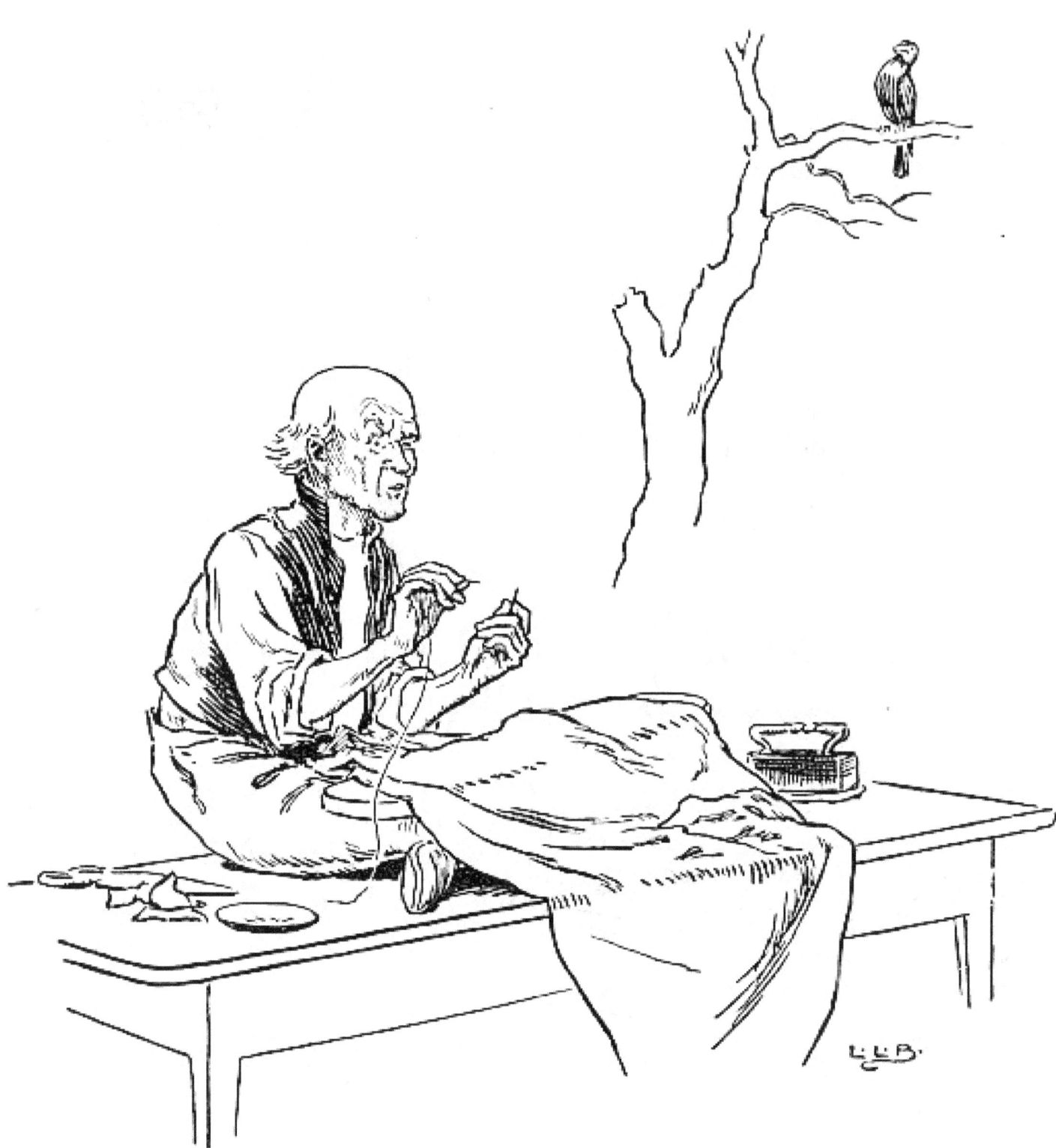

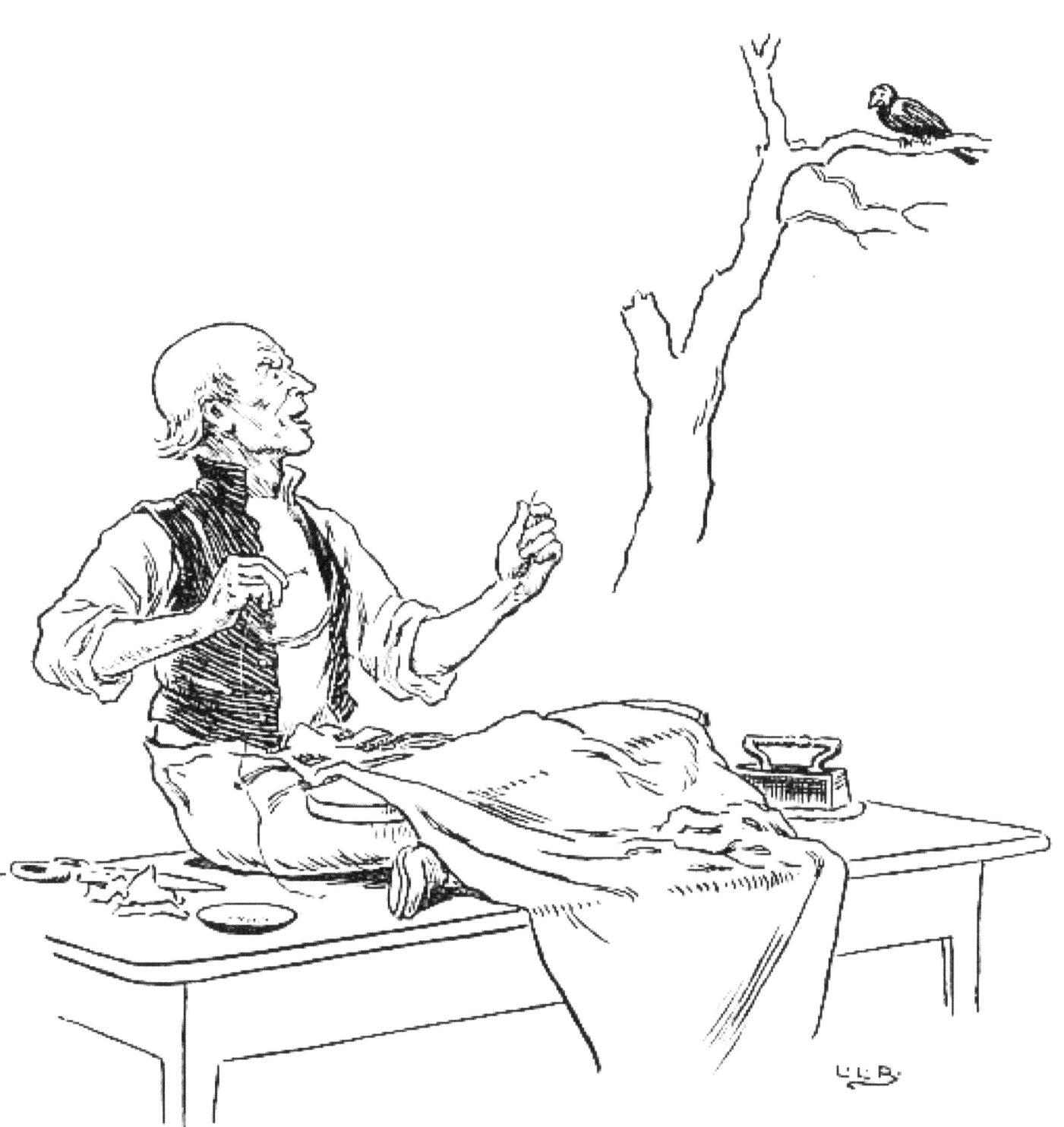

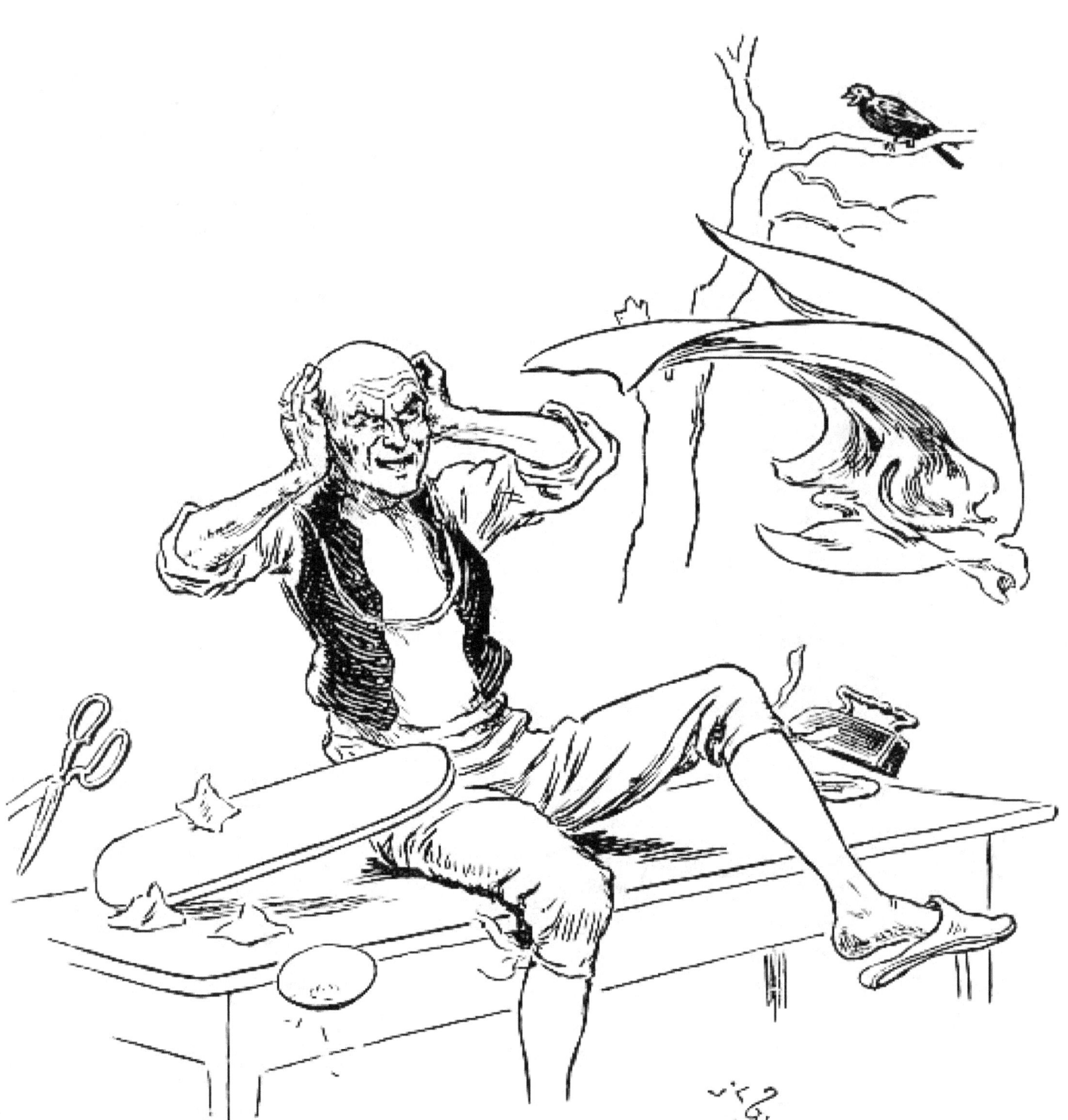

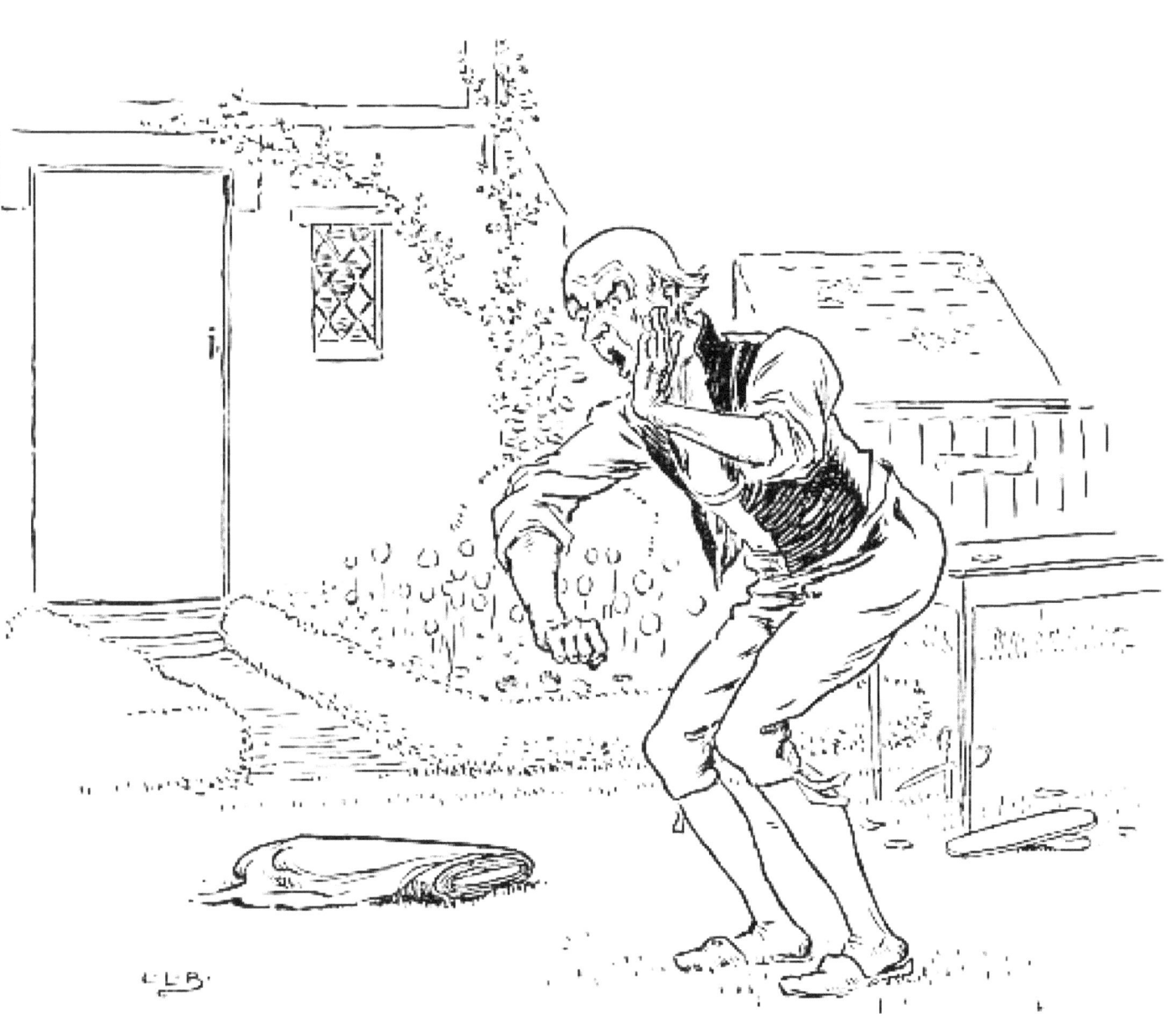

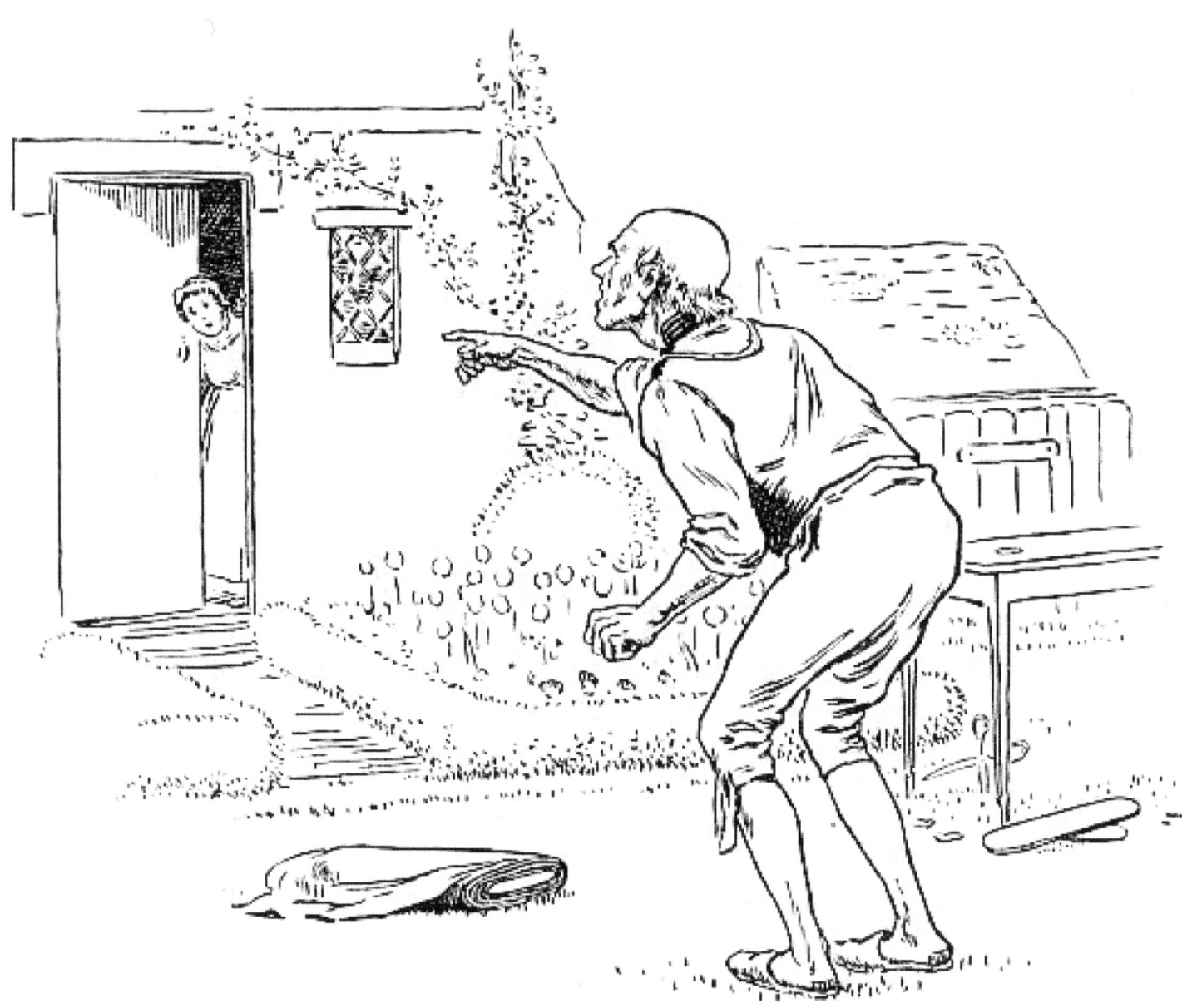

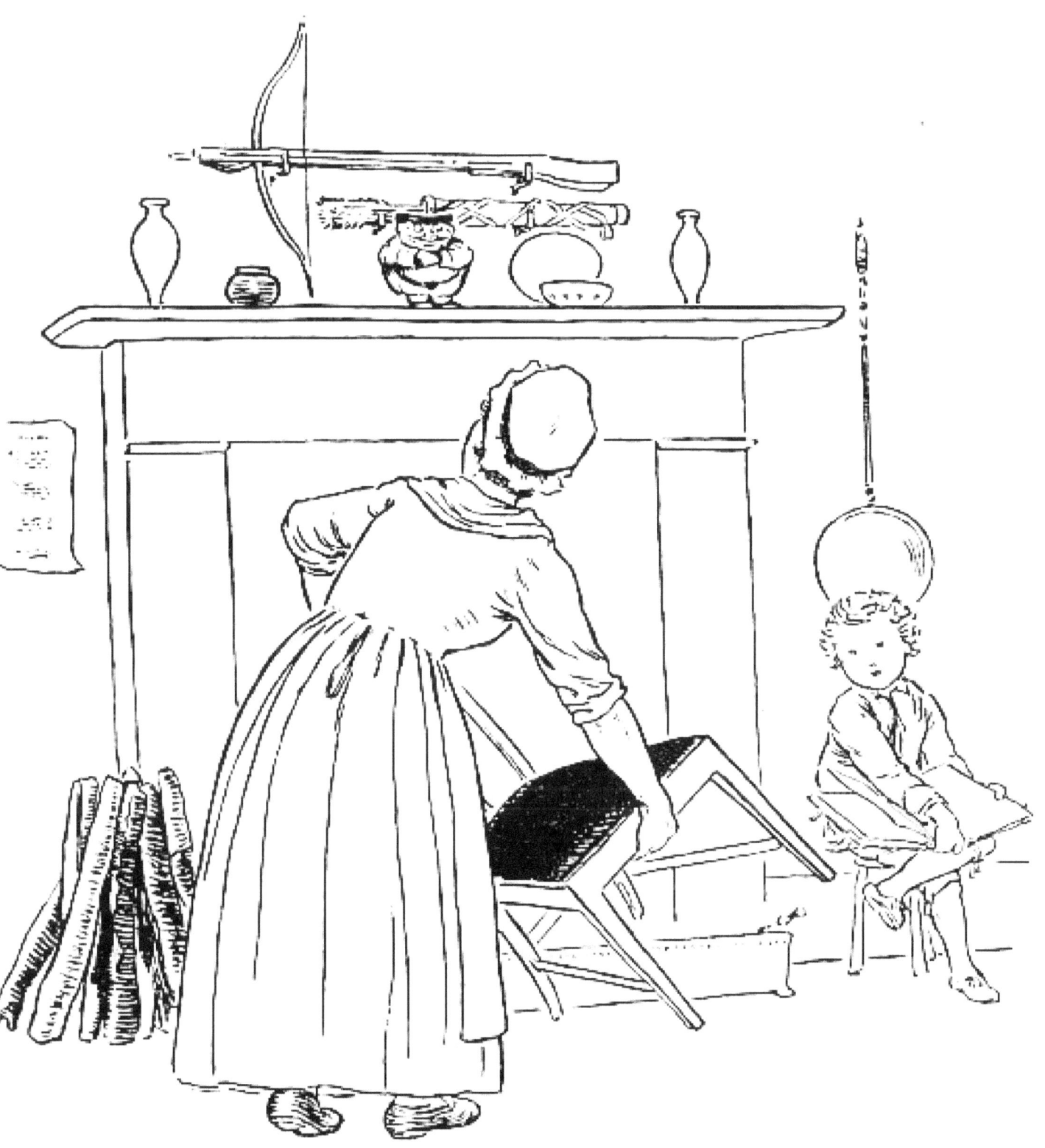

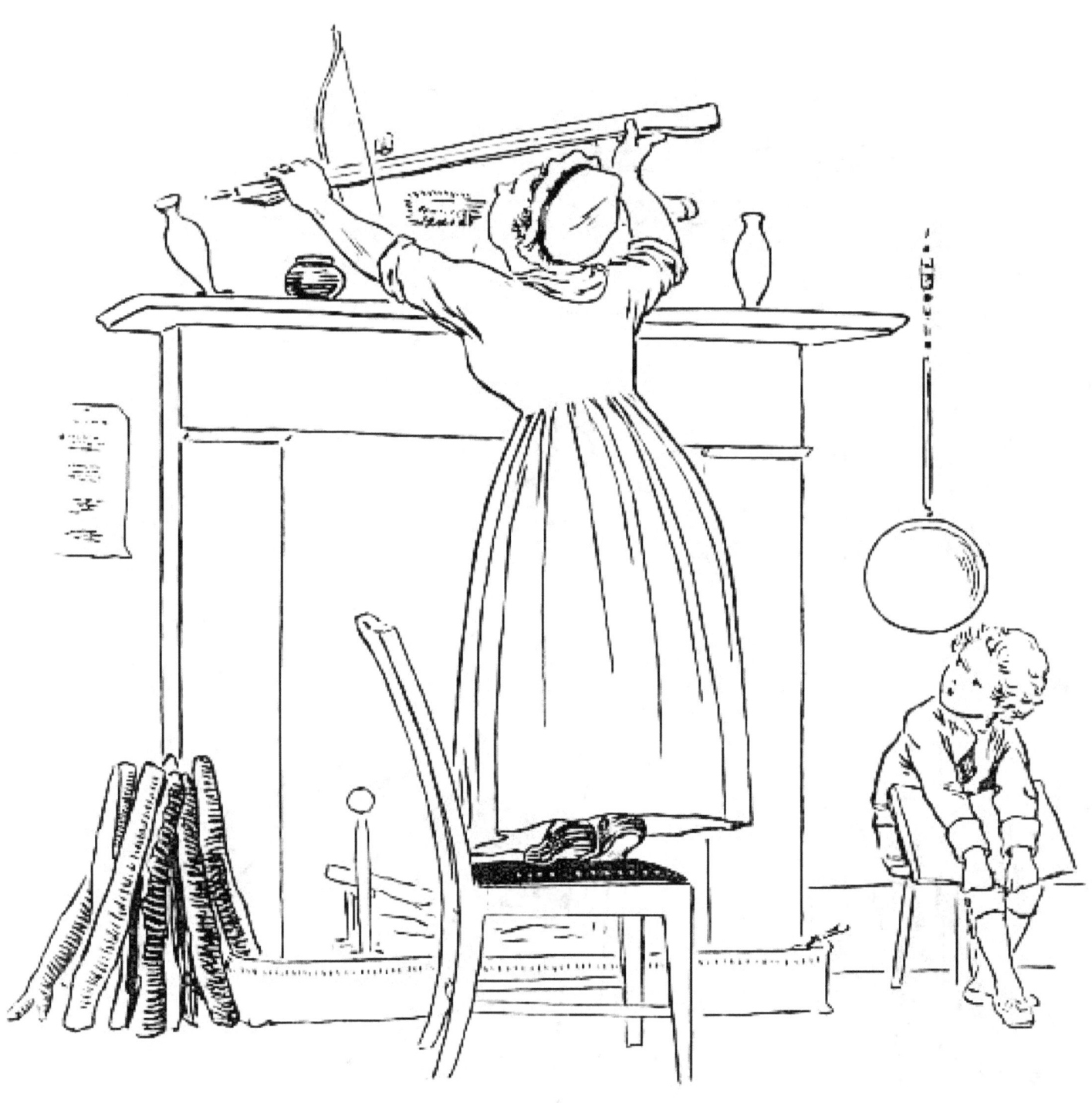

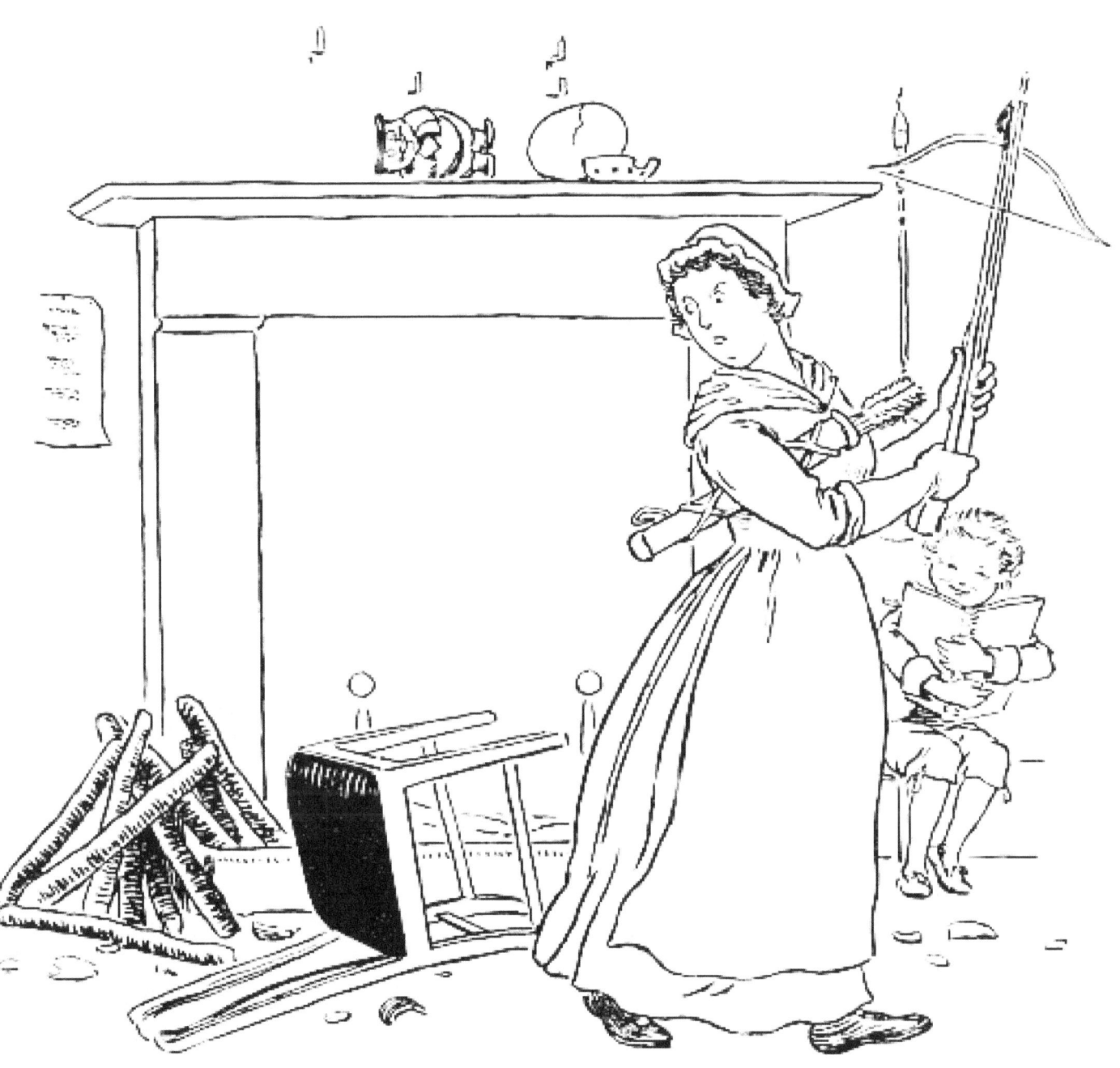

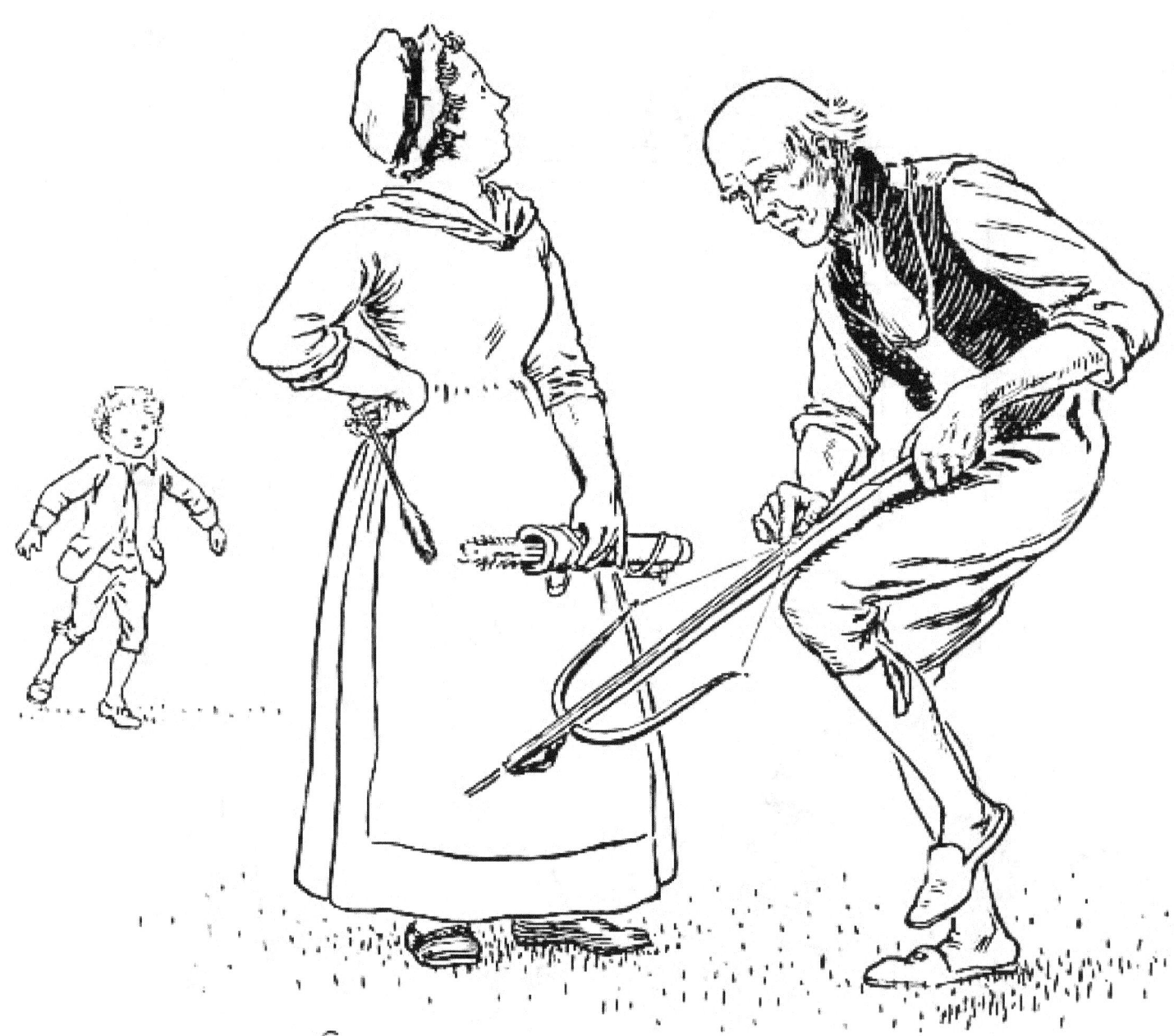

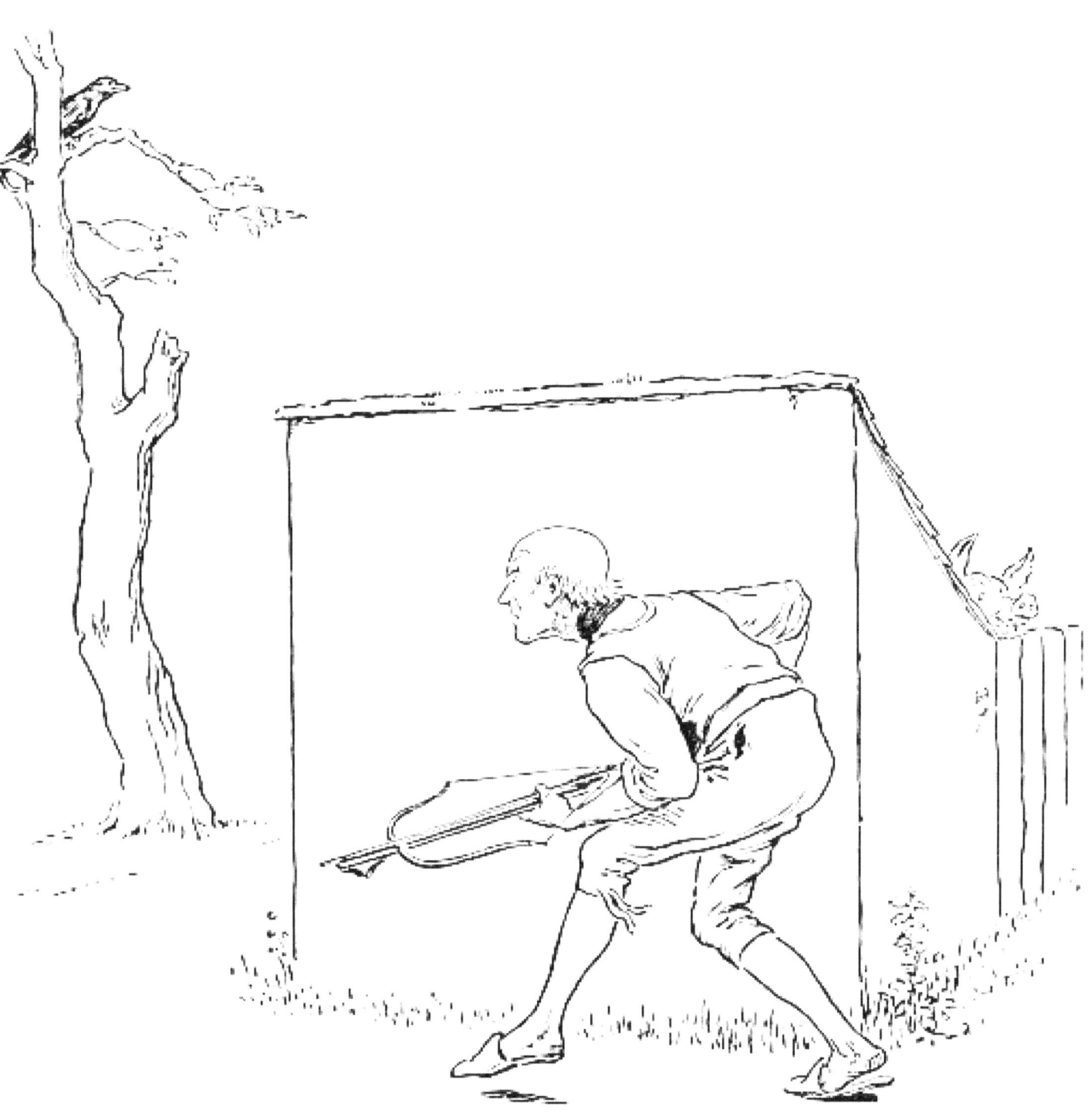

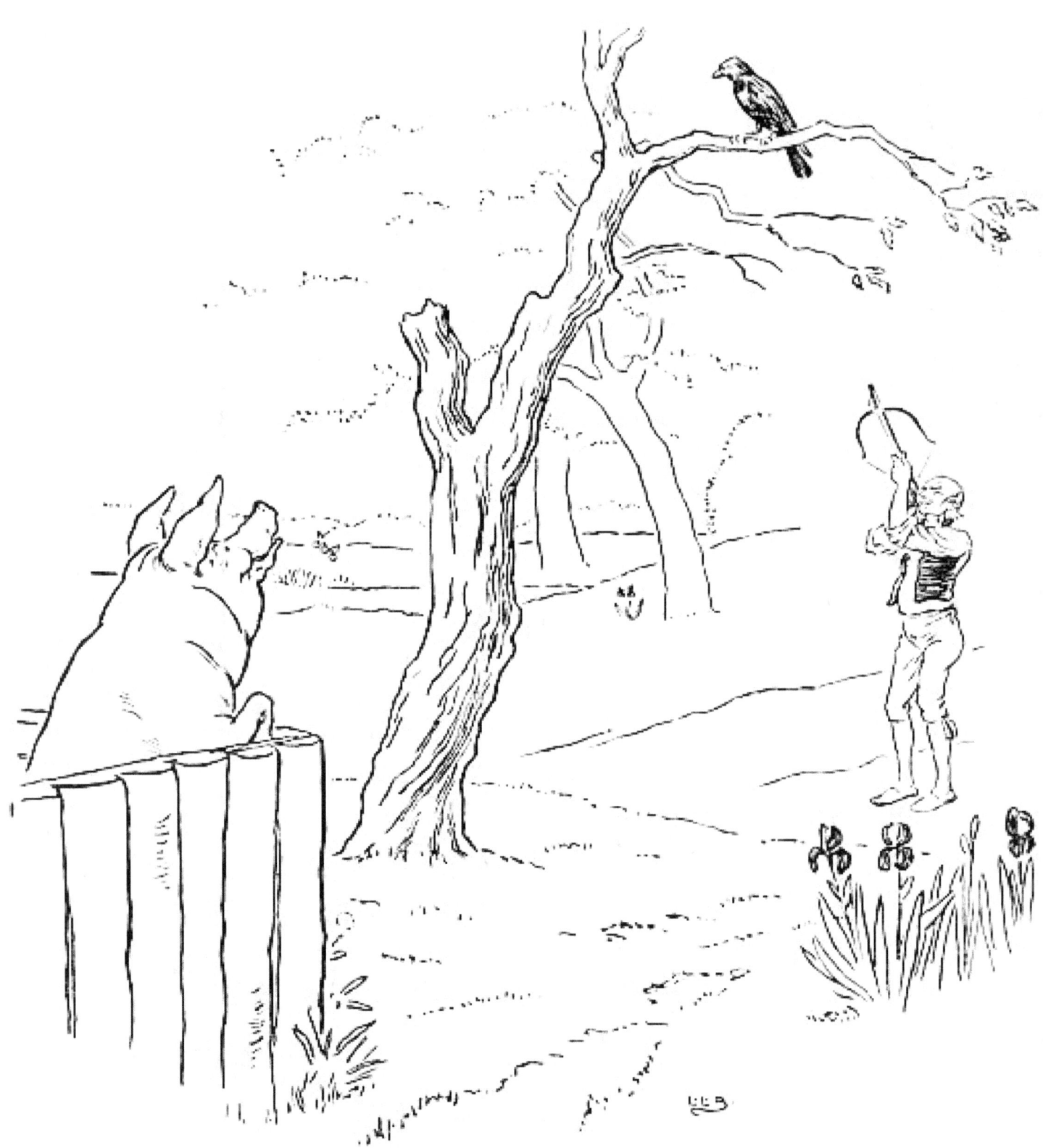

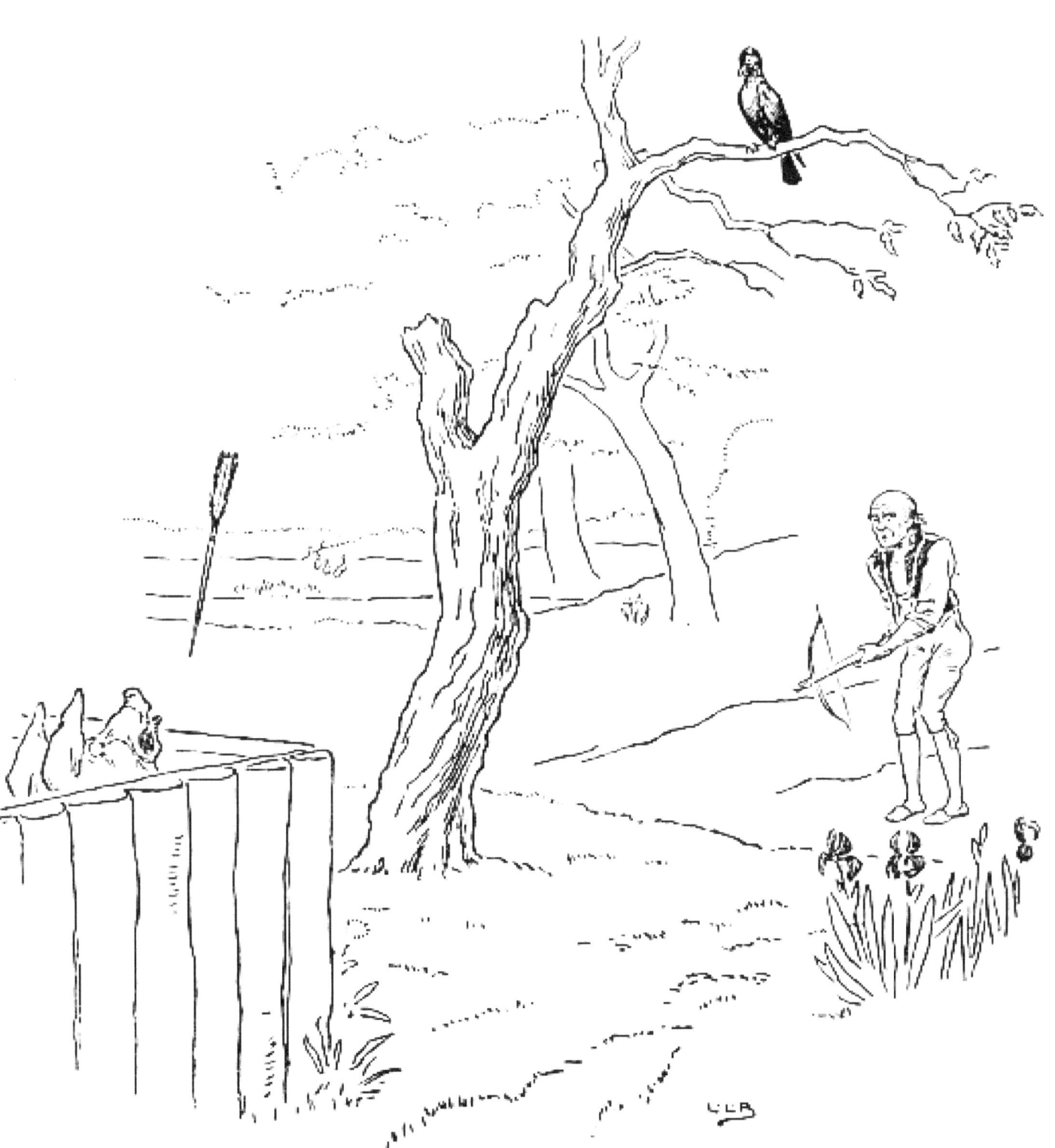

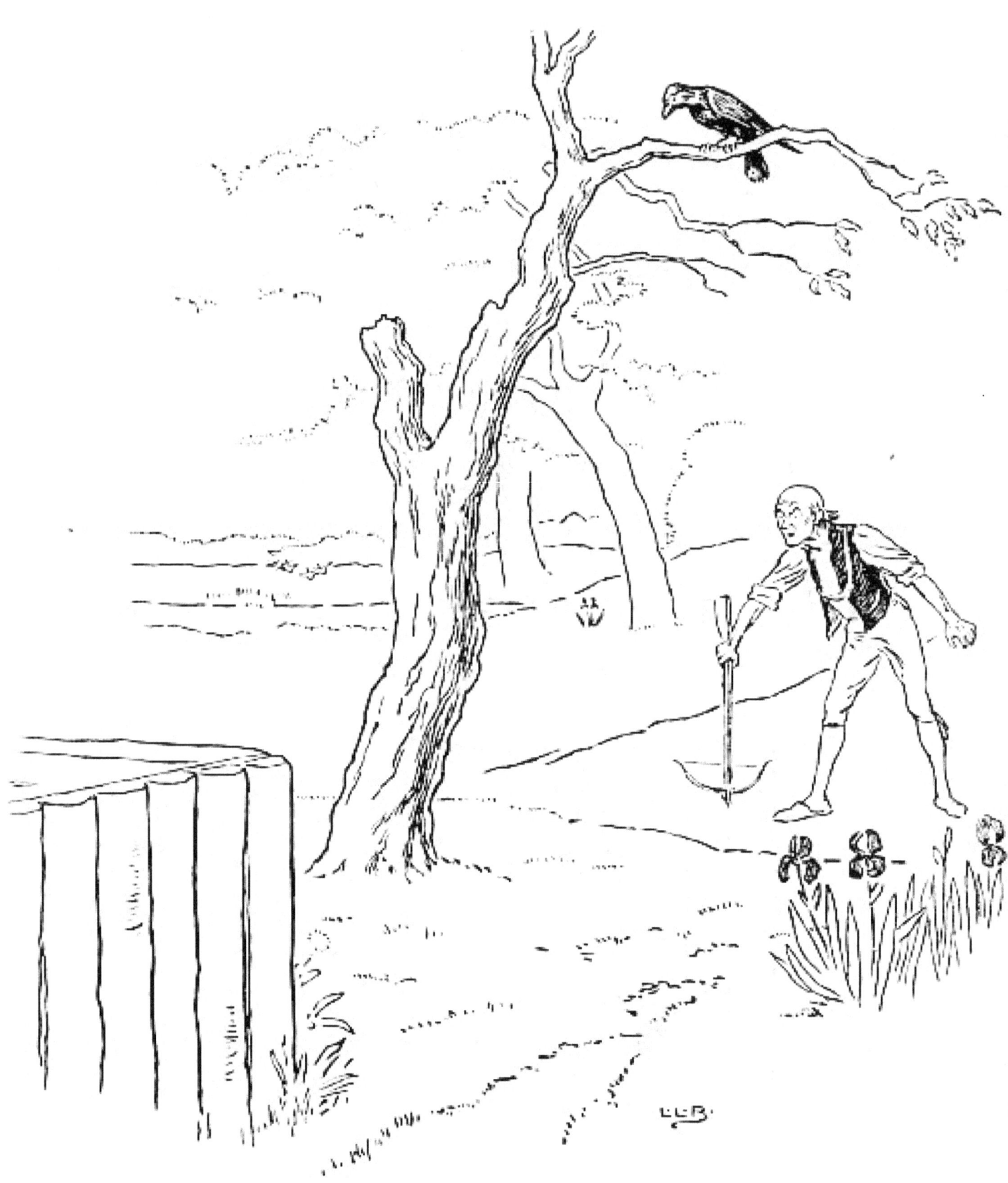

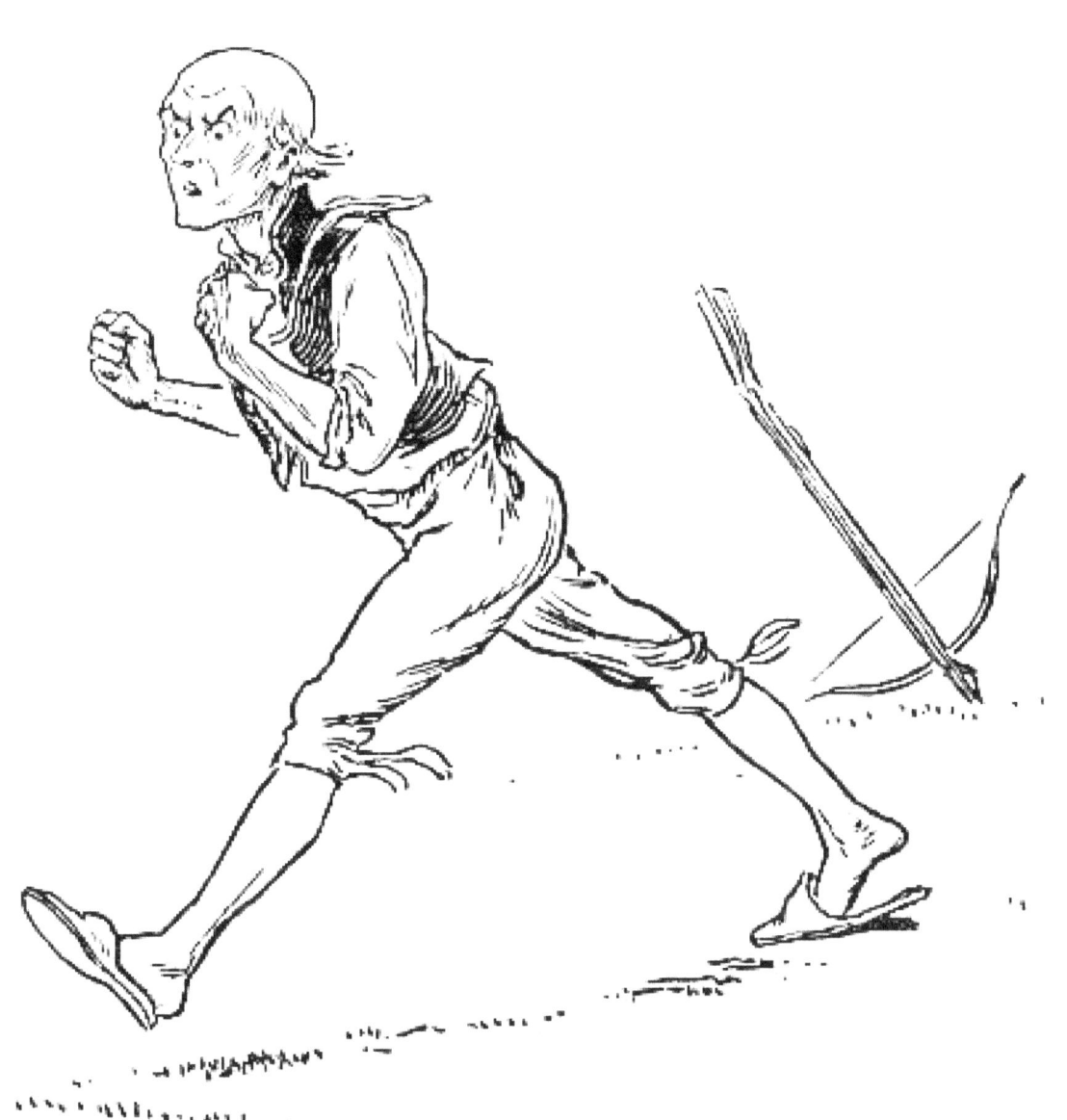

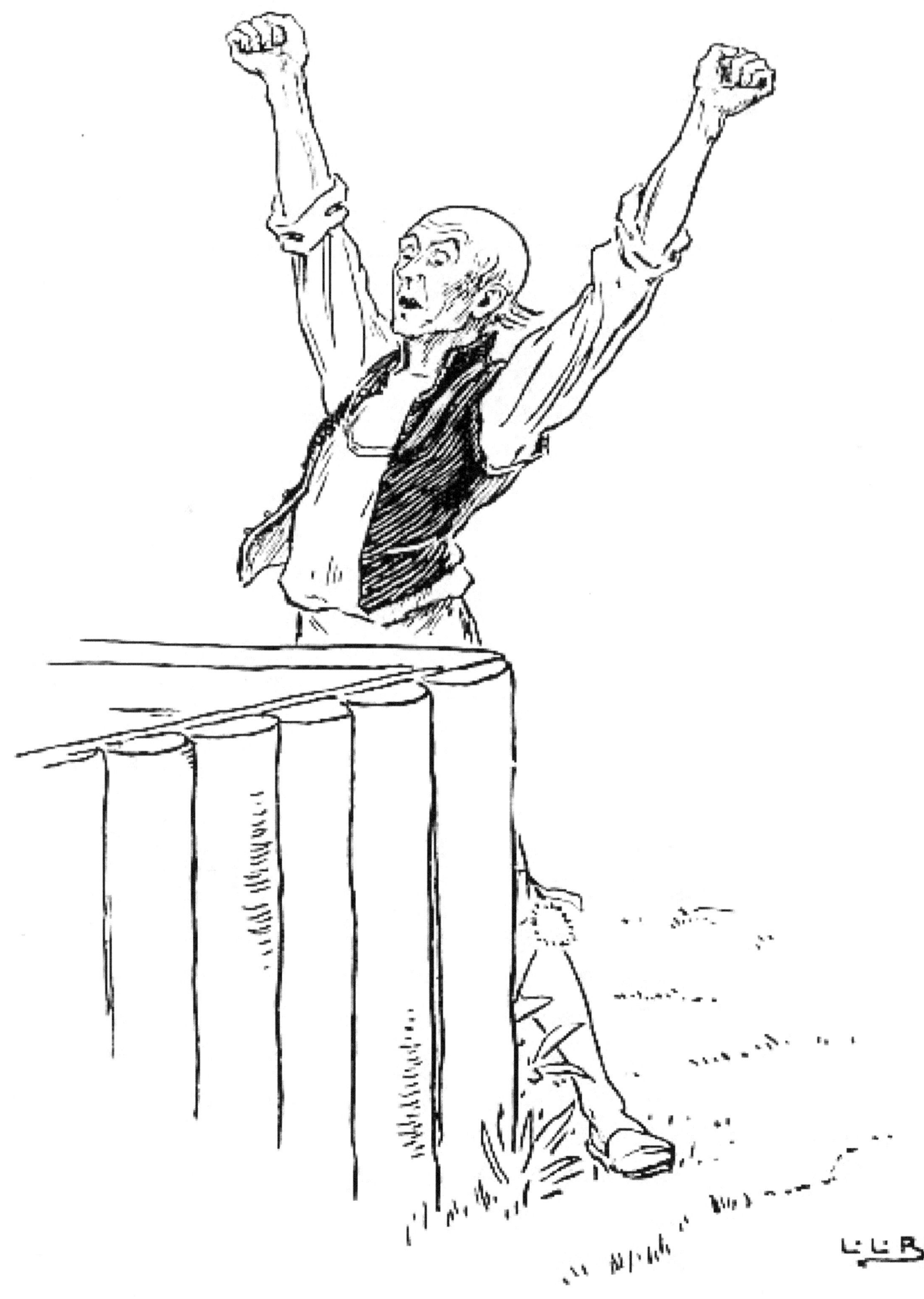

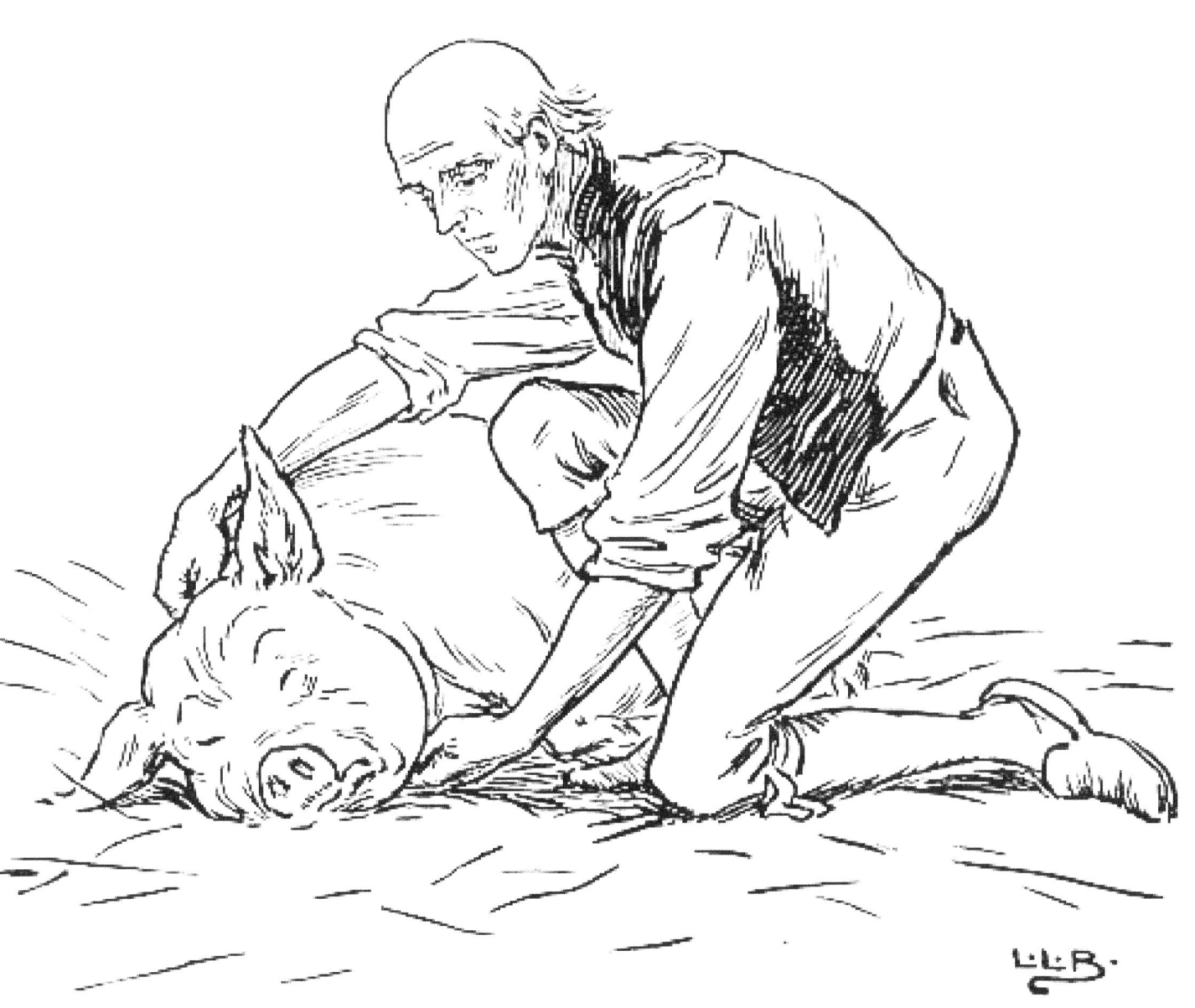

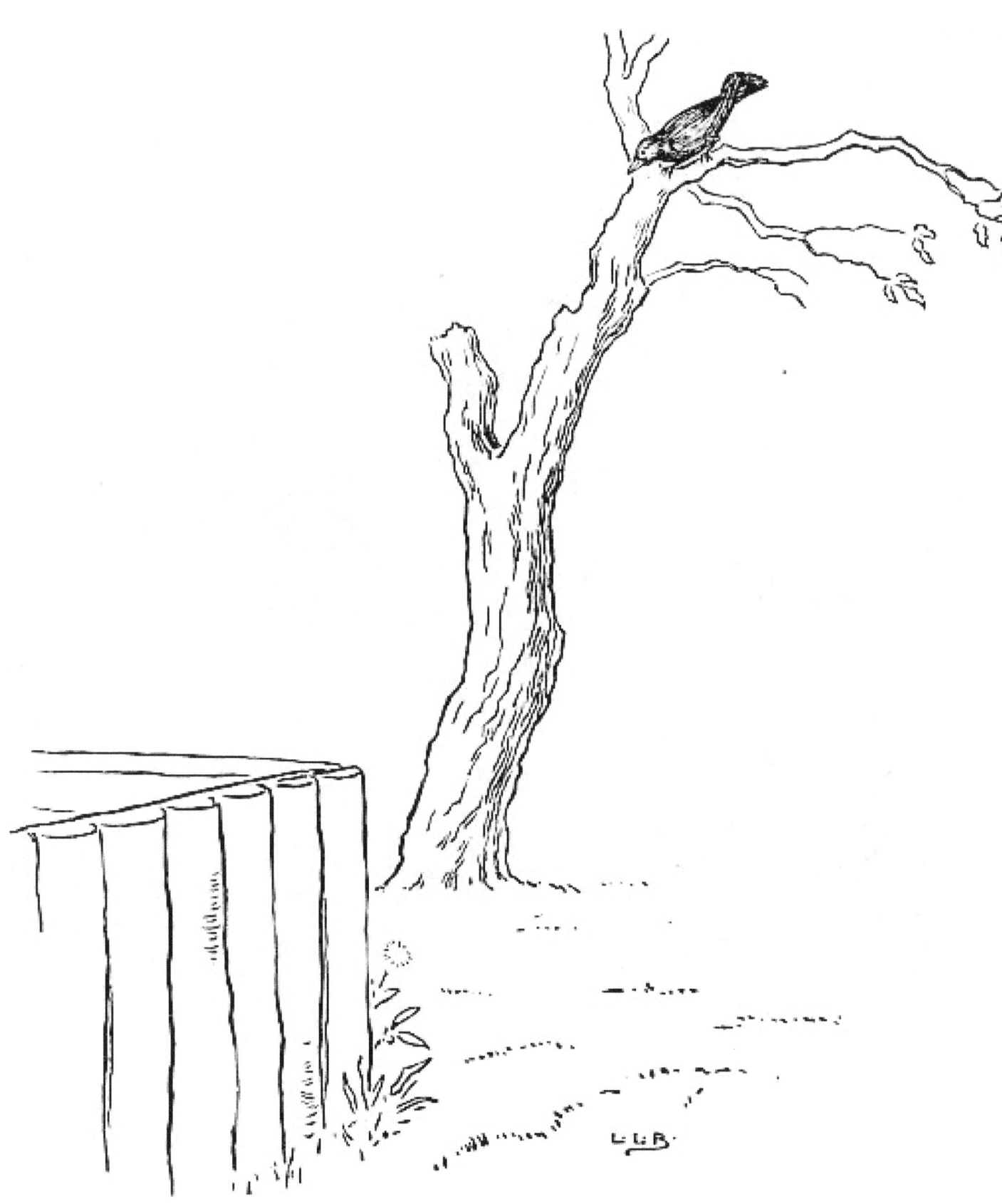

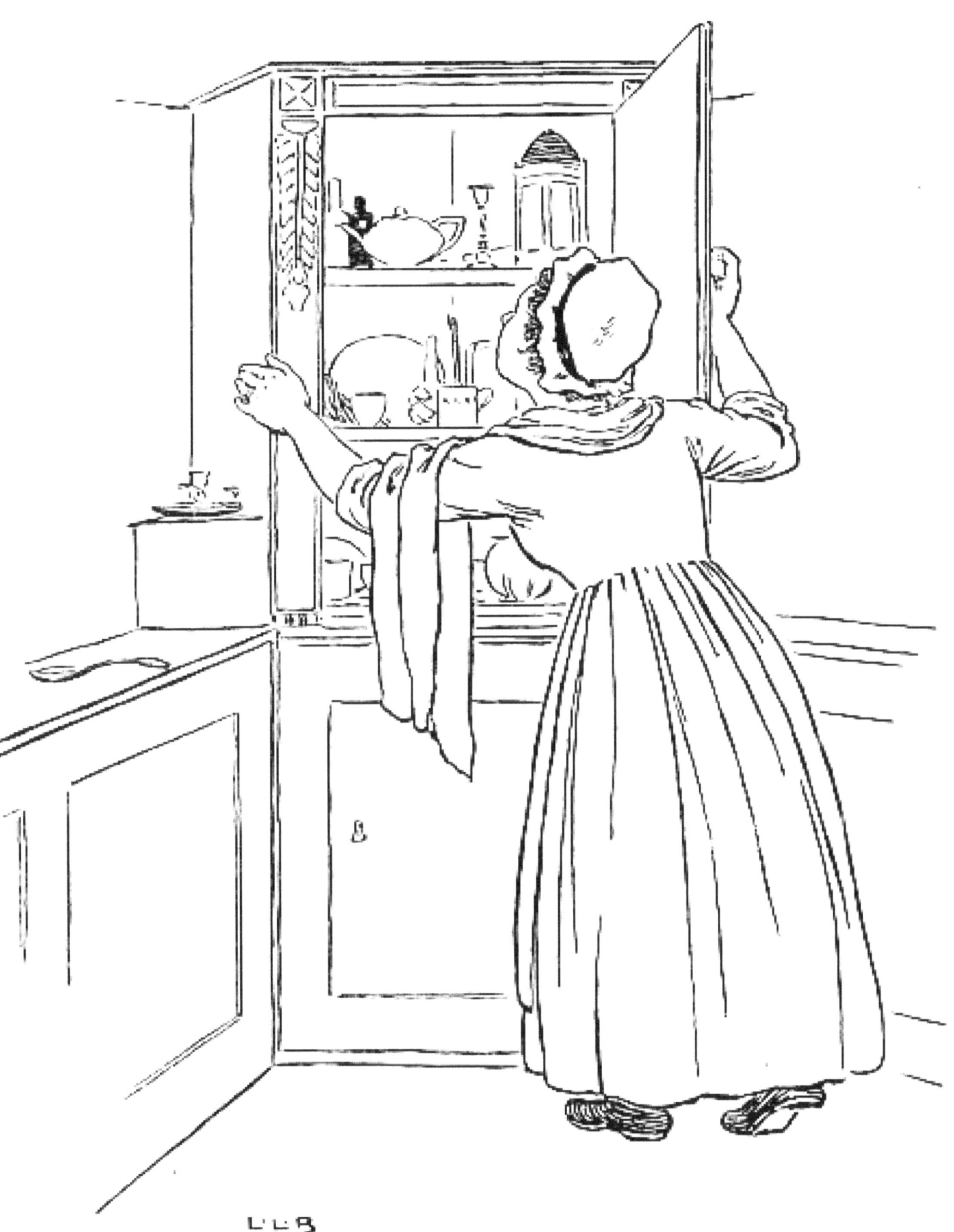

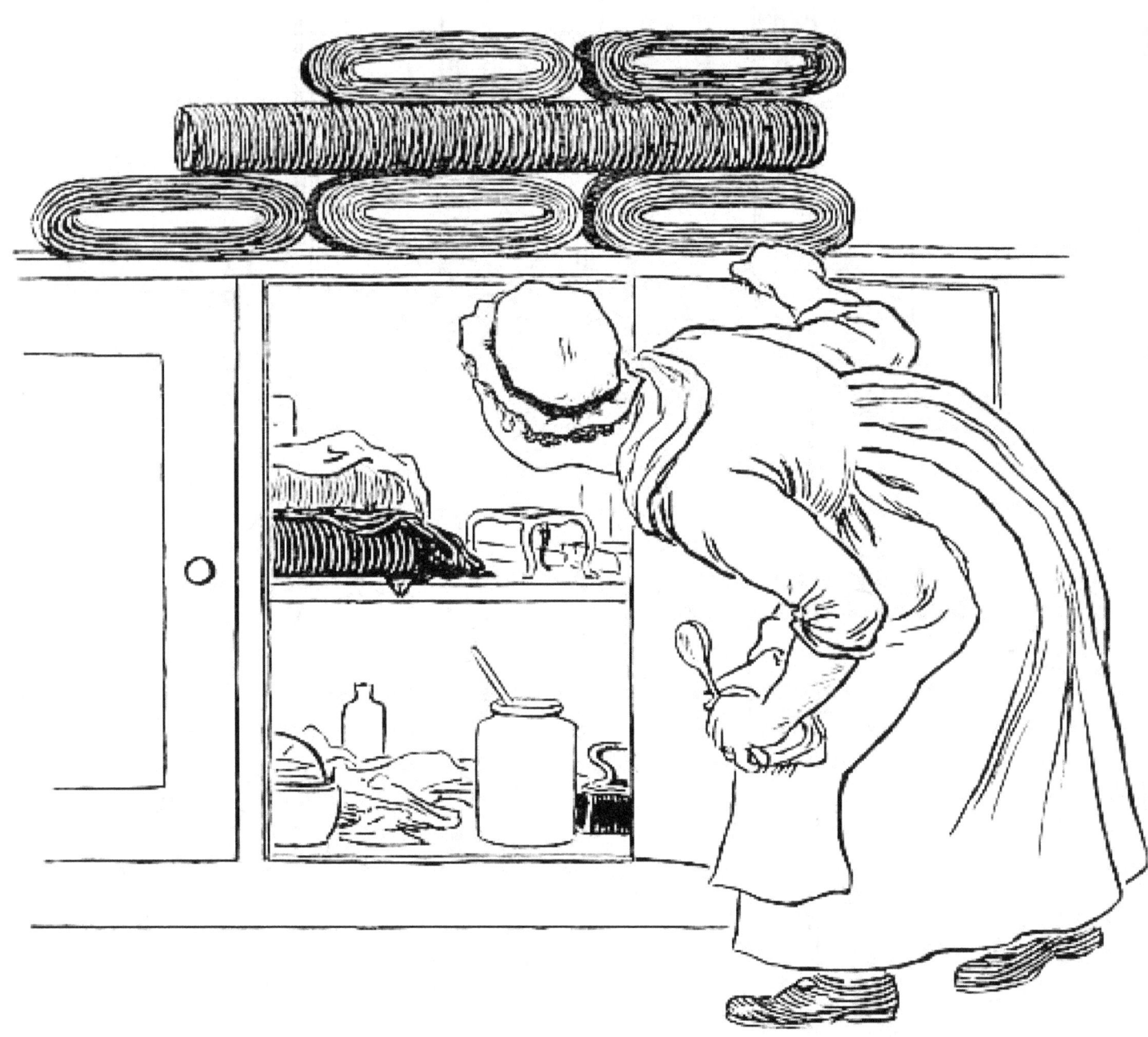

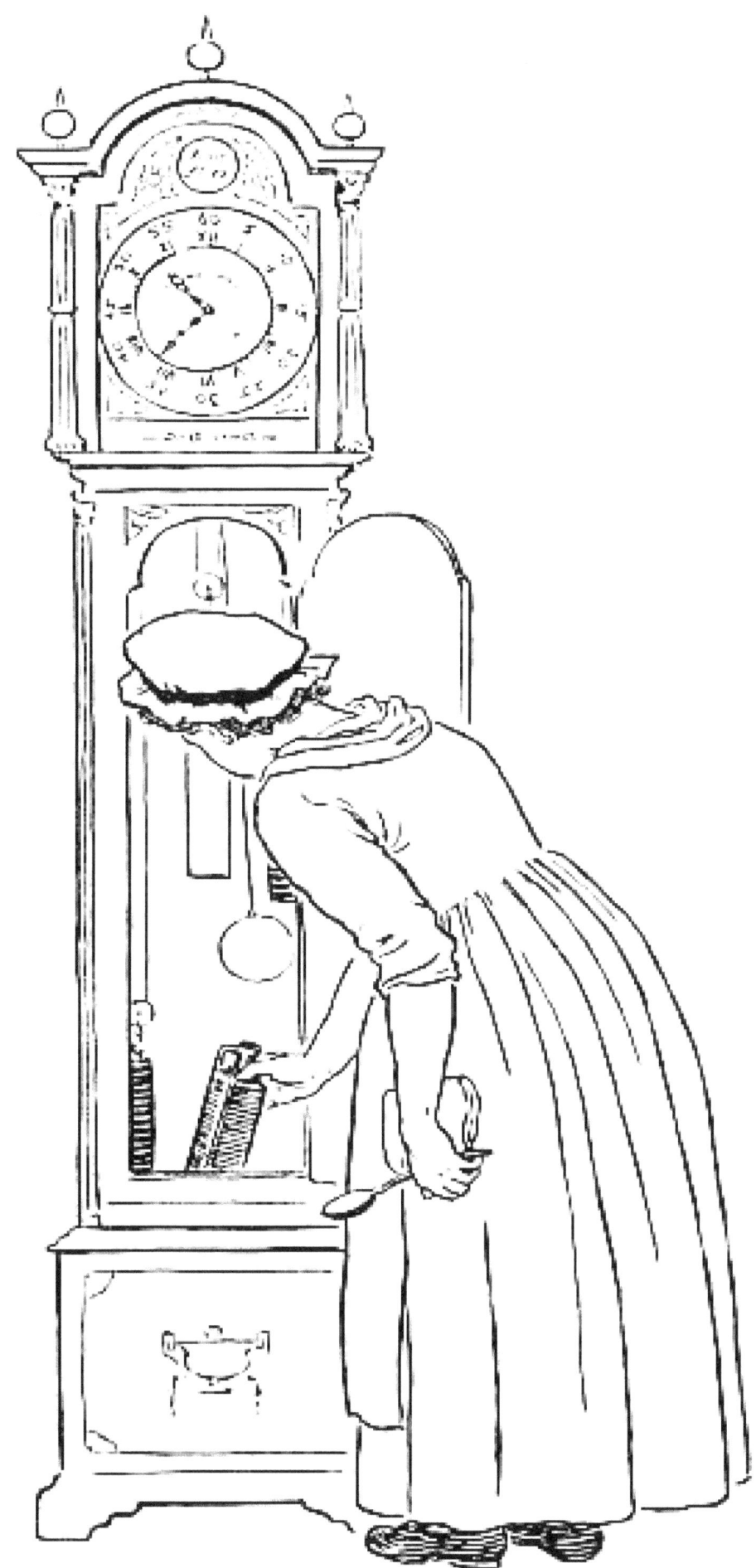

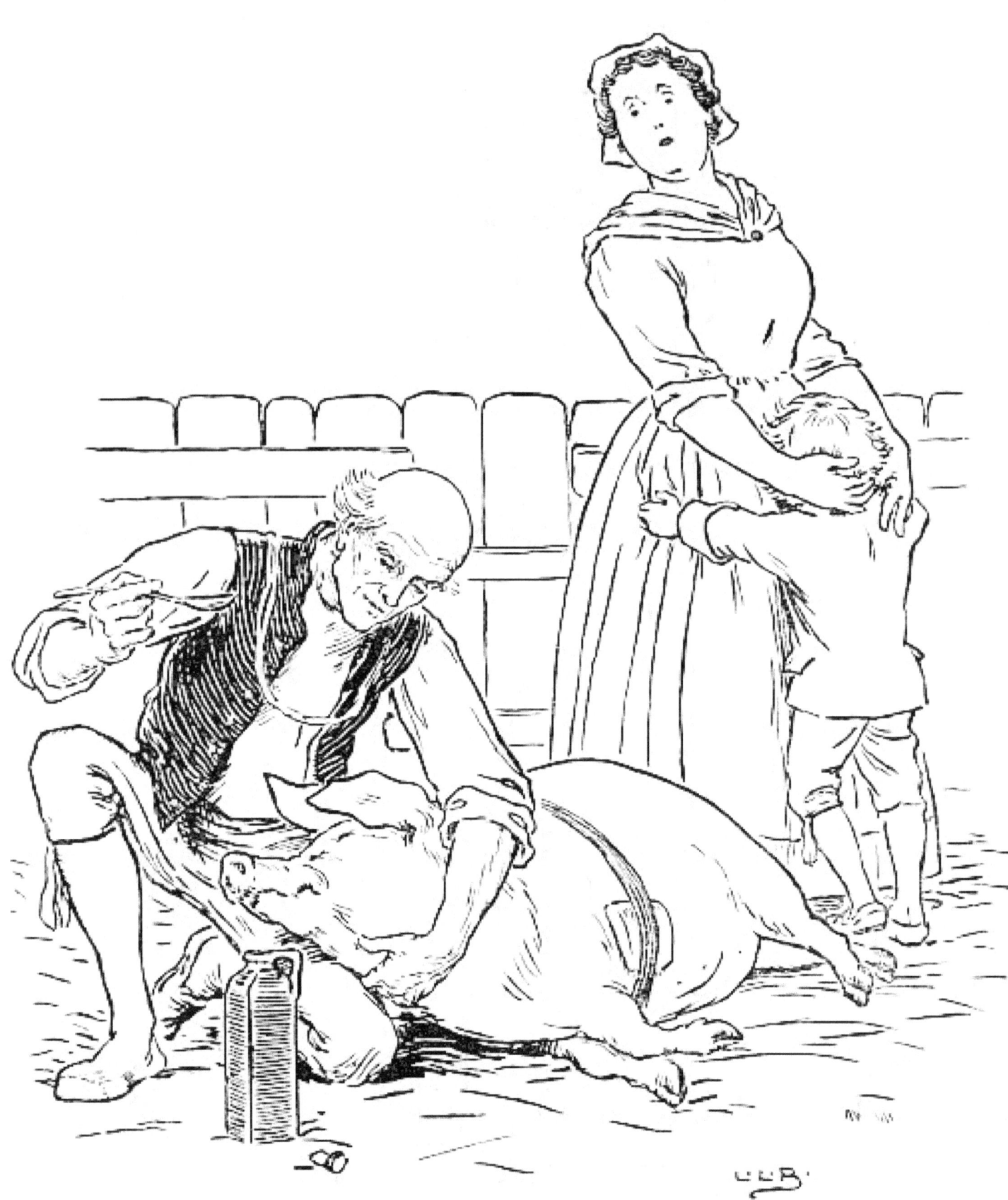

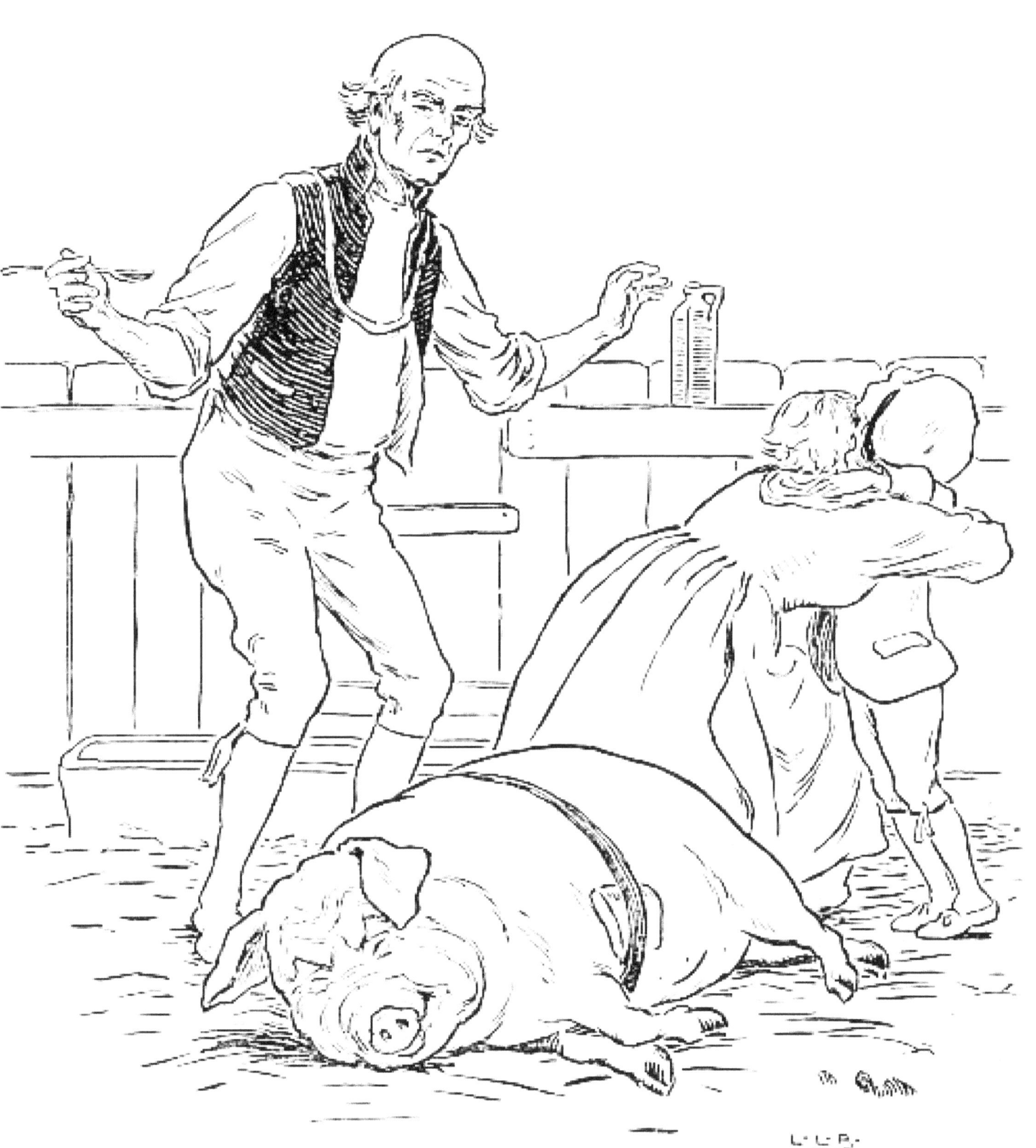

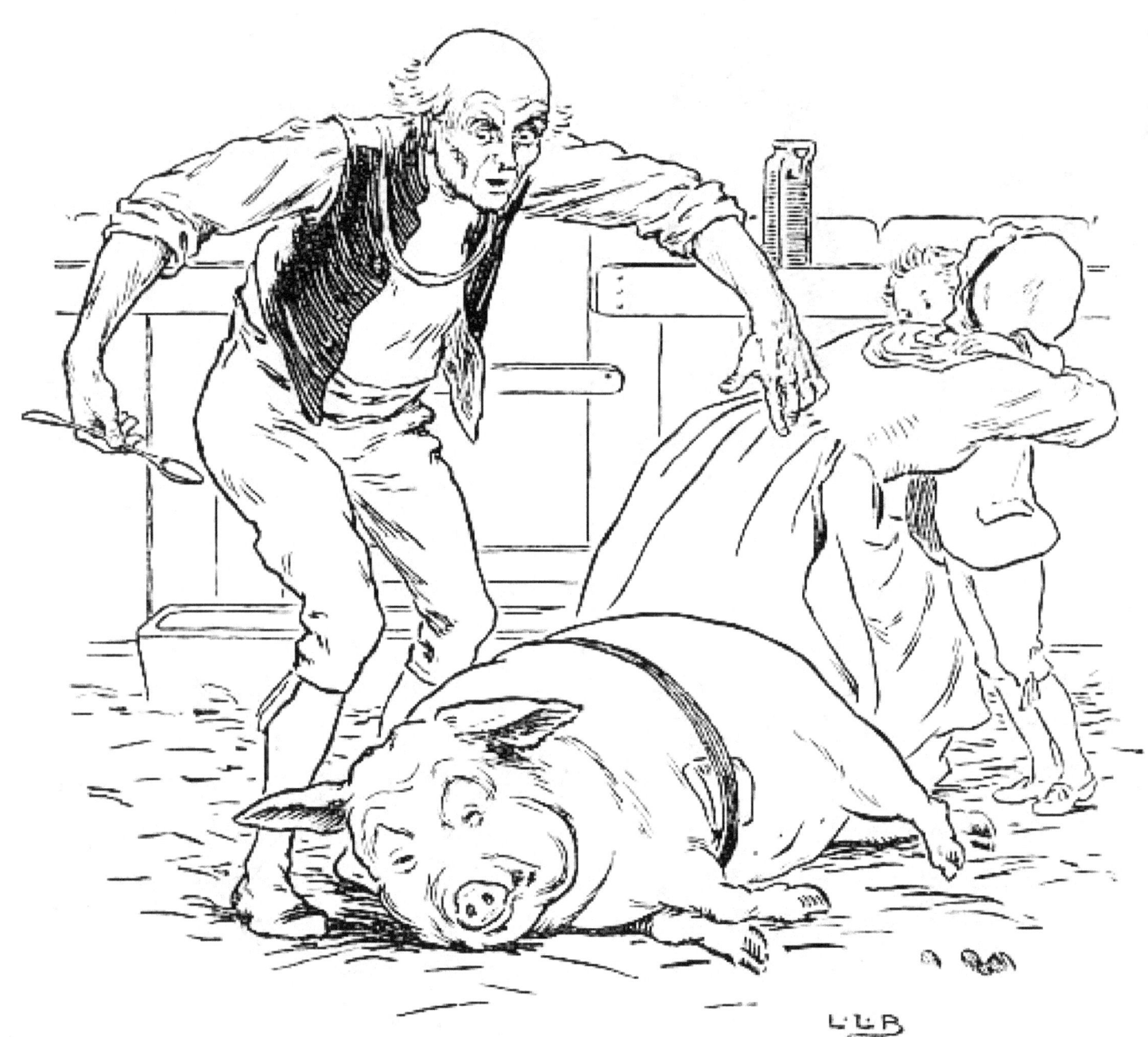

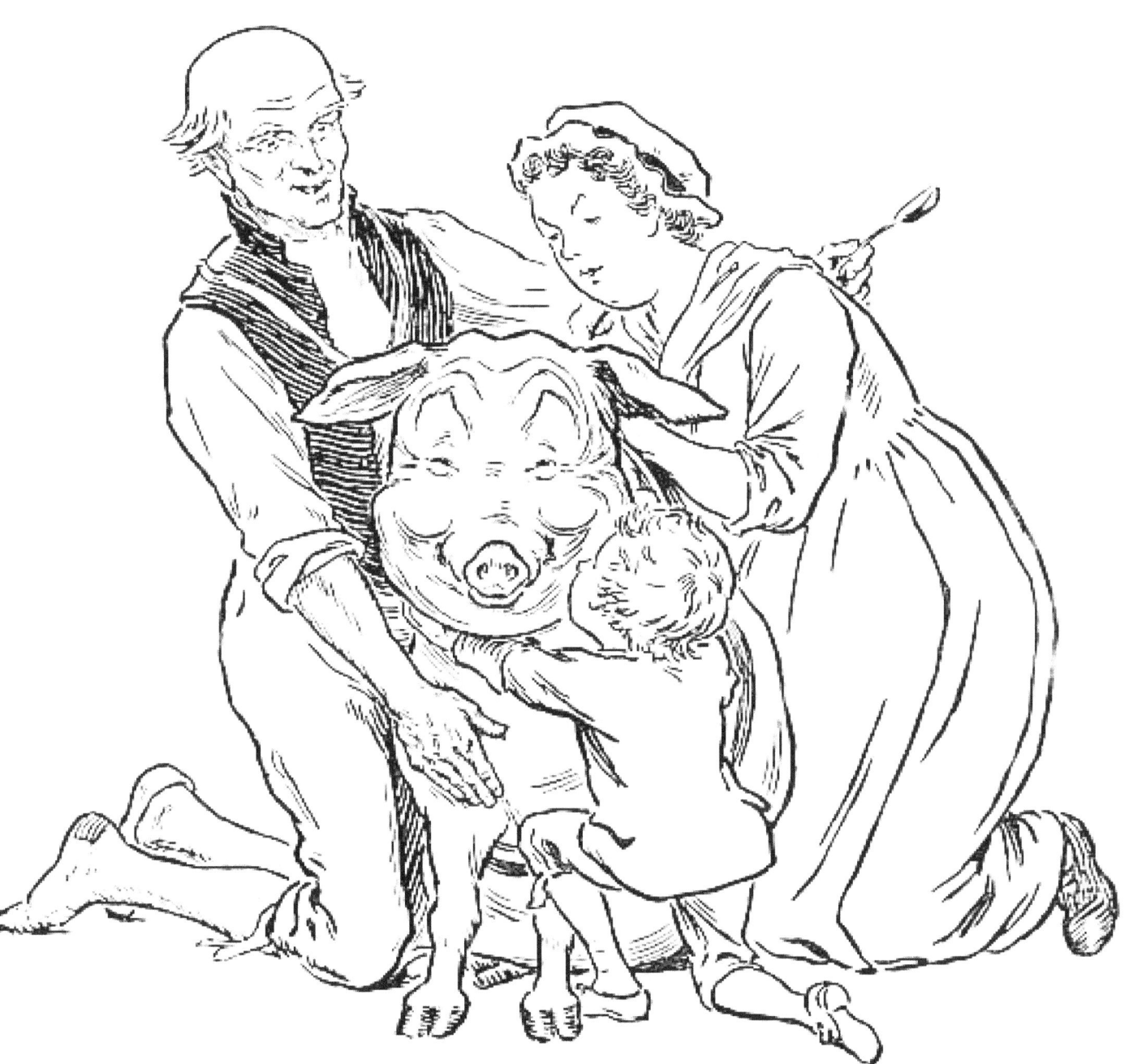

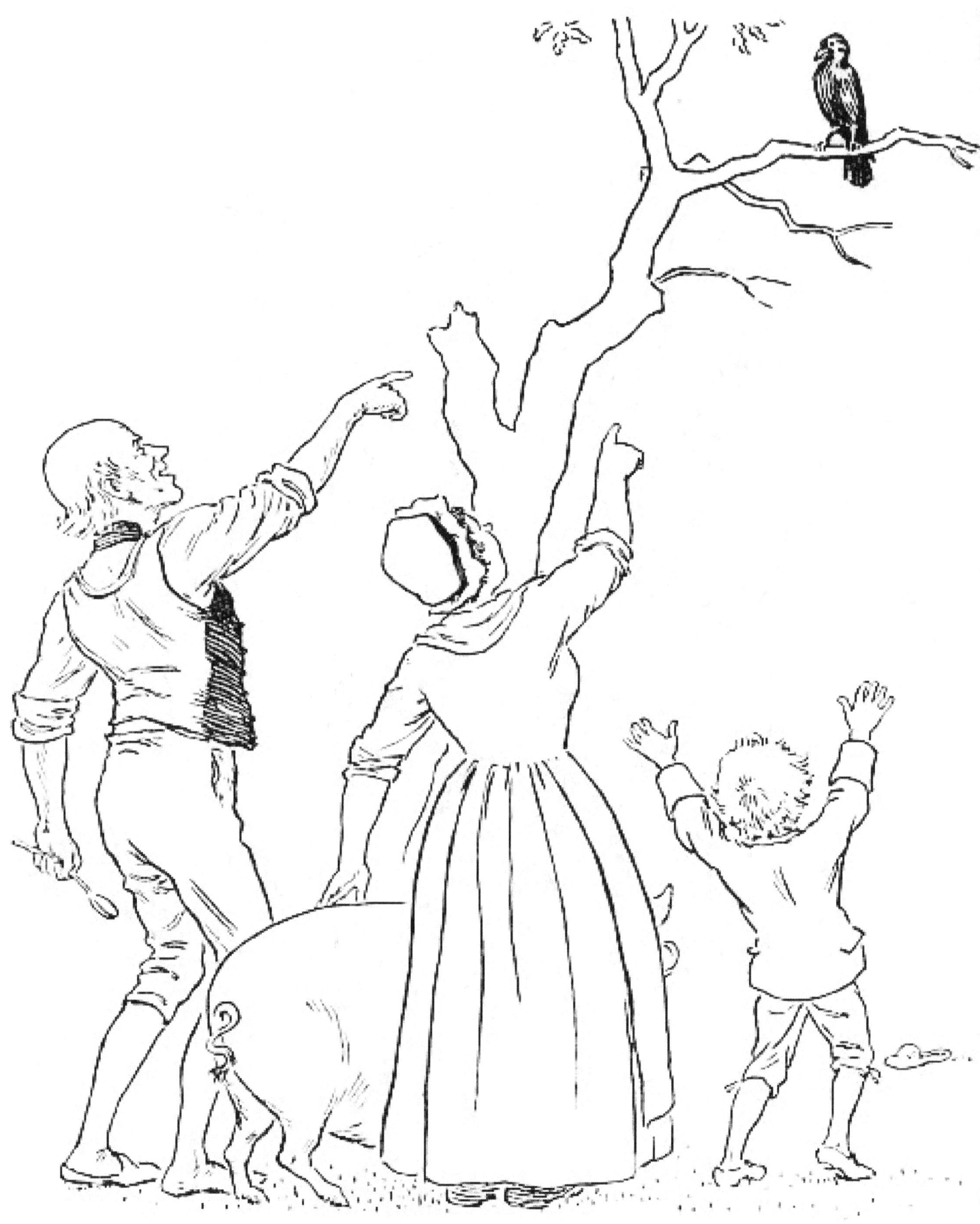

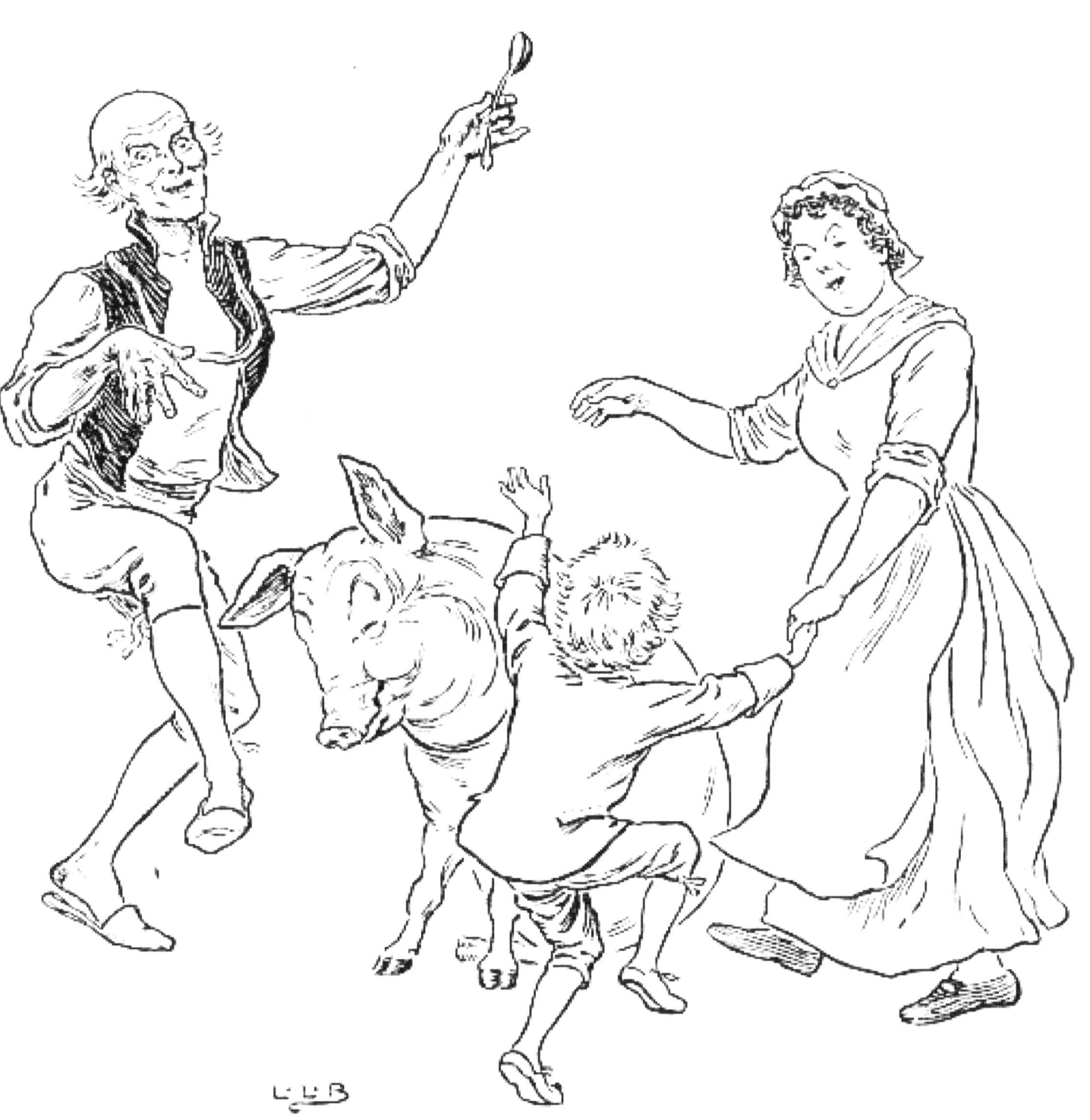

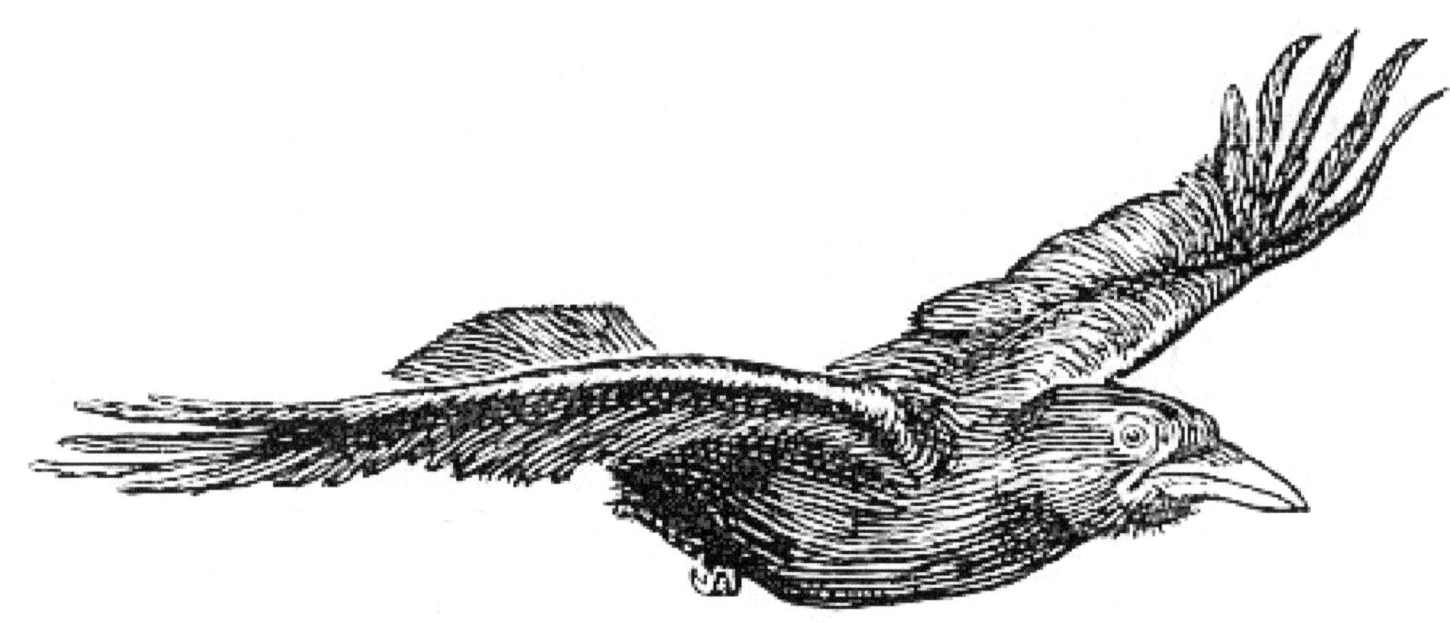

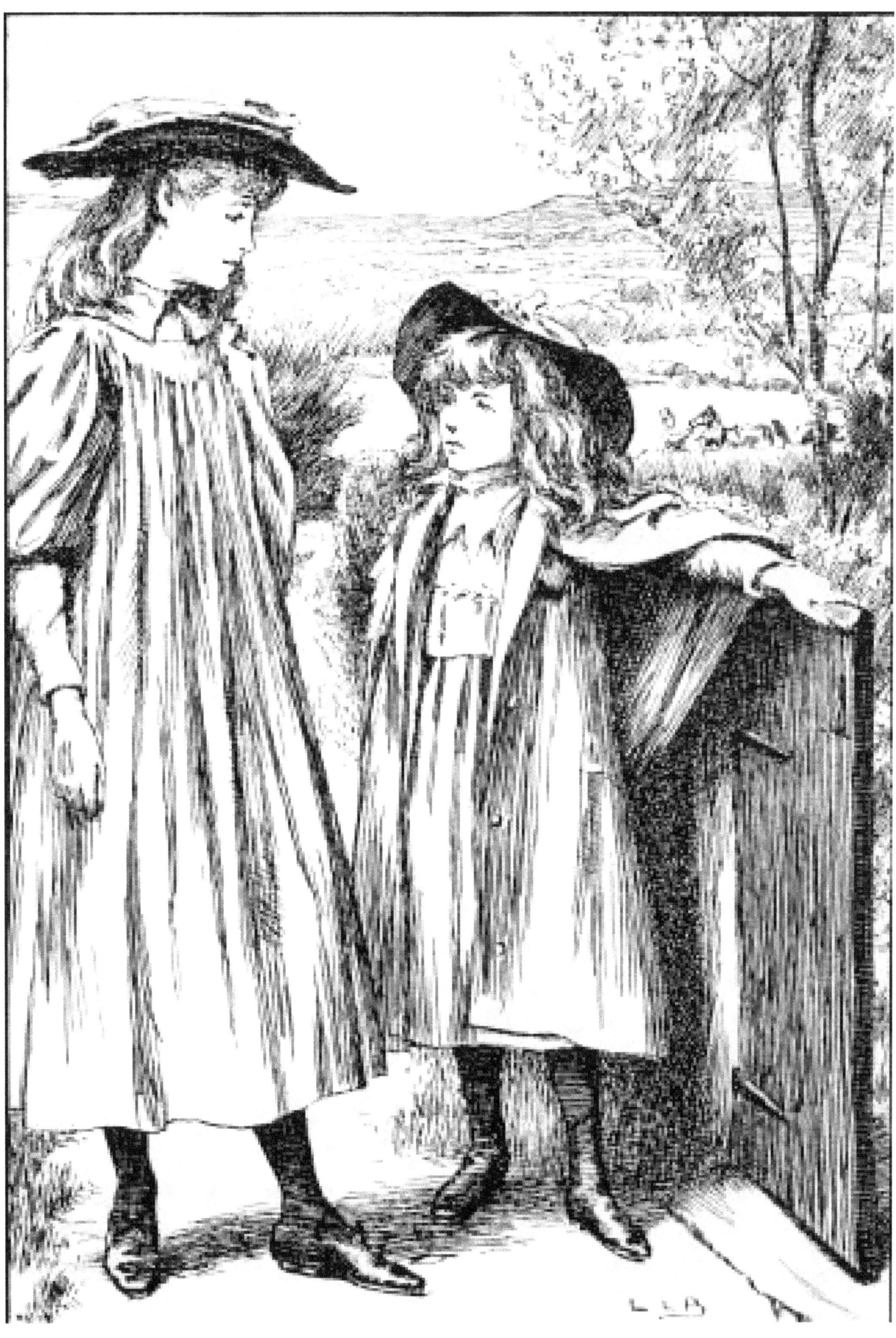

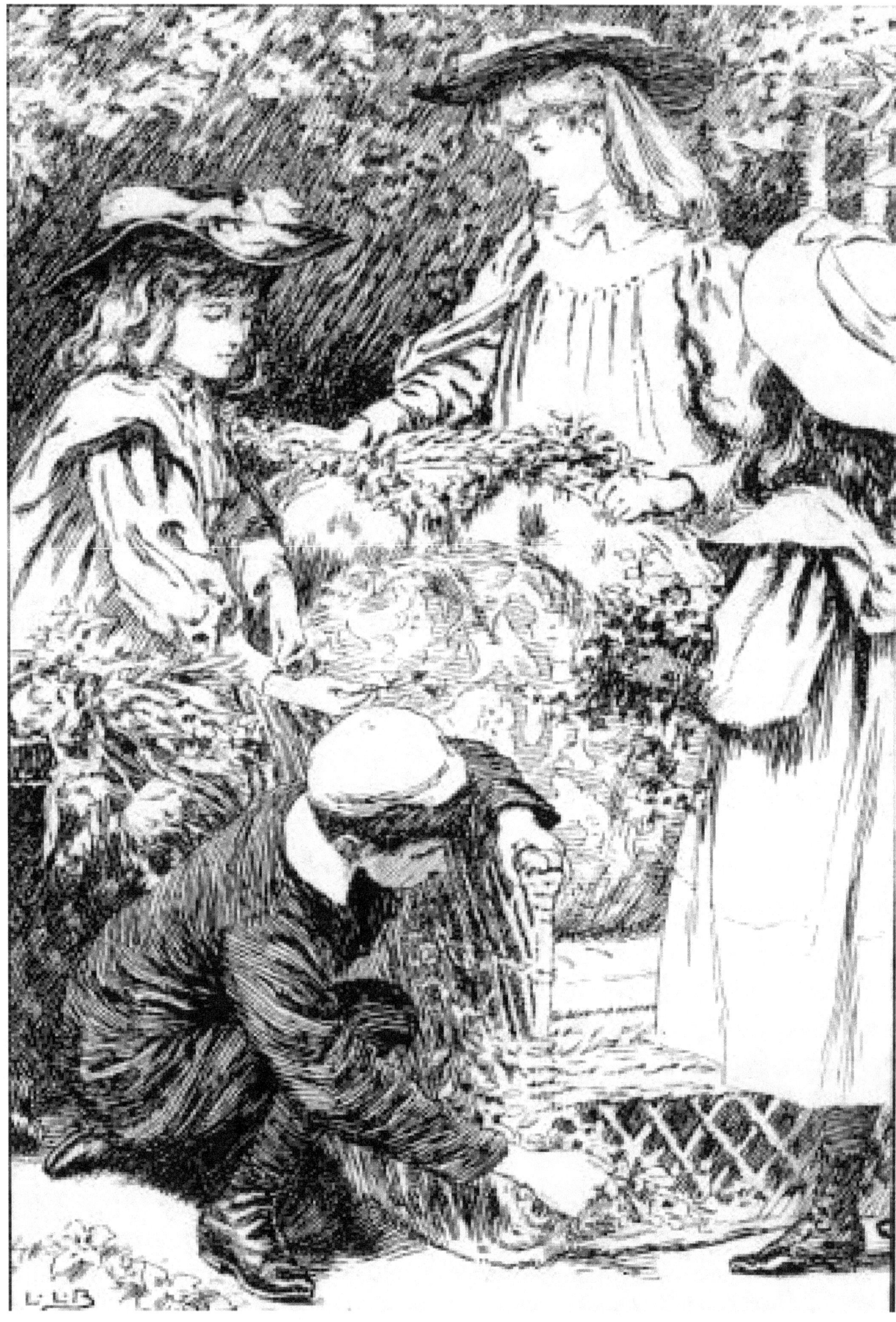

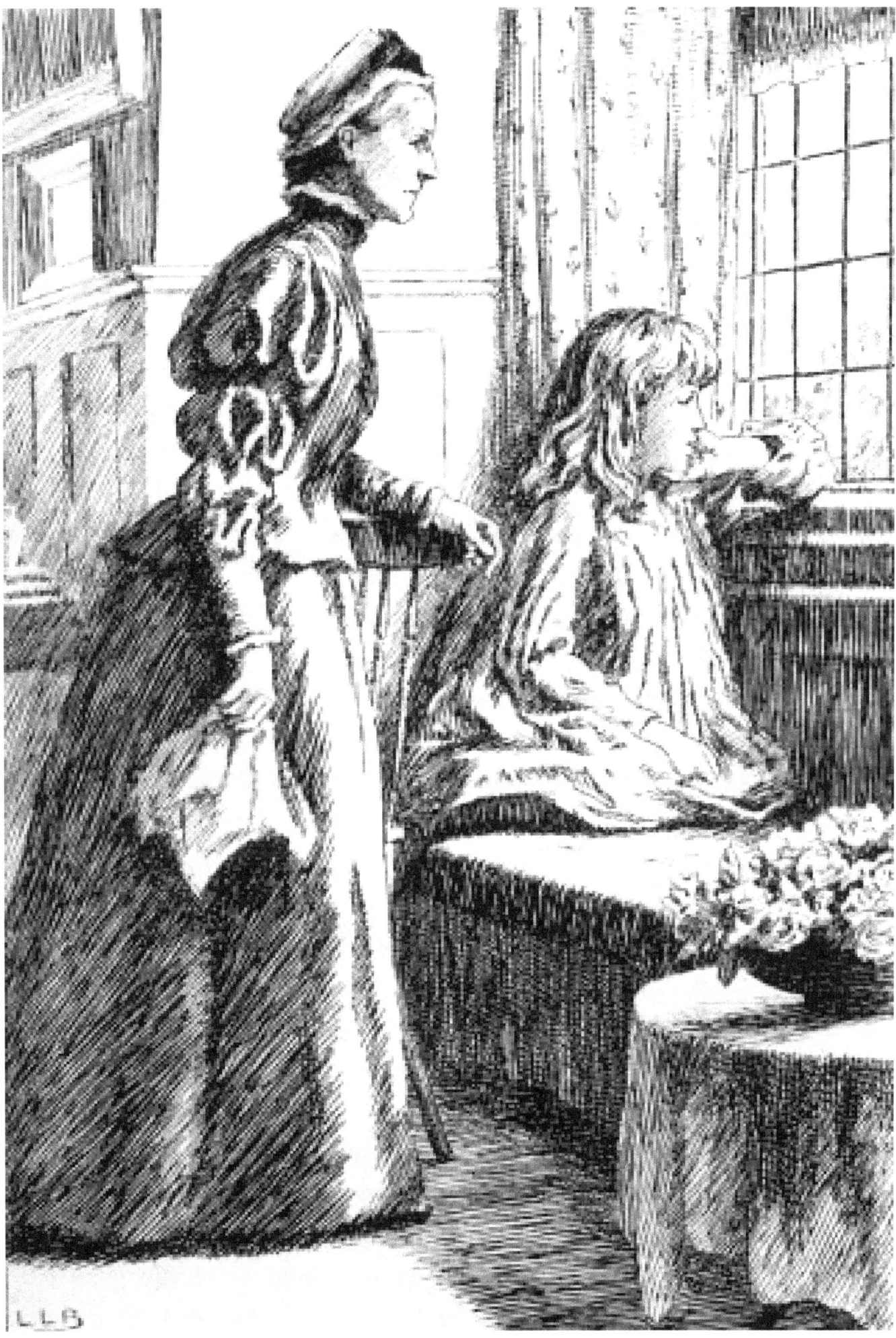

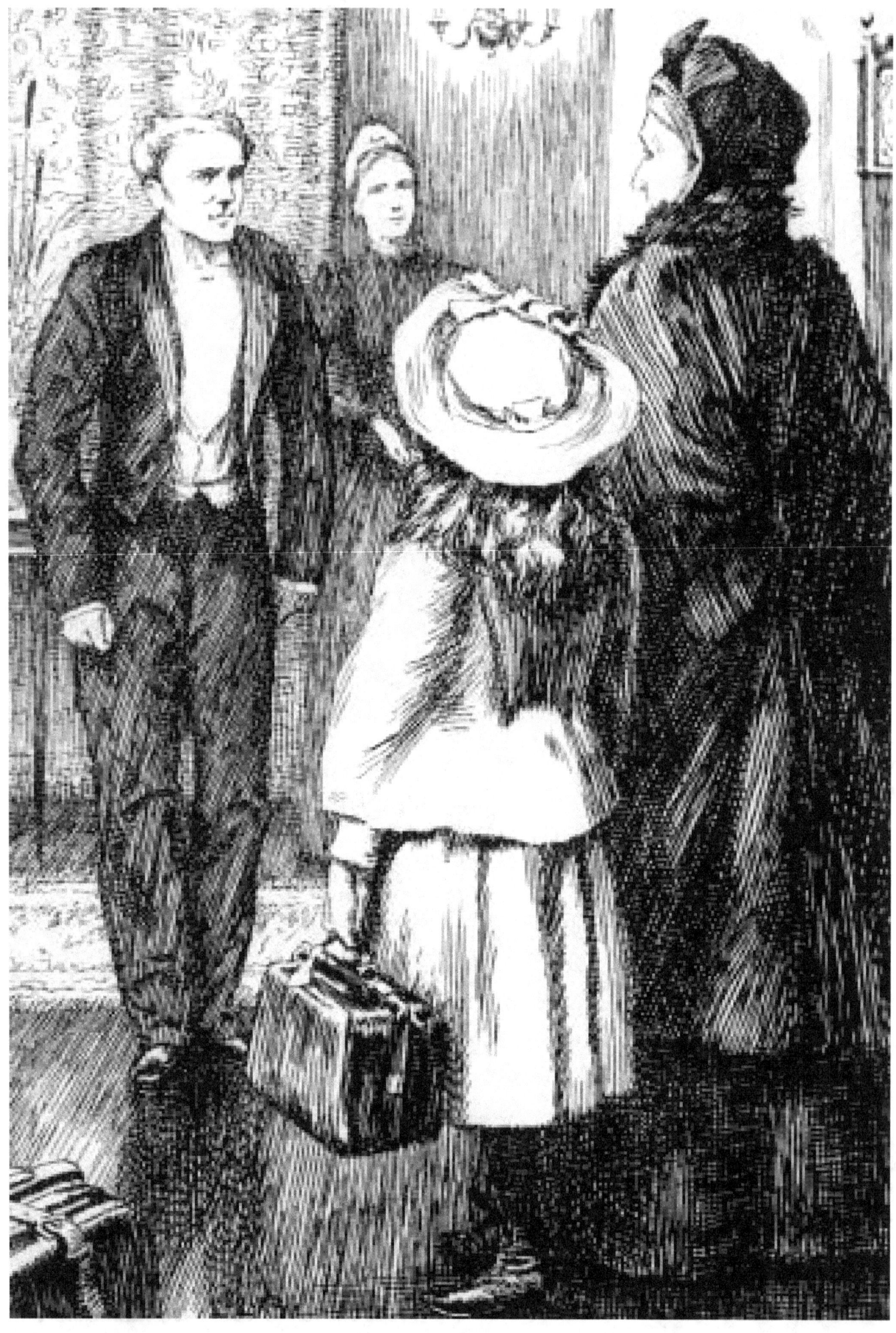

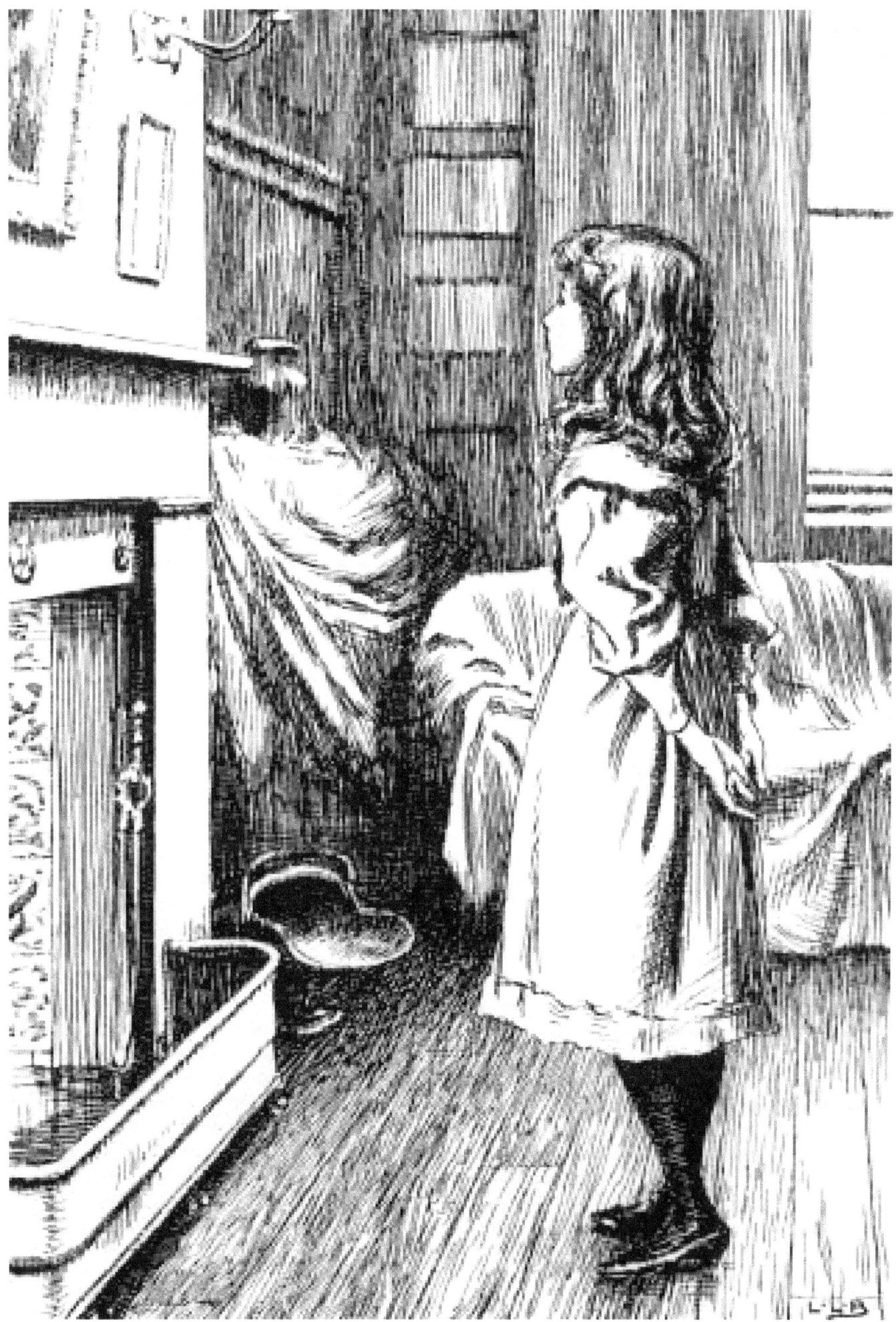

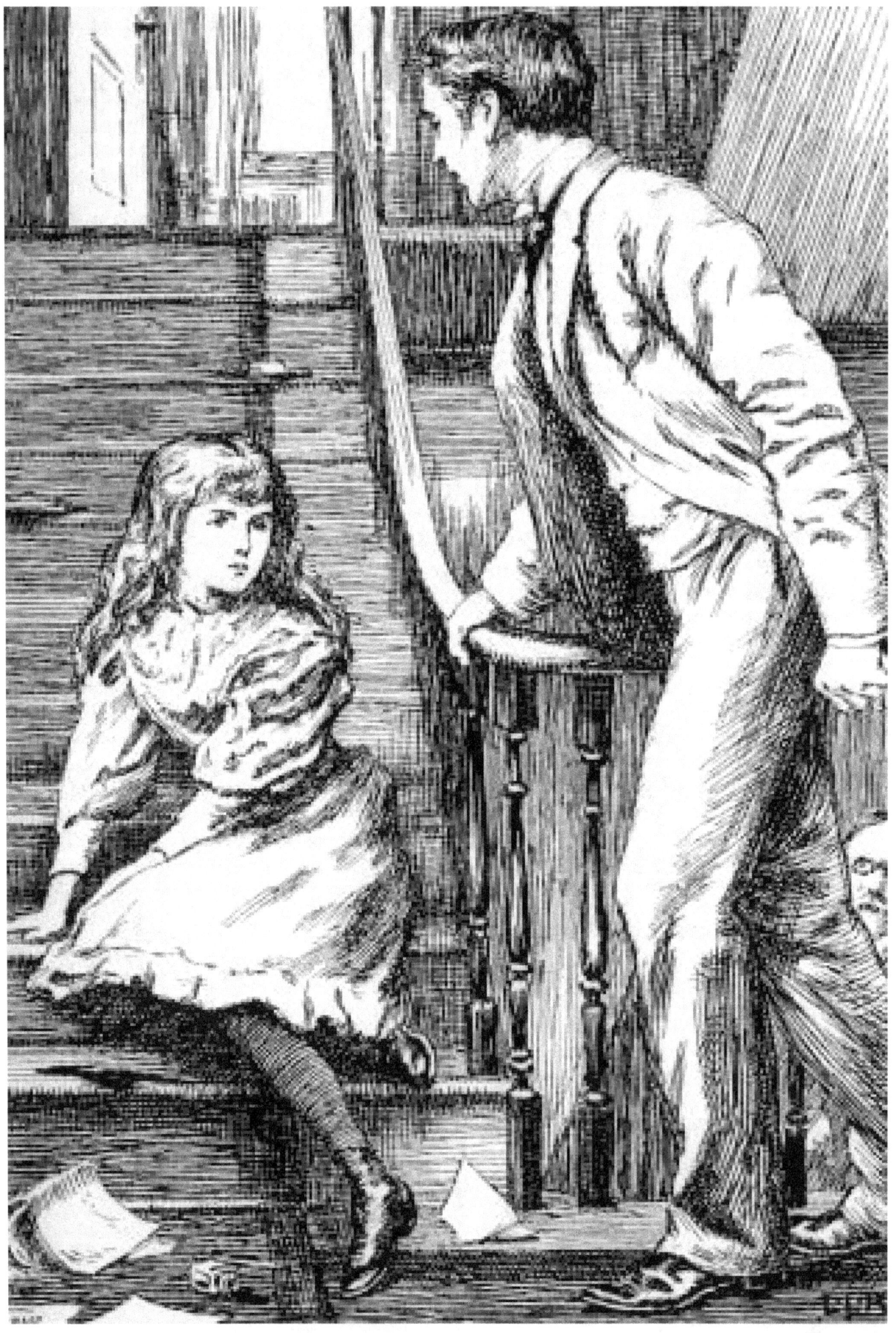

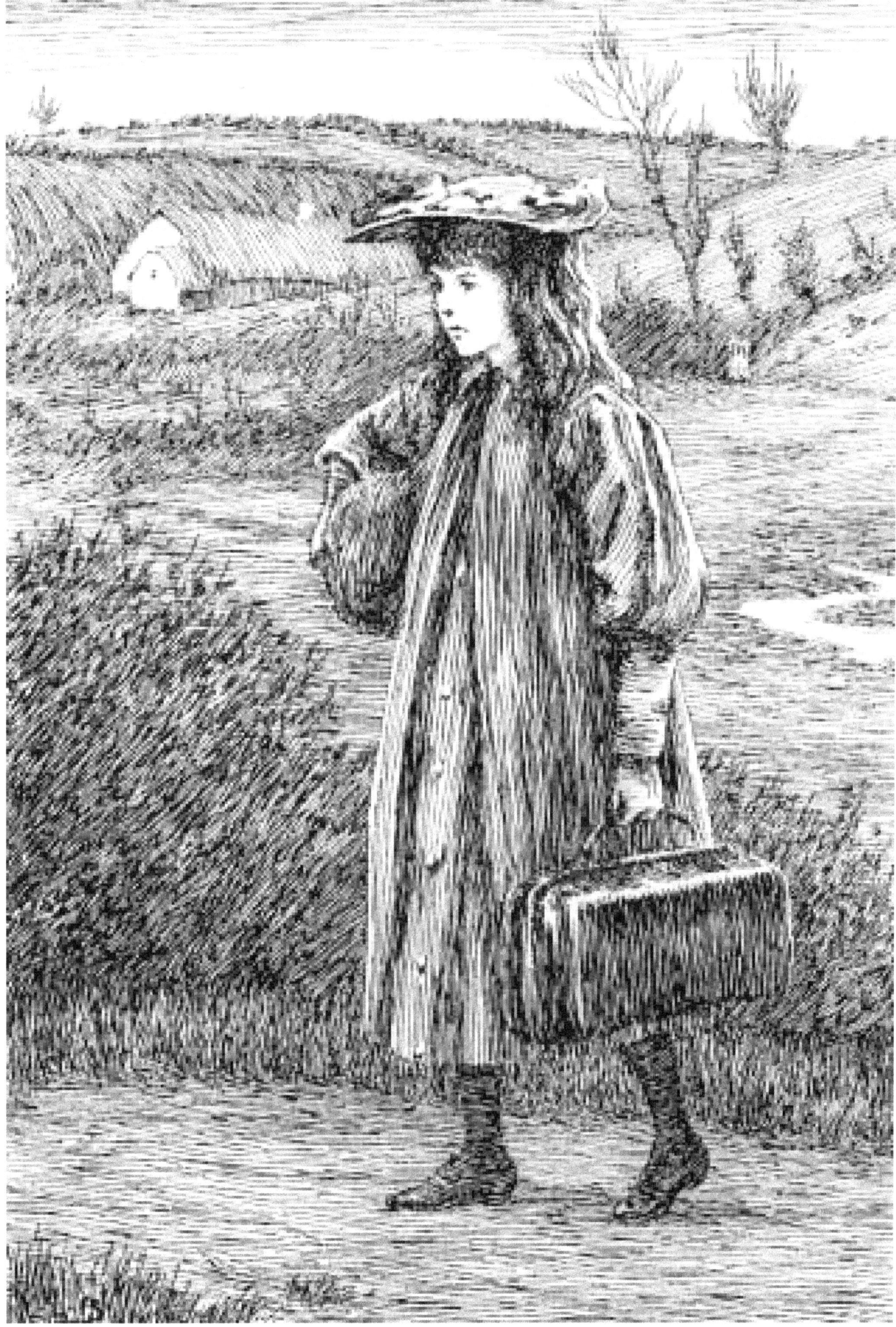

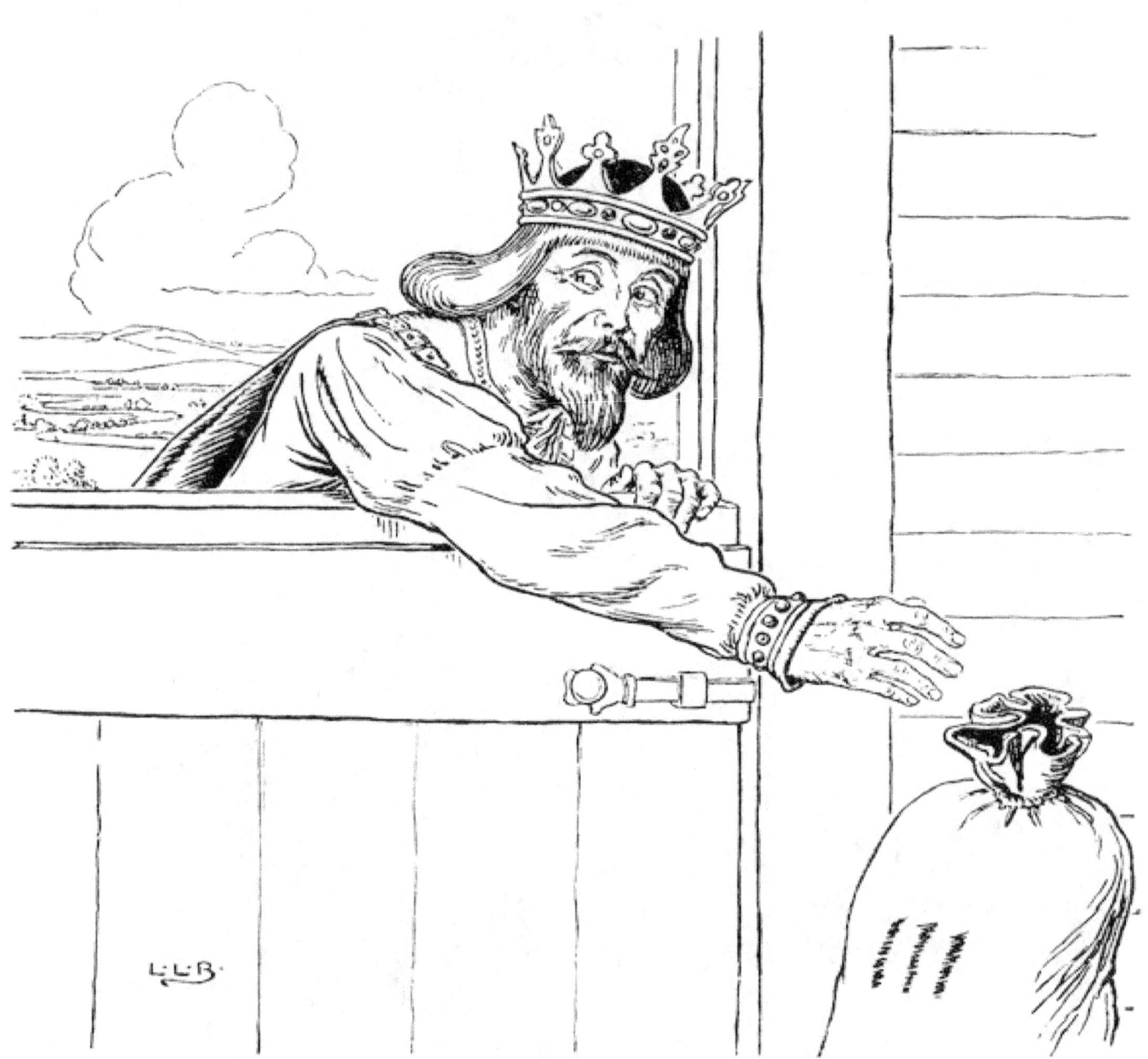

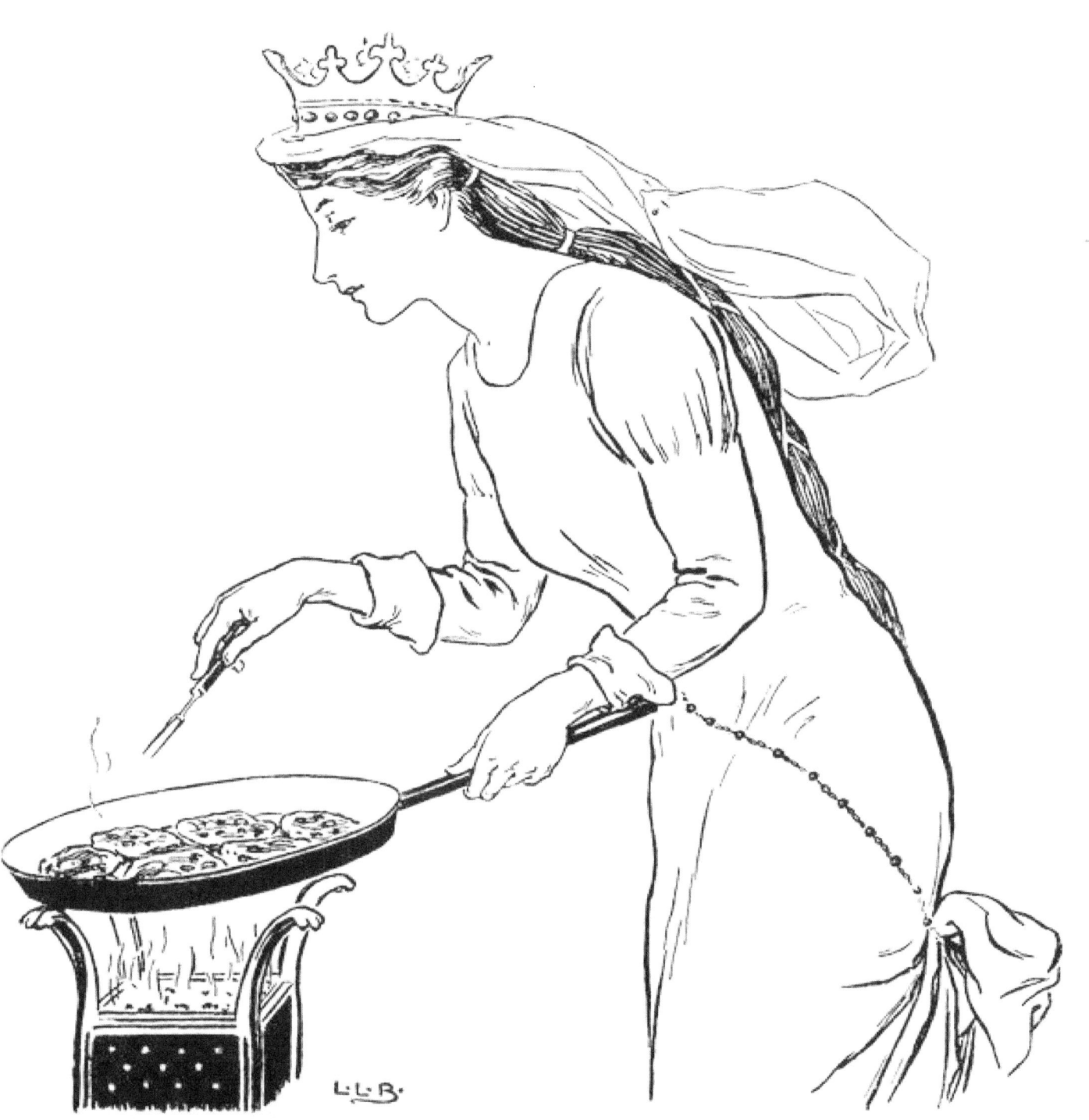

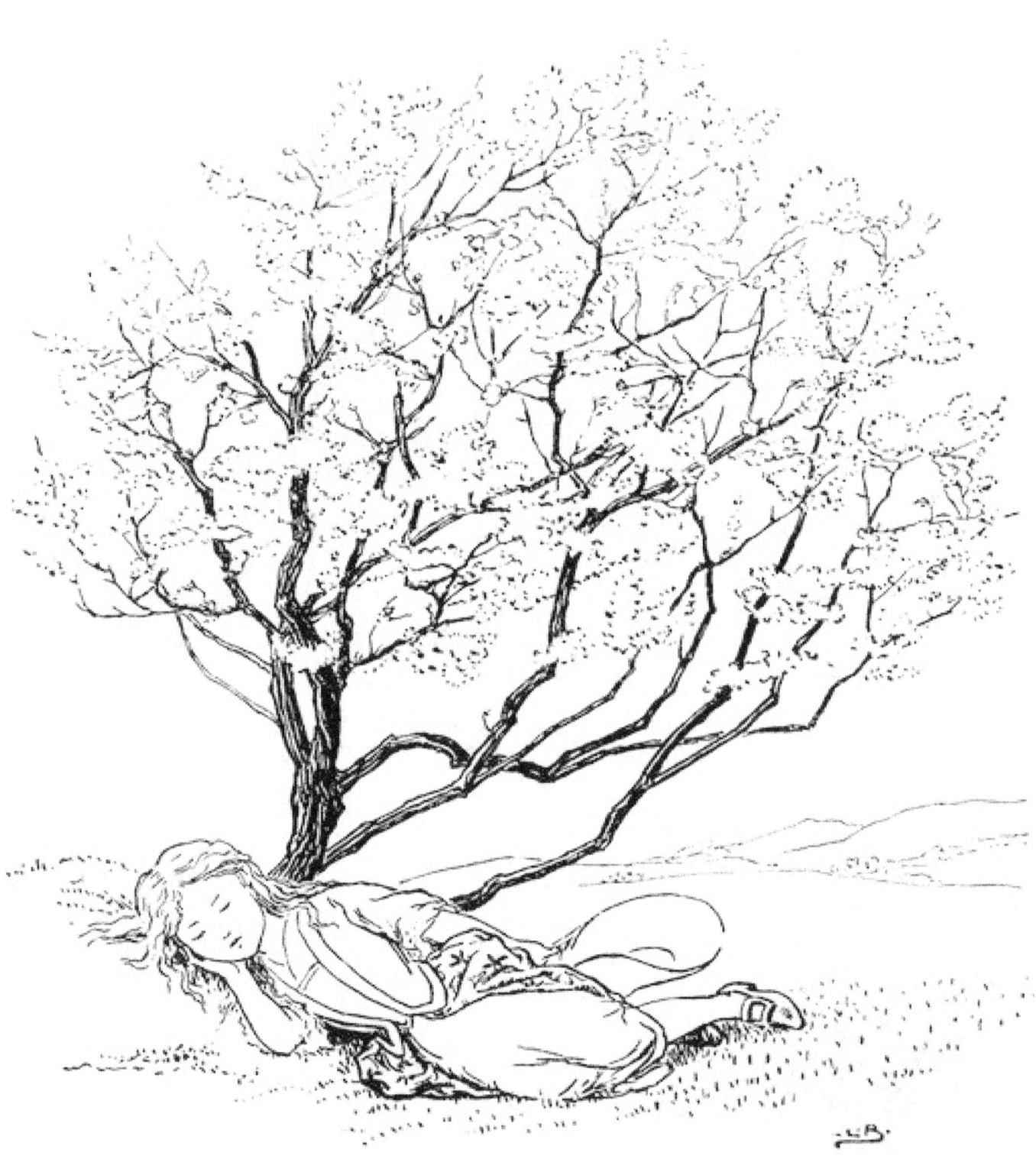

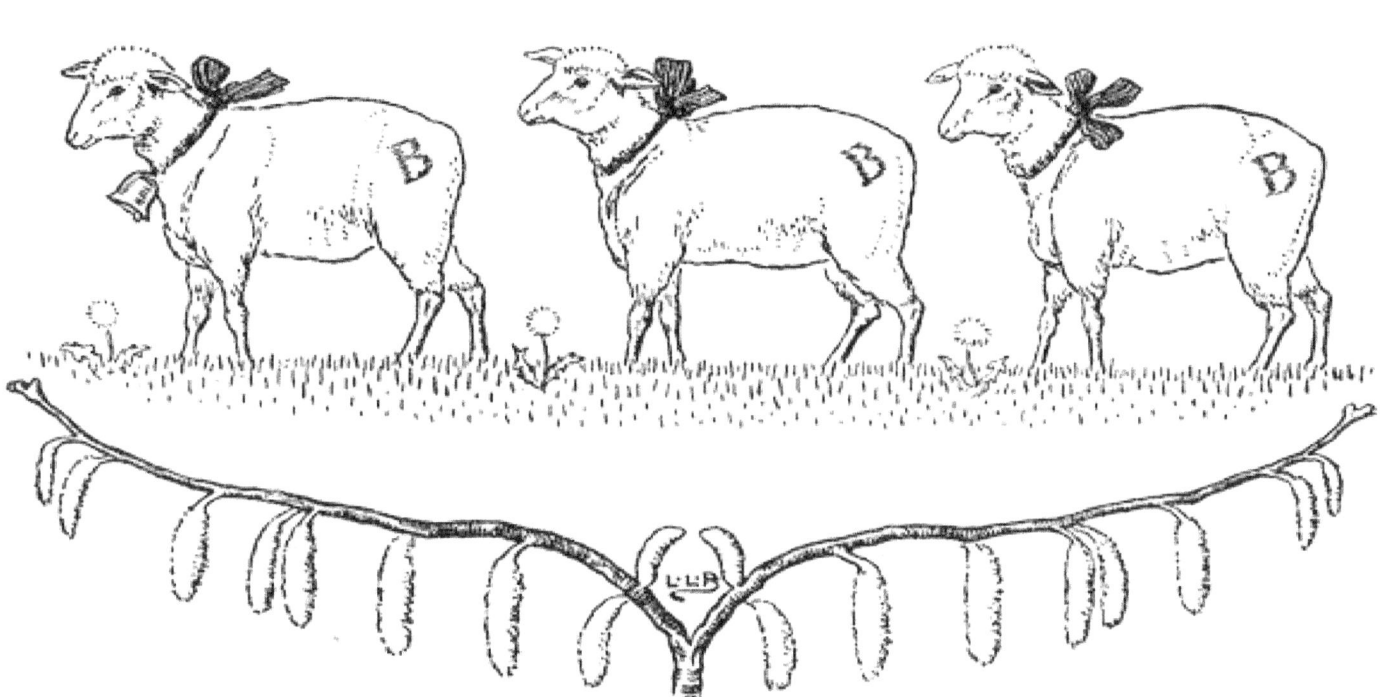

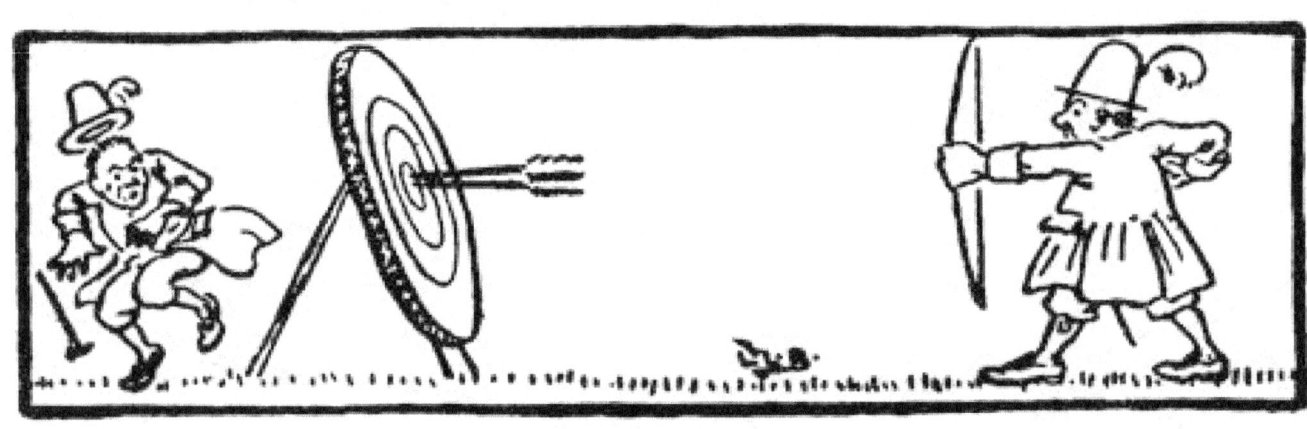

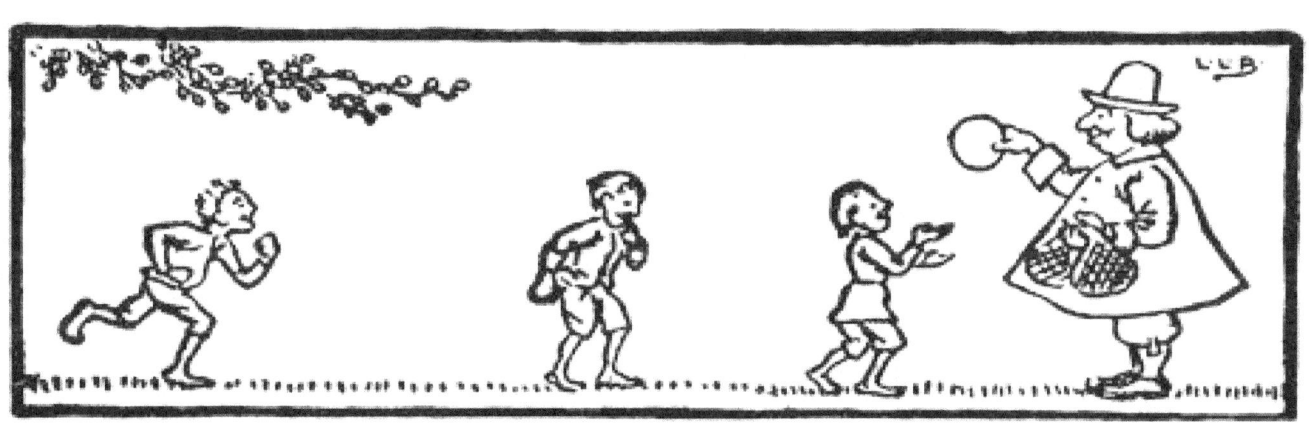

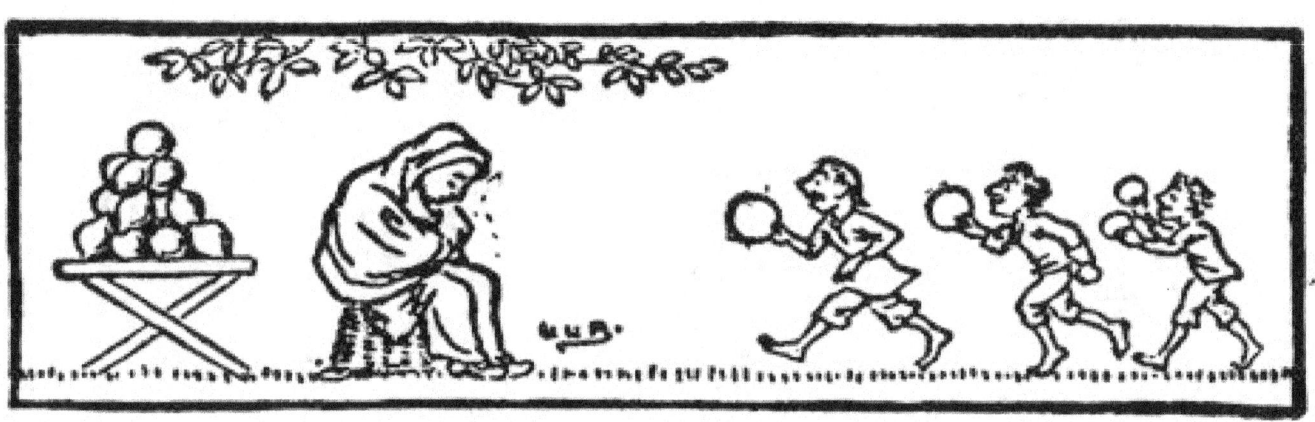

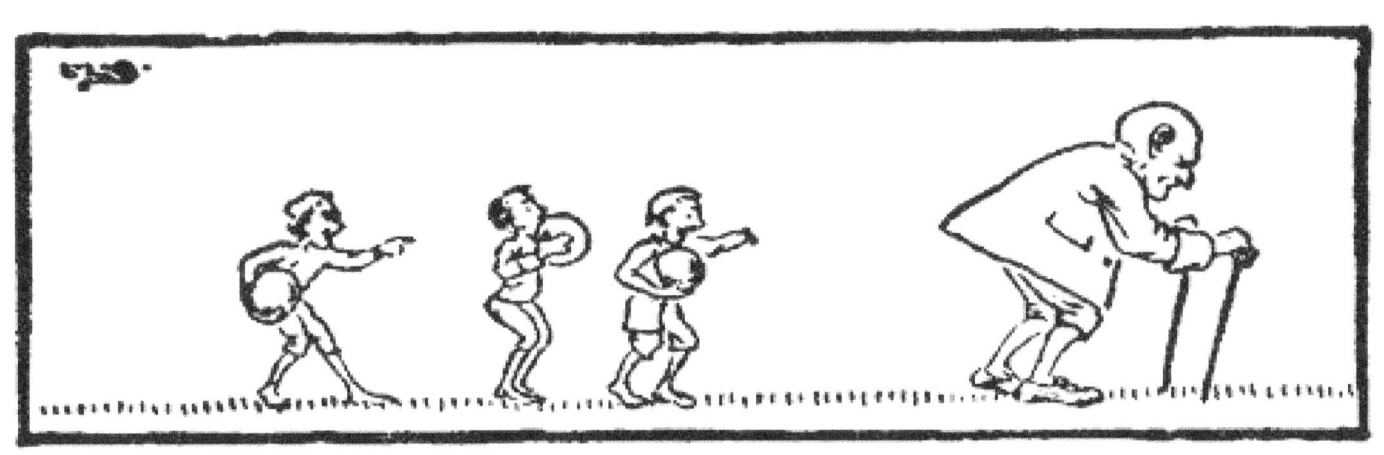

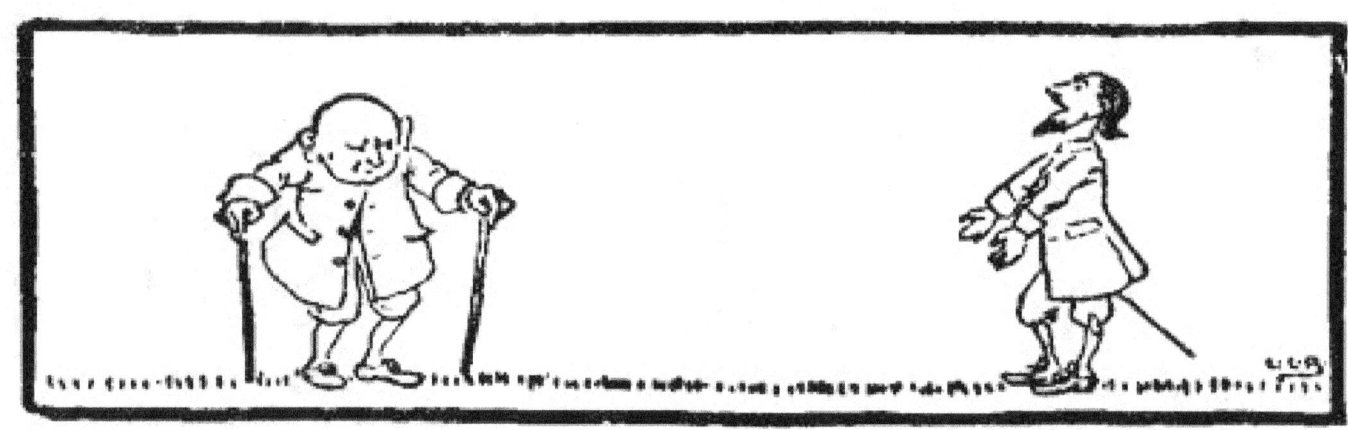

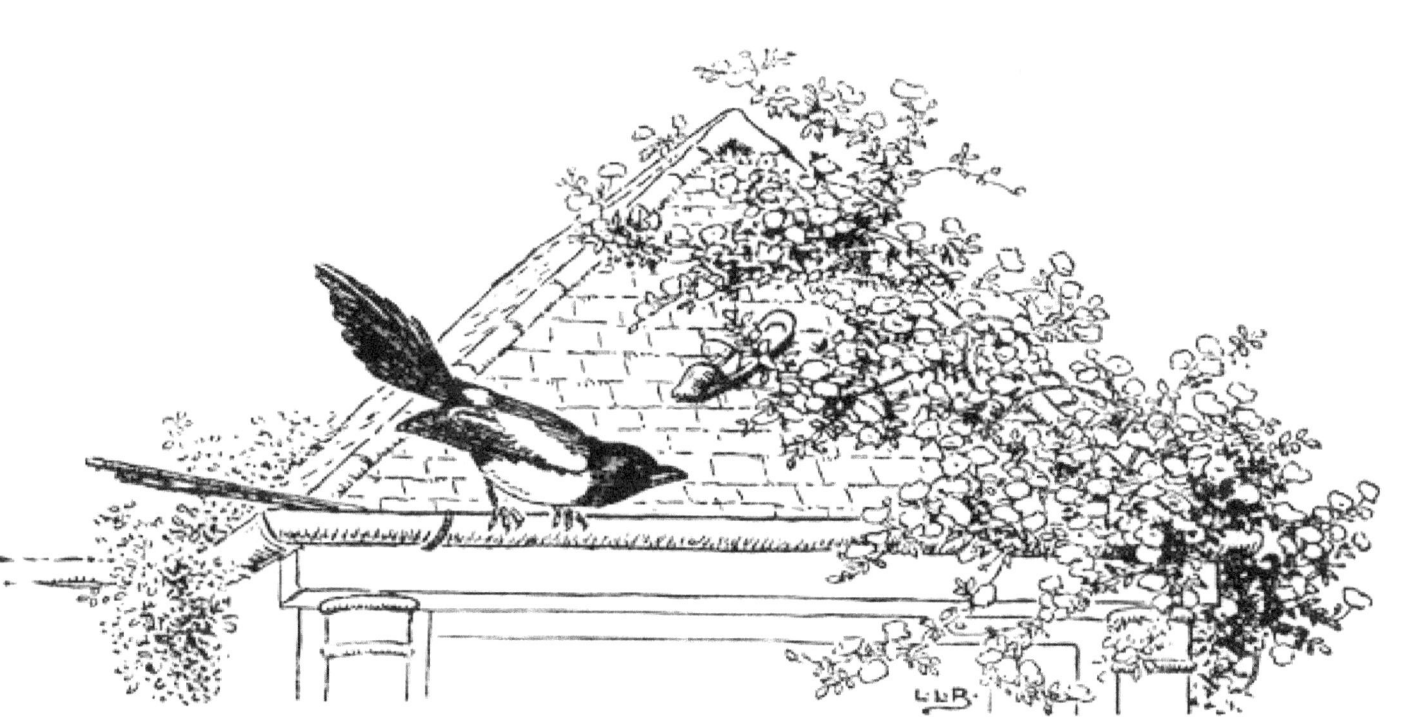

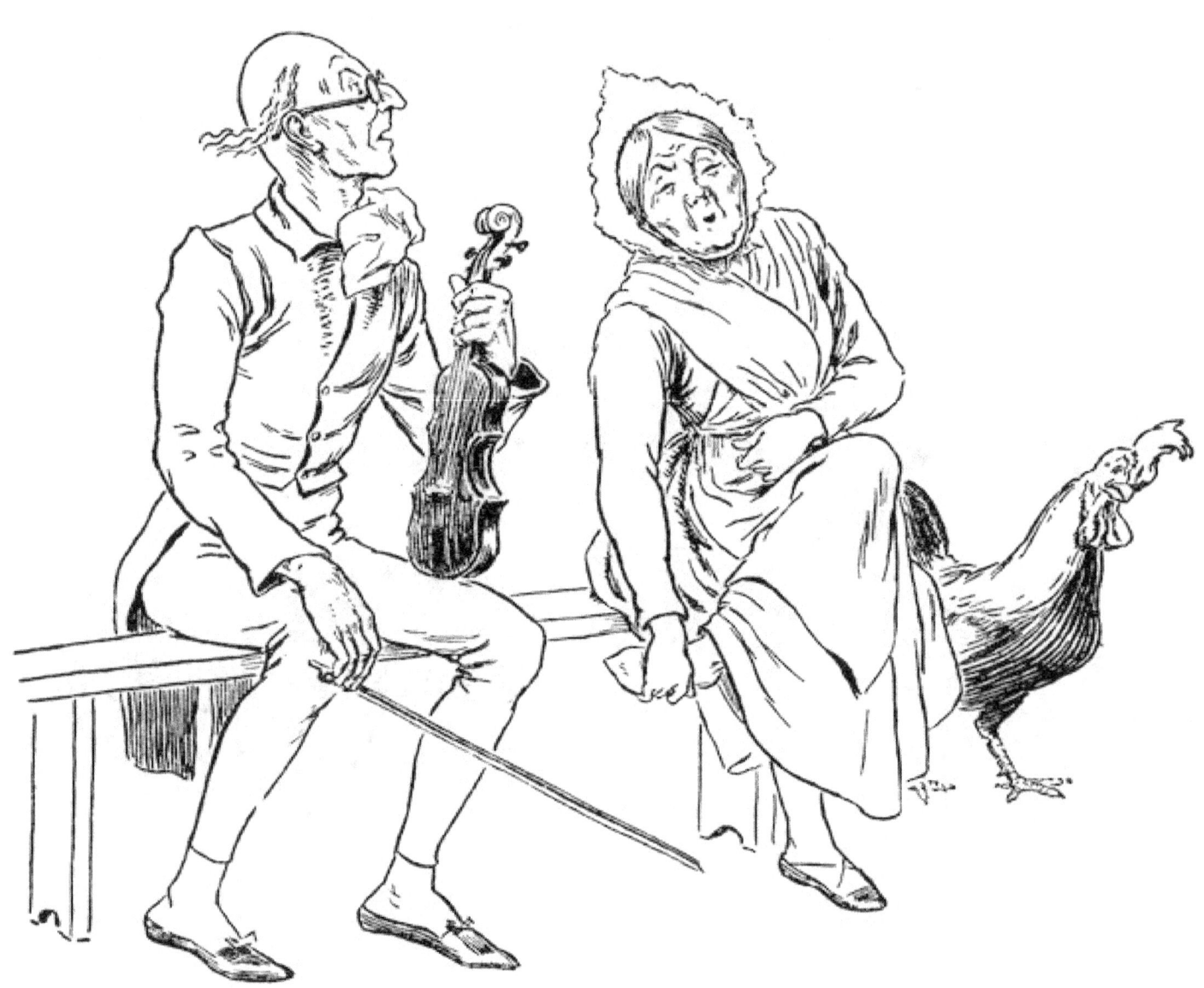

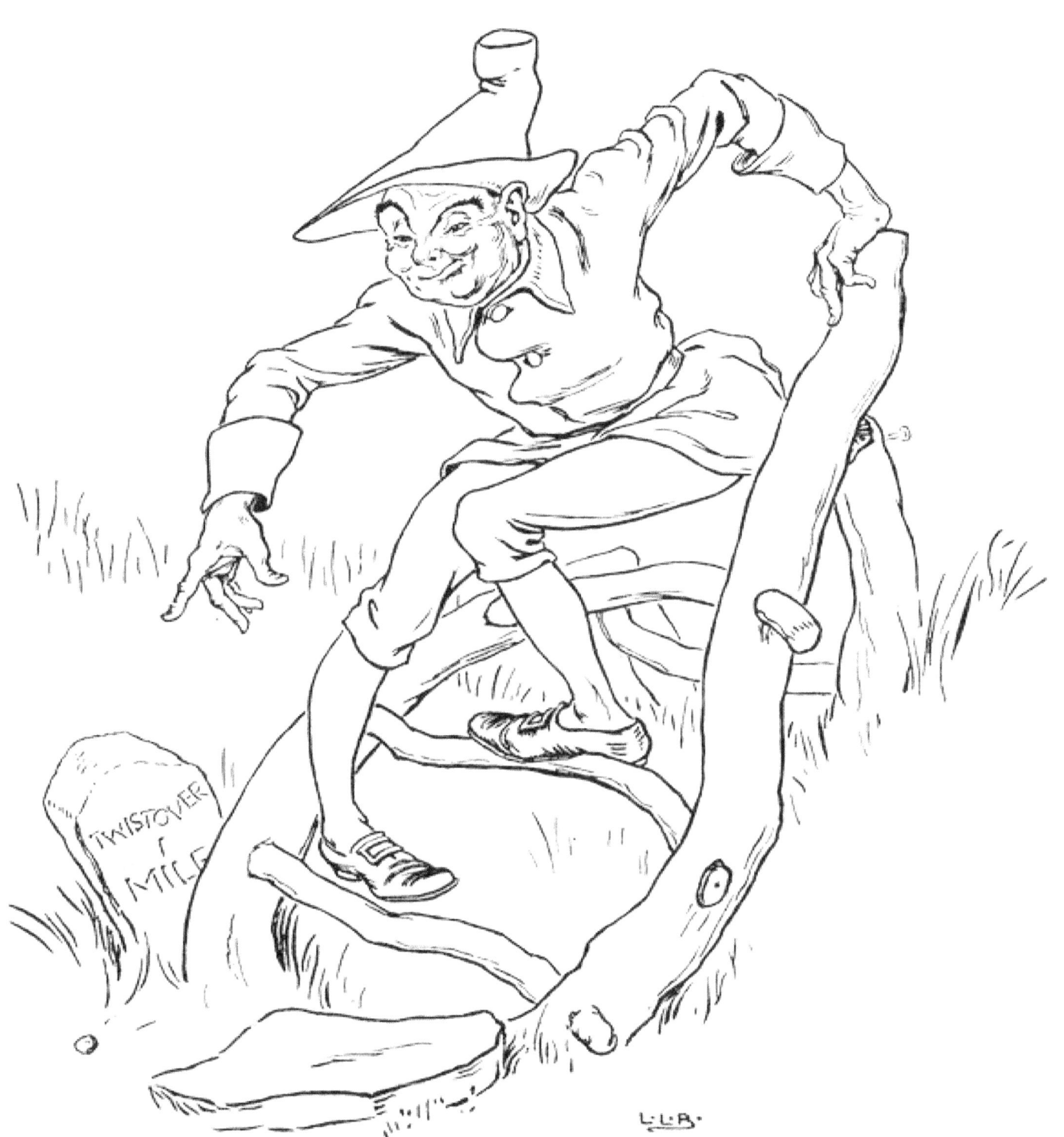

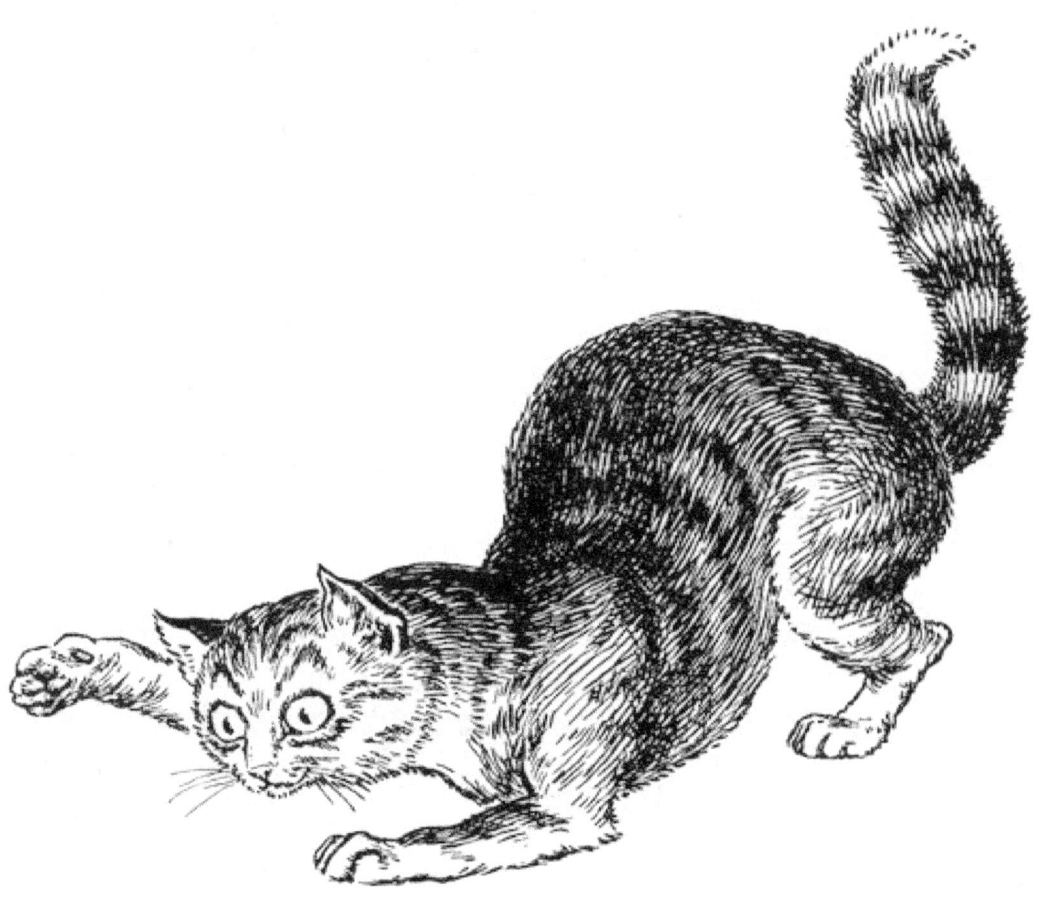
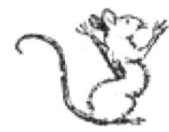

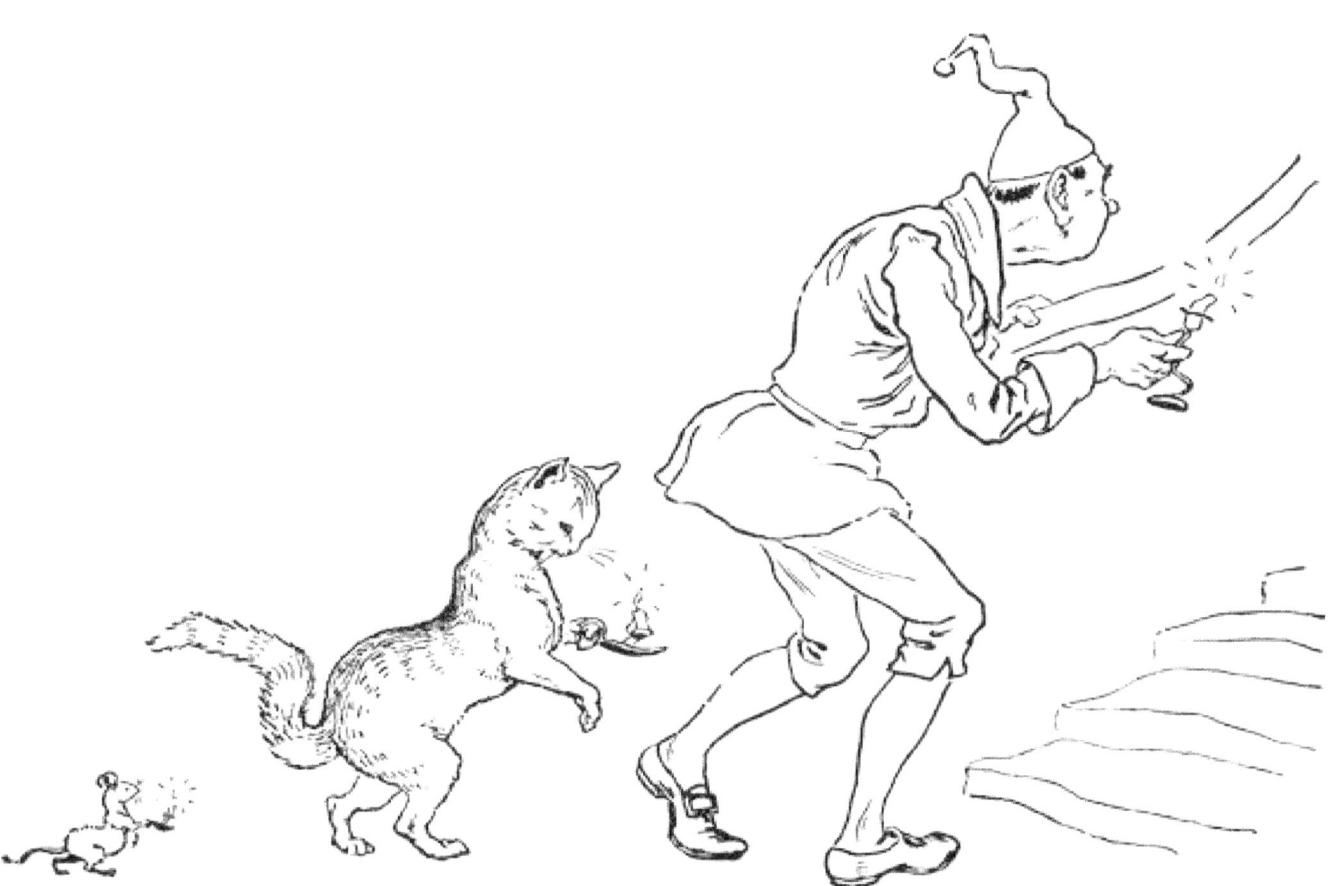

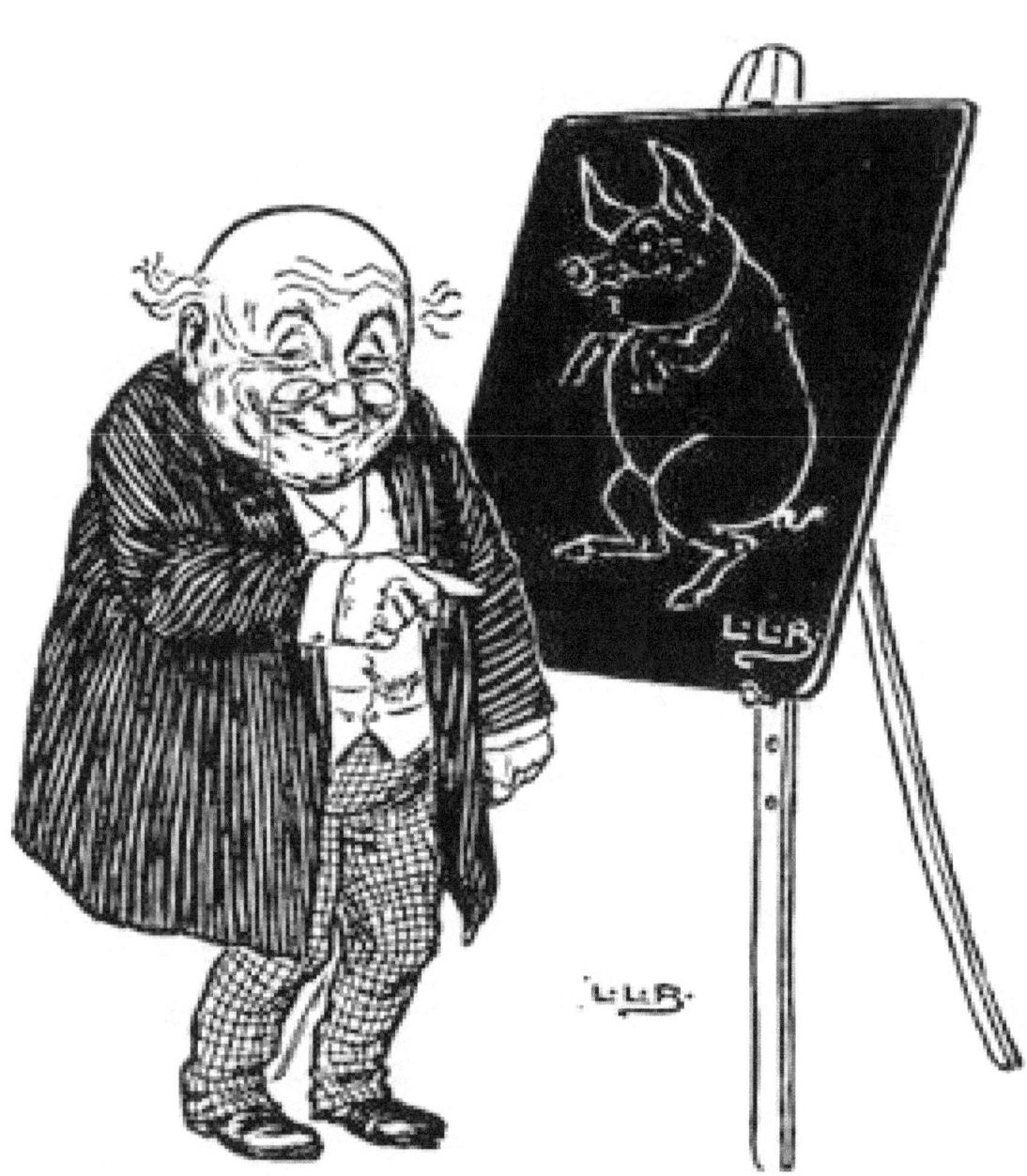

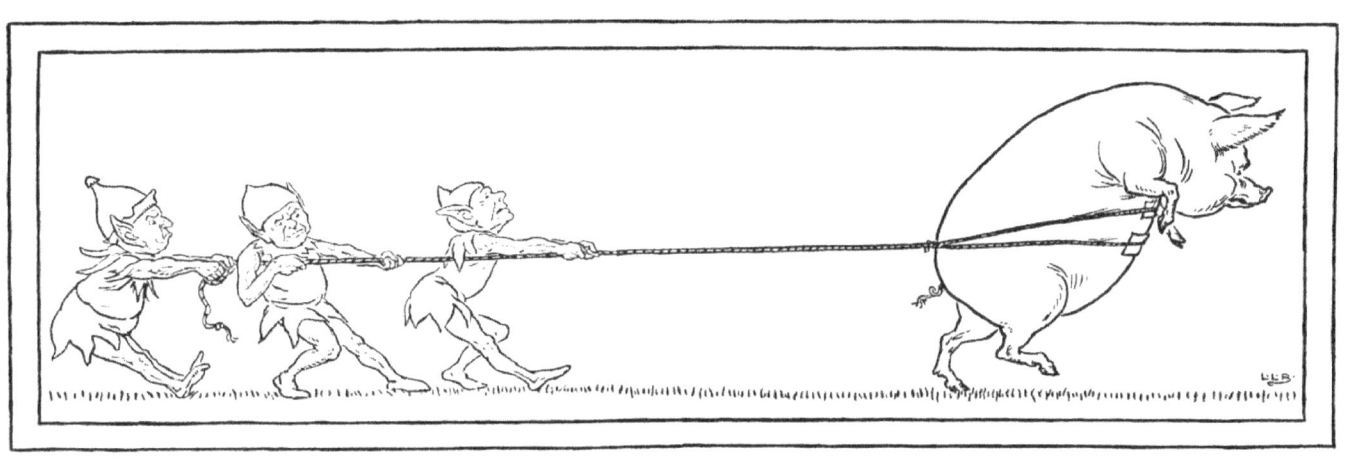

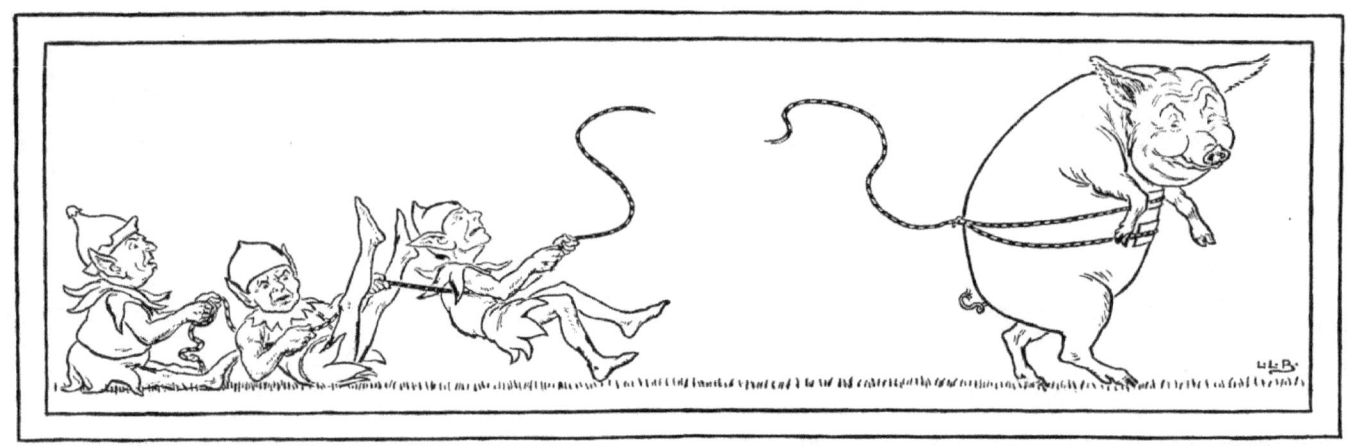

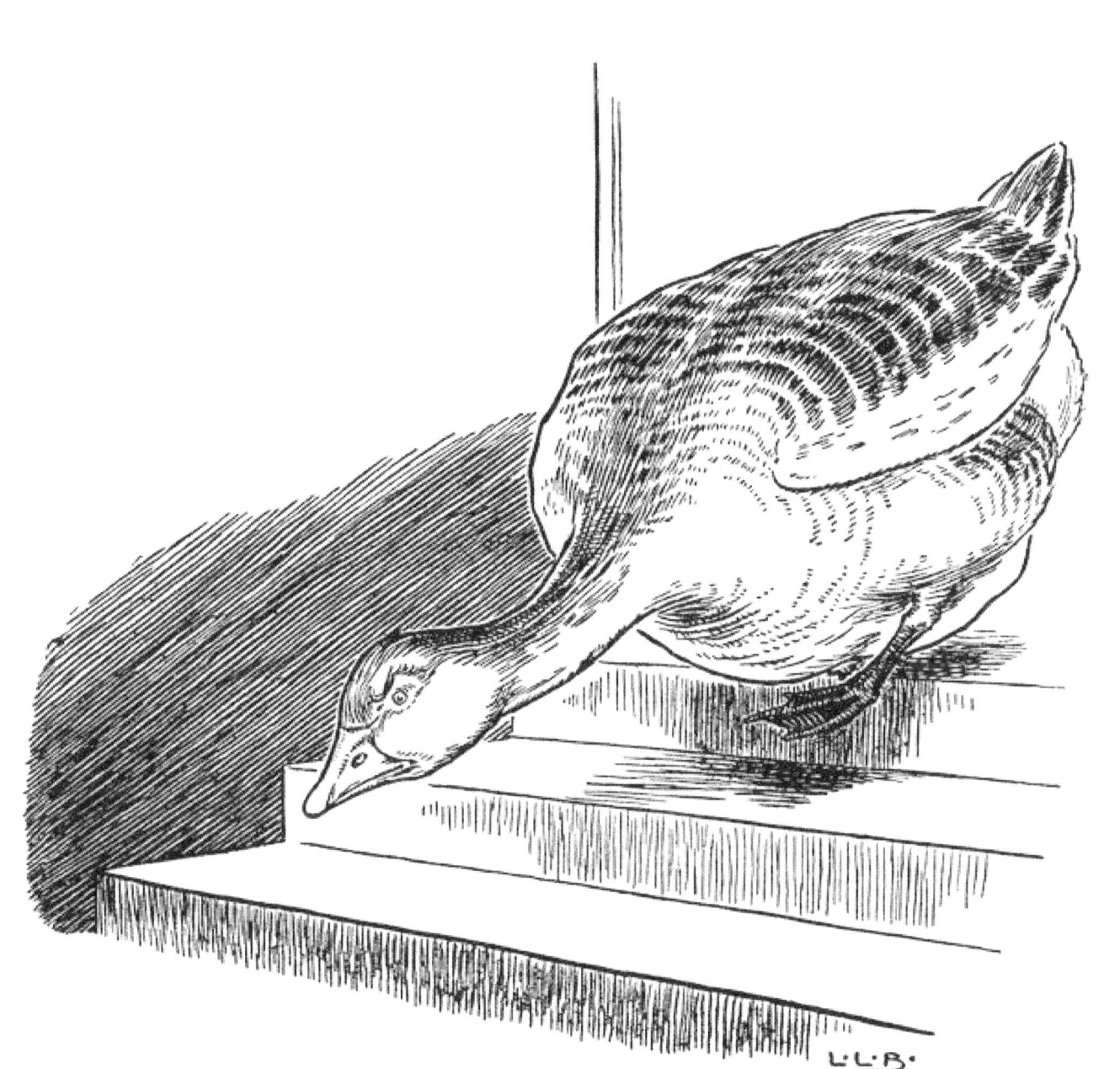

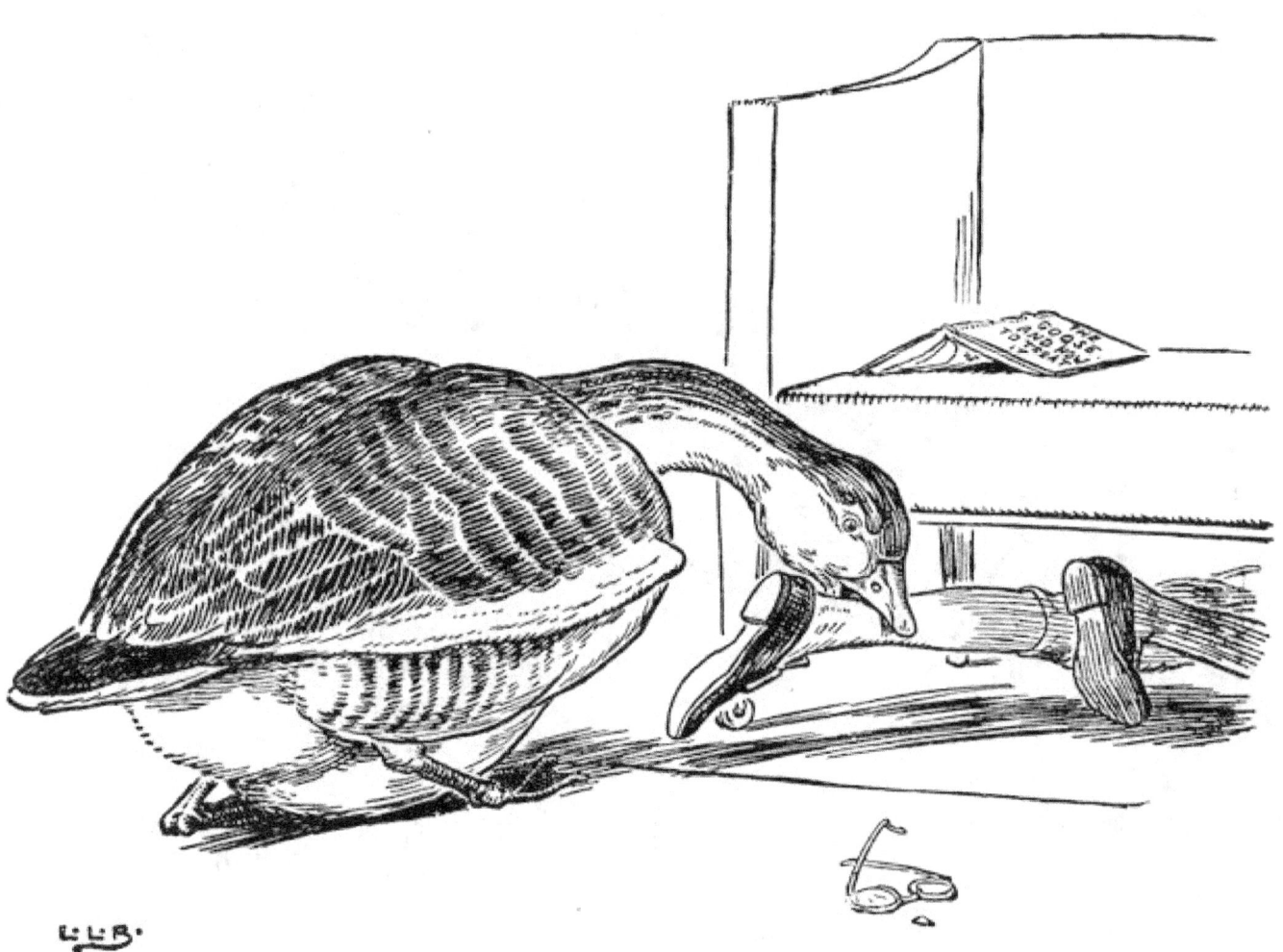

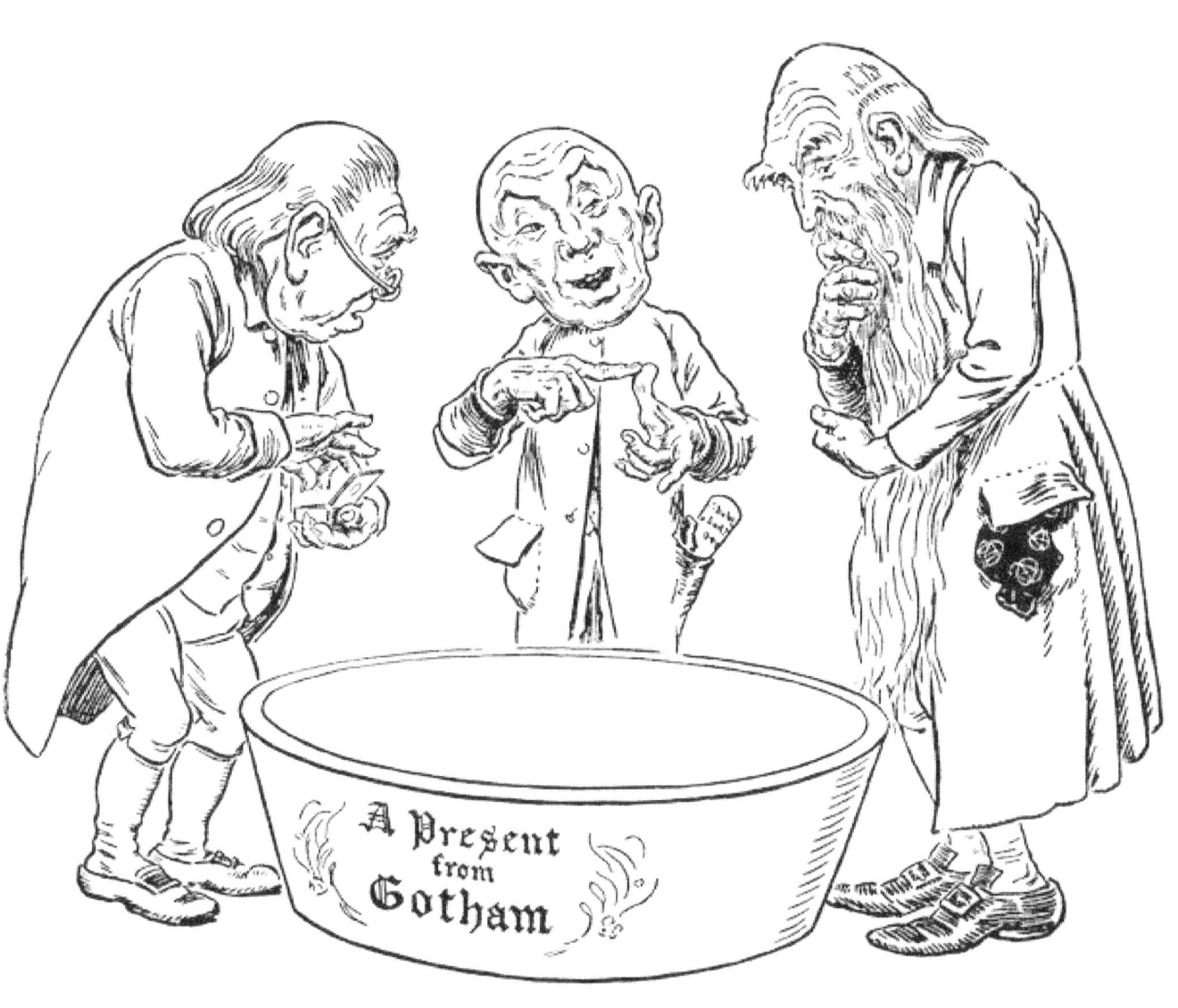

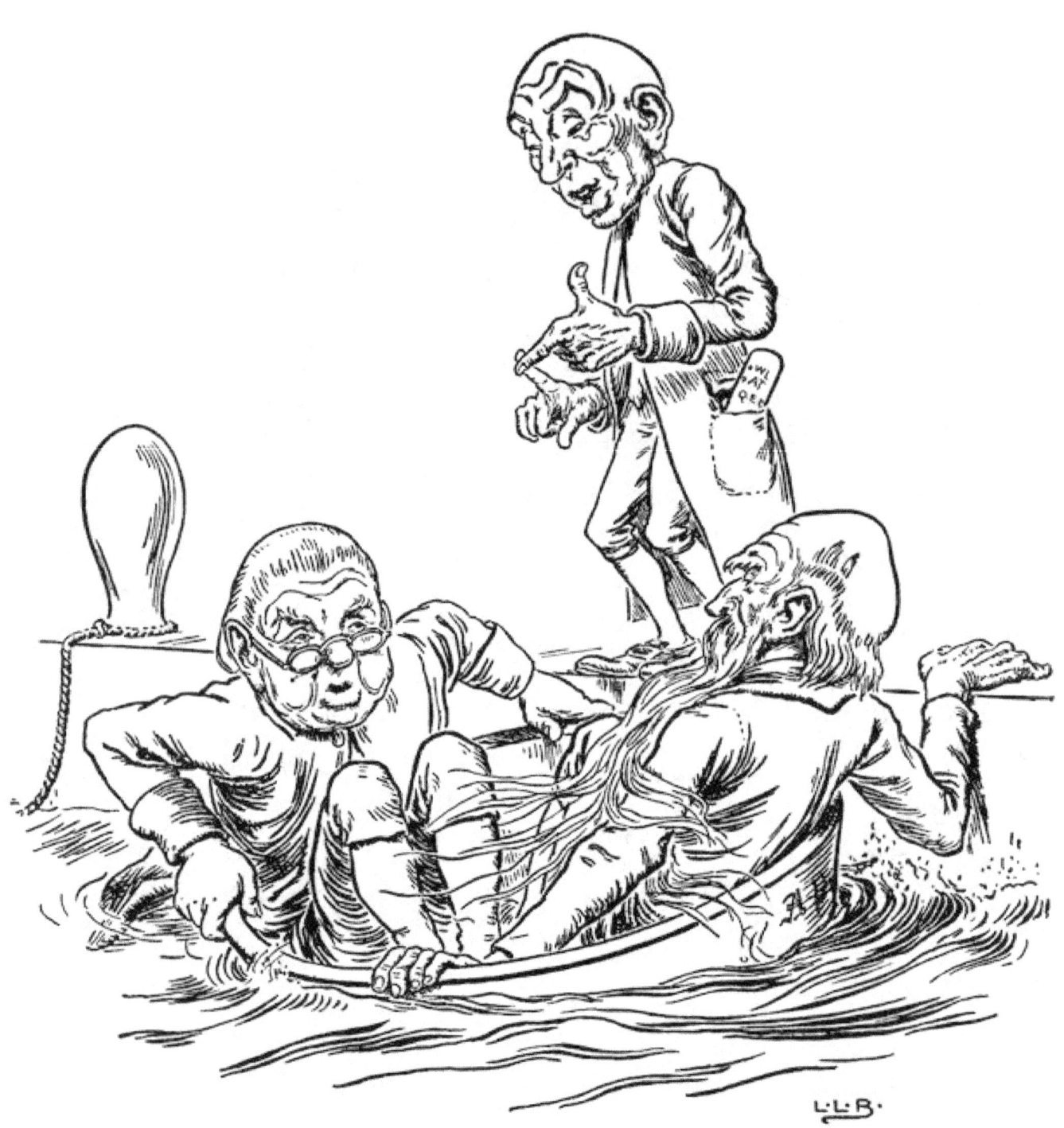

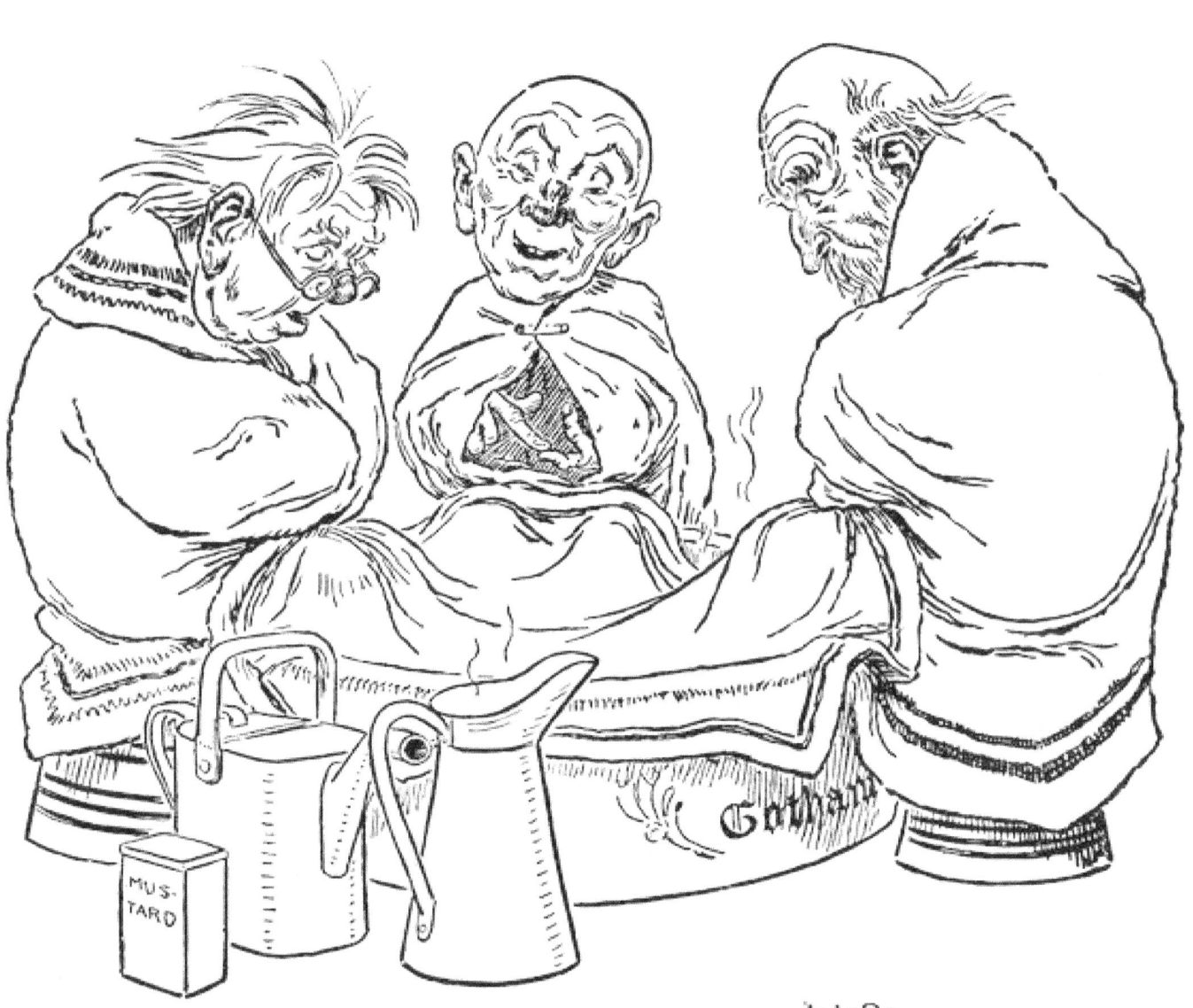

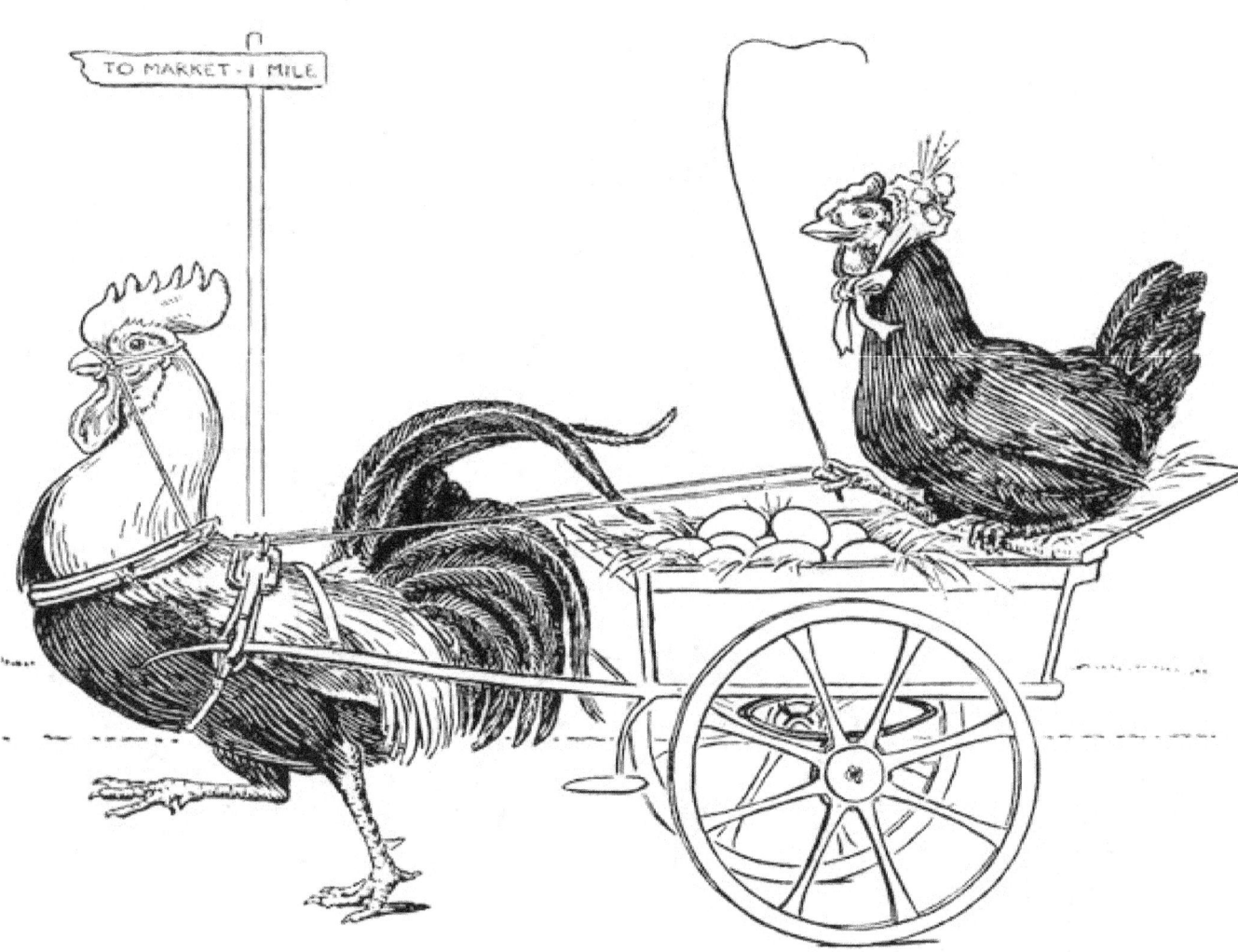

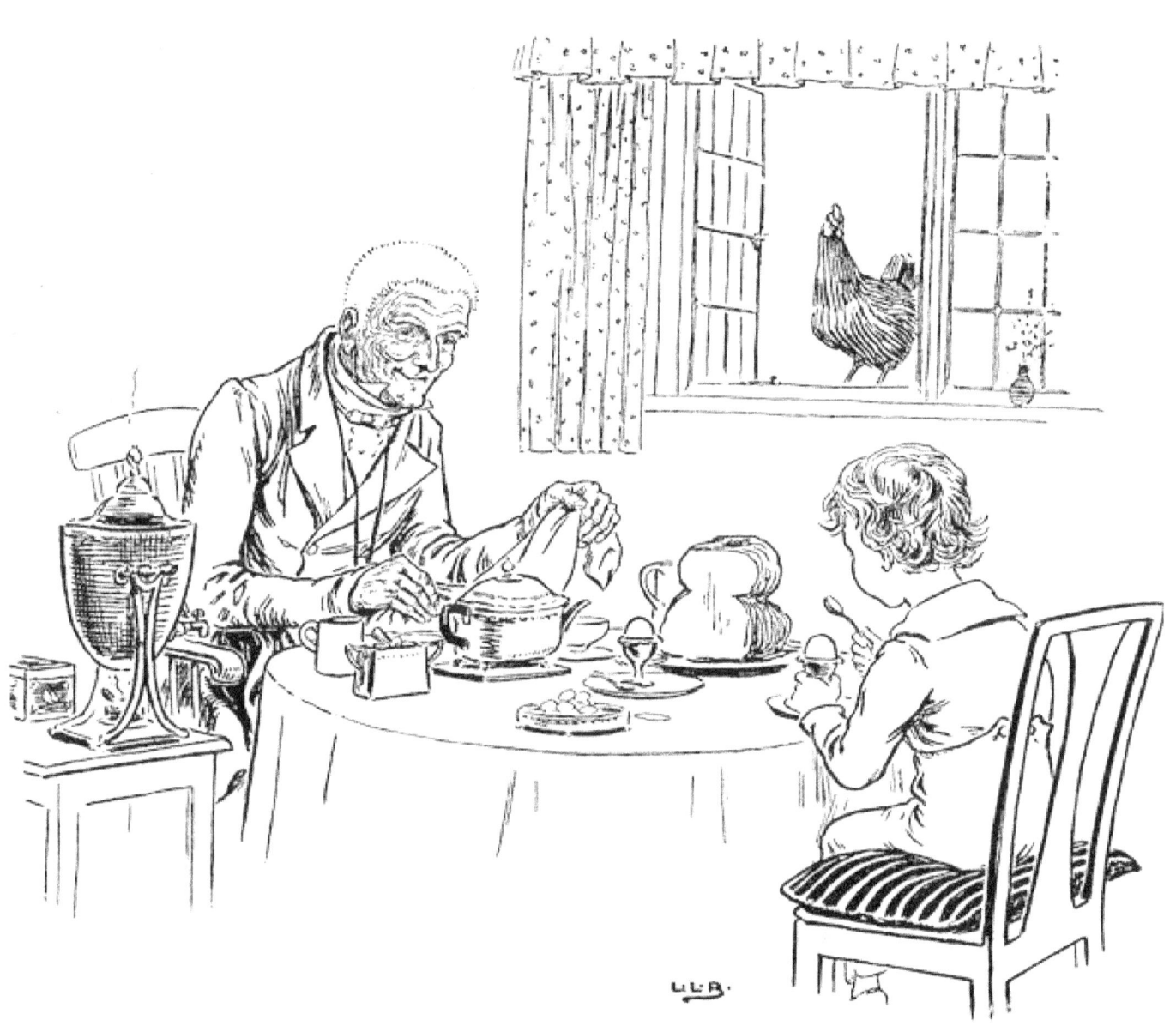

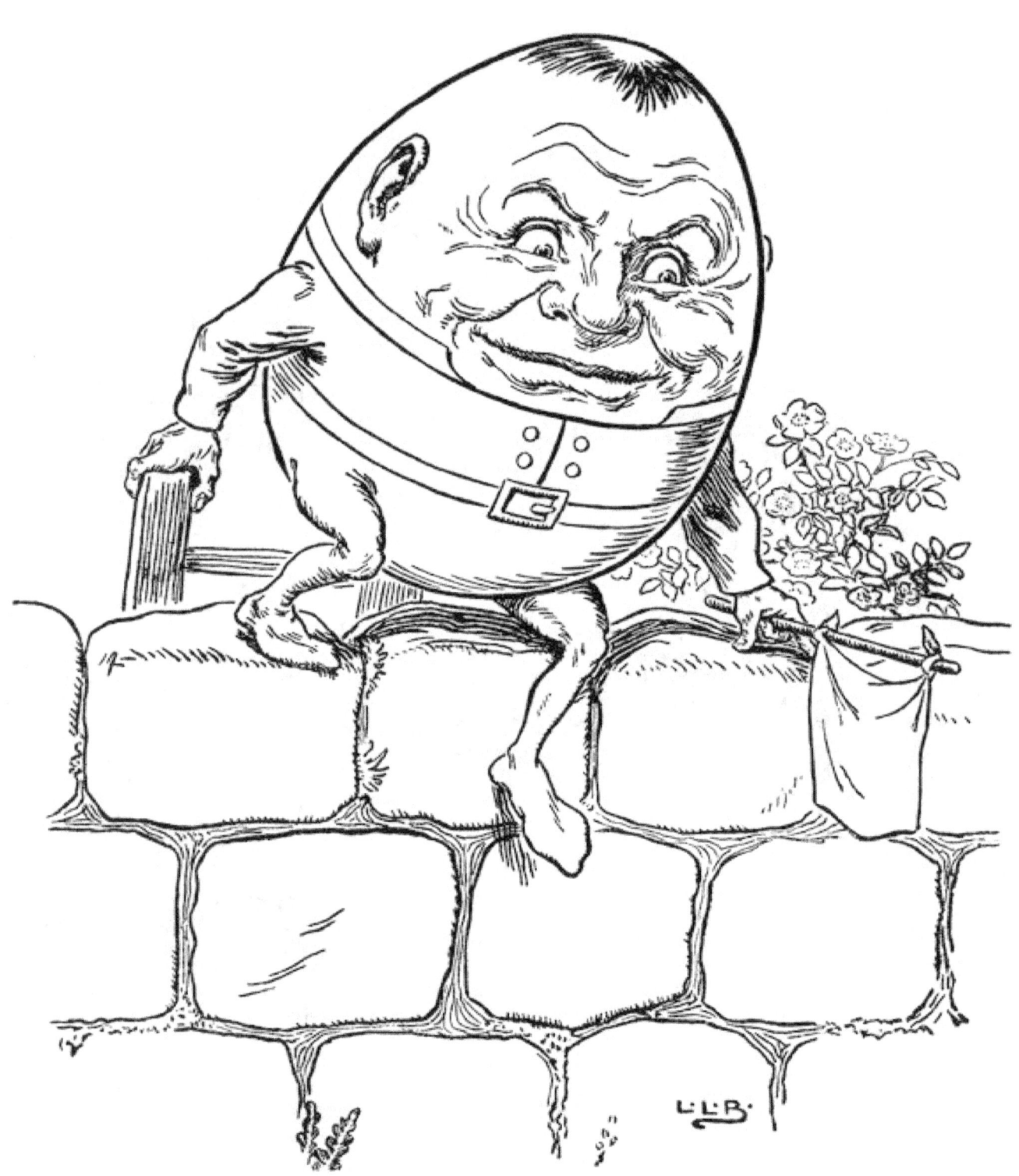

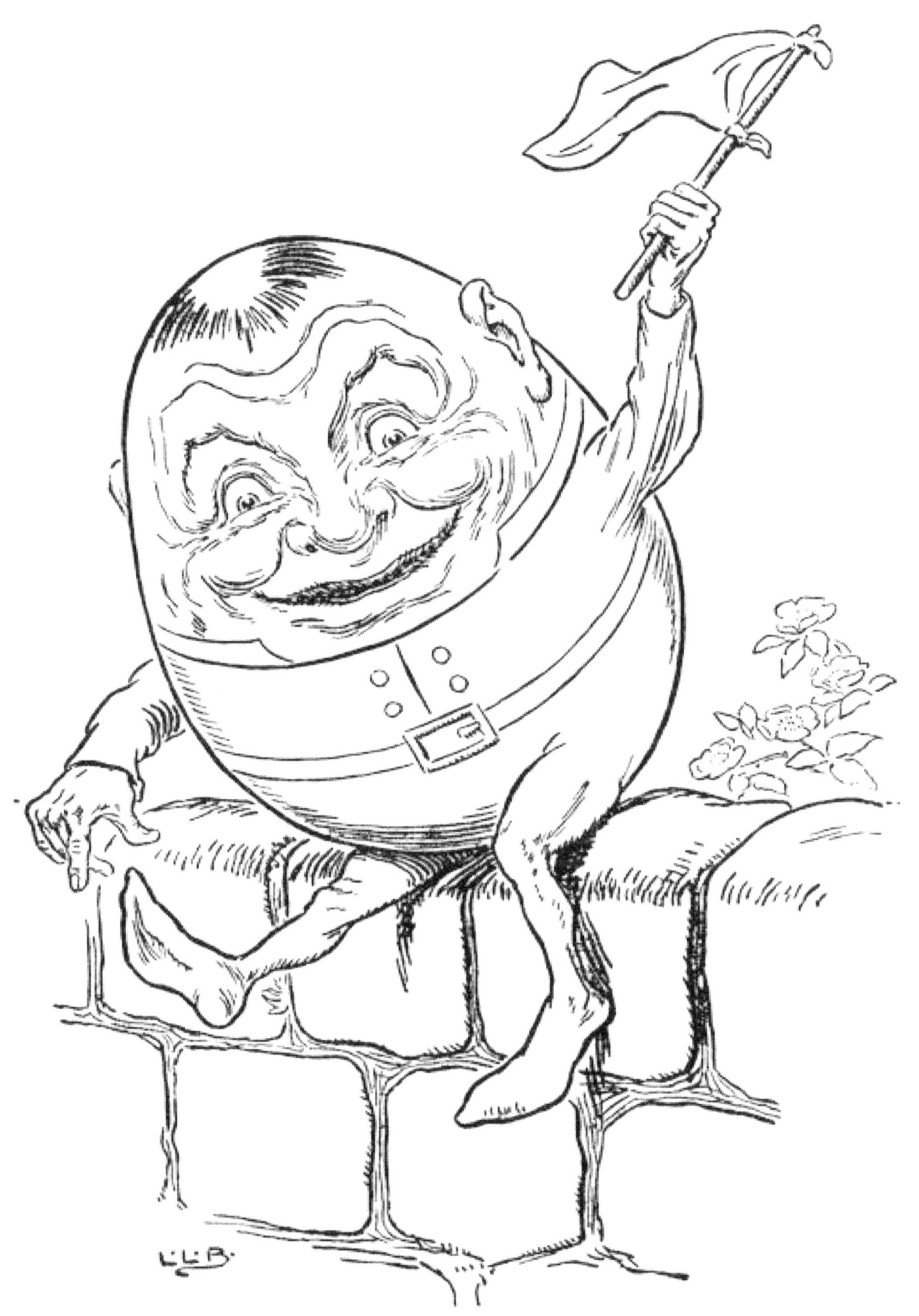

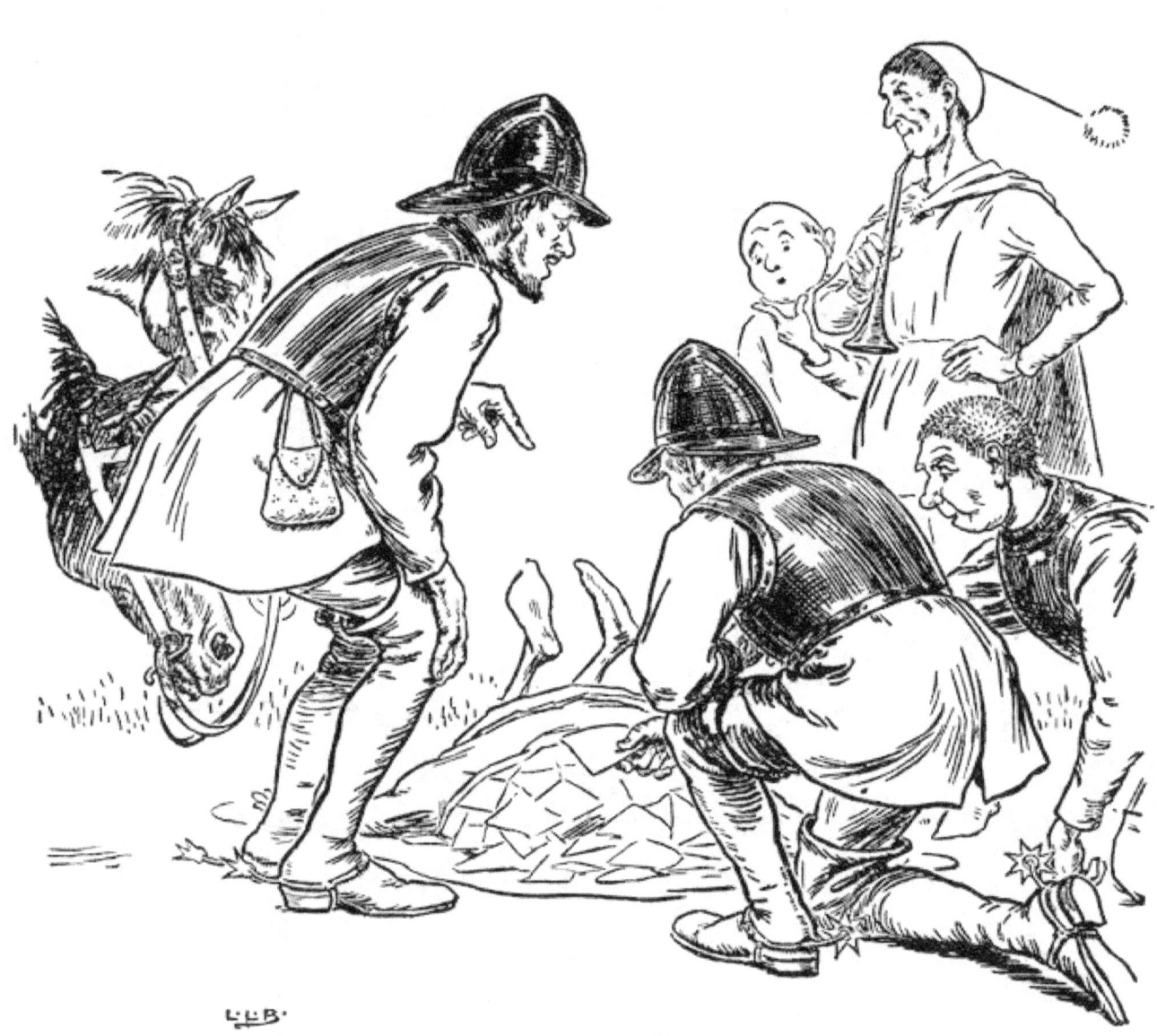

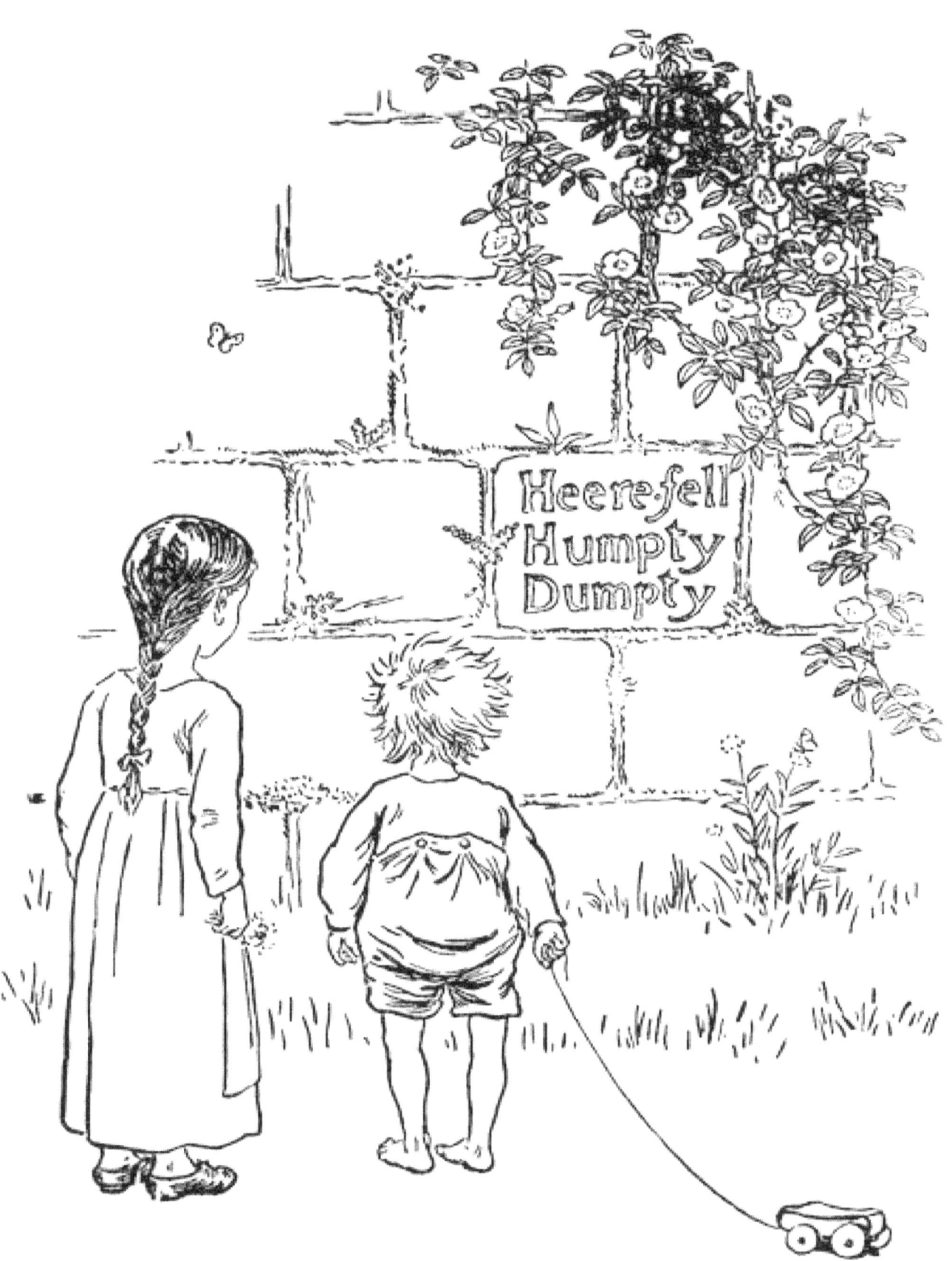

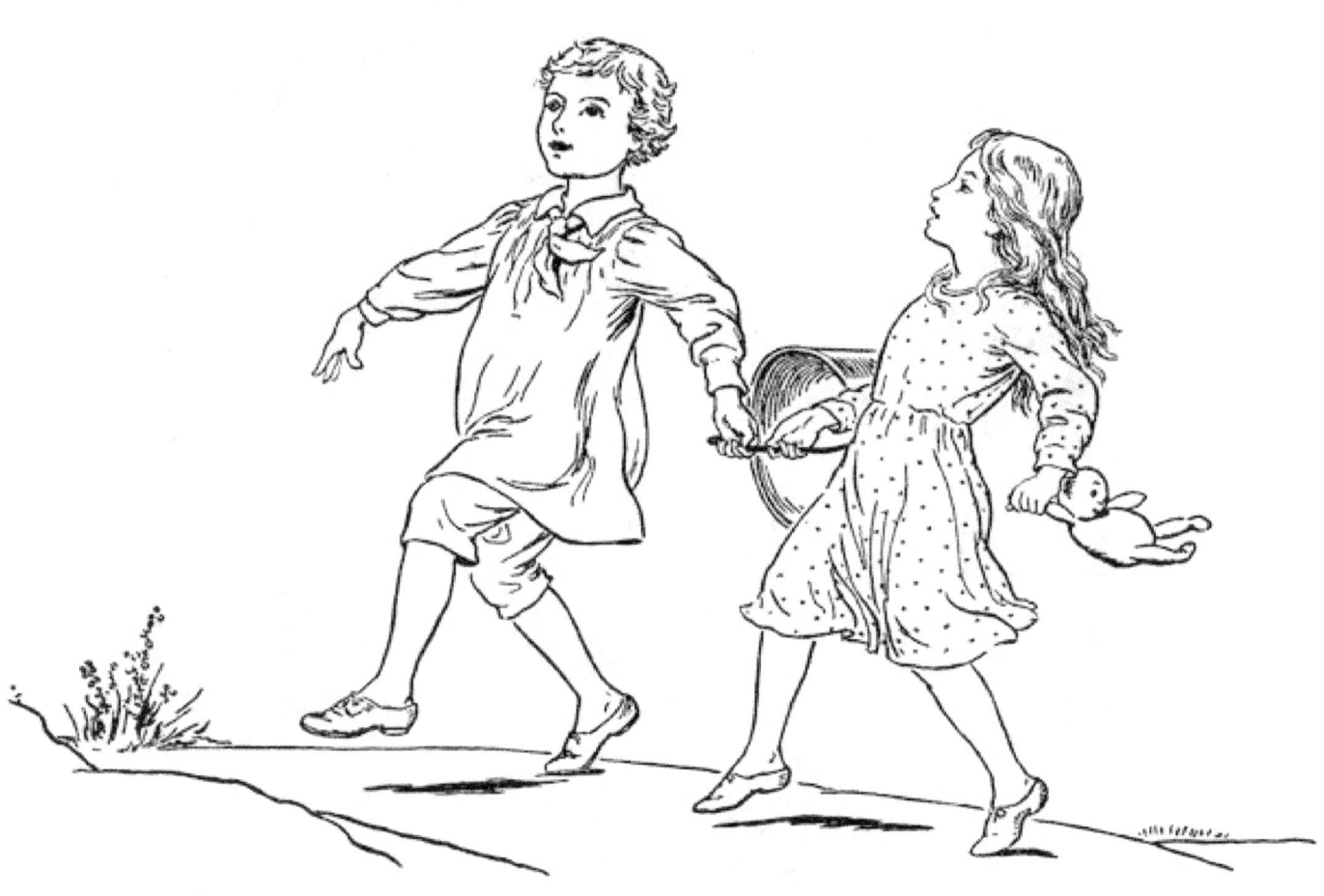

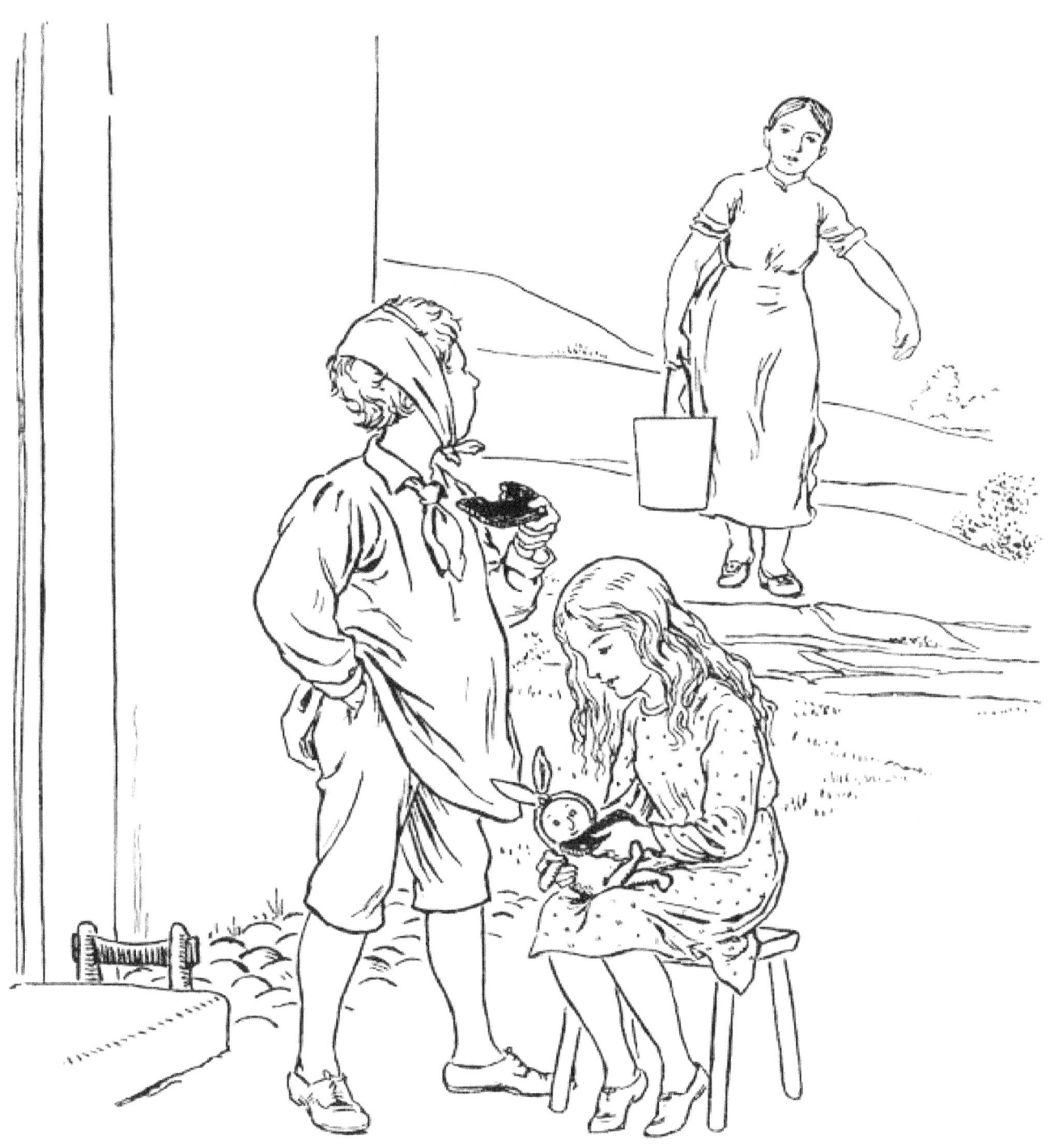

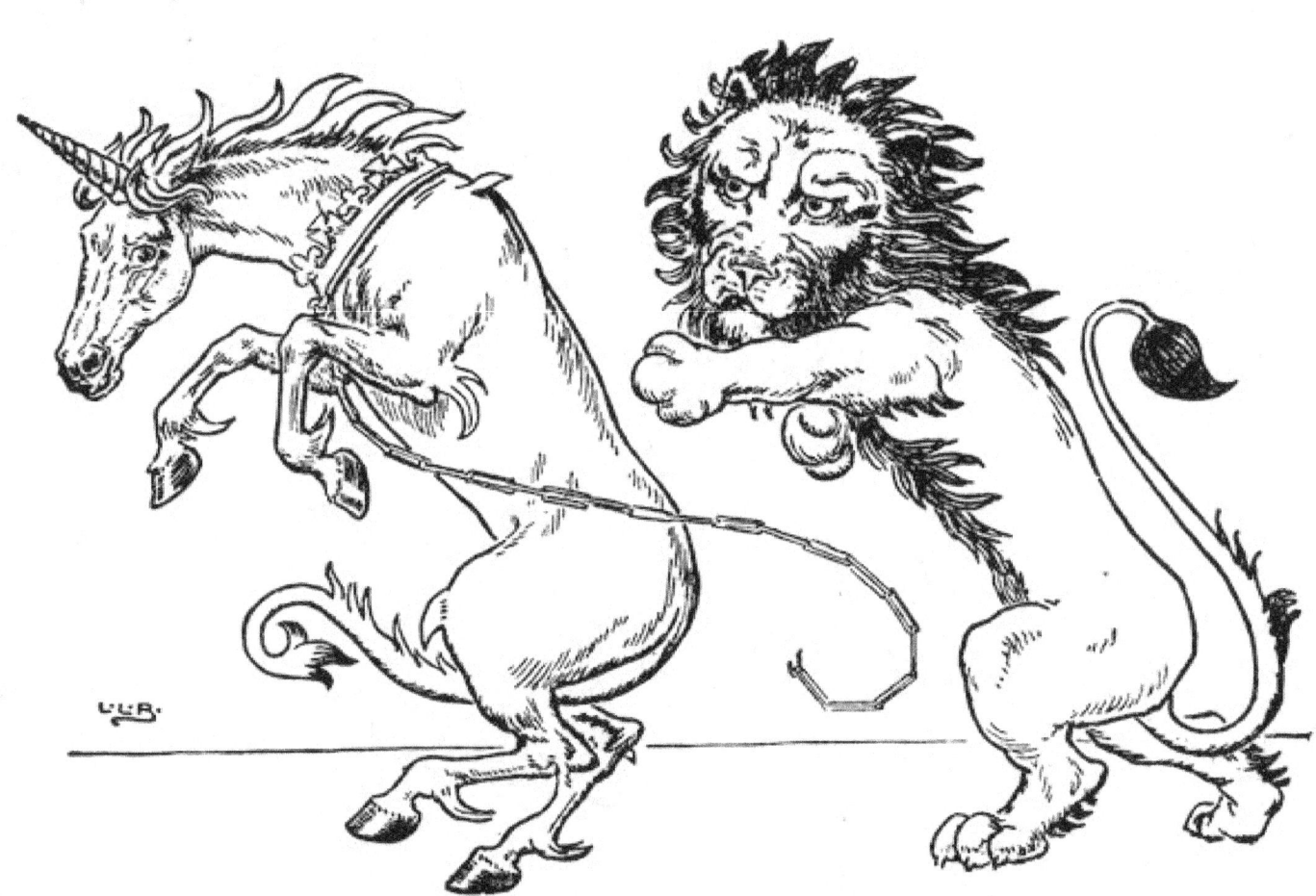

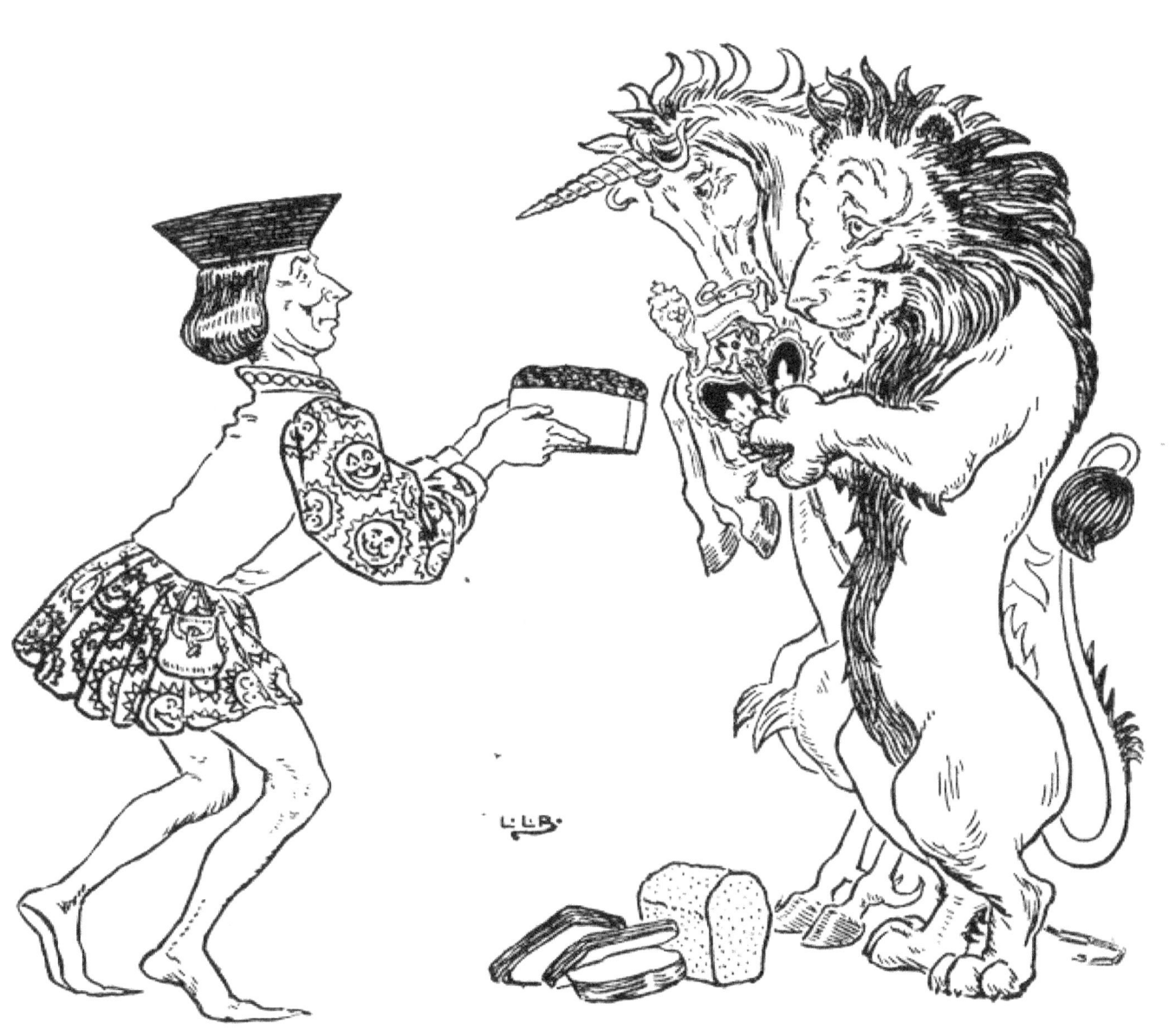

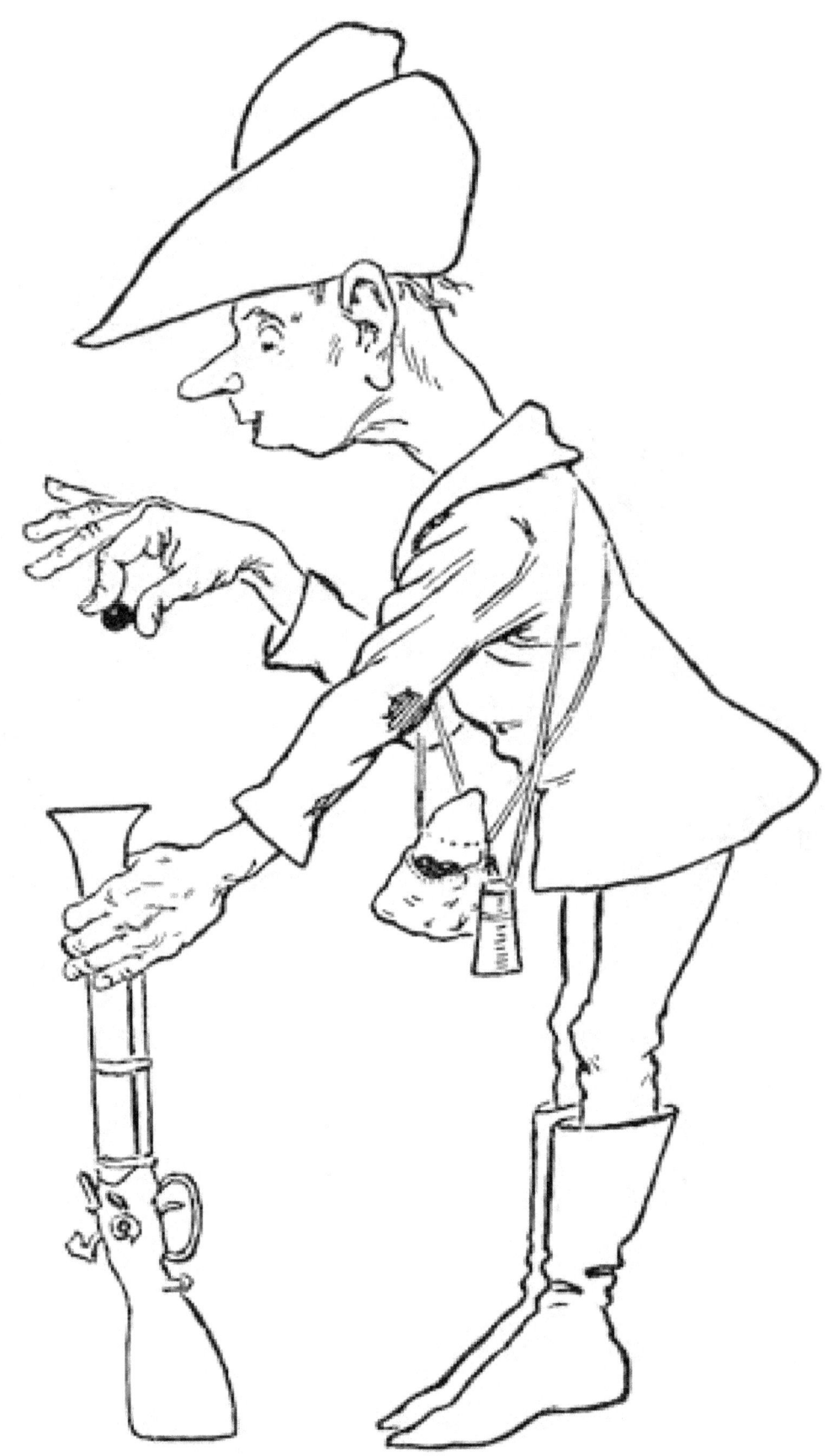

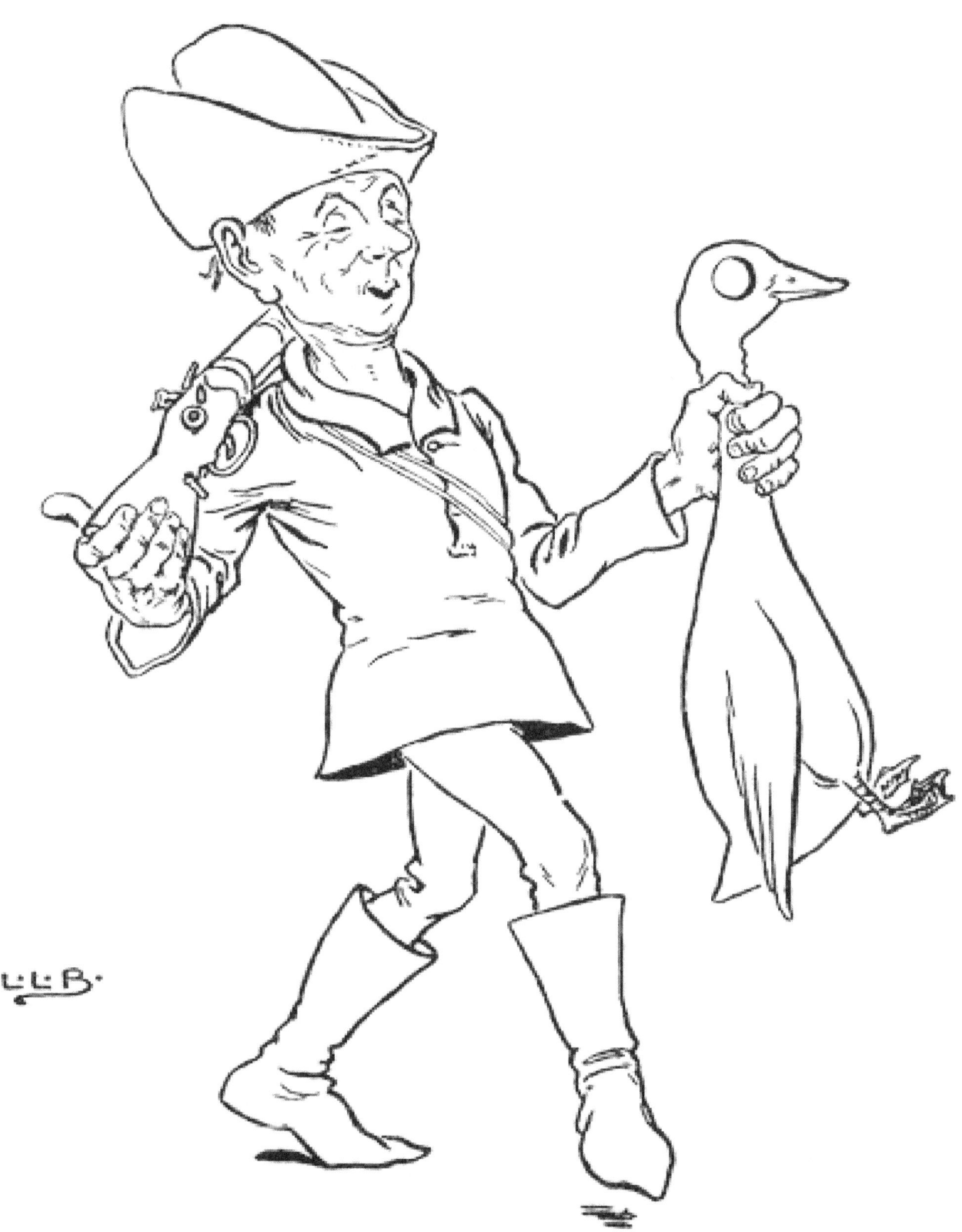

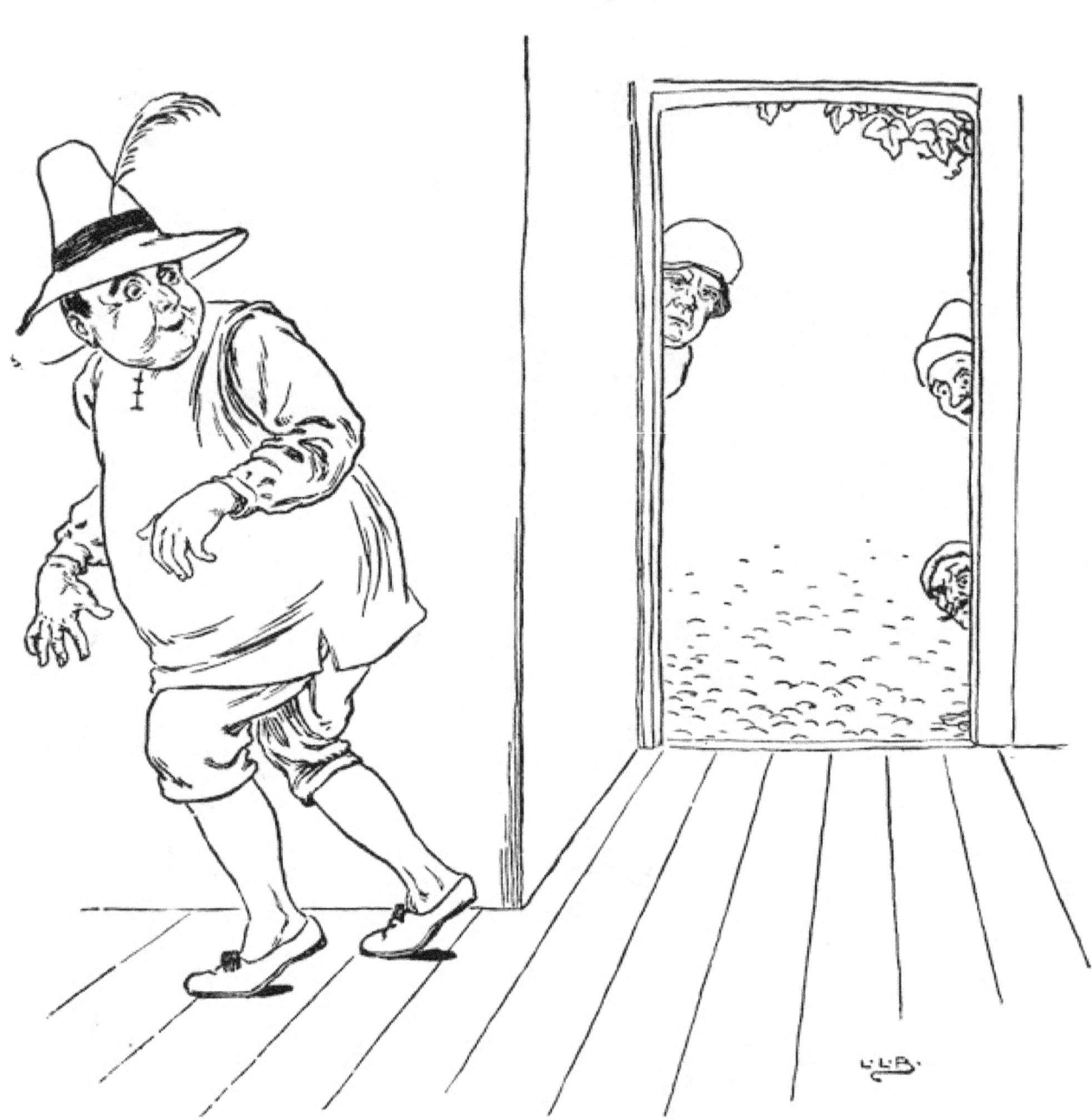

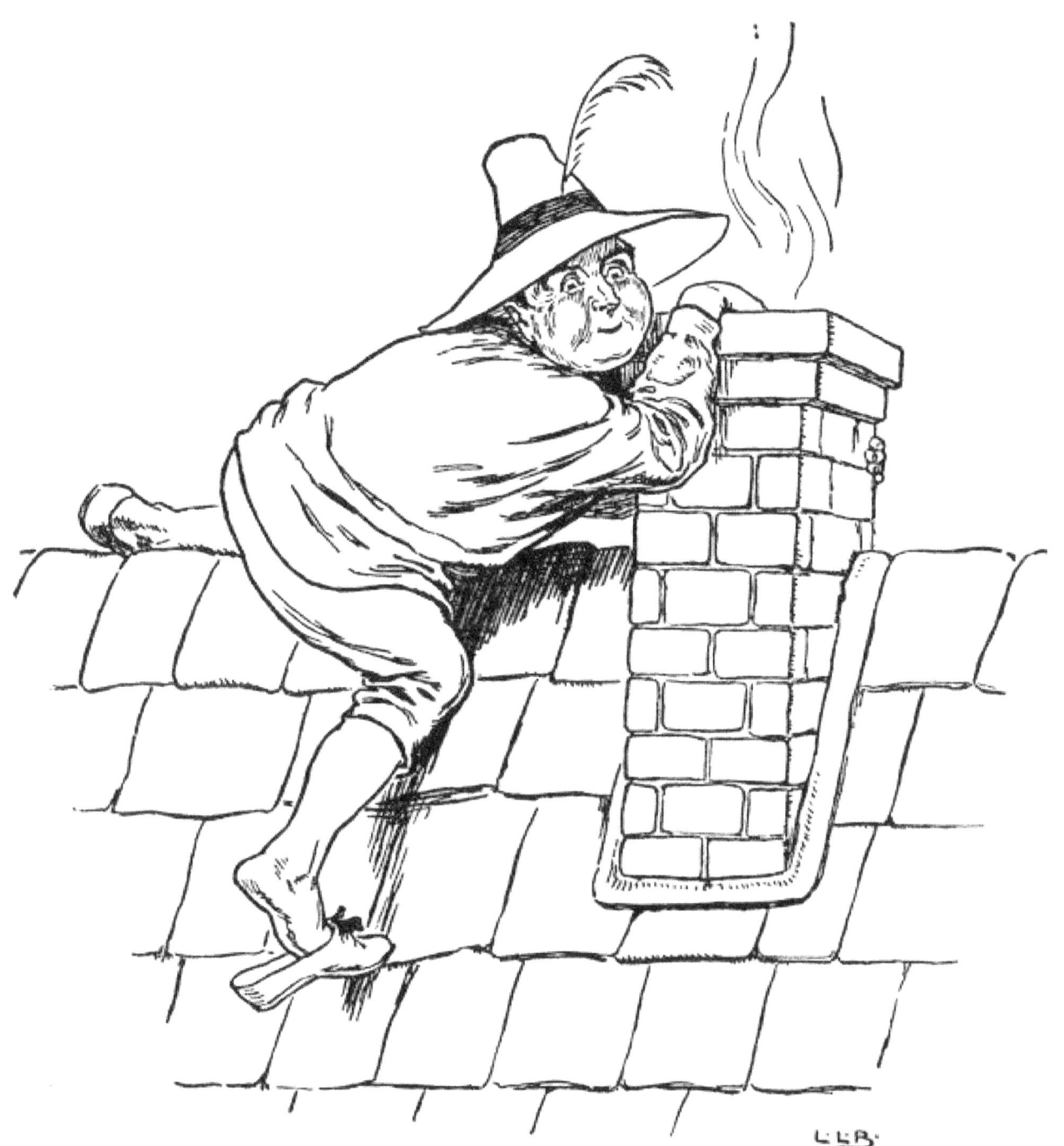

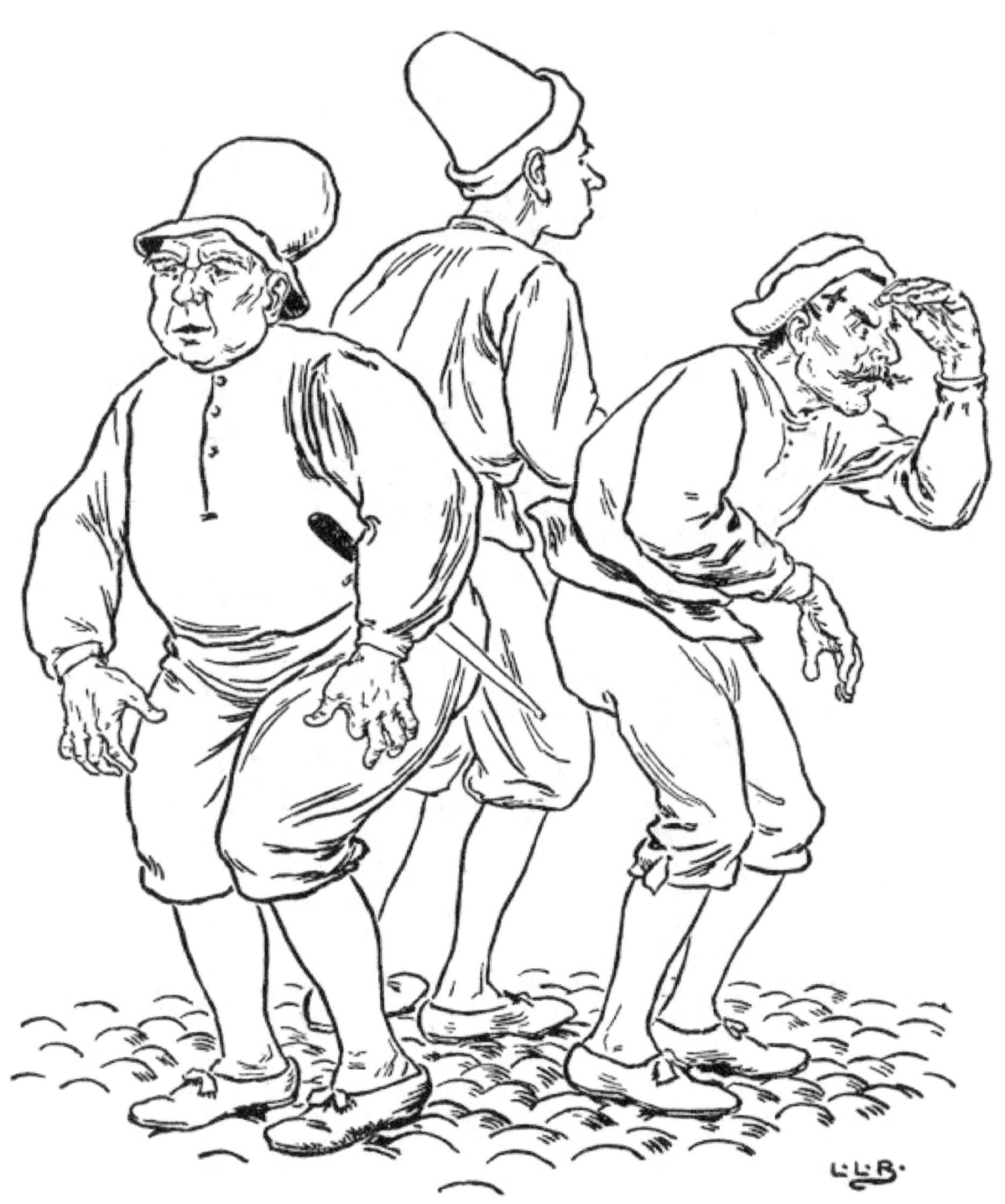

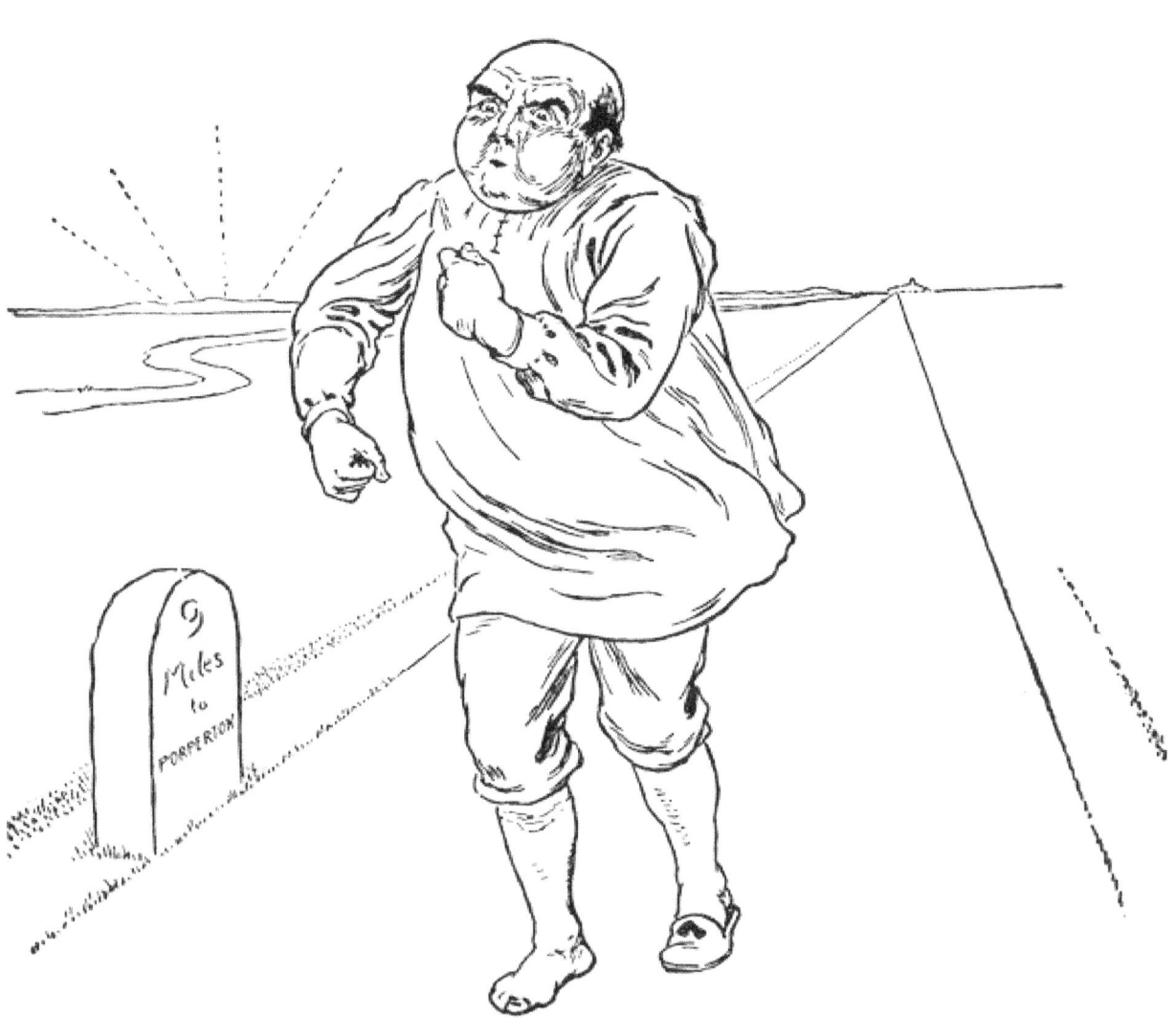

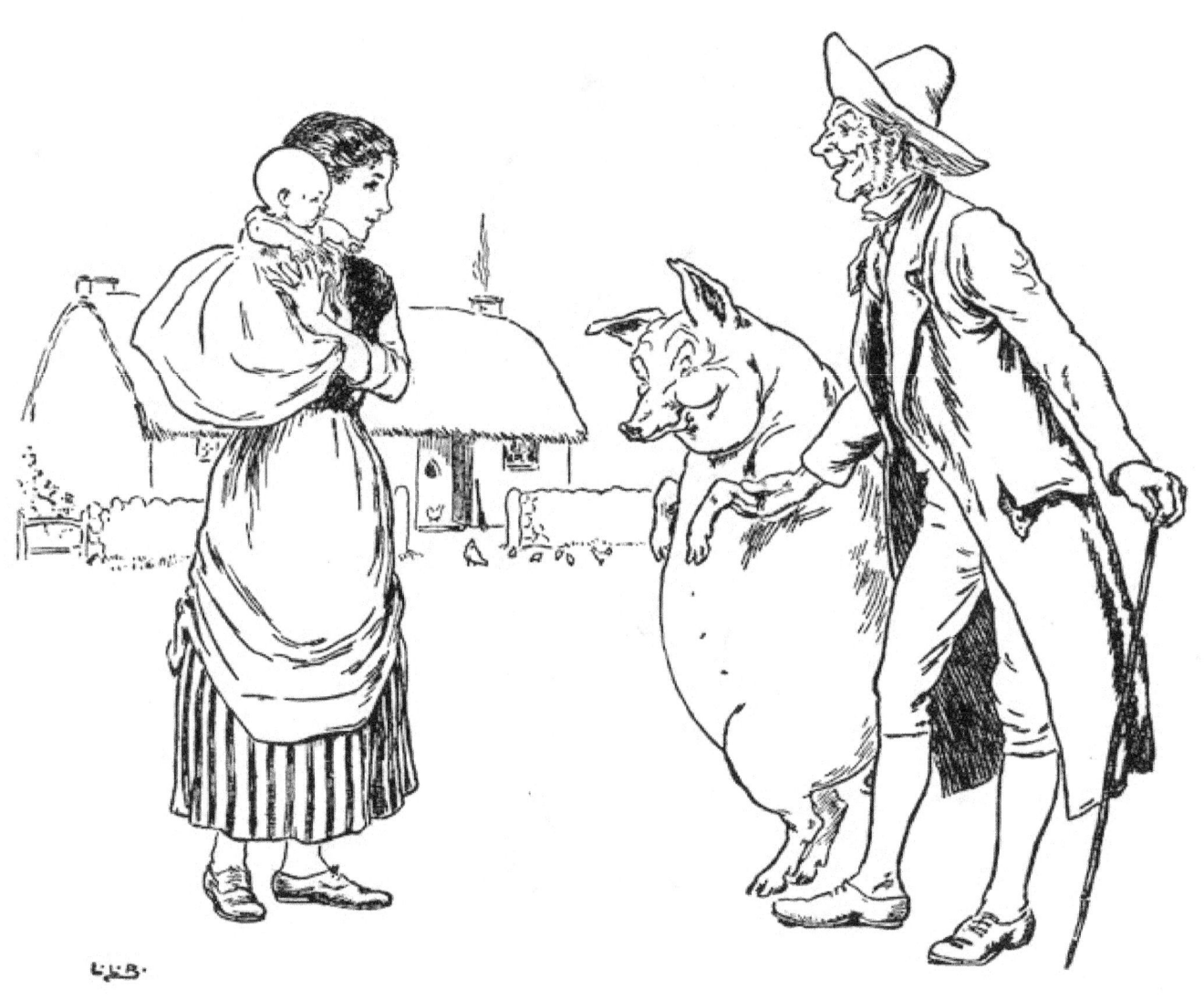

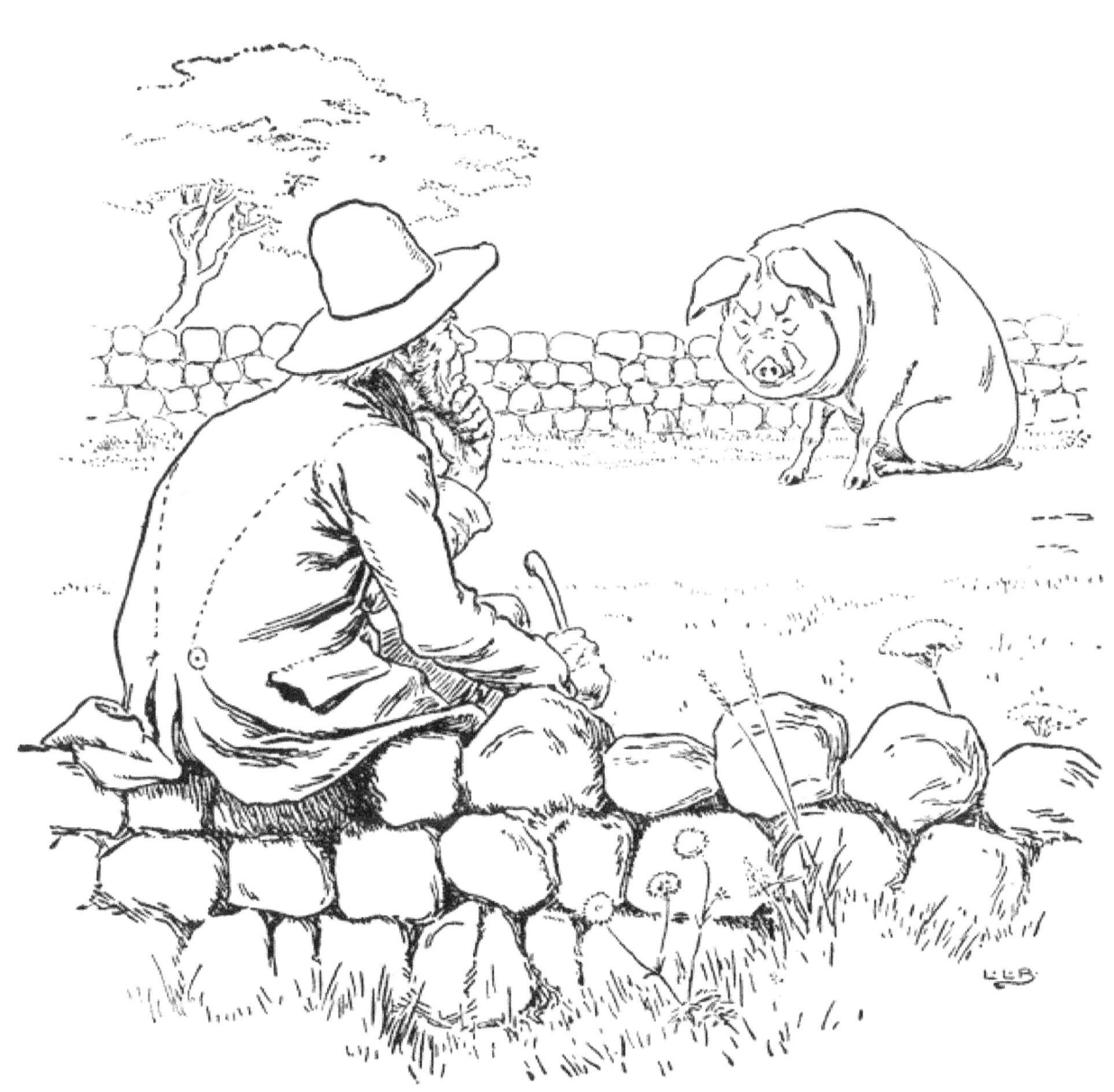

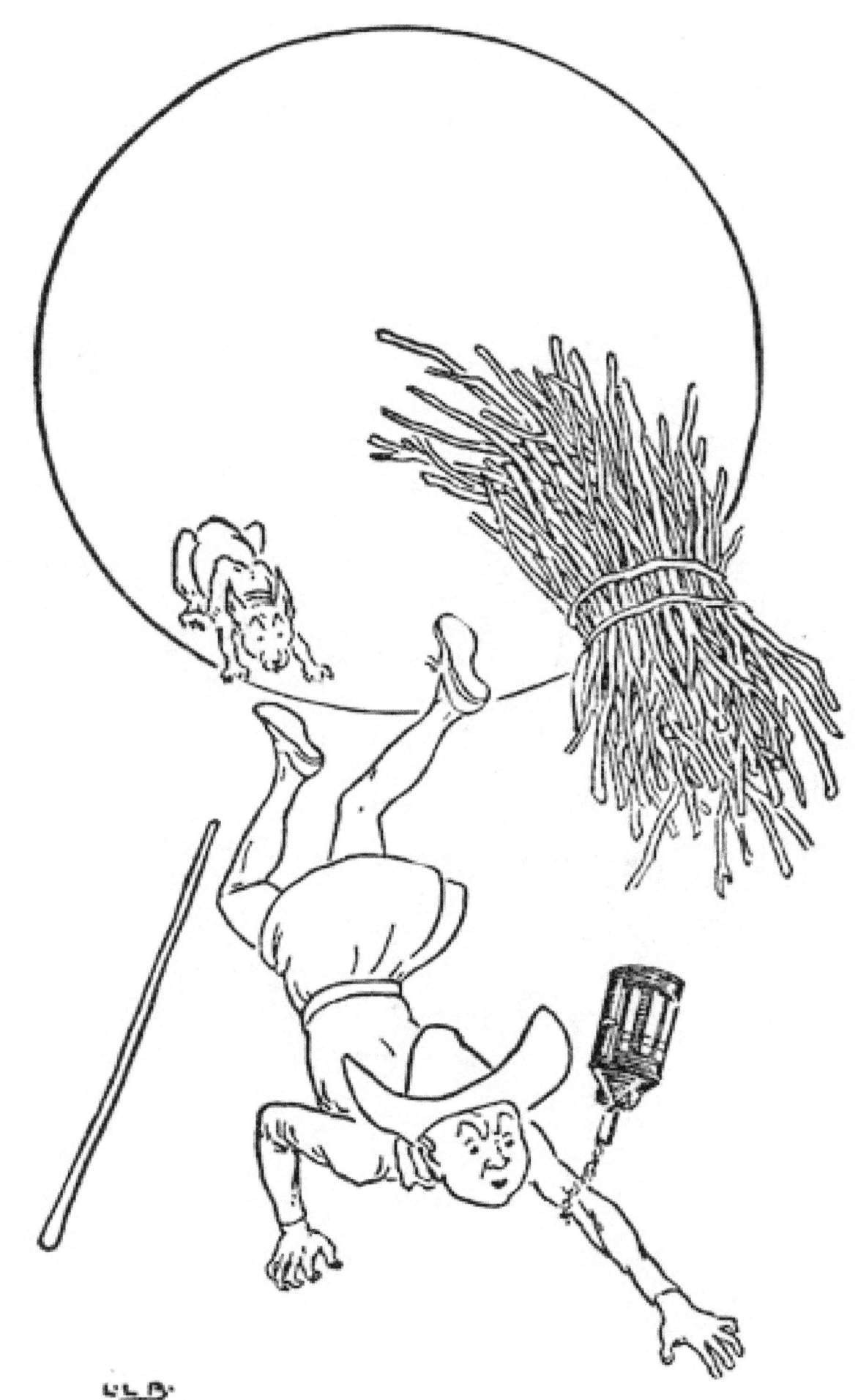

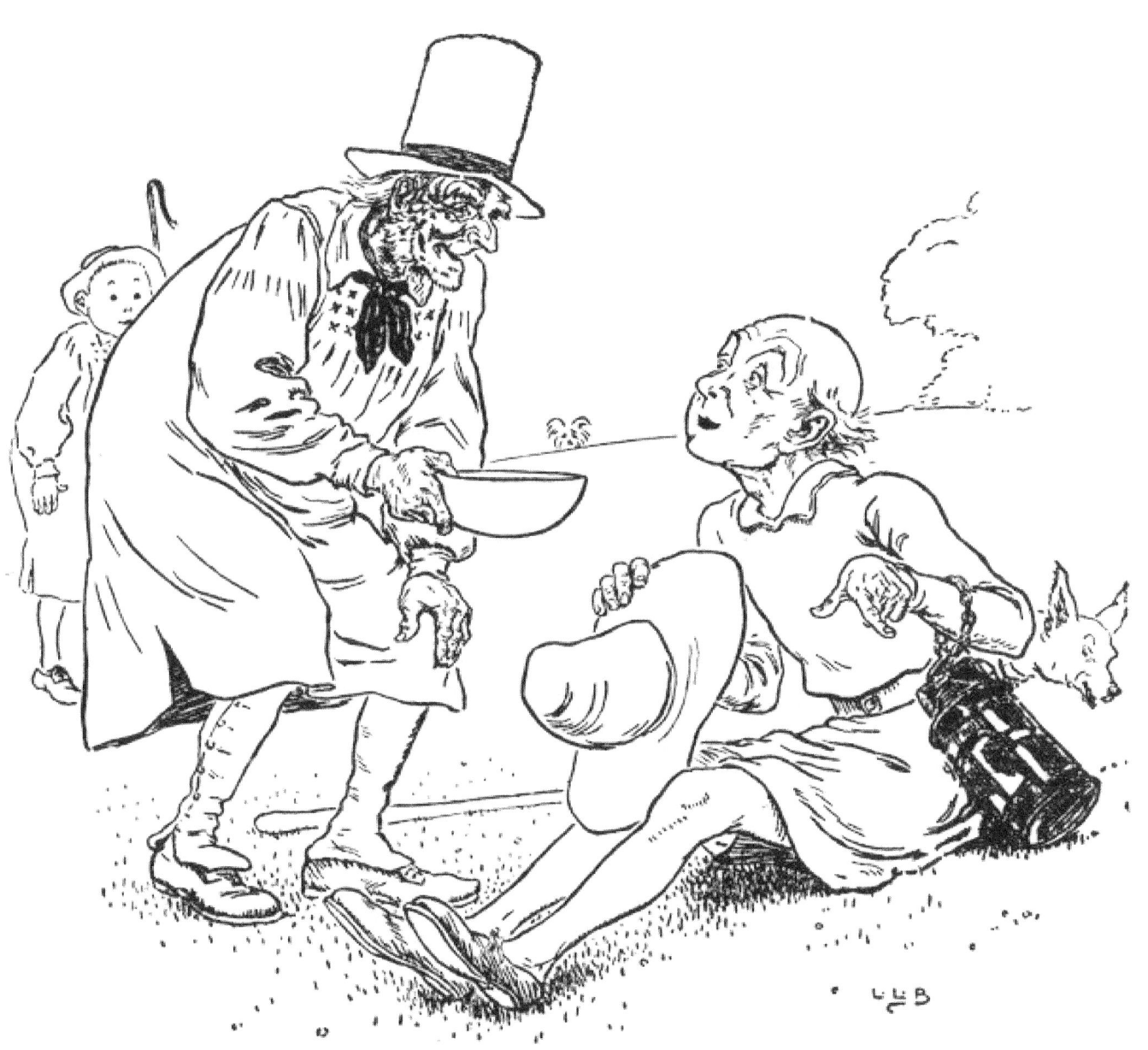

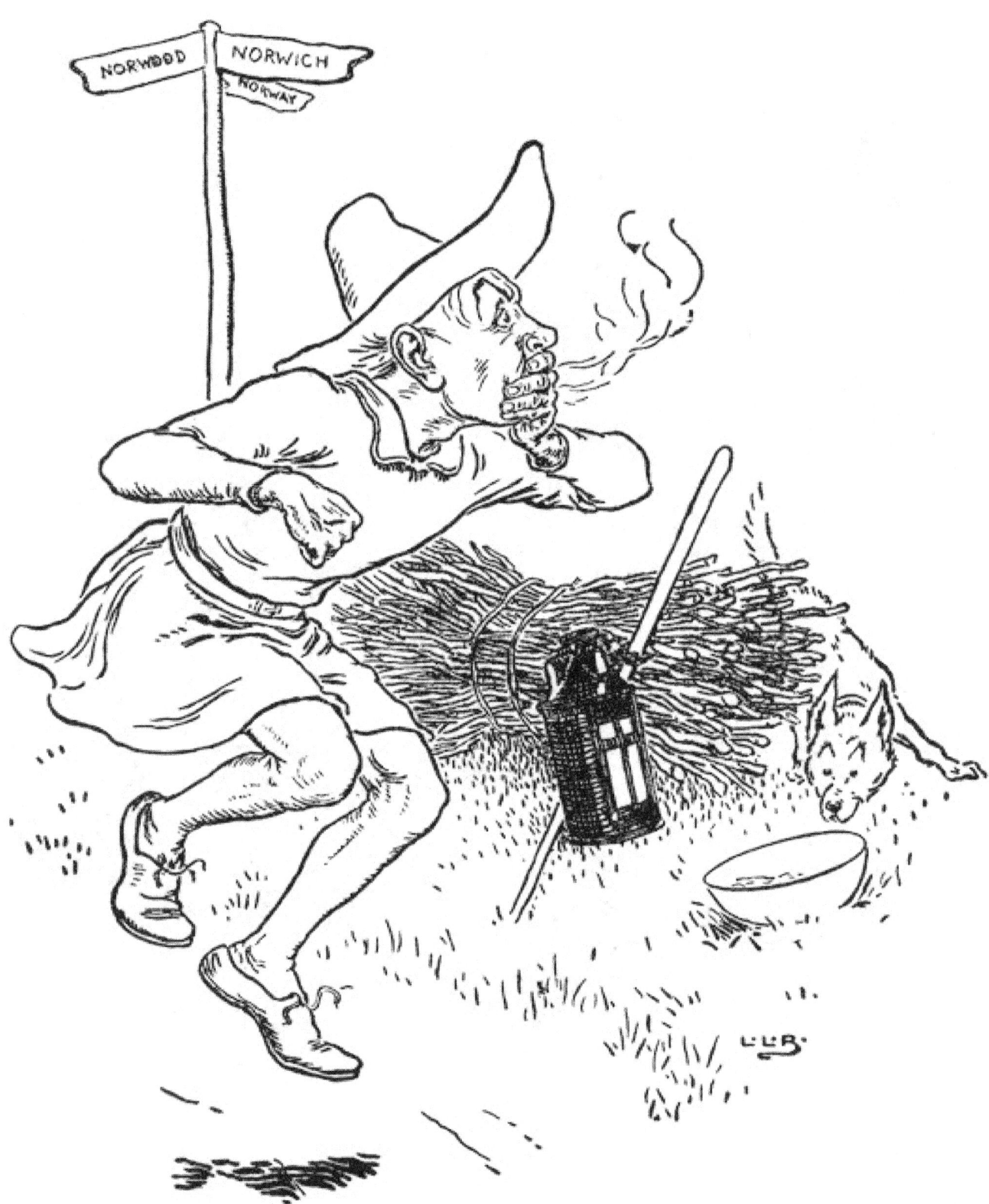

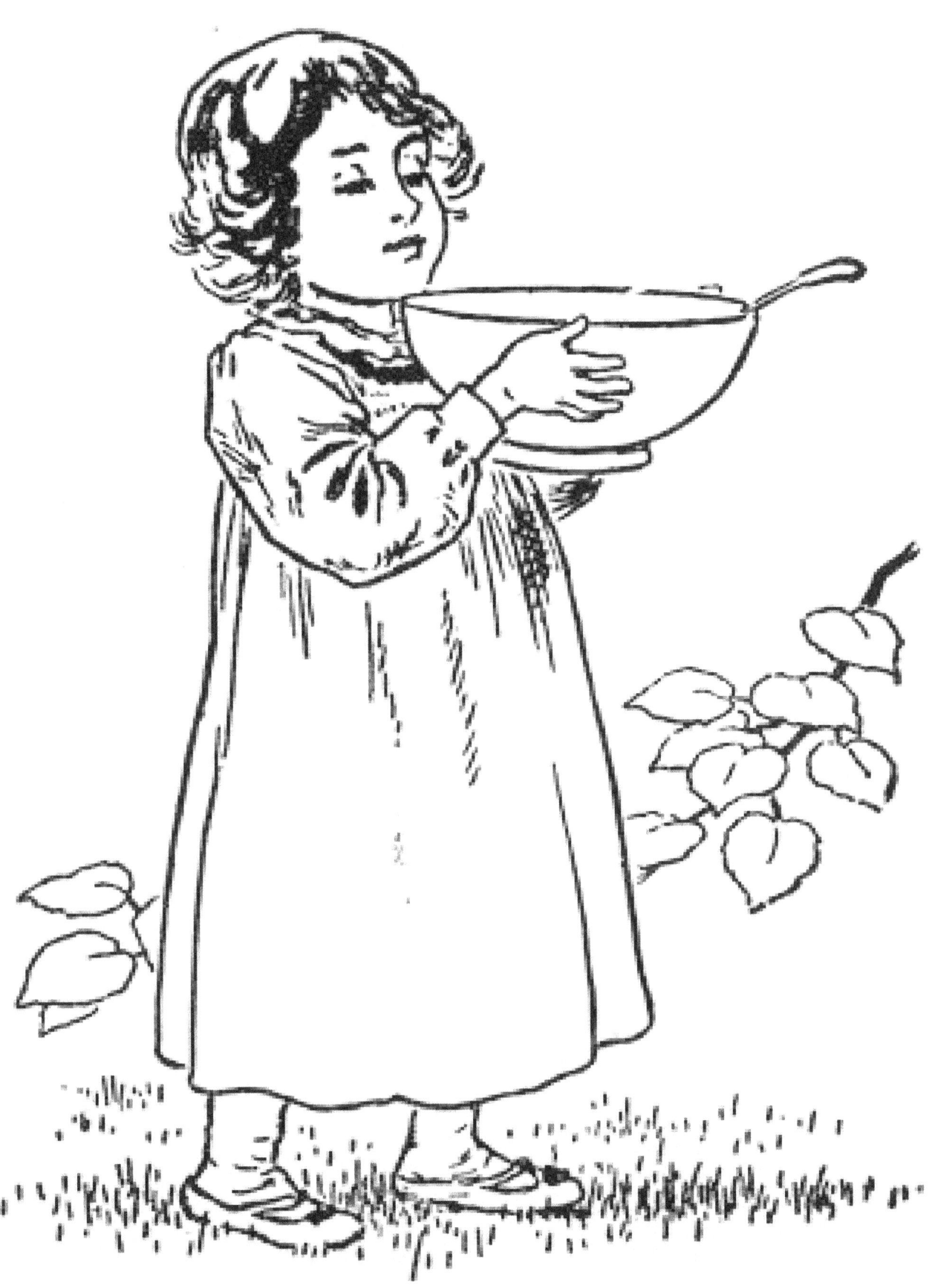

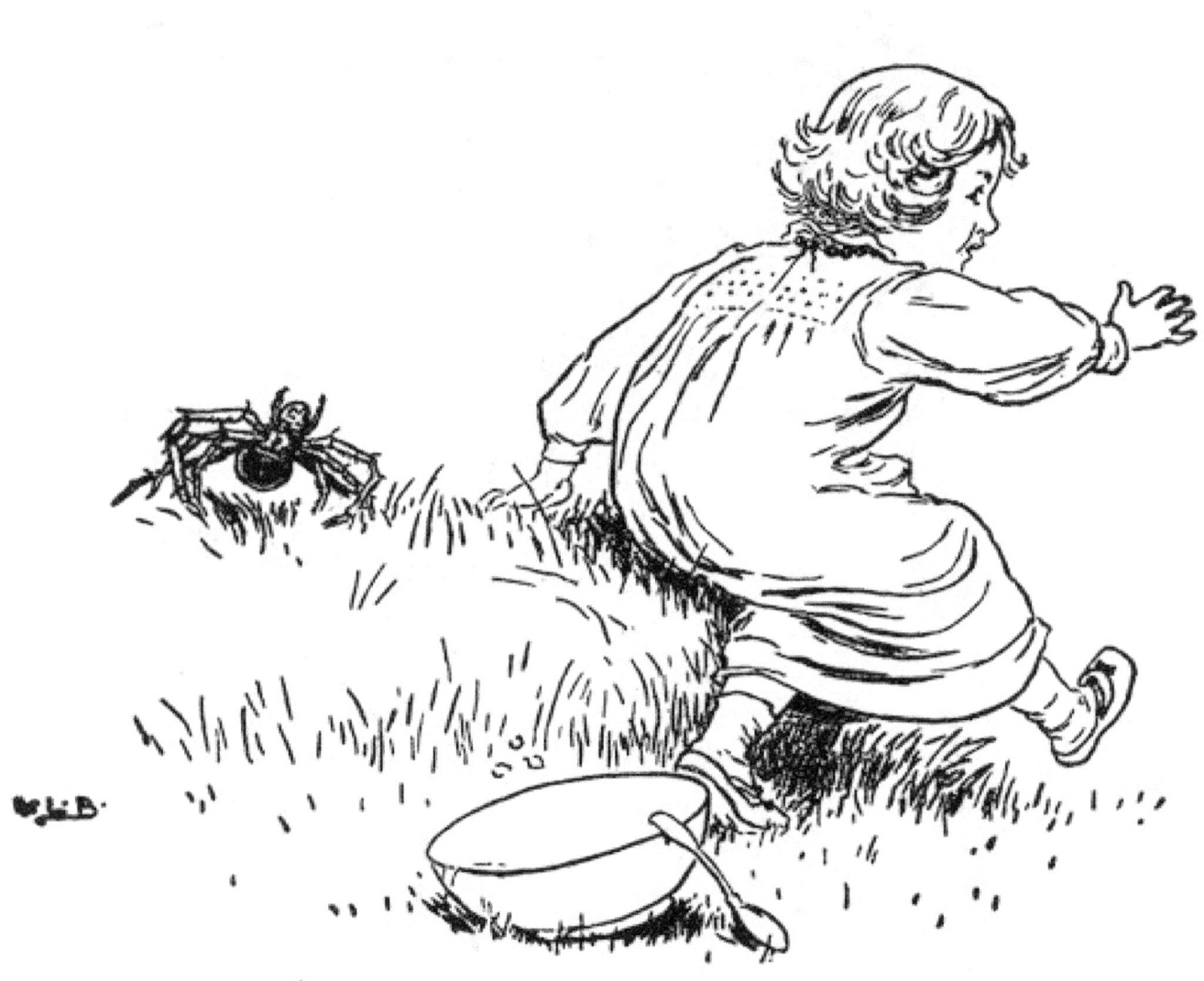

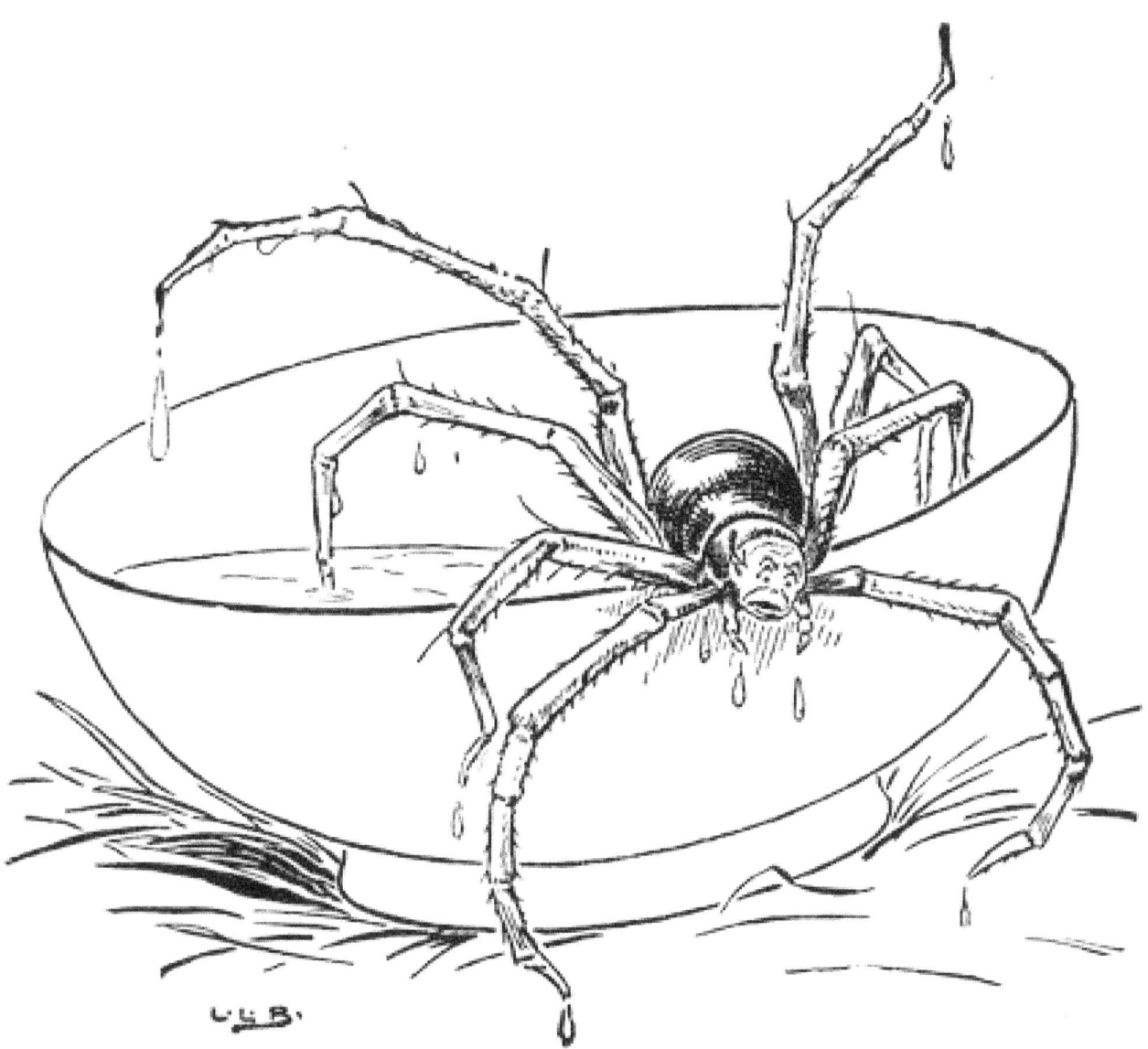

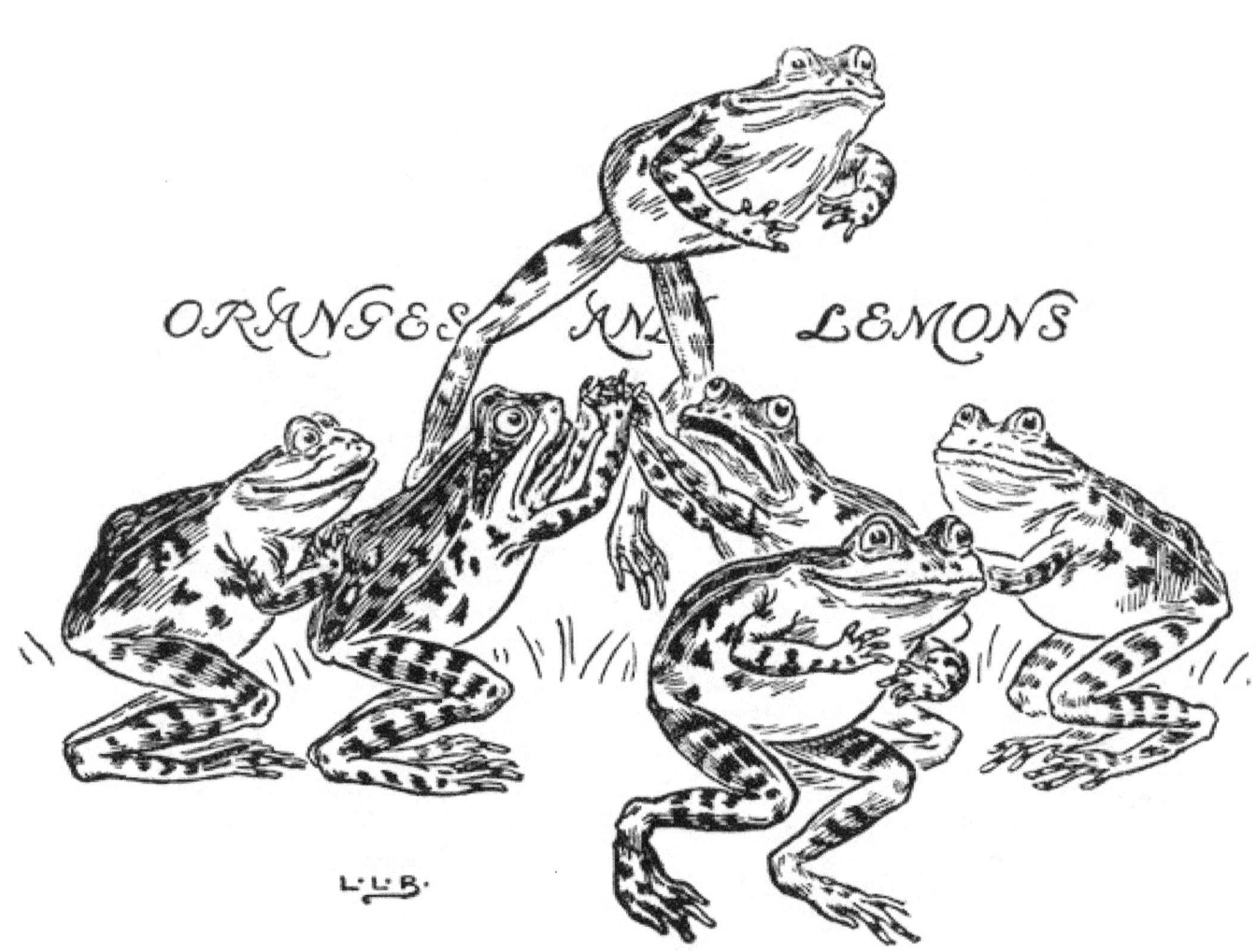

ORANGES AND LEMONS

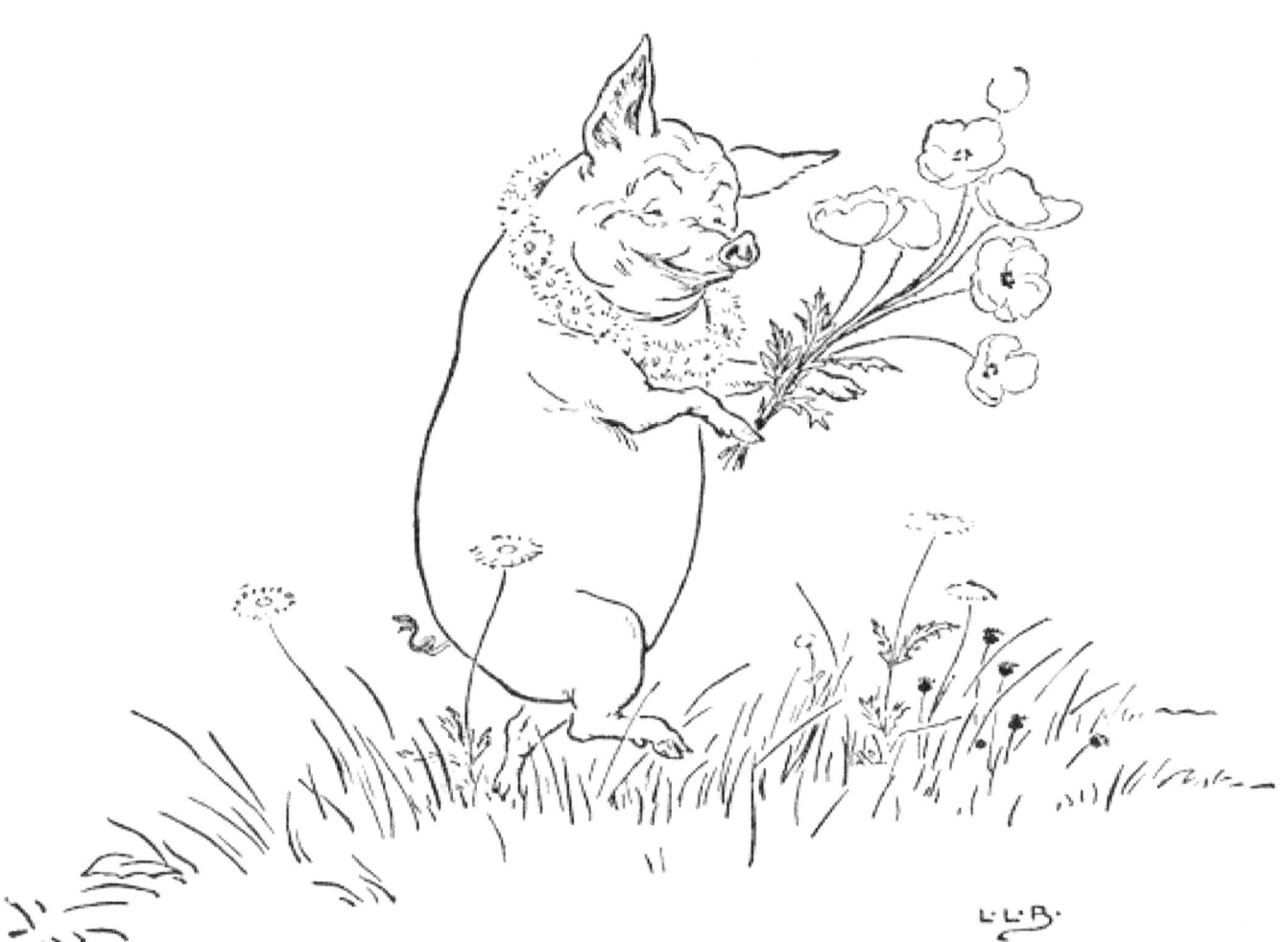

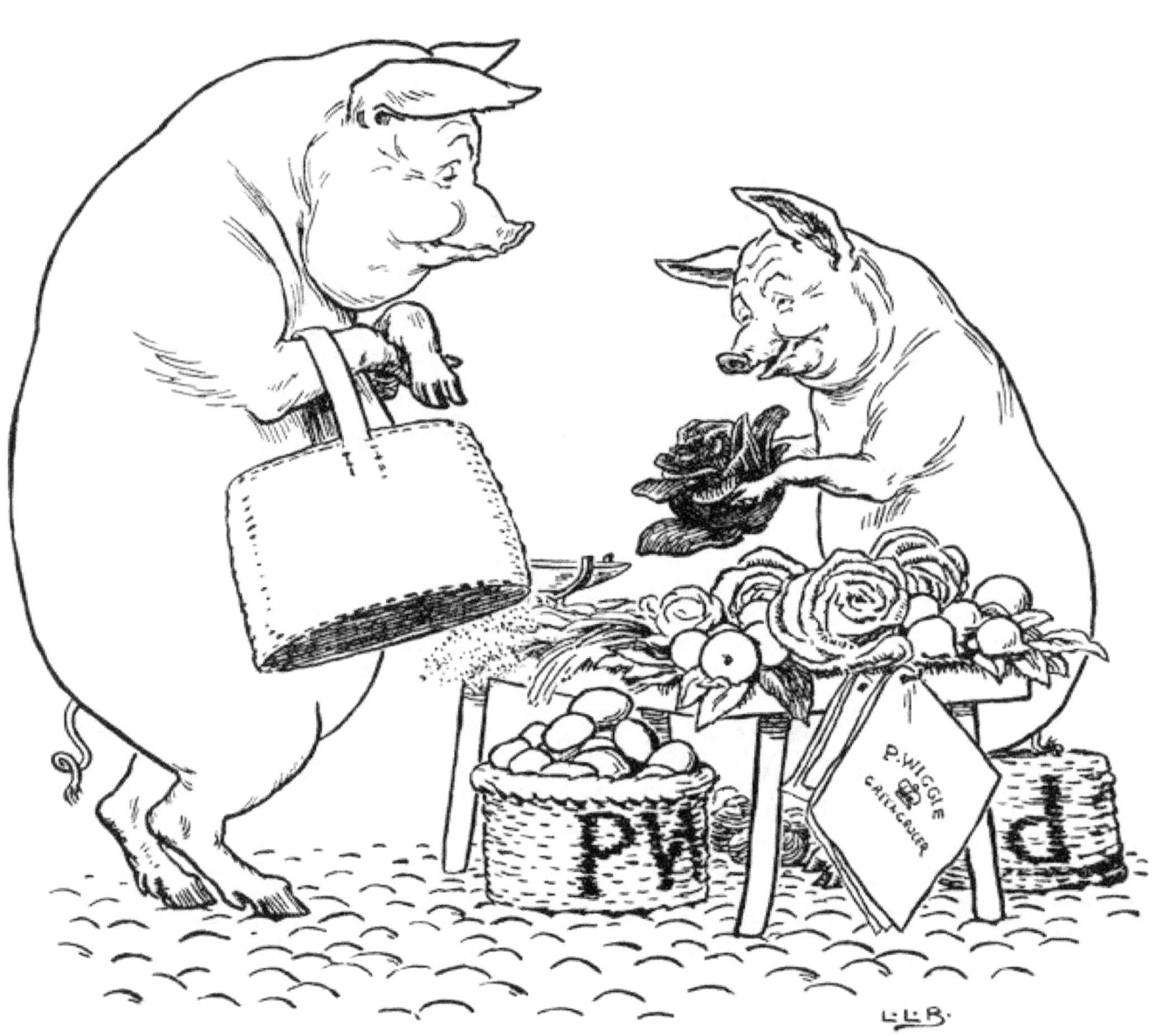

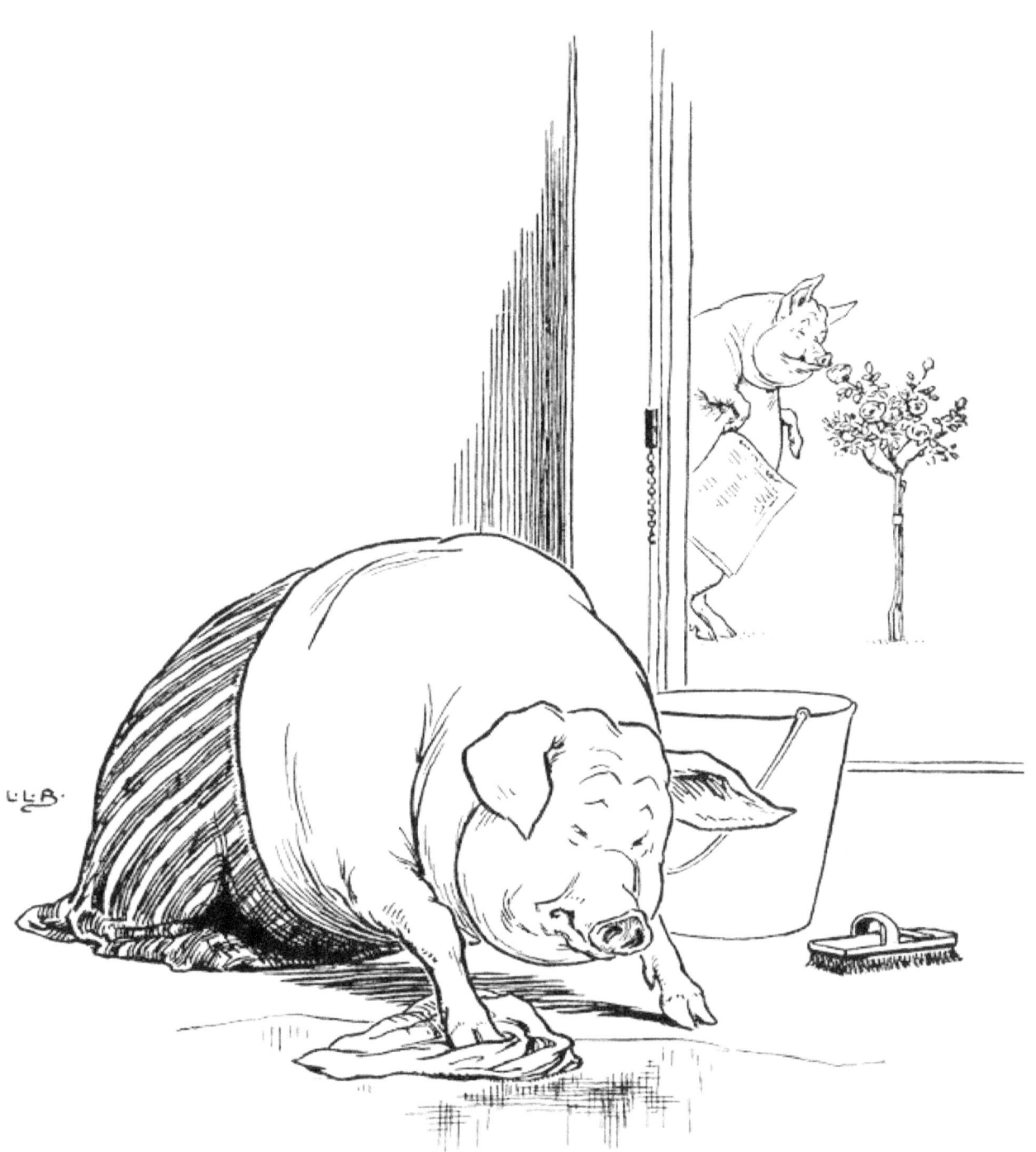

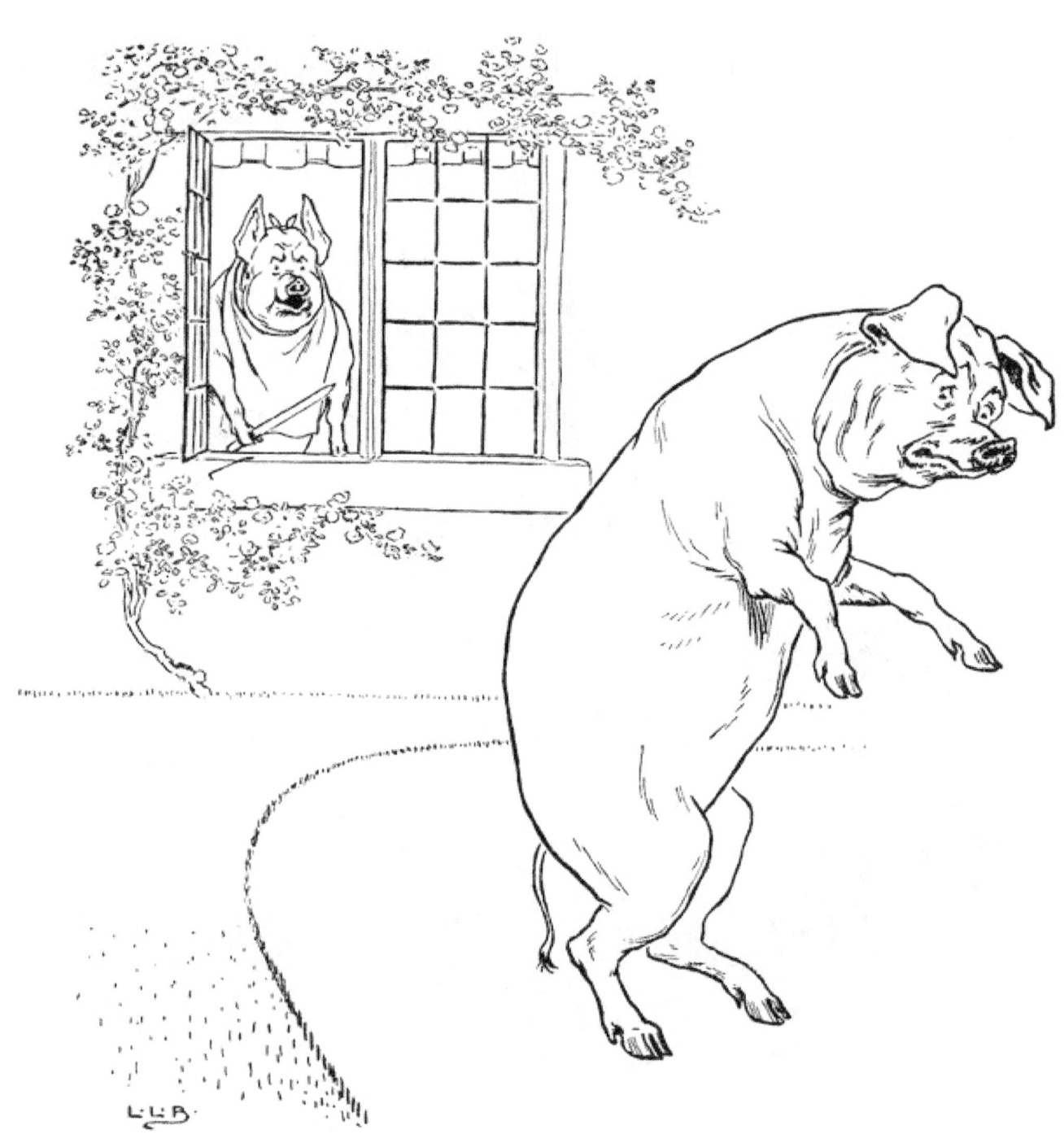

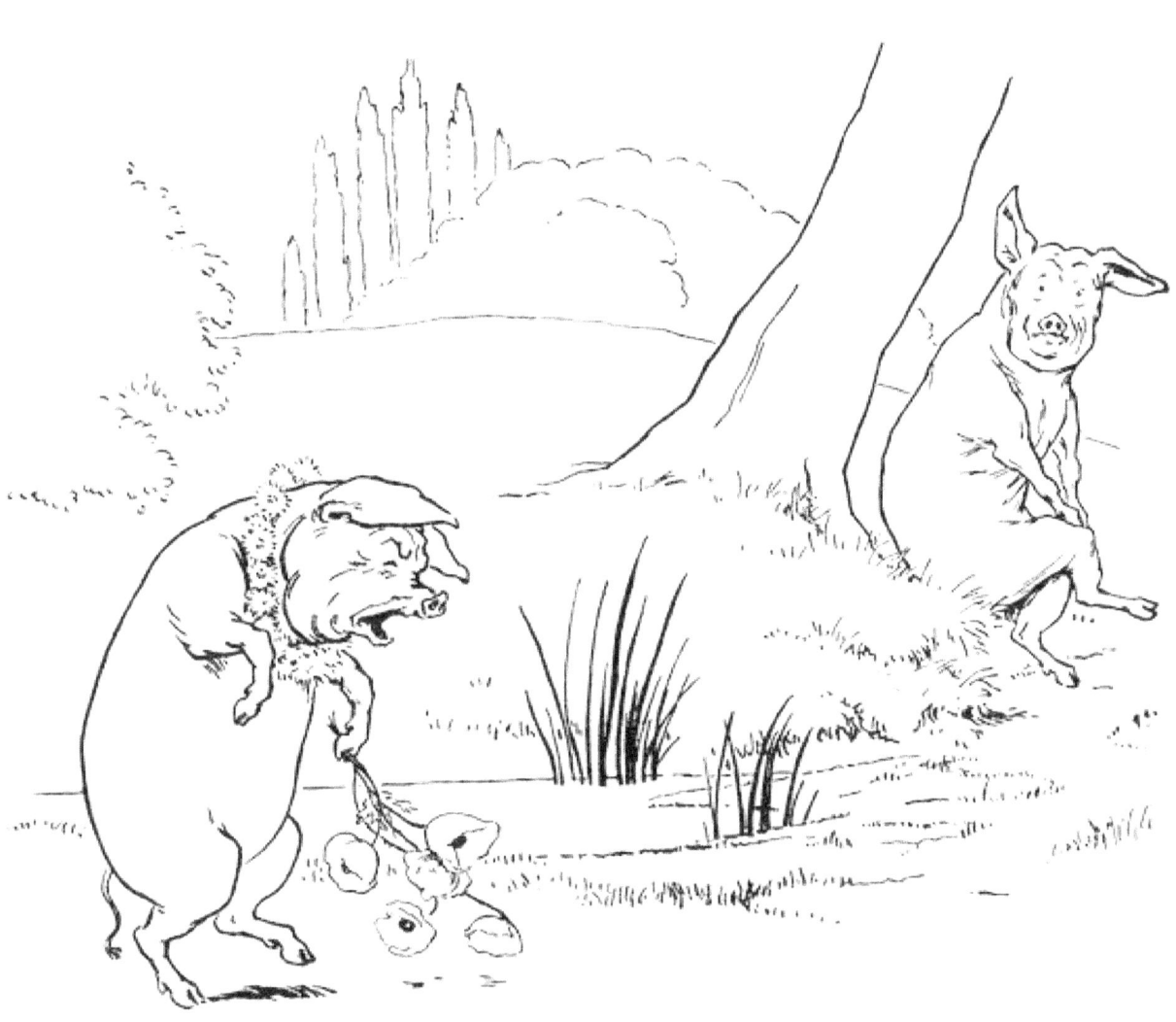

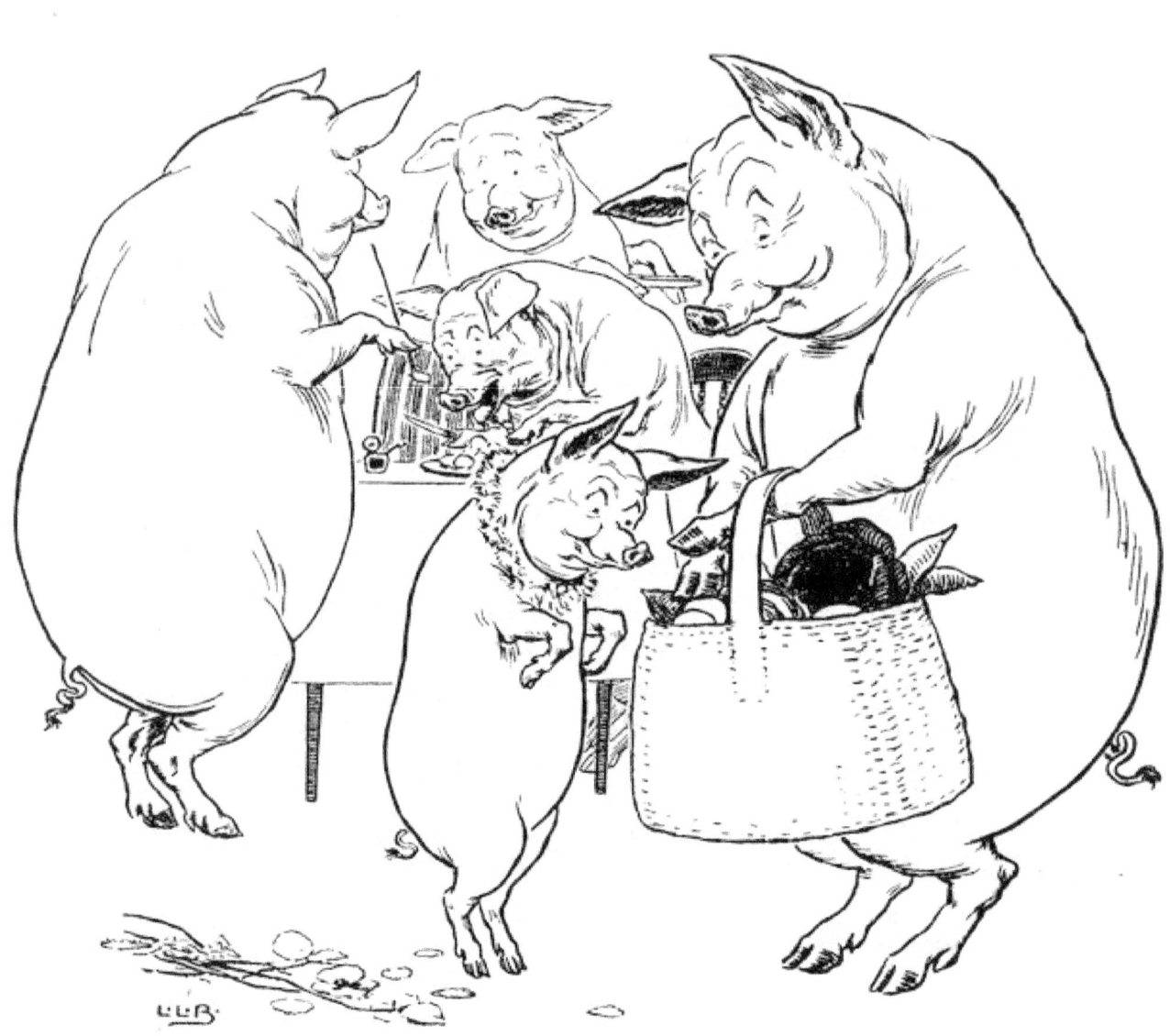

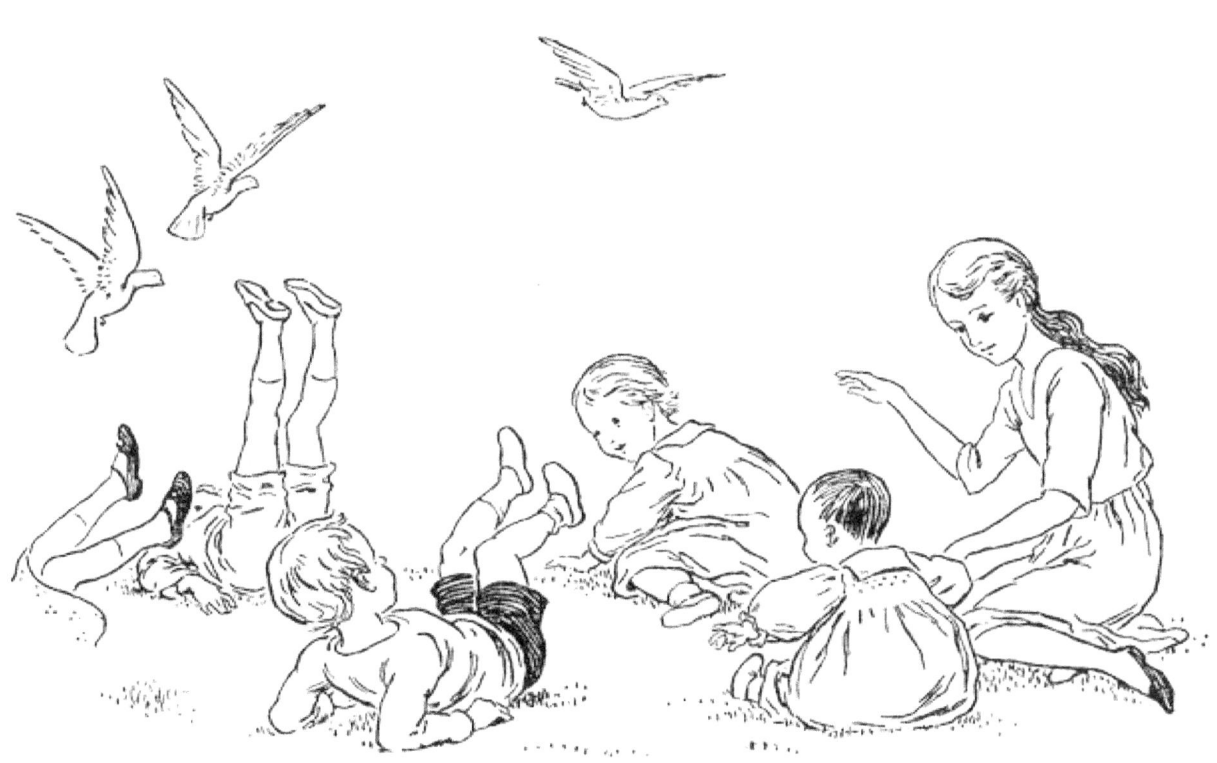

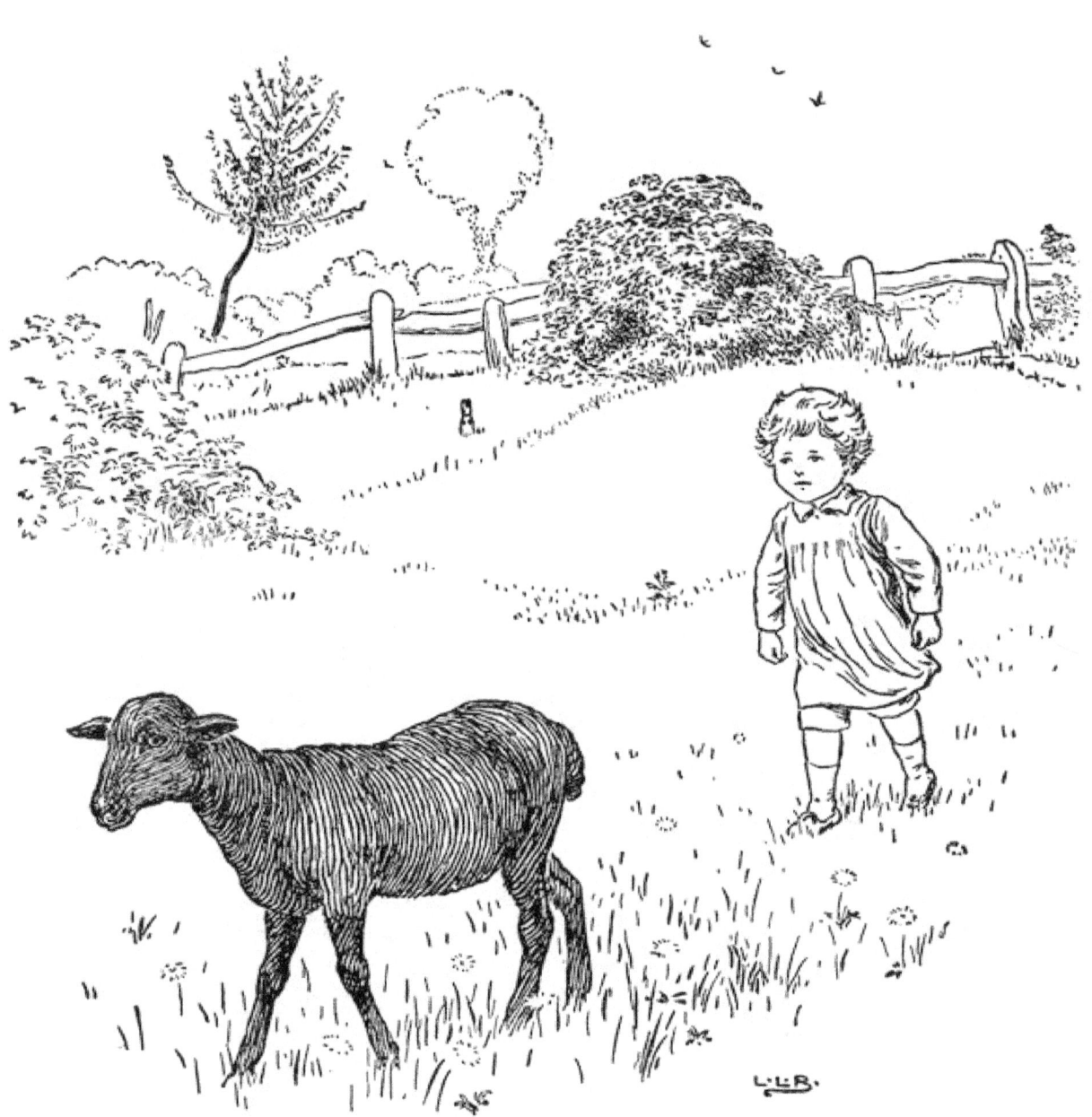

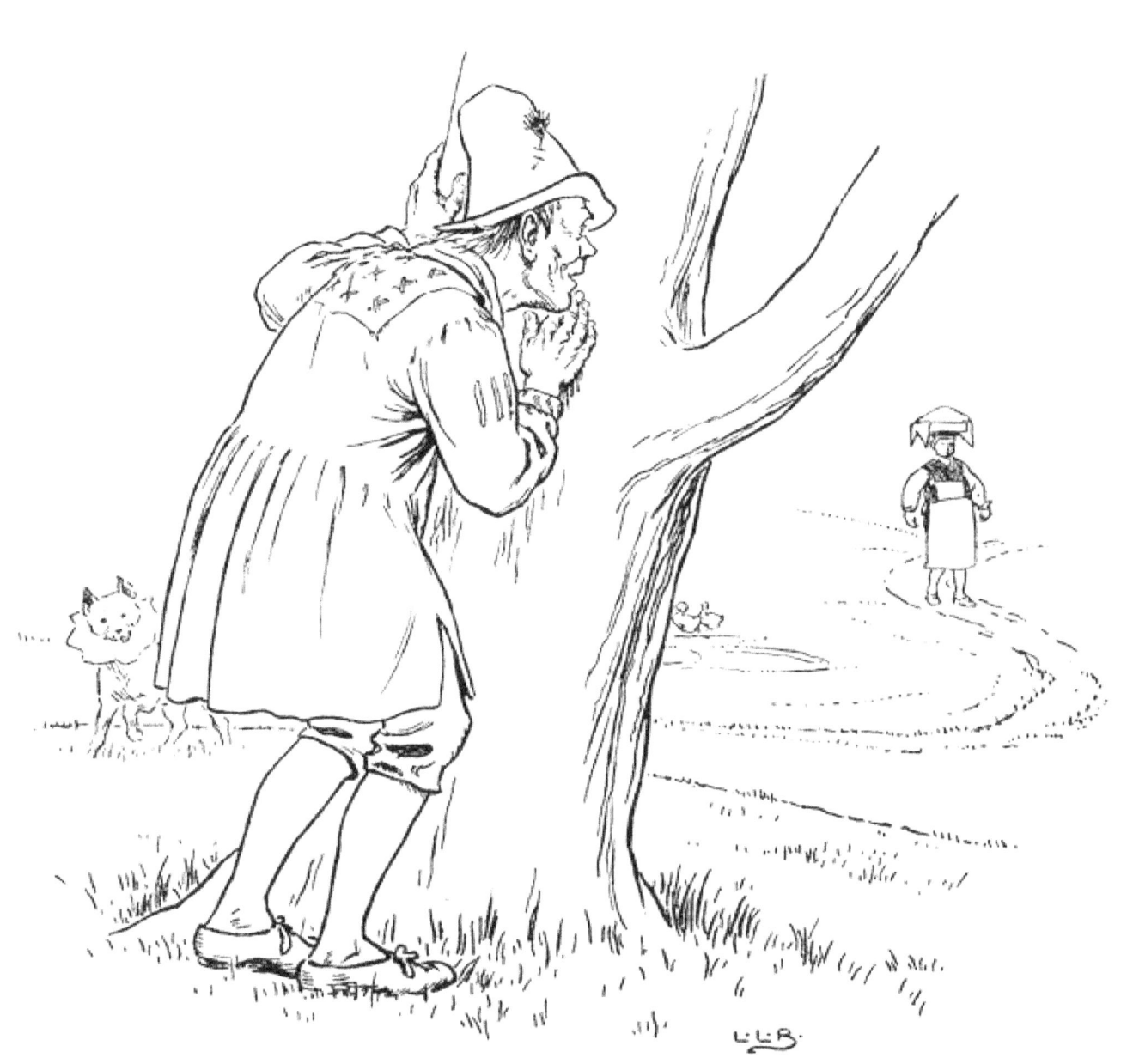

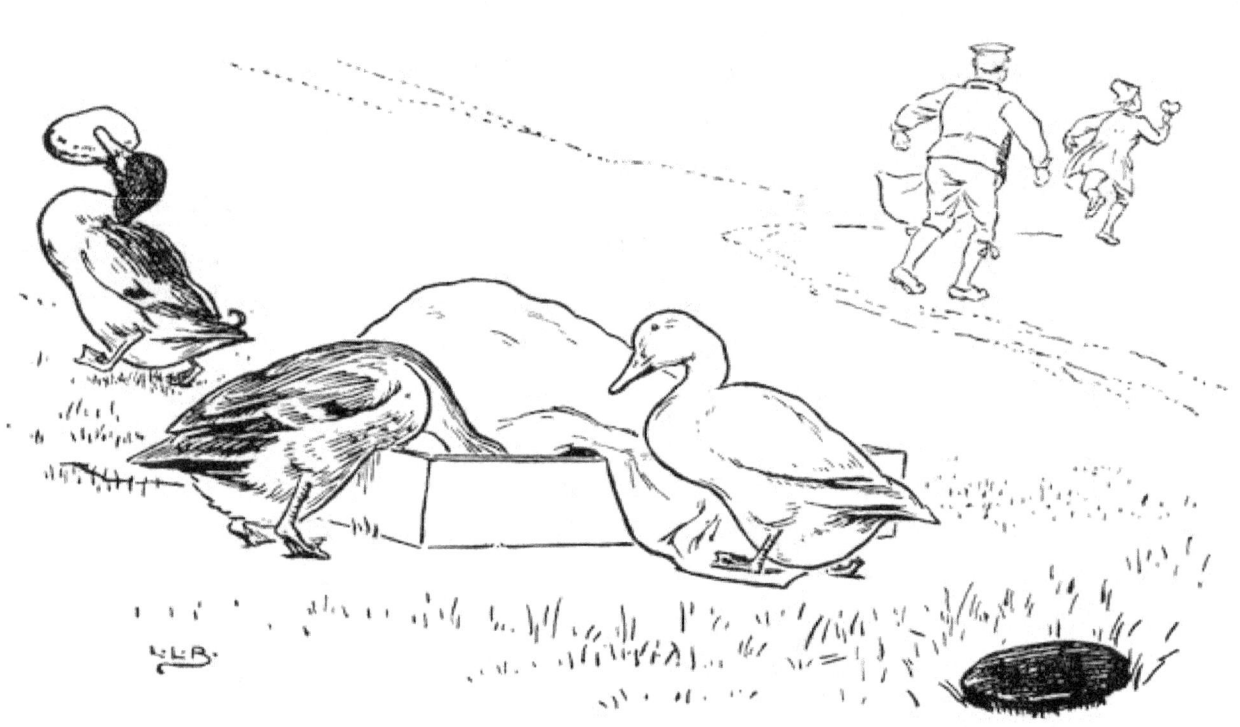

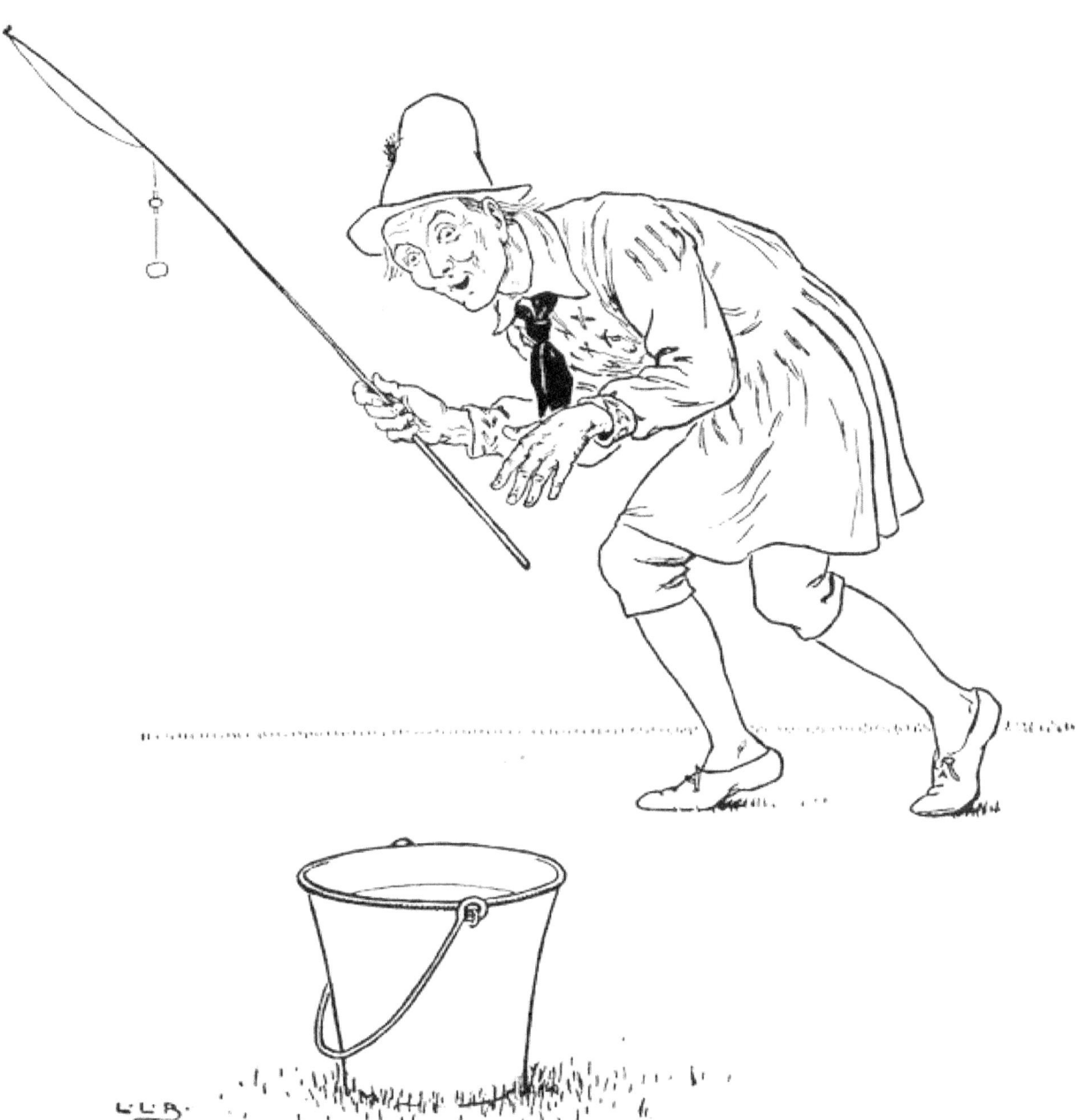

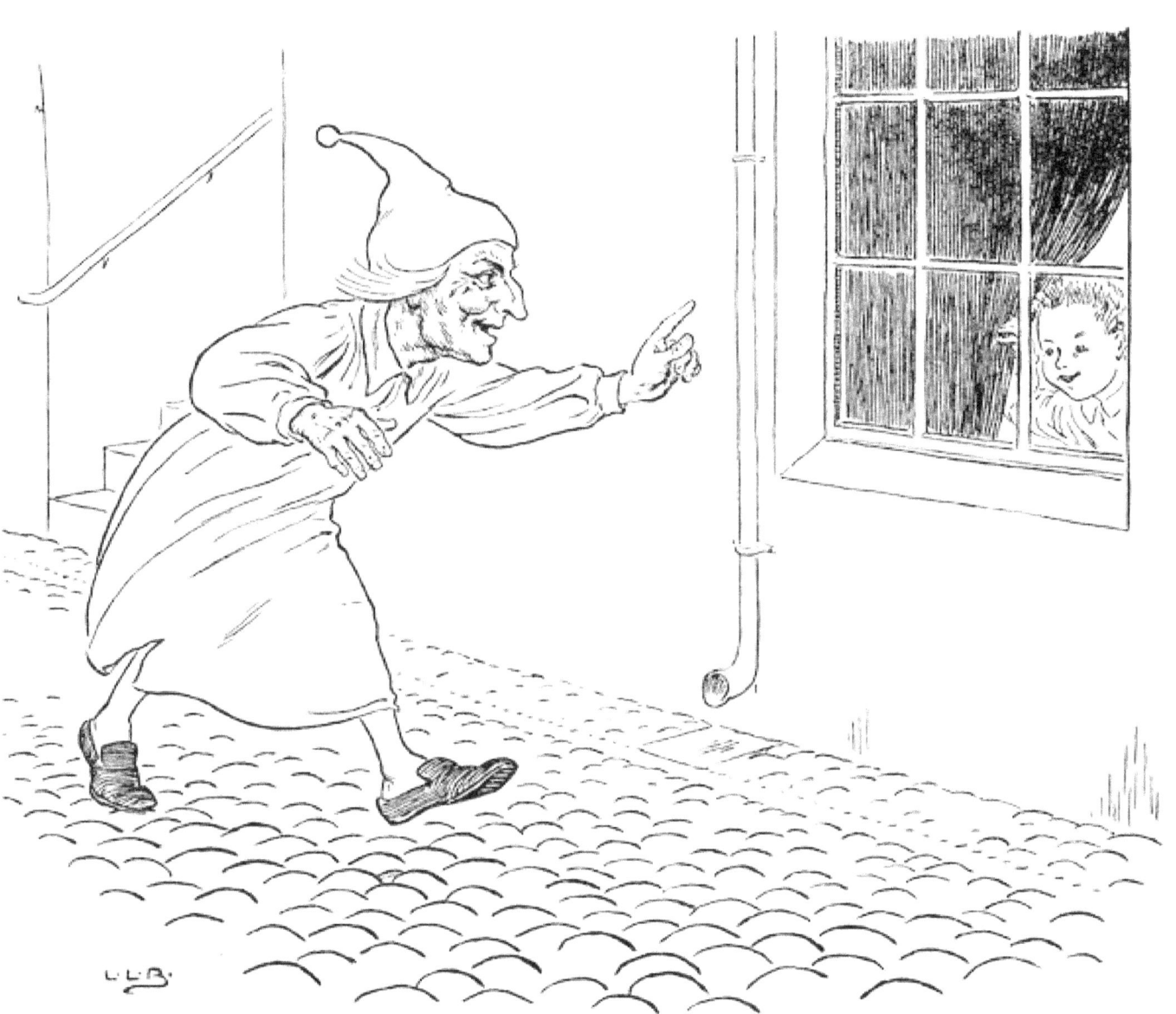

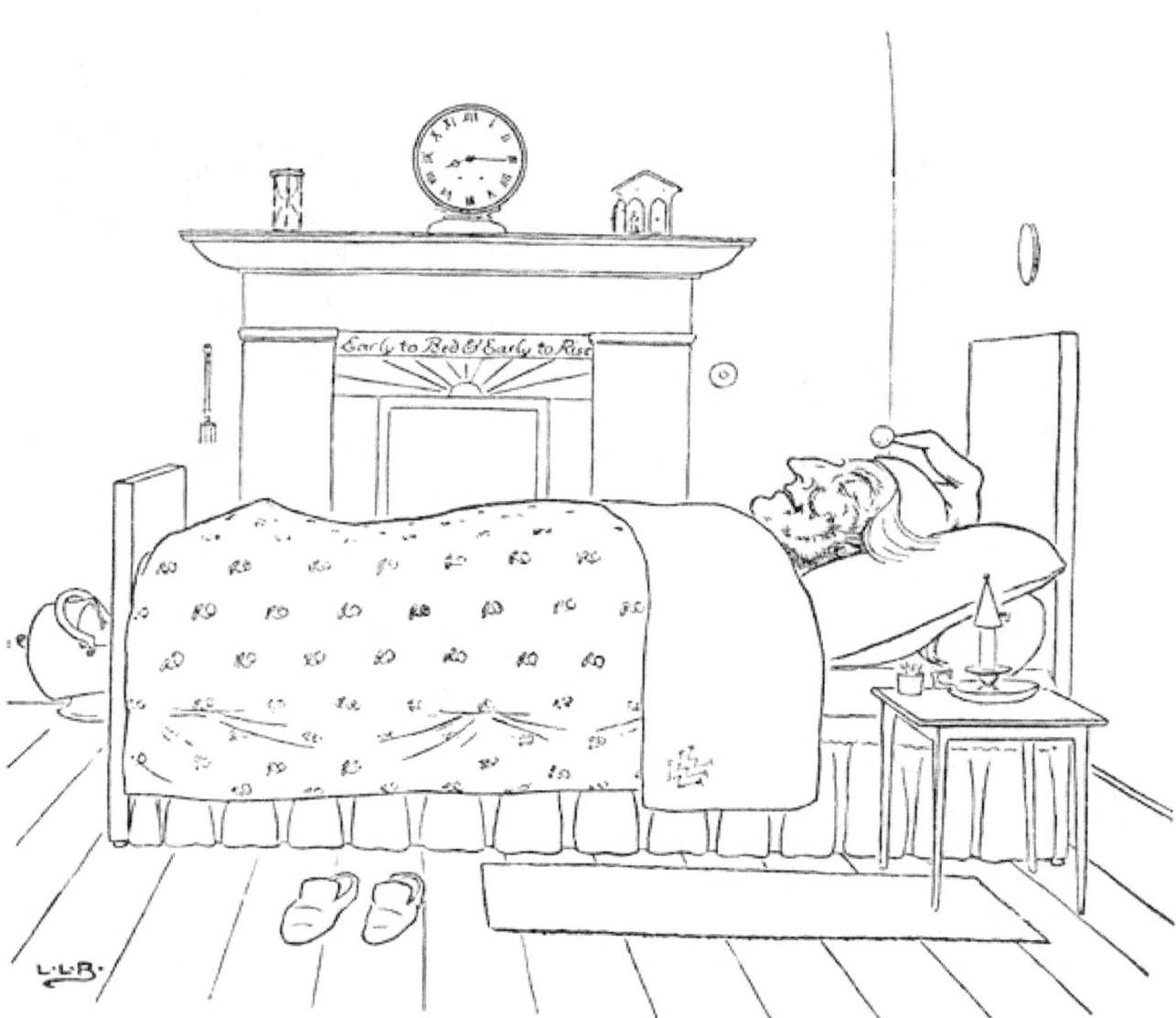